1950

THE NATURE AND SCOPE OF SEXUAL ABUSE OF MINORS
BY CATHOLIC PRIESTS AND DEACONS
IN THE UNITED STATES 1950-2002

2002

A RESEARCH STUDY CONDUCTED BY THE JOHN JAY COLLEGE OF CRIMINAL JUSTICE

THE CITY UNIVERSITY OF NEW YORK • FEBRUARY 2004

FOR THE UNITED STATES CONFERENCE OF CATHOLIC BISHOPS

Washington, D.C.

In June 2002 the full body of Catholic bishops of the United States in their General Meeting in Dallas approved the Charter for the Protection of Children and Young People. The Charter created a National Review Board, which was assigned responsibility to commission a descriptive study, with the full cooperation of the dioceses/eparchies, of the nature and scope of the problem of sexual abuse of minors by clergy. The National Review Board engaged John Jay College of Criminal Justice of The City University of New York to conduct research, summarize the collected data, and issue a summary report to the United States Conference of Catholic Bishops of its findings. This report by the John Jay College is authorized for publication by the undersigned.

Msgr. William P. Fay
General Secretary
USCCB

First Printing, June 2004

ISBN 1-57455-627-4

TABLE OF CONTENTS

LITERATURE REVIEW

PREFACE AND ACKNOWLEDGEMENTS

John Jay College of Criminal Justice was honored to have been asked by the United States Conference of Catholic Bishops to undertake the critically important task of obtaining a comprehensive description of sexual abuse of minors by Catholic priests. From the beginning, the College well understood its profound responsibility: to describe the dimensions of the abuse problem as accurately and completely as possible, to be scrupulously objective in carrying out the study, and to report the facts in an honest, forthright manner. The gravity of the assignment entrusted to the College cannot be overestimated.

Some advised the College to reject the request to do the study: it was too controversial; it was too complicated; it could expose the College to lawsuits; and it could engender negative publicity. After listening carefully to this counsel, I came to the conclusion that despite the problems which might arise, the College had a civic obligation to use its resources and academic talent to help provide facts about the sexual abuse phenomenon which has been such a sad chapter in the history of the Catholic Church. Because it is a significant part of the College's stated mission to engage in research dealing with public safety, I became convinced that we would be shirking our duty if we turned down the opportunity to do research on the victimization of children which hopefully will help protect them in years to come.

The administrators, faculty and students invited to participate in this endeavor shared my conviction. They committed themselves to making the study a high priority, to immersing themselves in the many tasks which had to be done, and to maintaining the highest level of professionalism in carrying out the sensitive mandate entrusted to us. This was a "fast track" project, taking less than a year from start to finish, but the faculty nevertheless faithfully adhered to the established norms of research ethics at every step along the way.

The findings presented in this report are very disturbing. As we at John Jay College pored over the data, we were deeply moved by the recitation of the large numbers of offenses committed against children and the seriousness of their nature. But we are genuinely hopeful that out of this excruciating inquiry will emerge not only a better understanding of the abuse problem but a series of sensible, effective measures to reduce the possibility that other children will suffer the kinds of abuses which we have uncovered.

I would like to thank the many men and women of good will without whose cooperation this study would have been impossible to accomplish. I thank with special gratitude the many Catholic bishops across the country who provided us in record time the detailed, revealing data from their files. The remarkable 98% response rate which we obtained from the dioceses is virtually unheard of in social science research. The National Review Board, all of whose lay members have very demanding responsibilities, worked with us endlessly as we met the various challenges that confronted us on an almost daily basis. I must also acknowledge my deep appreciation of the efforts of Kathleen McChesney, Executive Director of the Office of Child and Youth Protection of the United States Conference of Catholic Bishops, and her staff who repeatedly walked the extra mile to help us complete our assignment.

I would be remiss if I did not acknowledge the staff at John Jay College who facilitated the work of the team doing the study. Everything including finding space for the project office, installation of computers, providing logistical support for meetings, and posting this report on the John Jay College website happened because many individuals pitched in. This was truly a collective endeavor of the College, and as President I would like to thank each and every person who contributed to this historic social science research project.

The data which John Jay College collected will provide the basis for the development of hypotheses and analyses which explain the causes of the distressing sexual abuse phenomenon presented in this report. Even more important, it is my fervent hope that the facts which the John Jay study presents will ultimately work to prevent recurrence of such victimization of children in the future.

Gerald W. Lynch
President
John Jay College of Criminal Justice

EXECUTIVE SUMMARY

The study of sexual abuse of minors by Catholic priests and deacons resulting in this report was authorized and paid for by the United States Conference of Catholic Bishops (USCCB) pursuant to the *Charter for the Protection of Children and Young People* (*Charter*) unanimously adopted by the USCCB at its June 2002 meeting. The *Charter* called for many responses to this victimization of minors within the Catholic Church. Article 9 of the *Charter* provided for the creation of a lay body, the National Review Board, which was mandated (among other things) to commission a descriptive study of the nature and scope of the problem of child sexual abuse in the Catholic Church.

Accordingly, the Board approached John Jay College of Criminal Justice to conduct such a study. The College assembled an experienced team of researchers with expertise in the areas of forensic psychology, criminology, and human behavior, and, working with the Board, formulated a methodology to address the study mandate. Data collection commenced in March 2003, and ended in February 2004. The information contained in this report is based upon surveys provided by 195 dioceses, representing 98% all diocesan priests in the United States, and 140 religious communities, representing approximately 60% of religious communities and 80% of all religious priests.

The mandate for the study was to:

1. Examine the number and nature of allegations of sexual abuse of minors under the age of 18 by Catholic priests between 1950 and 2002.
2. Collect information about the alleged abusers, including official status in the church, age, number of victims, responses by the church and legal authorities to the allegations of abuse, and other characteristics of the alleged abusers.
3. Collect information about the characteristics of the alleged victims, the nature of their relationship to the alleged abusers, the nature of the abuse, and the time frame within which the allegations are reported.
4. Accumulate information about the financial impact of the abuse on the Church.

Three surveys provide the data for this study:

1. A profile of each diocese, providing information about characteristics of the diocese including region and size, the total numbers of allegations, and the total expenditures occasioned by allegations of abuse.
2. A survey of church records relating to individual priests against whom allegations of abuse had been made.
3. A survey of church records relating to the alleged victims of abuse and the nature of the alleged abuse.

Based upon the inquiries and communications that we received from the dioceses, eparchies and religious communities, it is our impression that, despite the complexity of the surveys and the difficulties of identifying relevant church records, these data reflect a conscientious and good-faith effort to provide exhaustive and reliable information regarding allegations of abuse made to church authorities.

Due to the sensitive nature of the abuse allegations, which form the core of this report, many steps were taken to assure the anonymity of alleged victims and priests who were the subjects of the study. The study used a double-blind procedure in which all reports were first sent to Ernst & Young, an accounting firm, where they were stripped of information that could be used to identify the area from which they were sent. Ernst & Young then sent the unopened envelopes containing survey responses to the John Jay researchers. The data set is thus stripped of all identifying information that may be linked to an individual diocese, eparchy or religious community, priest or victim.

OVERVIEW OF PREVALENCE AND REPORTING

PREVALENCE

- Priest surveys asked for birth dates and initials of the accused priests in order to determine if a single priest had allegations in multiple dioceses, eparchies or religious communities. To maintain anonymity, this information was encrypted into a unique identifying number, and birthdays and initials were then discarded. We detected 310 matching encrypted numbers, accounting for 143 priests with allegations in more than one diocese, eparchy or religious community (3.3% of the total number of priests with allegations). When we removed the replicated files of priests who have allegations in more than one place, we received allegations of sexual abuse against a total of 4,392 priests that were not withdrawn or known to be false for the period 1950-2002.

- The total number of priests with allegations of abuse in our survey is 4,392. The percentage of all priests with allegations of sexual abuse is difficult to derive because there is no definitive number of priests who were active between the years of 1950 and 2002. We used two sets of numbers to estimate the total number of active priests and then calculated the percentage against whom allegations were made.

  o We asked each diocese, eparchy and community for their total number of active priests in this time period. Adding up all their responses, there were 109,694 priests reported by dioceses, eparchies and religious communities to have served in their ecclesiastical ministry from 1950-2002. Using this number, 4.0% of all priests active between 1950 and 2002 had allegations of abuse.

  o The Center for Applied Research in the Apostolate (CARA) reports a total of 94,607 priests for the period 1960-2002. When we look at the time period covered by the CARA database, the number of priests with allegations of sexual abuse is 4,127. Thus, the percentage of priests accused for this time period is 4.3% if we rely on the CARA figures assessing the total number of priests.

  o If we examine the differences between diocesan and religious priests, then our numbers result in a total of 4.3% of diocesan priests with allegations of abuse and 2.5% of religious priests with allegations of abuse. The CARA numbers yield a total of 5% of diocesan priests from 1960-1996 with allegations of abuse and 2.7% of religious priests from 1960-1996 with allegations of abuse.

- Our analyses revealed little variability in the rates of alleged abuse across regions of the Catholic Church in the U.S.—the range was from 3% to 6% of priests.

- A total of 10,667 individuals made allegations of child sexual abuse by priests. Of those who alleged abuse, the file contained information that 17.2% of them had siblings who were also allegedly abused.

- It is impossible to determine from our surveys what percent of all actual cases of abuse that occurred between 1950 and 2002 have been reported to the Church and are therefore in our dataset. Allegations of child sexual abuse are made gradually over an extended time period and it is likely that further allegations will be made with respect to recent time periods covered in our surveys. Less than 13% of allegations were made in the year in which the abuse allegedly began, and more than 25% of the allegations were made more than 30 years after the alleged abuse began.

DISTRIBUTION OF CASES BY YEAR

- The distribution of reported cases by the year the abuse is alleged to have occurred or begun shows a peak in the year 1970. However, considering the duration of some repeated abusive acts, more abuse occurred in the 1970s than any other decade, peaking in 1980. But, these conclusions have to be qualified because additional allegations for those time periods may surface in the future.

- Alleged abuse sometimes extended over many years. In 38.4% of allegations, the abuse is alleged to have occurred within a single year, in 21.8% the alleged abuse lasted more than a year but less than 2 years, in 28% between 2 and 4 years, in 10.2% between 5 and 9 years and, in under 1%, 10 or more years.

- Approximately one-third of all allegations were reported in 2002-2003, and two-thirds have been made since 1993. Thus, prior to 1993, only one-third of cases were known to Church officials. The allegations made in 1993 and 2002-2003 include offenses that allegedly occurred within the full time period from 1950-1993 and 1950-2002. The distribution of allegations made in 2002-2003 resembles the distribution of offenses alleged at all other time periods—with the exception that allegations of abuse in recent years are a smaller share of all allegations.

COSTS OF ALLEGATIONS

- The amount of money already paid by the Church, as a result of allegations, to victims, for the treatment of priests and for legal expenses reported in our surveys was $472,000,000. That figure is not the total paid by the Church to date—14% of dioceses and religious communities did not report dollar figures. In addition, survey responses were filed over a 10-month period and would not include settlements and expenses incurred after surveys were submitted. In addition, no diocese reported the recent and highly publicized $85,000,000 settlement. If we include the $85,000,000 reported settlement, the total cost paid by the church exceeds $500,000,000.

PRIESTS AND ACCUSERS

PROFILE OF PRIESTS WITH ALLEGATIONS

- The majority of priests with allegations of abuse were ordained between 1950 and 1979 (68%). Priests ordained prior to 1950 accounted for 21.3% of the allegations, and priests ordained after 1979 accounted for 10.7% of allegations.

- Over 79% of these priests were between 25 and 29 years of age when ordained. For priests whose age at the time of the first alleged abuse was reported, the largest group—over 40% was between 30 and 39. An additional 20% were under age 30, nearly 23% were between 40 and 49, and nearly 17% were over 50.

- At the time abuse is alleged to have occurred, 42.3% of priests were associate pastors, 25.1% were pastors, 10.4% were resident priests and 7.2% were teachers. Other categories (e.g., chaplain, deacon, and seminary administrator) were under 3% each.

- The majority of priests (56%) were alleged to have abused one victim, nearly 27% were alleged to have abused two or three victims, nearly 14% were alleged to have abused four to nine victims and 3.4% were alleged to have abused more than ten victims. The 149 priests (3.5%) who had more than ten allegations of abuse were allegedly responsible for abusing 2,960 victims, thus accounting for 26% of allegations. Therefore, a very small percentage of accused priests are responsible for a substantial percentage of the allegations.

- Though priests' personnel files contain limited information on their own childhood victimization and their substance and/or alcohol abuse problems, the surveys report that nearly 7% of priests had been physically, sexually and/or emotionally abused as children. The surveys also indicate that nearly 17% had alcohol or substance abuse problems. There are indications that some sort of intervention was undertaken by church authorities in over 80% of the cases involving substance abuse.

- The surveys indicate that 32% of priests who were subject to allegations of sexual abuse were also recognized as having other behavioral or psychological problems.

OFFENSE CHARACTERISTICS

- The largest group of alleged victims (50.9%) was between the ages of 11 and 14, 27.3% were 15-17, 16% were 8-10 and nearly 6% were under age 7. Overall, 81% of victims were male and 19% female. Male victims tended to be older than female victims. Over 40% of all victims were males between the ages of 11 and 14.

- Of the total number accused, 37% of priests with allegations of sexual abuse participated in treatment programs; the most common treatment programs were sex-offender specific treatment programs specifically for clergy and one-on-one psychological counseling. The more allegations a priest had, the more likely he was to participate in treatment. However, the severity of the alleged offense did not have an effect on whether or not a priest participated in a treatment program. Those who allegedly committed acts of penetration or oral sex were no more likely to participate in treatment than priests accused of less severe offenses.

- Priests allegedly committed acts which were classified into more than 20 categories. The most frequent acts allegedly committed were: touching over the victim's clothing (52.6%), touching under the victim's clothes (44.9%), cleric performing oral sex (26%), victim disrobed (25.7%), and penile penetration or attempted penile penetration (22.4%). Many of the abusers were alleged to have committed multiple types of abuse against individual victims, and relatively few priests committed only the most minor acts. Of the 90% of the reported incidents for which we had specific offense details, 141 incidents, or one and one half percent, were reported that included only verbal abuse and/or the use of pornography.

- The alleged abuse occurred in a variety of locations. The abuse is alleged to have occurred in the following locations: in the priest's home or the parish residence (40.9%), in the church (16.3%), in the victim's home (12.4%), in a vacation house (10.3%), in school (10.3%), and in a car (9.8%). The abuse allegedly occurred in other sites, such as church outings or in a hotel room, in less than 10% of the allegations. The most common event or setting in which the abuse occurred was during a social event (20.4%), while visiting or working at the priest's home (14.7%), and during travel (17.8%). Abuse allegedly occurred in other settings, such as during counseling, school hours, and sporting events, in less than 10% of the allegations.

- In the 51% of cases where information was provided, half of the victims who made allegations of sexual abuse (2,638, or 25.7% of all alleged victims) socialized with the priest outside of church. Of those who did socialize with the priests who allegedly abused them, the majority had interactions in the family's home. Other places of socialization included in the church, in the residence of the priest, and in various church activities.

REPORTING AND ACTIONS TAKEN

- To date, the police have been contacted about 1,021 priests with allegations of abuse, or 24% of our total. Nearly all of these reports have led to investigations, and 384 instances have led to criminal charges. Of those priests for whom information about dispositions is available, 252 were convicted and at least 100 of those served time in prison. Thus, 6% of all priests against whom allegations were made were convicted and about 2% received prison sentences to date.

- Half of the allegations that were made (49.9%) were reported by the victim. In one-fifth of the cases (20.3%), the allegation of sexual abuse was made by the alleged victim's attorney. The third most common way in which the abuse was reported was by the parent or guardian of the victim (13.6%). Allegations made by other individuals, such as by a police officer, a sibling, or another priest, occurred in 3% of cases or less. These allegations were most commonly made by calling the diocese (30.2%), in a signed letter to the diocese (22.8%), or in a legal filing (10.5%). All other methods by which the allegations were made, such as in person, by telling a trusted priest, or through the media, occurred in less than 10% of cases. Cases reported in 2002 had a similar distribution of types of reporting as in previous years.

The full report contains more detailed and additional analyses related to the information provided above. This report is descriptive in nature. Future reports will examine the relationships among the variables described here in more detail and will be multivariate and analytic in nature.

THE MANDATE FOR THE STUDY

1.1 INTRODUCTION

In June 2002, the United States Conference of Catholic Bishops (USCCB) met in Dallas, Texas, and promulgated the *Charter for the Protection of Children and Young People*, in order to address the problem of child sexual abuse by Catholic priests. This *Charter* included a commitment to provide a thorough accounting of the nature and scope of the problem within the Catholic Church in the United States. Through the *Charter*, the USCCB formed two entities to address the problem of child sexual abuse in the Church: a group of lay Catholics who would comprise the National Review Board and the Office of Child and Youth Protection (OCYP), led by Kathleen McChesney, who served as executive director. The two groups would share a mandate to investigate and review the prevalence of sexual abuse in the Church, the causes of the abuse, and the procedures for responding to clergy who have been accused of abuse.

To carry out this mandate, the USCCB *Charter* indicated that two studies would be conducted—the first to describe the nature and scope of the problem and the second to examine its causes and context. This first study, entitled, "The Nature and Scope of the Problem of Sexual Abuse of Children by Catholic Priests and Deacons within the United States," was commissioned by the National Review Board and funded by the USCCB. The objectives of this study were to collect, organize, and summarize information available in Church files about the sexual abuse of minors (children under 18 years of age) by priests and deacons in the Catholic Church of the United States from 1950 through 2002. Specifically, Article 9 of the *Charter* states:

> The work of the Office for Child and Youth Protection will be assisted and monitored by a Review Board, including parents, appointed by the Conference President and reporting directly to him. The Board will approve the annual report of the implementation of this Charter in each of our dioceses/eparchies, as well as any recommendations that emerge from this review, before the report is submitted to the President of the Conference and published. To understand the problem more fully and to enhance the effectiveness of our future response, the National Review Board will also commission a descriptive study, with the full cooperation of our dioceses/eparchies, of the nature and scope of the problem within the Catholic Church in the United States, including such data as statistics on perpetrators and victims.

In December 2002, Kathleen McChesney, Director of the OCYP, approached the president of John Jay College of Criminal Justice, Gerald Lynch, Ph.D., to discuss the feasibility of the college conducting the first of the two mandated studies, as established by the *Charter*. The college was selected because it is a secular institution, with a national reputation in the fields of criminal justice, criminology, and forensic psychology.

President Lynch convened a group of faculty with relevant expertise who met with Kathleen McChesney and representatives of the USCCB to discuss the framework for the study on the nature and scope of child sexual abuse by priests in the Catholic Church. After a number of discussions, a contract was signed by USCCB and the Research Foundation of the City University of New York on behalf of John Jay College to conduct the study. Funding for the study was provided by the USCCB, with oversight by the

National Review Board. The overall purpose of the study was to provide the first-ever, complete accounting, or census, of the number of priests against whom allegations of child sexual abuse were made and of the incidents alleged to have occurred between 1950 and 2002.

To guide the study, Kathleen McChesney, on behalf of the USCCB, gave the College a specific set of questions to be answered, which defined the scope of the study. The questions focused on four specific areas of concern (see Appendix A.1.1.1 for a complete list of the questions). The first category involved information about the alleged offenses themselves (e.g., the number of allegations, the location in which the behavior is alleged to have occurred). Information about the priests against whom allegations were made was the focus of the second category of questions. These included questions about the age, status and duties at the time of the alleged offense, background information about the priest, whether the Church took action in response to the allegation, and what form that response took. The third category focused on information about those who made the accusations (e.g., their age at the time of the offense, their gender, the time between the offense and the report). Finally, information about the financial impact of these allegations on the dioceses and religious communities was requested.

In response to this mandate, a team of criminologists, forensic psychologists, and methodologists drawn from the John Jay faculty John developed three data collection instruments, or surveys (see Appendices A.1.1.2 – 5). The surveys were pre-tested, revised, and distributed to each of the 202 United States dioceses and eparchies (i.e. Eastern Church dioceses). The Catholic Church in the United States also includes 221 religious orders of men, formally called Religious Institutes of Men. Many of these groups are divided into provinces and include autonomous cloistered communities, monasteries or abbeys. The major superiors, leaders of the religious institutes, agreed to participate and sent the survey materials to the individual provinces or communities, where files on individual priests are kept. As a result, survey responses were submitted by three different types of religious communities: by religious institutes; by provinces of religious institutes; and by autonomous monasteries or abbeys. In this report, all three kinds of communities will be referred to as religious communities, to be understood in contrast to the dioceses and eparchies.

The John Jay College faculty developed detailed procedures to ensure complete confidentiality of the survey responders, which are discussed in chapter 1.2 (see also Appendices A.1.1.6 – 7). The faculty worked with the USCCB to maximize compliance with the survey by actively responding to questions and developing procedures to ensure that state-level confidentiality laws were not violated by any institution participating in the study. Surveys were returned by 195 of the 202 dioceses and eparchies, which constitutes a 97% compliance rate. Surveys were returned by approximately 60% of religious communities representing 80% of the religious priests in the United States.

The remainder of this report will describe in detail the findings of the study. The next sections of Part One explain in detail the methodology used in this study, the limitations of the study design, and the terminology used. Part Two presents an overview of the findings about the overall number and distribution of allegations. Part Three focuses on the characteristics of the accused priests themselves and Part Four provides details about and circumstances of the allegations.

Parts Five and Six discuss the reporting of these allegations and the actions taken by the dioceses and religious communities. Each Part begins by introducing the research context for the understanding the data and continues with a summary of the findings and subchapters that give detailed tables of data.

Appendices to each Part contain additional statistical information.

In presenting these findings in as clear, objective, and comprehensive manner as possible, it is the hope of the study team that an accounting of the scope of the problem over the last 50 years will ground future research and reform efforts.

1.2   METHODOLOGY - HOW THE STUDY WAS CARRIED OUT

The specific research questions posed by the United States Conference of Catholic Bishops (USCCB) (see Appendix A1.1.1) required a careful and thorough accounting at the national level of the number of priests against whom allegations of child sexual abuse had been made as well as the number of overall allegations that had come to the attention of the Church over the last 50 years. The study team had a unique opportunity to solicit this information from all 202 dioceses and 221 religious institutes, together comprising the population of Catholic priests in the United States. The study had the full backing of the USCCB to ensure, to the greatest extent possible, full cooperation from all levels of church hierarchy throughout the country.

STUDY APPROACH

It was clear from the outset that the study team would not itself have access to the confidential Church files, nor did we have sufficient time to conduct a study that would reach all 50 states including every diocese and religious community within the United States, and cover a 52-year timeframe.   Given this framework, the research team decided to collect the data necessary by constructing survey instruments and mailing them to each diocese, eparchy and religious institute in the country. Such a population-based survey approach provided the optimum strategy for fulfilling the mandate of the study to produce as complete a census as possible of the scope of the problem of sexual abuse of minors within the Catholic Church. Additionally, such an approach could make a significant contribution to the literature on child sexual abuse since no previous population-based research had been conducted.   While research on child sexual abuse in the general population by professionals and academic researchers is substantial, there has been, to date, no population-based research on the characteristics or patterns of behavior of sexual abuse in any single population. The information that was previously available on child sexual in the Catholic Church had been obtained from small samples, largely clinical samples, focused on a specific sub-population (e.g., one parish or diocese) or taken from public records. Therefore, it was our hope that by taking this approach, we would both fulfill the mandate of the Charter and make a significant contribution to this important literature.

STUDY DESIGN

As with any study, the questions to be answered drove the construction of the survey instruments. The study mandate suggested that we needed to address three specific targets: the dioceses/eparchies/religious communities, the priests against whom allegations had been made, and the incidents described in those allegations.   Thus, each diocese, eparchy or religious community would complete one survey focused on their institution as a whole, one survey for each priest against whom allegation(s) of abuse had been made, and one survey for each alleged incident(s) of abuse connected with each priest.   As a result we were able to construct three separate surveys, which taken together, provided a more comprehensive assessment of the scope of the problem.

The Diocesan Profile. The first survey was the "Diocesan/Order Profile" (Appendices A.1.1.2 and A.1.1.3). The aim of this survey was to establish aggregate numbers for the particular diocese/eparchy or religious community – the number of priests against whom allegations had been made and the total number of individuals making allegations. We were able to obtain a census of active and retired priests in the diocese/eparchy/religious community during the study period, 1950 – 2002. The survey consisted of ten questions, half of which provided us with demographic information about the units, and the other half, a profile of the scope of the problem within that unit. Dioceses and eparchies were asked to indicate the church region, the Catholic population, and the number of parishes within their boundaries. Religious communities were asked for the total number of members in the community. Because survey responses contained no identifying information (see our discussion of confidentiality issues later in this section), the broad demographic characteristics, presented in deciles, assisted us in evaluating the survey response rate. The survey then asked for a global number, based on the review of the church records, of the number of priests against whom allegations of abuse had been made and, of those, how many had been completely exonerated. It also requested the total number of individuals who made the allegations and asked specifically for the number of those allegations that had been shown to be false or that had been withdrawn. These unfounded or withdrawn allegations were not included in any further reporting.

The Cleric Survey. The second survey sent to study respondents was the "Cleric Survey" (Appendix A.1.1.4). This instrument included 17 questions, with 18 follow-up questions, and focused on individual priests. It was to be completed from existing files and records for each and every priest who had been named in a complaint or allegation of sexual abuse of a minor that was known to a diocese, eparchy or religious community. We were seeking answers to several types of questions in this survey. First, we wanted information related to the history of the individual priest who was accused of abuse, including specifications of the seminary he attended and the history of where he ministered in the Catholic Church (e.g., whether the priest had been transferred within or between dioceses). The relevant history also included information from the file concerning whether he himself had been abused and whether he had a known substance abuse problem or other medical/psychological conditions. The next set of questions related to the individuals who had made allegations against this particular priest, including their number, their age(s) and gender(s). The final section of the "Cleric Survey" focused on the actions taken by the Church in response to the allegations of abuse against this particular priest. These questions focused on the action taken by the church in response to the allegation (e.g., whether the priest was reprimanded, referred for treatment, or removed from duty). They also asked more specifically whether the priest participated in and/or completed any type of treatment, and the years in which those interventions would have occurred. The responses to the three sets of questions in this survey thus provided information on the scope and nature of the problem, information about those against whom allegations were made, and information about the church's response to the alleged offenses.

The Victim Survey. The third survey, titled the "Victim Survey," focused on incidents of alleged abuse. The aim of this survey was to capture information about each allegation that was made against a particular priest (Appendix A.1.1.5). In other words, for every priest against whom allegations were made, a separate and unique third survey was completed for each one of the alleged incidents. So, for example, if the "Cleric Survey" indicated that this particular priest had five allegations made against him, then five incident surveys would have been completed and submitted as part of the package of material on that particular priest. Surveys were neither requested nor submitted for those allegations that had been shown to be false or were withdrawn, or those for which the priest had been exonerated. This survey included 36 questions, with 18 follow-up questions. Like the "Cleric Survey," it was to be completed based on the information about the victim in the alleged abuser's file.

This incident survey was divided into two sections. The first section of the survey sought basic information on the person who brought an allegation against this particular priest[1] and about the incident or incidents themselves. This included information on the individual's gender; age at both the time of offense and time the offense was reported; method by which the allegation and follow-ups to the allegation were made; timeframe and type of alleged incident(s); threats, gifts, or enticements used to coax or coerce the individual into participating in sexual conduct and action(s) taken by the Catholic institution and/or civil authorities as a result of the incident(s). The second part of the survey sought information on the financial impact of the incident or incidents of alleged abuse reported in the preceding section. These questions asked about monies paid for treatment of both the victim and the priest, legal fees associated with the incident(s), and overall compensation to the accuser.

Pilot Testing of Surveys. During the development of the survey instruments, in February and March 2003, the research team consulted with many individuals associated with the Church, including members of the National Review Board, the Office of Child and Youth Protection, as well as numerous diocesan and religious priests who agreed to provide feedback to us on the content and wording of the survey instruments. Numerous meetings were held in which terminology categories of responses were refined, e.g., types of responses a diocese might have taken and manners in which allegations might have come to the Church's attention.

A formal pre-test was also conducted in one diocese. For this pre-test, a high-ranking official within the diocese, at the direction of the presiding bishop, completed the draft survey instruments using actual data from diocesan files, and provided detailed comments to the principal investigator about their content, readability and accessibility. These comments and suggestions were used to refine the study instruments.

STUDY PROCEDURE

In April 2003, a package containing one copy of each of the three separate survey instruments was sent to all 202 dioceses and eparchies in the United States. Prior to that mailing, a letter was sent to all dioceses and eparchies from Bishop Gregory, President of the USCCB, alerting bishops to the study, reminding them of the mandate to comply with the study as stated in the Charter, and requesting full compliance with it.

Unlike the dioceses and eparchies, whose participation was mandated by the Charter, the religious communities of men were invited to participate in the study. When their agreement was given in June 2003, the survey materials were sent to the 140 religious institutes of men in the United States. These religious orders then distributed the surveys to their provinces and autonomous monasteries or abbeys. The organization of religious communities is such that the files with the information being sought for the study were held in the provinces and autonomous communities of many religious orders, rather than at their central offices, so this second level of distribution by the religious institute was required.

Reliability of Data. With so many separate entities within the Catholic Church in the United States preparing to complete the surveys, a number of affirmative steps were taken to maximize the reliability and consistency of the data. First, the surveys were mailed to each diocese, eparchy and religious community with a packet of information that included two forms of instruction - written instructions (see Appendix A.1.1.6) and, a videotape with detailed instructions about how to fill out the surveys, how to handle the process of mailing the surveys once they were completed, and how to obtain additional guidance and information if needed during survey completion. Second, the research team provided anonymous telephone and email support five days a week from 10 am to 6 pm, adding an 800 number during the summer months. A number of research assistants were specially trained to answer the telephone and to keep a log of all calls, each of which was reviewed by a member of the study team. Notes were kept on the caller questions, and written responses were regularly updated. Third, as the volume of calls grew during the summer and a pattern of questions was discerned, a highly secure website with answers to frequently asked questions[2] was made available in July 2003. The telephone, email and web site support was continued throughout the study period until February 2004. Fourth, members of the John Jay College research team attended the biannual meeting of the USCCB in St. Louis to meet with the bishops and answer any questions they had about the study. And, finally, the structure of the survey instruments themselves assisted in ensuring reliability. The three surveys employed multiple measures of the same information, thus providing additional internal reliability checks for the results.[3]

Survey Responses. The data collection process lasted approximately eleven months. At first, many bishops and religious superiors had reservations about the study, and some explicitly opposed it. Through discussion, consultation, and the exchange of questions and responses, the research team was able to resolve the concerns of most of the bishops and major superiors, especially their worries about concealing the identities of accused priests. Because all states present unique legal issues, the research team also worked with diocesan attorneys around the country to reduce their concerns and to ensure that the data collection process would not affect pending or potential law suits involving the Catholic Church.[4] Ultimately, 97% of the dioceses and eparchies returned the surveys, an extraordinarily high response rate for any type of survey research, though perhaps not surprising given the mandate from the Charter and the significant efforts made by all parties to guarantee confidentiality and alleviate concerns. In general, the surveys were complete and showed careful attention to detail, as indicated by the many specific comments provided in the surveys. There was not, however, uniformity in terms of the amount of support, staff and resources that were available around the country, and so the responses did vary in terms of completeness and level of detail provided.

Data Entry. All aspects of data coding, entry, and analysis were directed by a data analyst, working in consultation with the study's principal investigator. Actual coding and data entry were done by 16 research assistants. All research assistants were thoroughly trained by both the principal investigator and data analyst, not only in the specific procedures for dealing with the survey data, but, most importantly, to equip them to understand the importance of the study's complex confidentiality provisions. All study materials and documents were recorded when they were received by John Jay College during the entire study period. Information from the surveys was recorded in files using both statistical and database software.

CONFIDENTIALITY

Ensuring the confidentiality of individuals mentioned in the Church's files was an important element that influenced the design of the study and, ultimately, allowed dioceses and religious communities to participate fully in the study. The research team was concerned about the confidentiality of and risks to those individuals who reported sexual abuse; their friends and family members; priests and deacons against whom allegations had been made; Church employees and the dioceses and religious institutes themselves.

A number of steps were taken to ensure confidentiality. The first decision was that no one on the John Jay College team would have direct contact with the files or records that were the property of the Church. The only persons who had any direct contact with the Catholic Church files used to complete the survey instruments were those persons designated by their bishop or major superior.

Secondly, the study team put into place complex procedures to ensure that no identifying information about any individual who made an allegation of abuse, any priest against whom an allegation had been made, nor any individual diocese, eparchy or religious community would be included on any study materials that came to John Jay College.

Our files contain no personal identifying information beyond age at the time of the alleged incident and gender for those persons who made allegations of abuse against priests. The information for the surveys was taken from existing files, so no new contact was initiated with any person who reported abuse by a priest or any member of his or her family.

With respect to the priests against whom allegations had been made, a challenge arose because one interest of the USCCB was to determine whether individual priests had allegations of child sexual abuse in more than one diocese, eparchy or religious community. In order to answer this question, the researchers needed to be able to give a unique identifying number to each priest, which would then permit us to track information about him from more than one diocese. To do this accurately the researchers needed to collect, at a minimum, the initials and date of birth of each priest who had been the subject of an allegation.

Given this necessity, the following steps were taken to protect the confidentiality of each priest and his community:

1. No survey, nor any study communication of any kind bearing a postmark, was sent directly to John Jay College from any Catholic Church group. An independent auditor, a certified public accountant at a nationally known accounting firm, was designated to receive all communications from Catholic Church representatives.

2. Clear instructions were provided to respondents that all completed survey instruments were to be placed in blank envelopes that were then sealed. Those sealed, blank envelopes were then placed in another envelope or box with a piece of diocesan or religious community stationary and sent to the auditor. When these packages were received by the auditor, the outer envelope and the letterhead were used to make a record of the sender, for purposes of response rate calculation only. A random code number was then assigned to each respondent unit of the Catholic Church. The codes were recorded on the blank envelopes, and the materials boxed and sent to John Jay College. From the time of receipt by John Jay College, the materials were only known by their code numbers. Only the completed surveys that had been placed in sealed envelopes and mailed were seen by the John Jay College research team.

3. All external envelopes, packaging and records that linked the sender to the survey data were destroyed by the auditor.

4. The study's principal investigator opened each one of the envelopes. She recorded the identifying information for each priest—initials and birthdate—and then removed that page from the survey. The identifying data was immediately encrypted and the surveys numbered with a unique numerical code for each priest. The pages with initials and dates of birth were segregated in a secure location, separate from the study office, until data collection was complete. These paper records, and the digital record, have been destroyed.

5. The principal investigator carefully inspected all surveys for accidental disclosure of sensitive or identifying data. If there was any identifying information written on the survey itself, this information was immediately redacted before the surveys were given to the research assistants for coding.

6. Although the formal procedures made it very unlikely that any accidental disclosure of sensitive data would occur, it is always possible that there would be a lapse and sensitive data about victims or abusers be transmitted. Accordingly, the study design included several levels of training in confidentiality protections for diocesan staff and study research assistants in order to reduce the possibility of accidental exposure.

The John Jay College research team sought and was granted approval to conduct the study by the College's Institutional Review Board which oversees protection of human subjects in research. Additionally, the team applied for a Certificate of Confidentiality, which can be granted by the United States Department of Health and Human Services (DHHS) to protect against "compelled disclosure of identifying information about subjects of biomedical, behavioral, clinical, and other research." The certificate protects the researchers against involuntary disclosure about the identities of research participants and is understood to bar any legal demand for testimony in court. Such a certificate does not prevent any individual priest, victim, diocese or religious community from voluntarily releasing data. After a number of meetings and discussions, DHHS in November 2003 declined not to grant a Certificate of Confidentiality for the study. A major reason for denying the certificate was the determination that the John Jay College researchers had taken adequate measures to ensure that all identifying information would be removed and the surveys would be confidential, thereby precluding the need for a certificate. Additionally, since the primary purpose of the certificate is to protect human subjects who have given their consent to participate in research related to confidential matters that may adversely affect them, this framework did not apply to the John Jay study since the priests were not voluntary research participants, and their consent had not been sought nor granted. Therefore, they were uncertain as to whether it was legally possible to issue a certificate, which is primarily used as a vehicle to encourage human subjects to participate in a research project. In their letter explaining the rejection of a certificate, it was stated that the confidentiality plan for the study "includes multiple and wide-ranging protections for subject identifiers" and as such, "a certificate is not necessary to achieve your research goals." (See Appendix A.1.1.7 for a copy of the letter.)

---

[1] The survey did not request any personal information about those making the allegations, other than age and gender.

[2] The study website employed multiple levels of security to ensure that the public could not locate the site or access the questions and answers. The identification name and password were sent directly to each bishop or major superior so that he or his staff could access the website.

[3] Although we worded the definitions carefully to ensure that those filling out the questionnaires would do so in a uniform manner, in a study of this type, it is impossible to create an infallible operational definition with criteria so specific that everyone supplying the information would do so in exactly the same way. Therefore, some degree of variance in the responses is inevitable.

[4] For instance, California law prohibits the disclosure of any identifying information related to sexual behavior. As a result, we worked out complicated procedures whereby identifying information (which was used only to allow us to identify priests who had been moved from one diocese to another) was encrypted prior to being sent to the study headquarters so that California respondents did not transmit any identifying information.

1.3   STUDY TERMINOLOGY

Allegation
Any accusation that is not *implausible* (see definition below). This includes allegations that did not necessarily result in a criminal, civil or diocesan investigation and allegations that are unsubstantiated.

> An *implausible* allegation is one that could not possibly have happened under the given circumstances (e.g., an accusation is made to a bishop about a priest who never served at that diocese). Erroneous information does not necessarily make the allegation implausible (e.g., a priest arrived at the diocese a year after the alleged abuse, but all other facts of the case are credible and the alleged victim might have mistaken the date).

Boundary Problem
Inability to maintain a clear and appropriate interpersonal (physical as well as emotional) distance between two individuals where such a separation is expected and necessary. Boundary problems can be mild to moderate, such as the case of a therapist or teacher who develops a personal relationship with his/her student or patient; or, they may be severe, as in the development of an intimate relationship.

Canon law
According to http://www.newadvent.org/cathen/09056a.htm, canon law is the body of laws and regulations made by or adopted by ecclesiastical authority, for the government of the Christian organization and its members. The word *adopted* is here used to point out the fact that there are certain elements in canon law borrowed by the Church from civil law or from the writings of private individuals, who as such had no authority in ecclesiastical society.

Diocese
A geographical division of the Catholic Church led by a bishop that includes Catholic communicants ("the faithful") and parishes.

Eparchy
A Catholic Church jurisdiction, similar to a diocese, of Eastern-rite Catholics living in the United States.

Ephebophile (also called hebophile)
A clinical term (though not included in the DSM-IV) that denotes one who is sexually attracted to adolescent or post-pubescent children.

Extern
A priest who has not been incardinated to the diocese where he is working and living.

False allegation
An allegation that was proven to be untruthful and fabricated.

Incardinated
A priest who has been formally affiliated to a diocese is said to be incardinated in that diocese

Incidence
Used to convey the number of new events occurring in a specific time period.

Institutional Review Board (IRB)
Each institution engaged in research involving human subjects that is supported by a department or agency to which the federal policy applies must establish an IRB to review and approve the research. Under the regulations, an institution can also establish more than one IRB, which may be necessary or appropriate, depending on the structure of the institution or the kinds of human subjects research that is performed at that institution. Alternatively, an institution can designate another institution's IRB to review its research upon approval of the appropriate department or agency. If the research is supported by the Department of Health and Human Services, such designations must have the prior approval of the Office for Protection from Research Risks.

Laicization
Conversion from an ecclesiastical to a lay condition.

Mean
The average value of a set of numbers.

Median
The mid-point in a set of numbers. In other words, fifty percent of cases fall above and fifty percent of cases fall below the median.

National Review Board (NRB)
Established by the United States Conference of Catholic Bishops in 2002 to commission a study on the "nature and scope" of child sexual abuse in the Catholic Church. See http://www.usccb.org/ocyp/nrb.htm.

Ordained/Ordination
The sacramental rite by which a "sacred order" is conferred (diaconate, priesthood, episcopacy). The ceremony of consecration to the ministry.

Permanent Deacon
According to the Official Catholic Directory (A-14), they are sometimes referred to as "married deacons," although the permanent diaconate is open to both married and unmarried men, with the understanding that after ordination, they may not marry even after the death of a spouse. Under the authority of the diocesan bishop, they perform the same functions as transitional deacons while, at the same time, retaining their roles in society as family and business men.

Prevalence
The total number (or estimate of the total number) of cases or events at a given time.

Region (of the Catholic Church in the United States)
One of fourteen geographical areas, or divisions, of the Catholic Church in the United States.

Reliability
Data that is consistent, yielding the same or similar results in different clinical experiments or statistical trials.

Religious community
A group that may include ordained clerics and/or non-ordained brothers who are professed members of a religious order, and who live subject to the rules of that order. This term is used in

this study to include members of religious orders or institutes as well as those who reside in cloistered communities, monasteries, and abbeys.

Restricted ministry/ restricted faculties
An administrative decision made by a bishop or major superior to limit the ecclesiastical and/or parish or community functions of an individual priest.

Seminary
An educational institute for men that are preparing for the Holy Orders. Major seminary--A school for the spiritual, academic, and pastoral education and formation of priesthood candidates. Focus is on philosophical and theological teachings. Minor seminary--A prerequisite to the major seminary. Focus is on required courses in the humanities and the sciences.

Sexual abuse of a minor
As per the Charter, sexual abuse includes contacts or interactions between a child and an adult when the child is being used as an object of sexual gratification for the adult. A child is abused whether or not this activity involves explicit force, whether or not it involves genital or physical contact, whether or not it is initiated by the child, and whether or not there is discernible harmful outcome.

Suspension (in Canon Law)
Usually defined as a censure by which a cleric is deprived, entirely or partially of the use of the power of orders, office, or benefice.

Transitional Deacon
The diaconate is the first order or grade in ordained ministry. Any man who is to be ordained to the priesthood must first be ordained as a transitional deacon (also see Permanent Deacon). Deacons serve in the ministry of liturgy, of the work, and of charity (see A-14 of The Official Catholic Directory).

Universe
The set of individuals, items, or data from which a statistical sample is taken.

THE PREVALENCE OF SEXUAL ABUSE OF YOUTHS BY PRIESTS

2.1 ESTIMATES OF THE PREVALENCE OF SEXUAL ABUSE OF YOUTHS UNDER 18 CHILDREN IN THE UNITED STATES

The estimation of any form of deviance in the general population is a very difficult task. It is impossible to assess the extent of sexual offending, either in general or with children as targets. Most estimates of the distribution of sexual offenders in the general population are derived from forensic sources, that is, samples of those who are arrested or convicted for sex offenses. All researchers acknowledge that those who are arrested represent only a fraction of all sexual offenders. Sexual crimes have the lowest rates of reporting for all crimes. Not all potential participants in such studies can be known or contacted, not all would use the same language to describe their experiences, and not all are willing to share information. The sexual abuse of children by Catholic priests and deacons is part of the larger problem of sexual abuse of children in the United States. This chapter is a summary of the estimates of child sexual abuse in the Catholic Church.

RESEARCH ESTIMATES

The prevalence of some event or behavior in a specific population represents the proportion of a population which has experienced the event or behavior. Since it is not known how many people in the United States experience a form of sexual abuse as children, some researchers select groups, or samples, of individuals to study and direct questions to them. If the selection of the group to be surveyed is not biased, the results of this study provide estimates of the prevalence of sexual abuse in the population from which the group is selected. In order to avoid bias in a sample, every person in the part of the population to be used as a framework for selecting the sample must have an equal chance of being asked to participate. Researchers use the data gathered from those who participate to estimate the proportion of the United States population who are sexually abused during childhood.

Studies of the incidence, as opposed to the prevalence, of sexual abuse of children concentrate on estimating the number of new cases occurring over a particular period of time and on whether the number of events or incidents is increasing or decreasing. Scholarly studies of both the incidence and the prevalence of sexual abuse of children in the United States began emerging in the 1960s and gained greater urgency after the cluster of day care center child abuse cases in the 1980s made the issue one of acute public interest. A look at victimization studies that focus on the sexual abuse of minor children suggests that the scope of this problem is extensive.

Although we do not have data reflecting the prevalence of abusers, there are data from several studies reporting the prevalence of victimization. The prevalence rates reported in these studies vary somewhat.

- 27% of the females and 16% of the males disclosed a history of childhood sexual abuse; 42% of the males were likely to never have disclosed the experience to anyone whereas 33% of the females never disclosed.[1]
- 12.8% of the females and 4.3% of the males reported a history of sexual abuse during childhood.[2]
- 15.3% of the females and 5.9% of the males experienced some form of sexual assault.[3]
- Only 5.7% of the incidents were reported to the police; 26% of the incidents were not disclosed to anyone prior to the study.[4]
- In summary, when compared with their male counterparts, females were more likely to have been sexually abused during childhood. Furthermore, females were more likely than males to disclose such information; however, disclosure rates are quite low regardless of the victim's gender.

Finkelhor and Jones have used data from National Child Abuse and Neglect Data System (NCANDS) to make a national estimate of the number of sexual abuse cases substantiated by child protective service (CPS) for the period from 1992 to 2000. Using data from more than forty states, they report that the number of substantiated sexual abuse cases peaked at approximately 149,800 in 1992, followed by annual declines of 2 to 11 percent per year through 2000 when the number of cases reached a low of approximately 89,355.[5]

Professional opinion is divided about why this drop occurred and how much of the drop is real or the result of factors such as changes in definitions, reporting and investigation by the states. Finkelhor and Jones examined other indicia of sex abuse rates and conclude that, taken together, they suggest that at least part of the drop in cases has resulted from a decline in sexual abuse of children.[6] The National Crime Victimization Survey (NCVS)—which asks about rape and sexual assault for victims ages 12 and older (including acts counted within the broader definition of child sexual abuse)—shows that sex offenses against children ages 12-17 declined 56 percent between 1993 and 2000. Virtually all the decline, 72 percent, occurred in offenses committed by known perpetrators (family and acquaintances) which declined.[7] Finkelhor and Jones observe that cases involving known perpetrators are the ones most likely to be categorized as sexual abuse.[8]

Another source of self-report data on sexual abuse is the Minnesota Student Survey, which has been administered to 6th, 9th, and 12th–grade students in Minnesota in 1989, 1992, 1995, 1998, and 2001.[9] Between 90 and 99 percent of Minnesota's school districts and more than 100,000 students have participated in the survey each year. The survey includes two questions about sexual abuse. Results indicate that sexual abuse by family and nonfamily perpetrators showed a slight rise between 1989 and 1992 followed by a 22-percent drop from 1992 to 2001.[10]

At the same time reports of sexual abuse have declined, there has been a significant drop in crime rates and measures of family problems such as violence among adult intimates, and a drop in out-of-wedlock teenage pregnancies and live births to teenage mothers (some of which are attributable to child sexual abuse)—all of these suggest a general improvement in the well-being of children.

Additionally, Finkelhor and Jones suggest that rates of sexual abuse have perhaps been reduced as a result of increased incarceration for sexual abuse offenders. They report that surveys of state correctional facilities indicate that between 1991 and1997, the number of individuals incarcerated in state correctional facilities for sex crimes against children rose 39 percent, from 43,500 to 60,700, having already more than doubled from 19,900 in 1986. They further note that these totals do not include large numbers of sexual abusers who receive sanctions which do not involve incarceration for a year or more.[11]

[1] David Finkelhor et al., "Sexual Abuse in a National Survey of Adult Men and Women: Prevalence, Characteristics, and Risk Factors." *Child Abuse & Neglect* 14 (1990): 20-21.

[2] Harriet L. MacMillan and Jan E. Fleming, "Prevalence of Child Physical and Sexual Abuse in the Community." *Journal of the American Medical Association* 278 (1997): 131-135.

[3] K. Moore, K. Nord, and J. Peterson, "Nonvoluntary Sexual Activity Among Adolescents." *Family Planning Perspectives* 21 (1989): 110-114.

[4] Sue Boney-McCoy and David Finkelhor, "Psychosocial Sequelae of Violent Victimization in a National Youth Sample." *Journal of Consulting and Clinical Psychology* 63 (Oct. 1995): 726-736.

[5] Lisa Jones and David Finkelhor. "Explanations for the Decline in Child Sexual Abuse Cases." *OJJDP Bulletin*. Washington, DC: U.S. Department of Justice, Office of Justice Programs, Office of Juvenile Justice and Delinquency Prevention (2004).

[6] Lisa M. Jones and David Finkelhor, "The Decline in Child Sexual Abuse Cases." *OJJDP Bulletin*. Washington, DC: U.S. Department of Justice, Office of Justice Programs, Office of Juvenile Justice and Delinquency Prevention (2001); Lisa M. Jones, David Finkelhor, and Kathy Kopiec. "Why is sexual abuse declining? A survey of state child protection administrators." *Child Abuse & Neglect* 25 (2001): 1139–1158.

[7] Rennison, C.M. "Criminal Victimization 2000: Changes 1999–2000 with Trends 1993–2000." *Bulletin*. Washington, DC: U.S. Department of Justice, Office of Justice Programs, Bureau of Justice Statistics, 2001.

[8] Jones, 2004.

[9] Harrison, P.A., Fulkerson, J.A., and Beebe,T.J. "Multiple substance use among adolescent physical and sexual abuse victims." *Child Abuse & Neglect* 21(1997): 529–539.

[10] Minnesota Department of Children, Families & Learning, Minnesota Department of Human Services. *Minnesota Student Survey: Key Trends Through 2001*. Roseville, MN: Minnesota Department of Children, Families & Learning, 2001.

[11] David Finkelhor and Richard K. Ormrod, "Factors in the Underreporting of Crimes Against Juveniles" *Child Maltreatment* 6 (2001): 219-230.

2.2 SUMMARY RESULTS: PREVALENCE OF SEXUAL ABUSE OF YOUTHS UNDER 18 BY CATHOLIC PRIESTS AND DEACONS

A paramount concern for all involved with the study has been the determination of the prevalence of the problem in the Catholic Church in the United States. The survey responses make it clear that the problem was indeed widespread and affected more than 95% of dioceses and approximately 60% of religious communities. Of the 195 dioceses and eparchies that participated in the study, all but seven have reported that allegations of sexual abuse of youths under the age of 18 have been made against at least one priest serving in ecclesiastical ministry in that diocese or eparchy. Of the 140 religious communities that submitted surveys, all but 30 reported at least one allegation against a religious priest who was a member of that community.

Researchers asked each diocese, eparchy and religious community to provide the total number of priests who were active, or serving in ministry, between 1950 and 2002 so that the number of the accused could be presented as a part of an overall total. In our effort to understand the scope and distribution of the problem for the dioceses and eparchies, researchers collected information on the region, a geographical division of the Catholic Church, the number of Catholics per diocese, and the number of parishes per diocese. Dioceses and eparchies were asked to indicate these numbers by choosing one of ten equal ranges for the number of Catholic communicants and the number of parishes. The range, i.e., 88,501 – 122,000, 122,001 – 170,000, and so forth, in Catholic population, was used to ensure confidentiality of each study participant. Religious communities were grouped into ten equal groups by their total membership and clerical membership, as reported in the Official Catholic Directory 2002. These different ways of looking at the scope of the problem were used to examine the extent of sexual abuse of youths under 18 by Catholic priests and deacons.

- Dioceses and eparchies reported that allegations of child sexual abuse had been made against 4,692 priests and deacons for incidents that took place while these men were serving in ecclesiastical ministry. Individual survey forms were submitted for 4,557 of these priests. Of these, some surveys had to be eliminated because the victim's was 18 or older or the date of the alleged incident was prior to 1950 or after 2002.

- Religious communities reported that allegations of sexual abuse had been made against 647 priests who were members of their communities. Dioceses reported additional religious priests, for a study total of 929 religious priests.

- When the multiple surveys for the 143 priests who were the subject of allegations in more than one diocese or religious community are condensed to a single record, the total number of Catholic priests and deacons in the United States who have been accused of sexual abuse of children is 4,392.

- When dioceses are grouped by the fourteen geographical regions of the Church, the average percent of all incardinated priests in a region's dioceses to have been accused of sexual abuse is consistent: all regions averaged between 3% and 6% of priests accused.

- If the total number of priests in religious communities who have had allegations made against them is presented as a percentage of all religious priests in ministry, as estimated form the study data, the percentage accused of child sexual abuse is 2.7%.

The consistency of the findings in dioceses across the United States is remarkable: whether region, number of Catholic communicants or number of parishes is used to array the dioceses, the results show allegations of sexual abuse have been made against 2.5% to 7% of diocesan priests. Similarly, whether religious priests are ranked by overall membership of religious clerical membership, the percent of priests in communities who have been accused ranges from 1% to 3%, or approximately half of that of the diocesan priests.

To estimate the percentage of all priests in ecclesiastical ministry between 1950 and 2002 who have been the subject of allegations requires a reliable overall total of priests in ministry during that time period. This calculation was done two different way—first by using the data collected through the Diocesan and Religious Order Profiles and then by using the estimates produced by the Center for Applied Research in the Apostolate[1]. These different methods both yielded the same statistic: approximately 4% of Catholic priests and deacons in active ministry between 1950 and 2002 have been accused of the sexual abuse of a youth under the age of 18.

Surveys for 90% of the priests and deacons reported to have had allegations of child sexual abuse included the year of ordination. If the yearly ordination totals for diocesan priests accused are compared to the overall number of diocesan priests ordained in that year, the percentages of accused priests range from a maximum of almost 10% in 1970, decreasing to 8% in 1980 and to fewer than 4% in 1990.

These prevalence estimates alone do not describe the extent of the problem of sexual abuse. Another way to understand the extent of the problem is to ask how many incidents of sexual abuse were alleged to occur each year of the study period or, alternatively, to ask how many priests were accused in each year. This distribution of alleged abuse events over time shows the pattern of the reported sexual abuse. When the incidents recorded in the surveys are tallied for each year of occurrence (of each incident), the resulting figure shows that 75% of the events were alleged to occur between 1960 and 1984. This result should be considered together with the declining percentage of priests ordained in each year. Additionally, understanding about sexual abuse and the treatment of sexual offenders has changed markedly between 1950 and 2002, and as a result both reporting and response to the problem are like to have been affected.

---

[1] Bryan T. Froehle, "Numbers of Priests in the United States 1960 – 1996" (working Paper, Center for Applied Research in the Apostolate, Georgetown University, Washington DC, 1997).

2.3 DETAILED DATA ON PREVALENCE OF SEXUAL ABUSE OF YOUTHS UNDER 18 BY CATHOLIC PRIESTS

The red (upper) line in Figure 2.3.1 represents the total incidents of alleged abuse for each year of the study while the blue (lower) line charts the total number of priests accused in each year of the study.

Figure 2.3.1

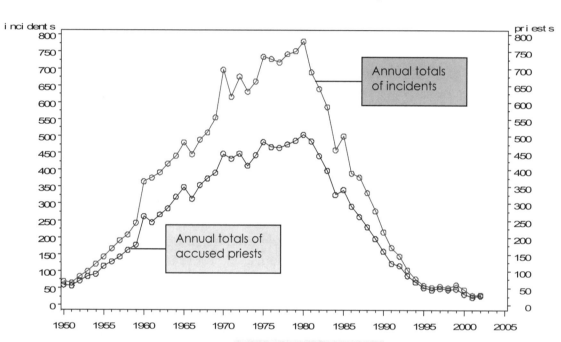

Annual Count of Incidents Reported and Priests Accused, by Year

The calculation of an overall percentage of priests in ministry was initially derived using information from the Diocesan Profiles for total numbers of priests and deacons subject to allegations compared to the total of those in ministry between 1950 and 2002. The surveys reported 75,694 diocesan priests and approximately 34,000 religious priests in ministry with 4,392 accused of abuse. If the total of the accused priests (4,392) is divided by the total of all priests in ministry between 1950 and 2002 (109,694), the result is 4%; for diocesan priests only, (3,282/76,694), the percentage is 4.27% and for religious priests, (929/34,000), 2.7%.[1]

Alternatively, the total of priests in ministry estimated by the Center for Applied Research in the Apostolate is 94,607 between 1960 and 2002. If the number of priests who had no allegations after 1959 is removed (265), the total of surveys for priests and deacons with allegations of child sexual abuse is 4,127, and the resulting percentage is slightly more than 4%.

Figure 2.3.2 DISTRIBUTION OF ALLEGED INCIDENTS OF ABUSE, BY DATE OF FIRST INSTANCE

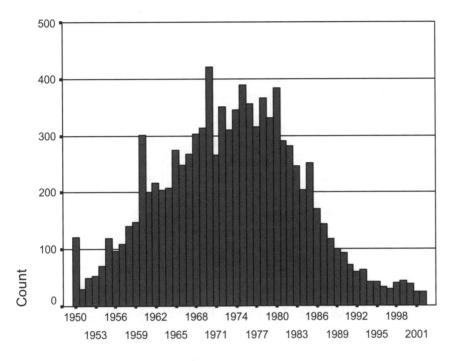

Year Alleged Abuse Began

The tables that follow show in detail the distribution of the allegations of child sexual abuse for each diocese or religious community, arrayed by a series of demographic variables. The results are fairly uniform across each of the three diocesan tables: the percentage of incardinated priests and deacons accused of child sexual abuse is consistently between 3% and 6% and the overall average is 5%. For the religious communities, a similar uniformity is evident although it is approximately half of the diocesan level. The tables that follow do not include priests who have been exonerated, or those who were determined to be ineligible for the study because they did not meet the protocol criteria.

Table 2.3.1 shows the average number of incardinated clerics who have been accused of sexual abuse and the percentage of accused clerics within the total number of incardinated clerics in an individual diocese, grouped by Catholic Region. These tables also show the dioceses with the lowest number (and percentage) of accused priests in a Region and the dioceses with the highest number (and percentage). Table 2.3.2 shows the United States dioceses grouped by the size of the Catholic population and Table 2.3.3 repeats this display by the number of parishes.

Tables 2.3.4 and 2.3.5 show the average number of religious community members who have been accused of sexual abuse, grouped by the overall membership of the community and then by clerical membership.

The average number of incardinated clerics in individual diocese or eparchy who have been the subject of an allegation of sexual abuse is 19. Another way of expressing this statistic is that the average diocese or eparchy had records or knowledge of allegations against 19 clerics. The total number of accused clerics incardinated to an individual diocese or eparchy, between 1950 and 2002, ranges from a minimum of 0 to a maximum of 165.

Table 2.3.1. PERCENT AND NUMBER OF INCARDINATED CLERICS PER DIOCESE OR EPARCHY ACCUSED OF SEXUAL ABUSE, GROUPED BY REGION

United States Dioceses Grouped by Catholic Region	Accused Clerics as a Percent of All Accused of Abuse			Number of Incardinated Clerics Accused of Abuse		
	Average Per Diocese	Minimum	Maximum	Average per Diocese	Minimum	Maximum
1	5%	0%	10%	40.42	0	165
2	4%	1%	9%	38.22	4	73
3	5%	0%	24%	26.13	0	69
4	5%	0%	10%	17.00	0	46
5	5%	0%	11%	8.24	0	30
6	3%	0%	8%	17.71	0	93
7	4%	1%	7%	24.47	5	116
8	5%	2%	16%	13.45	3	26
9	3%	1%	5%	16.50	2	64
10	5%	0%	19%	7.44	0	31
11	4%	1%	9%	15.07	1	71
12	4%	2%	9%	6.80	2	21
13	6%	0%	11%	9.89	0	24
14	5%	1%	10%	8.38	2	12

Table 2.3.2. PERCENT AND NUMBER OF INCARDINATED CLERICS PER DIOCESE OR EPARCHY ACCUSED OF SEXUAL ABUSE, GROUPED BY CATHOLIC POPULATION

United States Dioceses Grouped by Catholic Population	Accused Clerics as a Percent of All Incardinated Priests, 1950 - 2002			Number of Incardinated Priests Accused of Sexual Abuse		
	Average In Diocese	Minimum	Maximum	Average In Diocese	Minimum	Maximum
Group 1 (5,000 - 45,000)	4%	0%	9%	3.00	0	10
Group 2 (45,001 - 66,000)	4%	0%	11%	5.00	0	12
Group 3 (66,001 - 88,500)	6%	0%	19%	9.35	0	41
Group 4 (88,5001 – 122,000)	3%	0%	6%	7.63	0	23
Group 5 122,001 – 170,000)	5%	0%	10%	12.53	0	35
Group 6 (170,001 – 239,000)	4%	0%	10%	15.55	0	34
Group 7 (239,001 – 350,700)	4%	1%	9%	21.17	3	52
Group 8 (350,701 – 475,000)	4%	2%	7%	18.31	1	39
Group 9 (475,001 – 778, 700)	5%	0%	24%	23.85	0	64
Group 10 (788,701 – 4,500,000)	4%	0%	10%	45.47	0	165

Table 2.3.3. PERCENT AND NUMBER OF INCARDINATED CLERICS PER DIOCESE WHO HAVE BEEN ACCUSED OF SEXUAL ABUSE, GROUPED BY NUMBER OF PARISHES

United States Dioceses Grouped by Number of Parishes	Accused Priests as a Percent of All Incardinated Priests, 1950 - 2002			Number of Incardinated Priests Accused of Sexual Abuse		
	Average in Diocese	Minimum	Maximum	Average In Diocese	Minimum	Maximum
1 (1 - 35)	3%	0%	9%	1.10	0	3
2 (36 - 46)	5%	0%	11%	4.36	0	12
3 (47 – 56)	4%	0%	19%	5.73	0	23
4 (57 – 71)	5%	0%	12%	8.41	0	31
5 (72 – 84)	3%	0%	7%	7.42	0	17
6 (85 – 97)	5%	1%	9%	15.37	3	41
7 (98 – 119)	6%	2%	24%	16.80	5	35
8 (120 – 138)	5%	1%	10%	23.67	6	52
9 (139 – 185)	4%	1%	8%	27.04	9	93
10 (186 +)	4%	2%	8%	55.67	11	165

Table 2.3.4 PERCENT AND NUMBER OF ALL CLERICS IN RELIGIOUS COMMUNITIES ACCUSED OF SEXUAL ABUSE, GROUPED BY THE OVERALL MEMBERSHIP

U.S. Catholic Religious Communities Grouped by Overall Membership	Accused Priests as a Percent of All Priests in a Religious Community, 1950 - 2002			Number of Religious Priests Accused of Abuse		
	Average Per Community	Minimum	Maximum	Average Per Community	Minimum	Maximum
1 (1 – 10)	-0-	-0-	-0-	-0-	-0-	-0-
2 (11 – 20)	2%	0%	9%	.67	0	3
3 (21 – 30)	2%	0%	5%	1.55	0	4
4 (31 – 40)	3%	0%	13%	2.10	0	7
5 (41 – 75)	3%	0%	8%	2.71	0	9
6 (76 – 110)	3%	0%	7%	6.62	0	17
7 (111 – 150)	1%	<1%	2%	4.38	1	8
8 (151 – 305)	2%	<1%	5%	10.19	1	21
9 (306 – 540)	1%	<1%	4%	16.00	4	55
10 541 +	1%	<1%	1%	10.50	6	15

Table 2.3.5 PERCENT AND NUMBER OF ALL CLERICS IN RELIGIOUS COMMUNITIES ACCUSED OF SEXUAL ABUSE, GROUPED BY THE CURRENT CLERICAL MEMBERSHIP

U.S. Catholic Religious Communities Grouped by Clerical Membership	Accused Clerics as a Percent of All Clerics in a Religious Community, 1950 - 2002			Number of Religious Clerics Accused of Abuse		
	Average Per Community	Minimum	Maximum	Average Per Community	Minimum	Maximum
1 (1 – 6)	2%	0%	9%	.17	0	1
2 (7 – 14)	2%	0%	7%	1.57	0	4
3 (15 – 21)	2%	0%	5%	1.00	0	2
4 (22 - 35)	3%	0%	13%	2.45	0	9
5 (36 – 57)	2%	0%	5%	2.71	0	6
6 (58 – 80)	3%	0%	7%	5.58	1	17
7 (81 – 110)	2%	0%	5%	6.30	0	17
8 (111 – 176)	2%	0%	5%	9.41	1	21
9 (177 – 399)	2%	0%	4%	13.93	1	55
10 (400 +)	1%	0%	1%	8.67	4	15

FIGURE 2.3.3 PRIESTS ACCUSED AS A PERCENT OF ALL ORDINATIONS, BY YEAR

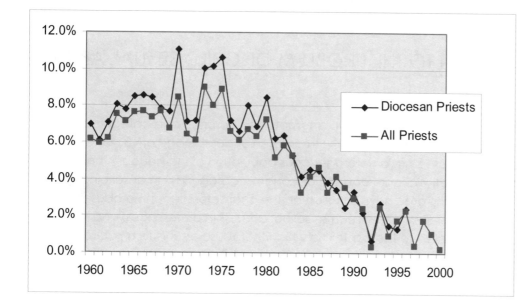

This figure shows the percentage of all priests ordained in each year from 1960 to 2002 who were subsequently accused of child sexual abuse. Data was not available for the total number of Catholic priests ordained for the years 1950 through 1959. The upper, or darker, line represents the percentage of ordained diocesan priests and the lower, or lighter, line is the percentage of all who were ordained. The Official Catholic Directory and the Center for Applied Research were the sources for the total numbers of yearly ordinations.

---

[1] Surveys were included in the study for 181 priests who were reported by their dioceses to have had allegations, but whose clerical status was not reported. The total number of individual priests and deacons includes the diocesan priests, the religious priests and those who status was not identified.

THE PRIESTS AND DEACONS ACCUSED OF SEXUAL ABUSE

3.1 INTRODUCTION TO THE PROBLEM OF CHILD SEXUAL ABUSE BY ADULT MEN

For many years, scholars and practitioners have attempted to describe and categorize adult men who engage in sexually abusive behavior with children under the age of 18. One clear finding is that child sexual abusers are a heterogeneous population of individuals. There are sexual offenders in all racial, ethnic, age, and socioeconomic categories. In describing child sexual abuse, researchers in this area have focused on the characteristics of the abusers themselves (e.g., static personal variables, such as sexual attraction preferences, and personality) and variables related to the context in which the abuse occurs (e.g., access to victims, isolation of the offender, and presence of substance abuse) as well as personal and situational characteristics of their victims in an effort to create typologies of abusers for assessment and treatment purposes.[1]

One way of categorizing offenders, for example, is by the type of victim they choose. Some child sexual abusers are diagnosed as pedophiles, meaning that they exhibit recurrent, intense, sexually arousing fantasies, urges or behaviors related to sexual contact with a prepubescent child over a period of at least six months duration.[2] However, not all sexual abuse occurs with young children, and not all child sexual abusers fit this clinical diagnosis. Some researchers have identified a similar condition, ephebophilia, which refers to individuals who exhibit these same fantasies, urges or behaviors towards post-pubescent youths.[3] While some offenders evidence a clear preference for particular types of victims with regard to age and gender, many do not. Individuals who molest children may be heterosexual, homosexual, or bisexual with regard to victim selection. Child sexual abusers who prefer female victims are more likely to be diagnosed as pedophiles than those who prefer male children while child sexual abusers who prefer male victims tend to target boys who are slightly older.[4]

A second way of categorizing offenders is based on the factors believed to produce the offending behavior. The most widely accepted classification of child molesters follows a dichotomous model consisting of fixated offenders and regressed offenders.[5] A fixated offender is characterized as having a persistent, continual, and compulsive attraction to children. In contrast, regressed offenders are individuals who are primarily attracted to adults, but who are perceived to engage in sexual activity with children in response to particular stressors (e.g., marital problems and unemployment) or contextual variables (e.g., stress or loneliness).[6] Subsequent research has demonstrated that while these two concepts are still important in terms of describing sexual abusing types, this classification alone is not sufficiently nuanced to describe the complexities of child sexual abusers.[7] Instead, fixation can be understood to exist on a continuum, meaning that all offending behavior is likely to result from some varying degrees of a combination of stable personal characteristics (e.g., substance abuse) with contextual variables (e.g., depression).[8] It is clear that multiple subtypes of offenders exist within the population of sex offenders; however, there is no single classification system that has strong empirical support.

Empirical studies on child sexual abuse in the Catholic Church are limited. However, a number of descriptive studies have been reported which have examined small, often clinical samples of clergy. These studies suffer from a number of methodological weaknesses, such as small, non-representative samples, which limit their findings and make it impossible to draw any type of meaningful generalization about child sexual abuse in the Church. This literature, however, has focused attention on a number of important topics to be considered in studying the issues within the Church, including the difference between sexually offending and non-offending priests,[9] the difference between sexually offending priests and sexual offenders in the general population,[10] personality characteristics or backgrounds of sexually offending priests,[11] the link between child sexual abuse and substance abuse,[12] and the emotional or psychological development of abusive priests.[13] The survey instrument completed for each priest against whom allegations of abuse had been made incorporated questions associated with these topics.

The followings sections of the report present information about the priests and deacons alleged to have committed child sexual abuse.

---

[1] Robert A. Knight & Raymond A. Prentky, "Classifying Sexual Offenders: The Development and Corroboration of Taxonomic Models." in *Handbook of Sexual Assault: Issues, Theories, and Treatment of the Offender*, 3rd ed., ed. William L. Marshall (New York: Plenum Press, 1990), 23-52; and Barbara K. Schwartz, "Characteristics and Typologies of Sex Offenders." in *The Sex Offender: Corrections, Treatment and Legal Practice*, 2nd ed., ed. Barbara K. Schwartz and Henry R. Cellini (New Jersey: Civic Research Institute, Inc, 1995)

[2] American Psychiatric Association, *Diagnostic and Statistical Manual of Mental Disorders: DSM-IV* (Washington, DC: American Psychiatric Association, 1999).

[3] Martin P. Kafka, "Sexual Molesters of Adolescents, Ephebophilia, and Catholic Clergy: A Review and Synthesis," in *Sexual Abuse in the Catholic Church: Scientific and Legal Perspectives*, ed. R. Karl Hanson, Friedemann Pfäfflin, and Manfred Lütz (Vatican: Libreria Editrico Vaticana, 2004).

[4] American Psychiatric Association, *DSM-IV*.

[5] A. Nicholas Groth, William F. Hobson, and Thomas G. Gary, "The Child Molester: Clinical Observations," in *Social Work and Child Sexual Abuse*, ed. Jon R. Conte and David A. Shore (New York: Haworth, 1982).

[6] Groth, Hobson, and Gary; David Finkelhor, *Child Sexual Abuse: New Theory and Research*, (New York: The Free Press, 1984).

[7] Lenore M. Simon, Bruce Sales, Alfred Kaszniak, and Marvin Kahn, "Characteristics of Child Molesters: Implications for the Fixated-Regressed Dichotomy," *Journal of Interpersonal Violence* 7 (2, 1992): 211-225.

[8] Simon, 211-225.

[9] Robert J. Camargo, "Factor, Cluster, and Discriminant Analyses of Data on Sexually Active Clergy: The Molesters of Youth Identified," *American Journal of Forensic Psychology* 15 (2, 1997): 5-24.

[10] Thomas W. Haywood et al., "Psychological Aspects of Sexual Functioning Among Cleric and Non-cleric Alleged Sex Offenders," *Child Abuse & Neglect* 20 (6, 1996): 527-536; and R. Langevin, S. Curnoe, and J. Bain, "A Study of Clerics Who Commit Sexual Offenses: Are They Different From Other Sex Offenders?" *Child Abuse & Neglect* 24 (4, 2000): 535-545.

[11] Calvin S.L. Fones et al., "The Sexual Struggles of 23 Clergymen: A Follow-up study. *Journal of Sex & Marital Therapy* 25 (1999): 183-195; Richard Irons and Mark Laaser, "The Abduction of Fidelity: Sexual Exploitation by Clergy- Experience with Inpatient Assessment." *Sexual Addiction & Compulsivity* 1 (2, 1994): 119-129; and Thomas G. Plante, "Catholic Priests Who Sexually Abuse Minors: Why Do We Hear So Much Yet Know So Little?" *Pastoral Psychology* 44 (5, 1996): 305-310.

[12] Mary F. Ruzicka, "Predictor Variables of Clergy Pedophiles," *Psychological Reports* 80 (1997): 589-590.

[13] Eugene C. Kennedy, Victor J. Heckler, and Frank J. Kobler, "Clinical Assessment of a Profession: Roman Catholic Clergymen," *Journal of Clinical Psychology* 33 (1, 1977): 120-128; and Thomas P. Doyle, "Roman Catholic Clericalism, Religious Duress, and Clergy Sexual Abuse," Pastoral Psychology 51(3, 2003): 189-231.

3.2   SUMMARY RESULTS: PRIESTS WHO HAVE ALLEGATIONS OF SEXUAL ABUSE

Priests who have allegations of sexual abuse of minors are a heterogeneous group of individuals. This is also the case with the general population of child sexual abusers, who have no consistent pattern of age, socioeconomic status, race or psychological problems.   The purpose of this chapter is to explain the characteristics of these priests, including their demographic characteristics (e.g., age at time of ordination and offense), their status in the Church, any behavioral and psychological problems they have experienced and any criminal penalties resulting from the allegations of abuse.

The study produced a number of interesting findings:

- The majority of priests with allegations of abuse from 1950-2002 were ordained between the 1950s and 1970s.

- The majority of priests with allegations of abuse are diocesan. Religious priests have slightly more than half as many allegations as diocesan priests. Additionally, religious priests have fewer multiple allegations and fewer allegations of "severe" offenses (e.g., those with penetration).

- Surveys indicated that some priests with allegations of sexual abuse also showed a variety of behavioral problems, the most common of which were personality problems.

- Few incidents were reported to the police. It is possible to speculate that one reason for this is because of the delay in reporting of abuse; consequently, the abuse was alleged beyond the statutes of limitation in many instances.

- When allegations were made to the police, they were almost always investigated, and about one in three priests were charged with a crime. Overall, few priests with allegations served criminal sentences; only 3% of all priests with allegations served prison sentences. The priests with many allegations of abuse were not more likely than other priests to be charged and serve prison sentences.

3.3 DEMOGRAPHIC CHARACTERISTICS OF PRIESTS AND DEACONS ACCUSED OF SEXUAL ABUSE OF YOUTHS UNDER 18

This chapter is based on survey data that describes 4,392 individual men ordained as Catholic priests or deacons. The following steps were taken to achieve that number:

- 4,627 surveys were submitted based on files of individual priests and deacons.
- 68 surveys were removed as ineligible for the study.
- 143 priests were accused of sexual abuse of minors in more than one diocese or religious community. These individuals were identified as having identically encrypted initials and birth dates. All were also confirmed by ordination year and seminary. The information about these men from multiple surveys has been collected into a single entry, and the duplicate entries deleted.
- There were 41 permanent deacons, 20 transitional deacons and 22 seminarians (who were later ordained) among the group of men accused of sexual abuse of minor children. Since there were few deacons, it should be understood that they are included when priests are mentioned.
- Not all questions were answered on each survey; as a result, each table shows the available responses, and the total will change from table to table.

Birth dates of the clerics accused of sexual abuse of minors during the study period span more than a century–from 1867 to 1973 (Table 3.3.1). The ordination dates show a similar range, from 1890 to 2000 (Table 3.3.2). However, the majority of men in this study were born between 1920 and 1950, and were ordained in their mid- to late-twenties. Almost 50% of these men were ordained at ages 26 or 27, and 75% were ordained between the ages of 26 and 30. The majority were ordained after 1950.

Table 3.3.1 DECADE OF BIRTH

Decade	Count	Percent	Cumulative
1860 - 1899	88	2.2%	2.2%
1900 - 1909	189	4.7%	6.9%
1910 - 1919	430	10.7%	17.6%
1920 - 1929	839	20.9%	38.5%
1930 - 1939	1,049	26.1%	64.6%
1940 - 1949	1,003	25.0%	89.5%
1950 - 1959	336	8.4%	97.9%
1960 - 1969	80	2.0%	99.9%
1970 - 1979	5	.1%	100.0%
Total	**4,019**	**100.0%**	

The year of a priest or deacon's birth was provided for 4,019 individuals, or 91.5% of those reported in the surveys.

Table 3.3.2 DECADE OF ORDINATION

Decade	Count	Percent	Cumulative
1890 - 1919	33	.8%	.8%
1920 - 1929	79	2.0%	2.8%
1930 - 1939	245	6.1%	8.8%
1940 - 1949	501	12.4%	21.3%
1950 - 1959	931	23.1%	44.3%
1960 - 1969	1,021	25.3%	69.7%
1970 - 1979	791	19.6%	89.3%
1980 - 1989	339	8.4%	97.7%
1990 - 2002	94	2.3%	100.0%
Total	4,034	100.0%	

The year of ordination was provided for 4,034 priests and deacons, or 91.6% of those reported in the surveys.

The average age at the time of ordination of those included in this study did not change between 1880 and 1979, but has risen significantly in the last 20 years to 35 in the period between 1990 and 2002. This change in age at time of ordination, observed in this subset of all men ordained to the Catholic priesthood, is consistent with an overall trend in the Catholic Church. If all are considered, the average age at the time of ordination for a diocesan priest in this study is 28 and for a religious priest, 29.

Canon law establishes the age for ordination. In 1983, Canon Law established the minimum age for ordination as 24. In earlier years, it would have been possible to be ordained to minor orders at a younger age. With respect to those ordained before the mid-1950s, we cannot be sure how those who completed the surveys understood ordination date and whether the date reported is ordination to a minor order or ordination to the priesthood.

Table 3.3.3 AGE AT TIME OF ORDINATION

Age	Count	Percent
18 - 24	175	4.4%
25 - 29	2,837	71.9%
30 - 34	649	16.4%
35 - 39	172	4.4%
40 - 49	77	2.0%
50 - 59	28	.7%
60 +	7	.2%
Total	3,945	100.0%

The age at ordination was calculated by subtracting the year of birth from the year of ordination. Information on both ages was available for 3,945 priests and deacons.

Only 1% of the men in this study were married at the time an allegation of sexual abuse was made against them.

Table 3.3.4 CLERIC'S MARITAL STATUS

Status	Count	Percent
Married	51	1.2%
Not Married	4,218	98.8%
Total	4,269	100.0%

The deaconate is the first stage of ordained ministry. Both married and unmarried men may be ordained as permanent deacons.

The clerical status at the time the allegation was made is shown below in Table 3.3.5. 172 individual priests held more than one status during the period covered by the accusation of abuse. Overall, 69.4 % of the accused priests were diocesan priests and 22.1% were religious priests.

Table 3.3.5 CLERICAL STATUS AT TIME OF ALLEGATION

Clerical status	Count	Percent
Diocesan Priest	2,915	69.4%
Religious Priest	929	22.1%
Extern Priest	208	4.9%
Eparchian Priest	14	.3%
Transitional Deacon	19	.5%
Permanent Deacon	42	1.0%
Bishop	12	.1%
Seminarian	21	.5%
Other	51	1.2%
Total	4,211	100.0%

Some priests held more than one clerical position during the period of alleged abuse. Twelve priests held the status of bishop at some point during the period of alleged abuse. Nine bishops who were the subject of allegations held more than one clerical status.

Seminarians or brothers who had been the subject of allegations before they were ordained were included in the study as long as they proceeded to ordination.

The total of 4,211 shown in Table 3.3.5 is less than the overall total of 4,392 because not all survey forms provided information about clerical status.

As a whole, the known population of sexual offenders is older than the population of other types of offenders. However, those who have more victims and are more serious offenders tend to have an earlier age of onset. Paraphilias often develop prior to adulthood, and adult sex offenders who had sexual convictions as adolescents generally commit both more offenses and more serious offenses as adults when compared with those who were not juvenile-onset offenders.

Table 3.3.6   AGE OF PRIEST AT FIRST INSTANCE OF
ALLEGED ABUSE

Age in Years	Count	Percent
18 – 24	105	3.3%
25 – 29	541	17.0%
30 – 34	718	22.6%
35 – 39	570	17.9%
40 – 44	406	12.8%
45 – 49	316	9.9%
50 – 59	345	10.9%
60 – 69	125	3.9%
70 – 90	50	1.6%
Totals	3,176	100.0%

Table 3.3.7   AGE OF PRIEST AT FIRST INSTANCE OF
ALLEGED ABUSE, DIOCESAN & RELIGIOUS

Age in Years	Diocesan Count	Diocesan Percent	Religious Count	Religious Percent
18 - 24	86	3.4%	18	3.1%
25 – 29	488	19.3%	45	7.7%
30 – 34	587	23.3%	112	19.2%
35 – 39	438	17.4%	123	21.1%
40 – 44	308	12.2%	89	15.3%
45 – 49	229	9.1%	77	13.2%
50 – 59	259	10.3%	75	12.9%
60 – 69	95	3.8%	28	4.8%
70 - 90	32	1.3%	15	2.6%
Total	2522	100.0%	582	100.0%

The average age of a priest at the first incident or allegation of child sexual abuse is 39 if all surveys are considered, and the median is 35. The average and median both rise gradually from late 30s to late 40s between 1950 and 2002.

Table 3.3.8 CHANGE IN AGE AT FIRST INSTANCE OF ALLEGED ABUSE, 1950 – 2002 BY DECADE

Time Period	Average Age	Median Age
1950 - 1959s	38	36
1960 - 1960s	37	35
1970 - 1970s	37	35
1980 - 1980s	42.5	39
1990 - 1990s	47	45
2000 - 2002	48	48
Overall	39	35

3.4 PRIESTS WITH BEHAVIORAL PROBLEMS

Mental health and treatment professionals have found that it is not uncommon for those who engage in child sexual abuse to demonstrate other behavioral and psychological problems as well. Studies on co-occurrence of sexual offending and other problems have consistently found high rates of personality dysfunction[1] as well as major mental disorders such as anxiety or depression.[2] Similarly, alcohol or substance abuse problems are frequently present among those who engage in child sexual abuse.[3] Studies which have examined clergy who sexually abuse minors with co-occurring problems have found them to exhibit fewer psychological problems than other sex offenders.[4] However, methodological limitations preclude firm conclusions about groups of clergy who offend.

To examine the co-existence of child sexual abuse and other problems, the study instruments inquired about other types of problems that were evident from a priest's files. The question asked specifically about whether the priest had a history of abuse that was either indicated in the record or known to the diocese; whether he had a history of substance abuse; whether there had been questions raised about his fitness for ministry and whether he had manifested other behavioral problems. Records of 1,400 priests and deacons, nearly one in three of those against whom allegations of sexual abuse of a youth under 18 were made, showed a history of substance abuse, questions about his "fitness for ministry" or behavioral problems.

According to information contained in Church records, very few priests accused of sexual abuse had themselves been victims of abuse. It should be kept in mind, however, that unless a priest self-disclosed his own prior abuse or it had been specifically raised as an issue, there might not have been an indication of abuse in Church files. Of the 4, 392 priests and deacons, 279, or 6.8% of the total number, were reported to have been abused (see Table 3.4.1 for breakdown of this number by type of abuse). Of these, a smaller number, 67 reported multiple forms of abuse. Almost half of the priests whose records indicated prior sexual or physical abuse also suffered verbal and emotional abuse.

Table 3.4.1 PRIESTS WITH A HISTORY OF VICTIMIZATION, BY TYPE OF ABUSE

Type of Abuse	Count	% of Total
Physical abuse	40	14.60%
Sexual abuse	178	64.96%
Physical & Sexual	20	7.3%
Emotional abuse	32	11.68%
Other	4	1.46%
Total	274	100%

The files for 68 priests included information indicating that they had experienced more than one form of abuse during childhood.

When there was a history of childhood abuse, the most frequent abuser was an adult man. As shown in Table 3.4.2, of the 274 priests reported to have been abused themselves, nearly half of them were abused by someone in their family. Thirty-five percent were abused by a parent and 25 percent by a father.

Table 3.4.2 PRIESTS WITH A HISTORY OF VICTIMIZATION, BY TYPE OF ABUSE

Decade	Count	% of Total
Mother	25	9.36%
Father	67	25.09%
Sibling	14	5.24%
Other family	24	9%
Teacher	5	1.87%
Peer/acquaintance	31	11.61%
Authority figure	23	8.61%
Priest	47	17.60%
Deacon	1	.38%
Other	30	11.24%
Total	267	100%

A total of 48 priests were reported to have been abused by a priest or deacon. This illustrates that 18 percent of priests with allegations of abuse had themselves been abused by a priest or deacon.

A history of substance abuse was reflected in the files of slightly fewer than one in five of the priests and deacons accused of sexual abuse. Alcohol abuse was reported much more frequently than drug abuse, implicated in 96% of the 753 priests with substance abuse information in their records.

Table 3.4.3 SUBSTANCE ABUSE HISTORY

Substance	Count	% of Total
Alcohol only	669	89%
Drugs only	23	3%
Alcohol & drugs	61	8%
Total	753	100%

The survey did not ask for a formal diagnosis of substance abuse or dependence. It was deemed sufficient that the personnel file included an indication that the problem of substance abuse had been observed.

Table 3.4.4 COMPARISON OF PRIEST VICTIMS

	Abuse History		No Abuse History	
Substance Abuse	93	34.4%	646	17.4%
No Substance Abuse	177	65.6%	3024	82.6%
	270	100%	3660	100%

Priests who had themselves been victims of abuse were twice as likely to have a history of difficulties with alcohol, illegal drugs or both.

For those priests with information about substance abuse problems in their files, nearly 72% were referred for evaluation or treatment, with no action reported for nearly 16% (see Table 3.4.5). However, it should be noted that evaluation and treatment referrals are likely to have been documented in the files whereas less formal handling of substance abuse issues might not have been included in the files, so these numbers need to be interpreted cautiously in terms of efficacy. Of those who were referred for treatment, Table 3.4.6 shows that more than 85% were sent for treatment outside of the diocese (76% of whom were referred for inpatient treatment).

Table 3.4.5 CHURCH RESPONSE TO SUBSTANCE ABUSE

Action by Church	Count	% of Total
Referred for evaluation	317	45.7%
Referred for treatment	180	25.9%
Provided spiritual counseling	12	1.7%
Recommended spiritual counseling	9	1.3%
Provided intervention	10	1.4%
No action taken	109	15.7%
Other	57	8.2%
Total	694	100%

Table 3.4.5 shows the initial response undertaken by dioceses and religious communities to care for a priest with a substance abuse problem. In the majority of cases, more than one response was made. According to data from the surveys, 63% of those priests recognized to have a substance abuse problem were referred for treatment.

Table 3.4.6 SUBSTANCE ABUSE TREATMENT

Type of treatment	Count	% of instances of SA treatment
Inpatient / in diocese	46	9.8%
Inpatient / outside the diocese	357	76%
Outpatient / in diocese	71	15.1%
Outpatient / outside diocese	44	9.4%

This is a Multiple Response Table. The categories are not mutually exclusive, since an individual may have participated in substance abuse treatment more than once.

Table 3.4.6 includes all instances of treatment reported in the surveys.

Forty six priests were treated twice for substance abuse problems and four were treated three times.

Church records for 476 priests, or 10.9% of the total in the study, raised questions about those priests' fitness for ministry. Another 774 were identified as having behavioral problems. The handwritten notes documenting these problems indicated they were largely psychological in nature (82.2% of those with noted behavioral or fitness for ministry problems were described as having psychological problems). If fitness and behavioral problems are considered together with other noted problems, 1,400 priests and deacons, or 32% of those who were later the subject of an allegation of sexual abuse had been recognized as having behavioral problems.

Table 3.4.7 CLASSIFICATION OF FITNESS AND/OR BEHAVIORAL PROBLEMS

Classification of Problem	Count	% of all responses
Sexual Relationship Problems		
Coercive Sex with Males	18	.8%
Coercive Sex with Females	10	.4%
Sex with Adult Women	131	5.8%
Sex with Adult Men	164	7.3%
Other Sexual Behavior	53	2.4%
Mental Health Problems		
Suicide	12	.5%
Depression	75	3.5%
Bipolar Symptoms	16	.7%
Other Axis 1	75	3.3%
Anxiety / Stress	36	1.6%
Personality Problems		
Social Inhibition, Immaturity	78	3.5%
Boundary Problems	479	21.3%
Narcissism	38	1.7%
Hostility	170	7.5%
Other Problems		
Substance Abuse	149	6.6%
Financial / Gambling	45	2%
Medical	90	4%
Legal -- Civil or Criminal	275	12.2%

The table is a Multiple Response Table. The categories are not mutually exclusive, as a priest may have exhibited multiple problems.

Table 3.4.7 provides a classification of the types of problems that were described in the surveys.

Table 3.4.7 includes information about 1,400 priests.

[1] Lisa J. Cohen et al. "Personality Impairment in Male Pedophiles," *Journal of Clinical Psychiatry* 63 (10, 2002): 912-919

[2] Peter J. Fagan, Thomas N. Wise, Chester W. Schmidt Jr., and Fred S. Berlin. "Pedophilia," *Journal of the American Medical Association* 288 (19, 2002): 2458-2465; and Nancy C. Raymond, Eli Coleman, Fred Ohlerking, Gary A. Christenson, and Michael Miner. "Psychiatric Comorbidity in Pedophilic Sex Offenders," *American Journal of Psychiatry* 156 (5, 1999): 786-788.

[3] Stephen H. Allnutt, John M.W. Bradford, David M. Greenberg, and Susan Curry. "Co-morbidity of Alcoholism and the Paraphilias," *Journal of Forensic Sciences* 41 (2, 1996): 234-239.

[4] Martin P. Kafka, "Sexual Molesters of Adolescents, Ephebophilia, and Catholic Clergy: A Review and Synthesis," in *Sexual Abuse in the Catholic Church: Scientific and Legal Perspectives*, ed. R. Karl Hanson, Friedemann Pfäfflin, and Manfred Lütz (Vatican: Libreria Editrico Vaticana, 2004).

3.5 PRIESTS AND DEACONS AND THE ALLEGATIONS

Statistics from recent United States Justice Department studies of the prevalence of youth victimization confirm what other surveys have found: a startling proportion of young people experience sexual victimization[1] In a sample of 4,023 adolescents ages 12 to 17 across racial and ethnic groups, the lifetime prevalence for sexual assault is 8.1%[2]

Of all female victims of forcible rape whose ages were reported to enforcement agencies in 1992 (from 15 states), girls under the age of 18 represented approximately half of the victims.[3] The younger the victim, the more likely that she knew the person who assaulted her.[4]

When similar research was done with data on all victims of sexual assault known to law enforcement between 1991 and 1996, juveniles represented the large majority of all victims of forcible fondling (84%), forcible sodomy (79%), and sexual assault with an object (75%)[5] One in seven victims of a reported sexual assault was under the age of six.[6] The single age with the greatest proportion of sexual assault victims among all victims reported to law enforcement was age 14.[7]

Table 3.5.1 ALLEGATIONS AGAINST PRIEST / DEACONS, GROUPED BY NUMBER OF ALLEGATIONS

Number of Allegations	Count	Percent
1	2,411	55.7%
2-3	1160	26.9%
4-9	600	13.9%
10+	149	3.5%
Total	4,311	100.0%

The Cleric Survey asked for the total number of victims who made allegations in the reporting diocese and for the total number off potential allegations that might be made about a particular priest or deacon. Respondents were also asked to complete a Victim Survey for each person making an allegation.

Table 3.5.1 is based on the data from the Cleric Survey.

If accused diocesan and religious priests are compared using the above classification into four groups, the results do not differ greatly

- 54% of diocesan priests had a single allegation compared to 61% of accused religious priests;
- 14.7 of diocesan priests have 4-9 allegations, compared to 10.9% of the accused religious priests;
- 4.2% of diocesan priests have ten or more allegations, compared to 1.5% of the religious priests.

Question 23 on the Cleric Survey asked the respondent to report the number of victims who had made formal allegations known to the diocese and religious community about an individual priest. These allegations are referred to in Table 3.5.2 as "Formal Allegations." The following survey question asked "Is there any indication that the cleric has abused more victims than the official allegations made?" The affirmative responses, and the numbers associated with them, are referred to as "Potential Allegations."

Table 3.5.2 FORMAL AND POTENTIAL ALLEGATIONS AGAINST PRIESTS, IN FOUR GROUPS

Number of Allegations	Count	Percent of all
1	2,154	50%
2-3	1138	26.4%
4-9	767	17.8%
10+	252	5.8%
Total	4,311	100%

If the formal allegations made against an individual priest or deacon are added to the potential allegations known to the diocese or religious community, the result is shown in Table 3.5.2.

Table 3.5.3 GENDER OF ALLEGED VICTIMS, BY NUMBER OF ALLEGED ABUSERS

Gender	Count	Percent of all
Male and Female	157	3.6%
Female only	991	22.6%
Male only	2,805	64%
Gender unknown	429	9.8%
Total	4,230	100%

Table 3.5.3 shows the percentage of all priests with allegations, grouped by the gender of the person who made the allegation.

In 429 surveys, the gender of the alleged victim was not identified.

Table 3.5.4 ALLEGED VICTIMS OF SEXUAL ABUSE INCIDENTS,
GROUPED BY GENDER AND AGE

Gender	1 – 7 years	8 – 10 years	11 - 14 years	15 – 17 years
Male	203	992	4,282	2,892
	41.7%	71.4%	85.4%	85.2%
Female	284	398	734	502
	58.3%	28.6%	14.6%	14.8%
Total per group	487	1,390	5,016	3,394
% of all incidents	5.8%	16%	50.9%	27.3%

The data for Table 3.5.4 are drawn from the Cleric Surveys. The question on that survey that asked for a listing of alleged victims' ages and gender was not completed for all surveys. Therefore the totals in Table 3.5.4, when summed, are not the same as the total number of alleged incidents.

Figure 3.5.1 GENDER RATIO OF ALLEGED VICTIMS,
BY DECADE OF ACCUSATION

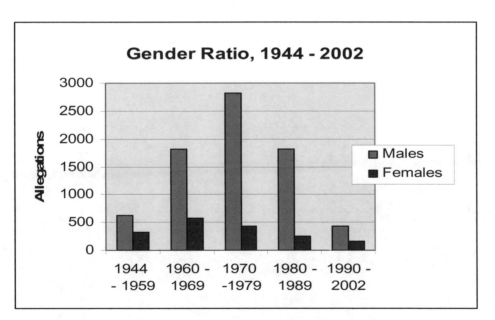

The year 1944 appears in this figure because one incident of abuse began in 1944, along with others that began in the late 1940s, but continued after 1950. The years of abuse before 1950 are not counted when the totals by year are derived, but are included here.

Table 3.5.5 ALLEGED MALE VICTIMS, AGE AT FIRST INSTANCE OF ABUSE
BY DECADE

Decade	Ages 1 - 7	Ages 8 - 10	Ages 11 - 14	Ages 15 - 17	Decade Total
1950 - 1959	20	115	266	87	488
	4.1%	23.6%	54.5%	17.8%	100%
1960 - 1969	74	298	950	314	1636
	4.5%	18.2%	58.1%	19.2%	100%
1970 - 1979	80	354	1461	668	2563
	3.1%	13.8%	57%	26.1%	100%
1980 - 1989	48	170	818	585	1621
	3%	10.5%	50.5%	36.1%	100%
1990 - 2002	10	29	141	222	402
	2.5%	7.2%	35.1%	55.2%	100%

Table 3.5.6 ALLEGED FEMALE VICTIMS, AGE AT FIRST INSTANCE OF ABUSE,
BY DECADE

Decade	Ages 1 - 7	Ages 8 - 10	Ages 11 - 14	Ages 15 - 17	Decade Total
1950 - 1959	79	87	89	24	279
	28.3%	31.2%	31.9%	8.6%	100%
1960 - 1969	92	129	207	98	526
	17.5%	24.5%	39.4%	18.6%	100%
1970 - 1979	46	97	164	119	426
	10.8%	22.8%	38.5%	27.9%	100%
1980 - 1989	28	48	110	75	261
	10.8%	18.5%	41.7%	29%	100%
1990 - 2002	11	16	75	43	145
	7.5%	11%	51.7%	29.7%	100%

The information in Tables 3.5.5 and 3.5.6 is taken from the Victim Surveys and available only for those surveys that included answers to the three questions about gender, date of incident and age at the time of the incident. Complete responses were received for 82%, or slightly more than four out of five, of the incident-level surveys.

Table 3.5.7 SUMMARY OF ALLEGED ACTS OF SEXUAL ABUSE

	Number of priests accused	Number of incidents reported	Percent of priests accused of each act
Verbal Abuse	626	1,105	15.2%
Victim Disrobed	1,057	1,442	25.17%
Priests Disrobed	695	1,129	16.9%
Touching over Victim's Clothes	2,161	3,600	52.6%
Touching over Priest's Clothes	494	968	12.0%
Touching under Victim's Clothes	1,848	4,022	44.9%
Touching under Priest's Clothes	553	968	13.4%
Shown Pornographic Video	107	150	2.6%
Shown Pornographic Magazine/Photo	149	240	3.6%
Photos of Victim	126	202	3.1%
Masturbation	466	741	11.3%
Mutual Masturbation	587	1,089	14.3%
Manual Penetration	283	389	6.9%
Penetration with Object	64	87	1.6%
Cleric Performed Oral Sex	1,068	1,477	26.0%
Victim Performed Oral Sex	585	922	14.2%
Penile Penetration/Attempt	920	1,219	22.4%
Hugs and Kissing	339	501	8.2%
Other	363	580	8.8%
No Record	754	991	18.3%
Unspecified Sexual Abuse	853	1,184	20.7%
Sexual Games (Strip Poker, Skinny Dipping)	78	104	1.9%
Group Sex or Coerced Sex w/ Others	14	52	0.3%
This table is a Multiple Response Table. The categories are not mutually exclusive, as an individual may have participated in more than one act during the course of an incident.			

[1] Dean G. Kilpatrick, Benjamin E. Saunders, and Daniel W. Smith. *Youth Victimization: Prevalence and Implications. NIJ Research in Brief.* (Washington, DC: U.S. Department of Justice, Office of Justice Programs, 2003), 1.

[2] Kilpatrick, 7.

[3] Patrick A. Langan and Caroline Wolf Harlow, *Child Rape Victims, 1992,* (U.S. Department of Justice, Office of Justice Programs, Bureau of Justice Statistics, 1992, Washington, D.C.), 1.

[4] Langan., 2.

[5] Howard N. Snyder, *Sexual Assault of Young Children as Reported to Law Enforcement: Victim, Incident, and Offender Characteristics, NIBRS Statistical Report,* (Washington, DC: U.S. Department of Justice, Office of Justice Programs Bureau of Justice Statistics, 2000), 2.

[6] Snyder, 2.

[7] Langan, 2.

3.6 SERIAL ABUSERS: PRIESTS WITH MULTIPLE ALLEGATIONS

Many individuals who commit a sexual offense, such as child sexual abuse, do so as a result of situational or impulsive factors. These are often single-victim offenders who may never repeat their crime or may repeat the act only if the same or similar circumstances recur. For example, such individuals may only act out when their controls are reduced due to intoxication, when experiencing significant situational stress, or when an opportunity is present. Thus, their behavior is often unplanned and considered a "regression," triggered largely—but not entirely—by external conditions.

However, there is a much smaller number of serial sex offenders who act out not as a result of the effects of external stress or a weakening of inhibitory controls; instead, they behave in a more methodical fashion using a high degree of planning. In these cases, there is a strong compulsion to act—a compulsion derived from a fixation on the type of victim desired and the type of acts performed. These offenses are often preceded by years of intense fantasy in which the act is rehearsed and strategies are developed. Offenders of this type have a very high potential to repeat their crimes. Such individuals can be quite manipulative in the way they approach victims and in the methods they employ to avoid apprehension. Because their crimes are highly planned and often target particular types of victims, they may abuse large numbers of children before they are apprehended.

Those priests who have been accused of abusing a large number of young people have attracted significant, often sensationalized, nationwide attention. These cases are frequently discussed along with the cases of those priests who have been transferred from diocese to diocese and who have continued to be accused of sexual abuse of youth under 18. Data from this study has found these two groups to be different in many aspects.   Those priests who have ten or more allegations differ in many respects from the average for all priests in the study, but this is not as true for the group having allegations in more than one diocese or religious community. The study received 149 surveys for priests who had ten or more allegations of child sexual abuse—although if potential allegations (from potential victims known to the diocese) are included, the number of priests is 252. After careful analysis, 143 priests out of the total number of 4,392, were identified as having been the subject of allegations in more than one diocese. Of that group, nine had allegation made in three dioceses and one priest was accused of sexual abuse in four dioceses.

- The group of 149 priests, the "10+ group," account for 26% of all incidents reported in the study. The 143 priests who were accused in more than one diocese, the "Transfers," had a lower rate of accusation, but account for 8.7% of all incidents reported in the study (see Table 3.6.1).

- The group of 143 priests who received accusations in at least two dioceses or religious communities were more likely to be identified with substance abuse and behavioral problems and more likely to be reported to the police. Overall, 64% of the "Transfer" group saw their ministry restricted.

Table 3.6.1 PRIESTS WITH MULTIPLE ALLEGATIONS: COMPARISON OF TWO GROUPS

	Transfers (N=143)	10+ Group (N=149)	All Priests (N=4,392)
Total Allegations	992	2,960	11,404
	8.7%	26%	100%
Median for Allegations, per Priest	4	14	1
Allegations And Potential Allegations	1,078	3,248	4,840
	9.5%	28%	100%
Substance Abuse	30%	22%	18.7%
Behavioral Problems	36%	33%	23%
Ministry Restricted	64.5%	53.7%	27%
Police Contact	7,6%	4%	14%
Charged with a Crime	4.6%	3%	3%

These data are taken from the Cleric Surveys. The total number of allegations reported there exceeds the number of Victim Surveys received.

The Cleric Survey asked for the total number of allegations that had been made against a priest or deacon in the responding diocese or religious community. It also asked for the number of other incidents not yet reported that were associated with or suspected of a particular priest.

The distribution of the number of allegations per priests is similar for diocesan and religious priests except with respect to 10+ group. There are only 14 religious priests in the 10+ group of 149.

Table 3.6.2 SERIAL ABUSERS BY CLERICAL STATUS

No. of Allegations	Diocesan Priests		Religious Priests	
1	1,752	54%	558	61%
2 - 3	883	27.2%	244	26.7%
4 - 9	476	14.6%	99	10.8%
10+	135	4.2%	14	1.5%
Total	3,246		915	

3.7 CRIMINAL PROSECUTIONS AND PENALTIES

Despite the gravity of the crime of child sexual abuse and the public policy interest in dealing effectively with it, very little systematic data has been collected that would provide a clear profile of those who are prosecuted, convicted or incarcerated for child sexual abuse.[1] As a U.S. Department of Justice publication explains, despite a few highly publicized cases of sexual assaults of young children, "there is little empirically-based information on these crimes."[2] The National Crime Victimization Survey, for example, collects data on victims over the age of 12. There is reason to believe, however, that sexual assault crimes against juvenile victims comprise a large proportion of sexual assaults handled by law enforcement agencies.[3]

In the last ten years or so, a new reporting system has been in place, the National Incident-Based Reporting Systems (NIBRS), which has the potential to provide much more detailed information about those who are arrested for sexual assaults against children and the methods of arrest clearance.[4] However, it is limited in representativeness because law enforcement agencies are not mandated to participate; for example, data from a July 2000 report draws from only 12 states.[5] Nevertheless, it does provide relevant contextual information. It reports that, in general, sexual assaults of juvenile victims were more likely to result in an arrest (29%) than were adult victimizations (22%) although rates were lower for victims under 6 (19%) versus approximately 32.5% for victims ages 6 to 17.[6] Overall, these results indicate that juvenile victims of sexual assault who were reported to law enforcement agencies were more likely to be male (18%) than were adult victims (4%); nearly one-fourth of the victims under 12 were male. Sexual assaults of children under the age of 6 were "the least likely of all such crimes to result in arrest or be otherwise cleared."[7] Law enforcement was able to identify the offender in just a third of the sexual assaults of children under age 6 and 45% of those for victims between 6 and 11.[8]

The following tables summarize whether each particular incident or allegation of abuse against a priest led to follow-up in the criminal justice system. Of course, the range of behaviors described in the allegations varied substantially (see Table 4.4.1), which might have affected whether law enforcement contact was initiated or resulted in any follow-up. Overall, fifteen percent of priests were reported to the police by a victim. A much smaller number were reported by a diocese or religious community.

A report to the police resulted in an investigation in almost all cases (see *Tables 3.7.1 and 3.7.2*). Only 384 of the 4,392 priests and deacons were criminally charged (see *Table 3.6.3*). The comparative percentages for diocesan, religious and extern priests investigated by the police and subsequently charged are generally equivalent.

Table 3.7.1 ABUSE REPORTED TO THE POLICE, BY CLERICAL STATUS

	Diocesan	Religious	Extern	Total
Police Report	778	191	54	1,021
	25.2%	20.6%	26%	24.2%
No police report	2298	738	174	3,190
	74.8%	79.4%	74%	75.8%

Table 3.7.2 ABUSE INVESTIGATED BY POLICE

	Diocesan	Religious	Extern	Total
Police investigation	709	174	56	939
	23.1%	18.7%	26.9%	22.3%
No police Investigation	2,365	755	152	3,272
	76.9%	81.3%	73.1%	77.7%

Table 3.7.3 PRIEST CHARGED WITH A CRIME

	Diocesan	Religious	Extern	Total
Priest charged	285	70	29	384
	9.3%	7.5%	13.9%	9.1%
Priest not charged	2,789	859	179	3,827
	90.7%	92.5%	86.1%	90.9%

According to the information in the Church's files, approximately 24% of priests accused of abuse were reported to the police, and some were independently detected.

Tables 3.7.1 – 3.7.4 report information on 4,211 priests and deacons, the total number for whom data was available on both clerical status and police contact.

Overall, 9.1% percent of priests were charged with a criminal offense (see Table 3.7.3). Although this is 41% of those cases in which a police investigation was carried out, the percentage of charges that proceeded to adjudication would be smaller.

Of the 384 priests who were charged with a crime, a majority (252) were convicted.

Table 3.7.4 PRIESTS CONVICTED OF A CRIME

	Diocesan	Religious	Extern	Total
Priests convicted	193	48	11	252
	6.3%	5.2%	5.3%	6%
Not convicted	2,881	881	197	3,959
	93.7%	94.8%	94.7%	94%

Table 3.7.4 is based on a total number of 4,211 priests.

Of those who were convicted (priests), the following table summarizes the type of sentence the priest was given for the offense. Criminal penalties are specific to localities or jurisdictions, and the charges against the priests varied widely.

Table 3.7.5 CRIMINAL PENALTIES

Penalty	Number of Priests	Percent
Prison	100	73%
Jail	61	44%
House arrest or electronic monitoring	7	5%
Probation	122	88%
Fine	25	18%
Community service	18	13%
Other	28	20.5%

Three men were sentenced to spend the rest of their lives in prison, and two others were required to register as sex offenders.

This is a Multiple Response Table. The categories are not mutually exclusive, since an individual may have been sentenced to several different penalties by the court.

Table 3.7.6 PRIESTS, BY NUMBER OF INCIDENTS CHARGED

Incidents	Count s	Percent	Cum. Percent
1	166	62.2%	62.2%
2	49	18.4%	80.5%
3	12	4.5%	85%
4	16	6%	91%
5	8	3%	94%
6	2	.7%	94.8%
8	3	1.1%	95.9%
9	1	.4%	97.3%
10 - 19	5	1.9%	98.1%
20 - 33	3	1.1%	99.2%
55	1	.4%	99.6%
131	1	.4%	100.0%
Total	226	100%	

In trying to better understand the types of incidents that led to criminal justice system involvement, the allegations made against priests have been divided into two categories: those involving direct sexual contact either by mouth to genitals (e.g., oral sex, penetration or masturbation) and those without such direct sexual contact (e.g., hugging, kissing or sex talk). The type of incident did not seem to influence whether the alleged victim contacted the police or whether the priest was ultimately charged or convicted (see Tables 3.7.7, 3.7.8 and 3.7.9).

Table 3.7.7 POLICE REPORT BY SEVERITY OF ALLEGATION

	Severity of Offense		
	Acts Involving Sexual	Acts Not Involving Sex	Row Total
Police Contacted	437	620	1,057
	28.4%	21.7%	24.1%
Police Not Contacted	1,103	2,232	3,335
	71.6%	78.3%	75.9%
Total	1,540 100.0%	2,852 100.0%	4,392 100.0%

Tables 3.7.7 – 3.7.9 show the comparative criminal justice system contact for priests accused of acts or attempts involving penetration or oral sex and those involving an act of masturbation. All other incidents, including those with allegations of unspecified " sex abuse" or "other" abusive behavior are counted in these tables as not involving sex.

Table 3.7.8 CRIMINAL CHARGE BY SEVERITY OF
ALLEGATION

	Severity of Offense		
	Acts Involving Sex	Acts Not Involving Sex	Row Total
Priest Charged	173	223	396
	5.1%	4.9%	5.0%
Priest Not Charged	1,367	2,629	3,996
	94.9%	95.1%	95.0%
Total	**1,540** **100.0%**	**2,852** **100.0%**	**4,392** **100.0%**

Table 3.7.9 CRIMINAL CONVICTION BY SEVERITY OF
ALLEGATION

	Severity of Offense		
	Acts Involving Sex	Acts Not Involving Sex	Row Total
Priest Convicted	107	152	259
	6.9%	5.3%	5.9%
Priest Not Convicted	1,433	2,700	4,133
	93.1%	94.7%	94.1%
Total	**1,540** **100.0%**	**2,852** **100.0%**	**4,392** **100.0%**

If the accused priests are grouped not just by the number of formal allegations, but by the number of actual and potential allegations (to include the number of potential victims) the results show that investigation, arrest, and conviction are more likely for priests with more allegations.

Table 3.7.10 POLICE INVESTIGATION–ALLEGATIONS PLUS POTENTIAL VICTIMS

	Allegations and Potential Victims per Priest			
	1	2-3	4-9	10+
Police Investigation	357	264	232	110
	16.5%	23.2%	30.3%	43.7%
No Police Investigation	1,807	874	534	142
	83.5%	76.8%	69.7%	56.3%
Total	2,164 100.0%	1,138 100.0%	766 100.0%	252 100.0%

The term "potential victims" refers to Question 24 on the Cleric Survey, which asks for any third-party allegations noted in the records. Tables 3.7.10 - 3.7.2 include both actual and "potential" allegations.

Table 3.7.11 PRIEST CHARGED - ALLEGATIONS AND POTENTIAL VICTIMS

	Allegations and Potential Victims per Priest			
	1	2-3	4-9	10+
Priest Charged	117	113	105	59
	5.4%	9.9%	13.7%	23.4%
Priest Not Charged	2,047	1,025	661	193
	94.6%	90.1%	86.3%	76.6%
Total	2,164 100.0%	1,138 100.0%	766 100.0%	252 100.0%

Table 3.7.12 PRIEST CONVICTED—ALLEGATIONS PLUS POTENTIAL VICTIMS

	Allegations and Potential Victims per Priest			
	1	2-3	4-9	10+
Priest Convicted	69	72	72	44
	3.2%	6.3%	9.4%	17.5%
Priest Not Convicted	2,095	1,066	694	208
	96.8%	93.7%	90.6%	82.5%
Total	**2,164** **100.0%**	**1,138** **100.0%**	**766** **100.0%**	**252** **100.0%**

---

[1] David Finkelhor and Lisa M. Jones. "Explanations for the Decline In Child Sexual Abuse Cases," *ODJJP Bulletin*, (Washington, DC: OJJDP, January 2004): 11.

[2] Howard N. Snyder. *Sexual Assault of Young Children as Reported to Law Enforcement: Victim, Incident, and Offender Characteristics*, (Washington, DC: U.S Department of Justice, Office of Justice Programs, 2000), 1.

[3] Snyder, 12.

[4] Snyder, 1.

[5] Snyder, 1.

[6] Snyder, 11.

[7] Snyder, 13.

[8] Snyder, 13.

INCIDENTS AND ALLEGATIONS OF CHILD SEXUAL ABUSE

4.1   INTRODUCTION TO INCIDENTS AND ALLEGATIONS OF CHILD SEXUAL ABUSE

Child sexual abuse is complex problem that encompasses psychological, social and legal considerations. Research and theory have sought to understand the various motivations for abuse as well as characteristic offender behaviors that lead up to and occur during abuse. In order to understand child sexual abuse, it is important to understand the motivation to begin offending (the preconditions to child sexual abuse), how child sexual abusers get children to participate in sexual activity ("grooming"), and how and why the abusers are able to maintain this course of abusive actions through rationalizations of the behavior.

When considering why men sexually abuse children and adolescents, researchers have identified a number of preconditions to child sexual abuse. These include, but are not limited to: the offender's "emotional congruence" to youths (the link between the offender's emotional needs and the children's characteristics), low self esteem, deviant sexual arousal, "developmental blockage" (the failure to develop the appropriate social skills and self-confidence necessary to form effective intimate relations with adults), "situational blockage" (when an adult's sexual interests are blocked from normal sexual expression owing to the loss of a relationship or some other transitory crisis), and disinhibition (the factors that help a child sexual abuser overcome his inhibitions so that he allows himself to abuse a child or adolescent, e.g., use of alcohol or other substances).[1] These preconditions are each variable in strength; while some abusers may act out as a reaction to transitory stress, others seem to be driven by such a strong compulsion that situational factors play only a minor role, if any at all.

In order to get the children to go along with the abuse, many child sexual abusers indulge in what is termed "grooming," or premeditated behavior intended to manipulate the potential victim into complying with the sexual abuse.[2] Grooming tactics include verbal, emotional and/or physical intimidation, seduction, and the use of enticements such as candy, money, or other gifts. Emotional manipulation and verbal coercion seem to be the most common tactics used by offenders to groom their victims, including doing favors for the victim in exchange for sex and/or emotionally blackmailing the victim into compliance.[3]

In order for the child sexual abuse to continue, child sexual abusers often rationalize their behavior through "cognitive distortions," or distorted thinking patterns. Like any other type of offender, child sexual abusers may subconsciously use a "neutralization technique" to defuse any feelings of remorse or guilt they have for committing the abusive act or for the consequences of that act.[4] They do so by excusing or justifying their actions, often acknowledging their guilt but not taking responsibility for the acts. Commonly, they blame the victims for their offenses or justify their offenses through the victims' actions.

We used the extensive body of research findings that describe offender characteristics and the circumstances of childhood victimization as a guide in crafting the questions (e.g., the type of enticements used to "groom" children and to understand this sub-group of abusers.

---

[1] David Finkelhor, *Child Sexual Abuse: New Theory and Research* (New York: The Free Press, 1984).

[2] American Psychiatric Association, *Diagnostic and Statistical Manual of Mental Disorders: DSM-IV TR* (Washington, D.C.: American Psychiatric Association, 2000).

[3] Douglas W. Pryor, *Unspeakable Acts: Why Men Sexually Abuse Children* (New York, NY: New York University Press, 1996).

[4] Greshan M. Sykes and David Matza, "Techniques of neutralization: A theory of delinquency," *American Sociological Review*, 22 (1957):664-670.

4.2   SUMMARY: CHARACTERISTICS OF THE INCIDENTS OF ALLEGED SEXUAL ABUSE BY CATHOLIC PRIESTS

One of the most important tasks of this report is to provide a better understanding of the situations in which sexual abuse of children by Catholic priests occurred. The purpose of this chapter is to describe who has alleged child sexual abuse in the Church, his or her situational characteristics (e.g., age, gender and family situation), the relationship between the priest and the accuser. and the circumstances of the abuse (when and in what situation the abuse allegedly occurred). Through an appreciation of these characteristics, the Church would be better able to design policies aimed at removing opportunities in which such abuse could occur.

The study produced some important findings about the nature of child sexual abuse in the Catholic Church.

- Unlike in the general population, more males than females were allegedly. In fact, there was a significant difference between genders, with four out of five alleged victims being male.

- The majority of alleged victims were post-pubescent, with only a small percentage of priests receiving allegations of abusing young children.

- The allegations of sexual abuse involved a variety of sexual acts, and most of the priests involved were alleged to have committed multiple acts per victim. Indeed, much of the sexual abuse reported involved serious sexual offenses.

- According to the allegations of sexual abuse, the most frequent context of the sexual incidents occurred during a social event. Additionally, many of the priests with allegations of abuse socialized with the family of the alleged victim.

- The most common place of occurrence was the residence of the priest though incidents of abuse allegedly occurred in a wide variety of locations.

Whatever the motivation of men to sexually abuse children, the abuse is less likely to occur if there are fewer opportunities for the abuse to happen. This chapter paints a picture of priests who are friendly with the families of their alleged victims and who spend much social time with those they allegedly abused. Several of the priests allegedly bought gifts or gave other types of enticements (e.g., let the youths drive cars or took them to sporting events) to those who made allegations against them. Thus, like in the general population, child sexual abuse in the Catholic Church appears to be committed by men close to the children they allegedly abuse. Many appear to use grooming tactics to entice children into complying with the abuse and the abuse frequently occurs in the home of the alleged abuser or victim.

4.3   CHARACTERISTICS OF CHILDREN WHO ALLEGED SEXUAL ABUSE BY CATHOLIC PRIESTS

This chapter is based on survey data that describes 10,667 incidents of alleged sexual abuse of youths under 18 by a Catholic priest or deacon, at least part of which occurred between the beginning of 1950 and the end of 2002.   The following steps were taken to achieve that number:

- Dioceses, eparchies and religious communities submitted 10,822 incident-level surveys based on files for individual priests and deacons who had been accused of child sexual abuse.
- Allegations determined to have been documented by more than one survey have been unified as a single incident-level file.
- 155 surveys that were submitted for allegations made about acts that occurred when the person making the allegation was 18 or older, and about alleged events that occurred or ended before 1950, or that were associated to seminarians or religious brothers not eligible for the study were deleted and diocesan/religious community totals corrected.
- Not all questions were answered on each survey; as a result, each table shows the available responses, and the totals change from table to table.

The extent of childhood sexual victimization is difficult to estimate though it is a phenomenon that has been studied extensively over the last few decades. Despite the claim by many that it occurs in epidemic proportions, most of these studies have disagreed with respect to the true prevalence figure. Prevalence estimates of childhood sex abuse range from 2 to 62 percent, depending largely upon the methodology used in the research design (including the definition of child sexual abuse, sampling procedures, type of questions asked during one-on-one interviews, and gender of the respondents). One analysis of the various studies on victim prevalence found that the overall prevalence for male children who are sexually abused is 13 percent, and the prevalence of female children who are sexually abused ranges from 30 to 40 percent.[1] This study also identified three significant explanations as to why there is such a wide range in childhood sexual victimization rates, including the number of screening questions used to identify abuse victims, the size of the sample, and the year in which the study was conducted.[2]

The results of our study indicated that of all victims whose gender was reported, (Table 4.3.1) 81% were male and 19% were female.

Table 4.3.1 GENDER OF ALLEGED VICTIM

Gender	Count	% of Total
Male	8,499	80.9%
Female	2,004	19.1%
Transsexual	2	.0%
Total	10,505	100.0%

98.5% of surveys reported the gender of the alleged victim.

Table 4.3.2 represents the age of the alleged victim at the time of the alleged event. If the event continued for multiple years, this table represents the age at which the abuse allegedly began. Each alleged victim is only represented once. Therefore, this table does not represent the duration of abuse or the ages of the alleged victims throughout the time they were abused. For instance, if a child was sexually abused from the age of three to nine, he or she is represented in this table at age three.

The majority of victims are males between the ages of 11-17, and just over half (50.7%) of all individuals who made allegations of abuse were between the ages of 11-14. The average age of all alleged victims is 12.6. This number has increased over time, however. In the 1950s, the average age was 11.5; in the 1960s it was 12; in the 1970s it was 12.87; in the 1980s it was 13.2; and by the 1990s it was 13.87.

Table 4.3.2 VICTIM'S AGE AT FIRST INSTANCE OF ABUSE

Age in Years	Count	% of Total
1	4	.0%
2	11	.1%
3	22	.2%
4	41	.5%
5	82	1.0%
6	158	1.8%
7	220	2.5%
8	369	4.1%
9	362	4.0%
10	752	8.4%
11	895	10.0%
12	1,323	14.7%
13	1,141	12.8%
14	1,188	13.2%
15	1,042	11.6%
16	769	8.6%
17	577	6.5%
Total	8,956	100%

Eighty-four percent of surveys included the age of the alleged victim at the time the abuse occurred or at the time the abuse began. It is important to understand that in retrospective studies, particularly where there is a delay in the reporting of the events, the possibility that alleged victims did not remember the specific dates correctly must be considered. (See Section 5.1 for a review of the research on this phenomeon, called "telescoping.")

The substantial majority of alleged victims of child sexual abuse, or almost four out of five, lived with both parents. Information about the residence of the alleged victim was provided on 70% of the Victim Surveys.

Table 4.3.3 VICTIM'S RESIDENCE / LIVING SITUATION

	Count	% of Total
Mother only	843	11.2%
Father only	81	1.1%
Both parents	5,905	78.6%
Brother(s)	29	.4%
Sister(s)	14	.2%
Other guardian	17	.2%
Grandparents	53	.7%
Boarding school	172	2.3%
Foster parents	29	.4%
Orphanage	159	2.1%
Home of priest	67	.9%
Church-related residence	53	.7%
Other	92	1.2%
Total	7,514	100%

---

[1] Rebecca Bolen and Maria Scannapieco, "Prevalence of Child Sexual Abuse: A Corrective Metanalysis" *Social Service Review* (1999): 281.

[2] Bolen and Scannapieco.

4.4 CHARACTERISTICS OF ACTS OF SEXUAL ABUSE BY CATHOLIC PRIESTS

Many efforts have been made to assess the abuse experiences of those who have been victims of child sexual abuse, from attempts to collect population data at the national level to small clinical studies done with a few survivors of sexual abuse. These studies generally tend to chronicle the types of behaviors engaged in by child sexual abusers, and primarily report percentages of the sample that experienced each form of abuse (e.g., intercourse, oral sex, fondling, pornography). A number of studies have compared male and female victims, although most of the male victim samples have been too small to allow for broad generalizations.

Looking at Table 4.4.1, it is clear that many of the allegations of abuse include more than one type of sexual act[1]. Several points are significant:

- The categories are not mutually exclusive. In other words, the abusers could have committed multiple types of abuses.

- Very few priests have allegations of only the least severe of the abuses. Only 148 priests (2.9%) allegedly committed act of verbal abuse and/or pornography offenses without more severe offenses. Only 395 priests (9.0%) allegedly committed offenses involving touching over the clothes only without also committing a more severe offense.

- Touching under the victim's clothes is the most common act alleged. However, only 695 (15.8%) priests committed that as the only or the most serious of their alleged offenses. This means that when this abuse was alleged, it usually included a more serious offense as well.

- There are 69 incidents for which the most serious act alleged is sexual talk. These incidents represent seven-tenths of one percent, or .7% of the 9,630 surveys that reported details about the behavior that was alleged to have taken place. If sexual talk and the use of pornography are counted together, for cases where no further sexual abuse was alleged, there are 141 incidents, or 1.5% of the total.

- If talk and/or pornography use are considered together with either touching under the priest's or victim's clothing, and nothing more serious is alleged, the total number of such incidents is 1,196, or 12.4% of the total.

- If hugging and kissing, the removal of clothing, or masturbation is counted along with the acts outlined above, the total number of incidents jumps to 4,167, or 43% of the total.

- If incidents that include acts of oral sex or sexual penetration are counted alone, they total 3,280, or 34%.

Table 4.4.1   ALLEGED ACTS OF ABUSE, BY GENDER

Behavior Alleged	GENDER		Combined
	Males	**Females**	**Totals**
Verbal (sexual talk)	885	215	1,100
	11.5%	12%	11.6%
Shown Pornography	223	9	232
	2.9%	.5%	2.4%
Shown Porn videos	142	6	148
	1.8%	.3%	1.6%
Touch Over Cleric's Clothes	704	165	869
	9.1%	9.2%	9.2%
Touch Over Victim's Clothes	2,862	691	3,553
	37.2%	38.6%	37.4%
Touch Under Victim's Clothes	3,280	701	3,981
	42.6%	39.2%	42%
Cleric Disrobed	944	177	1,121
	12.3%	9.9%	11.8%
Victim Disrobed	1,112	303	1,415
	14.4%	16.9%	14.9%
Photos of Victim	169	32	201
	2.2%	1.8%	2.1%
Sexual Games	96	8	104
	1.2%	.4%	1.1%
Hugging & Kissing	324	175	499
	4.2%	9.8%	5.3%
Masturbation	663	71	734
	8.6%	4.0%	7.7%
Mutual Masturbation	1,049	29	1,078
	13.6	1.6%	11.4%
Cleric Perform Oral Sex	1,186	274	1,460
	15.4%	15.9%	15.4%
Victim Performed Oral Sex	799	115	914
	10.4%	6.4%	9.6
Manual Penetration	192	195	387
	2.5%	10.9%	4.1%
Penetration with Object	61	26	87
	.8%	1.5%	.9%
Penile Penetration	990	213	1,203
	12.9%	11.9%	12.7%
Group or Coerced Sex	48	4	52
	.6%	.2%	.5%
Unspecified Sex Act	942	204	1,146
	12.2%	11.4%	12.1%
Other	490	87	577
	6.4%	4.9%	6.1%

The category of "other" includes a wide array of behaviors, including voyeuristic and sadistic acts. Unspecified sex act refers to surveys that indicate sexual acts but do not identify particular acts.

This is a Multiple Response Table. The categories are not mutually exclusive.

The majority of allegations of sexual abuse were made against priests who were accused of having committed abusive acts more than one time. Only slightly more than one quarter (29%) of the allegations involve only a single instance of abuse.

Table 4.4.2   NUMBER OF TIMES ABUSED, PER VICTIM

No. of times abused	Count	Percent
Once	2,759	29%
More than once	1,734	18.3%
Numerous times	5,002	52.7%
Total	9,493	100%

Question 8 on the Victim Survey asked how many times the victim was abused. The choices were 'once,' 'more than once,' and 'numerous.'

Child sexual abusers who plan their abusive acts indulge in what is termed "grooming" behavior. Grooming is a pre-meditated behavior intended to manipulate the potential victim into complying with the sexual abuse. Some methods by which child sexual abusers approach and initiate sexual activity with their victims include verbal and/or physical intimidation, seduction, emotional blackmail, and the use of enticements such as candy, money, or other gifts The tactics used by offenders depend somewhat on the potential victim's response to the tactic. If an offender encounters little to no resistance from the potential victim, he will continue to use the same tactic repeatedly. If, however, some resistance is encountered, the offender may either change the tactic and/or become more forceful in his endeavor. Table 4.4.3 shows the number of priests who allegedly threatened those who accused them of abuse, and Table 4.4.4 shows the type of threat that was used. Both tables display the information by gender.

Table 4.4.3   THREATS BY VICTIM'S GENDER

Victim Threatened?	Male	Female	Total
Yes	527	208	835
	14%	16.8%	14.6%
No	3,853	1,033	4,886
	86%	83.2%	84.5%
Gender Totals	4,480	1,241	100%

Approximately half of the incident-level surveys (5,761) included information on the use of threats. Table 4.4.3 is therefore based on only 50% of the reported incidents. If the number of incidents that involved a threat to the victim is expressed as a percentage of all reported incidents, 7.8% of all alleged victims were threatened in some way.

Table 4.4.4 TYPE OF THREATS BY VICTIM'S GENDER

Type of Threat	GENDER		
	Male	Female	Totals
Physical Threat with Weapon	30	13	43
	3.6%	5.0%	4.0%
Physical Threat without Weapon	74	21	95
	8.9%	8.1%	8.7%
Verbal (Harm to Victim)	179	65	244
	21.6%	25%	22.4%
Verbal (Harm to Cleric)	34	8	42
	4.1%	3.1%	3.9%
Threatened Family	26	12	38
	3.1%	4.6%	3.5%
Threatened Exposure	65	24	89
	7.9%	9.2%	8.2%
Spiritual Manipulation	173	55	228
	20.9%	21.2%	21%
Other	128	40	168
	15.5%	15.4%	15.4%
All of the Above	128	22	141
	14.4%	8.5%	13%
Gender Totals	828	260	1088
	100.0%	100.0%	100.0%

The use of gifts and other enticements to participate is sexual behavior is a common method of grooming potential victims. Tables 4.4.6 and 4.4.7 show the extent of and types of gifts and enticements made to alleged victims of sexual abuse by Catholic priests and deacons.. Gifts and enticements were recorded separately, and surveys showed that in 837 alleged incidents, a gift had been given. Accused priests used enticements in 1,834 incidents, or 17% of the total number of reported incidents.

Table 4.4.5 GIFTS TO VICTIMS

Gifts Given to Victim?	Count	Percent
Yes	837	18.2%
No	3,769	81.8%
Total	4,606	100%

Table 4.4.6 ENTICEMENTS OFFERED BY PRIEST

Type of Enticement	Count	Percent of Incidents
Allowed to Stay Up	130	7.1%
Allowed to Drive	148	8.1%
Access to Pornography	151	8.2%
Special Church Activities	89	4.9%
Alcohol/Drugs	712	38.8%
Taken to Sports/Rec. Events	427	23.3%
Stay Overnight with Cleric	559	30.5%
Sports-Related	22	1.2%
Travel	67	3.7%
Food	33	1.8%
Toys, Other Gifts	7	.4%
Money	377	20.6%
Other	281	15.3%

This is a Multiple Response Table. The categories are not mutually exclusive, as a priest may have employed more than one form of enticement. Percentages are of the 1,834 incidents involving enticements.

If the number of incidents that involved gifts is added to the number of incidents that involved enticements, the results is 2,231 incidents, or 20.9% of all reported incidents of abuse.

Some sex offenders in the general population use alcohol or drugs as a disinhibitor, or as a way to reduce their inhibitions and allow them to offend with reduced feelings of guilt and shame. Some sex offenders also offer drugs and/or alcohol to their victims to entice them to participate in sexual behavior. Tables 4.4.8 and 4.4.9 display drug/alcohol use by alleged offenders and victims respectively.

Table 4.4.7 DRUG/ALCOHOL USE BY PRIEST

Priest Used Drugs/Alcohol	Count	Percent
Yes	988	21.6%%
No	3,596	78.4%
Total	4,584	100%

Question 31 on the Victim Survey asked whether the victim was under the influence of alcohol or drugs at the time of the alleged incident, and Question 32 asked about the accused priest or deacon. The study does not have detailed information about the source or type of intoxicant used.

Table 4.4.8 DRUG/ALCOHOL USE BY VICTIM

Victim Used Drugs/Alcohol	Count	Percent
Yes	854	15.1%
No	4,789	84.9%
Total	5,643	100.0%

The percentages in Tables 4.4.7 and 4.4.8 are based on the total number of surveys that included answers to the Questions 31 and 32.

[1] A very substantial number of surveys recorded sexual acts without giving any further information about them.

4.5 CIRCUMSTANCES OF THE ABUSE ALLEGATIONS

The following section describes characteristics of the alleged abuse. Information from this section was obtained through the surveys of the incidents completed for each allegation of abuse of a child by a priest or deacon. These data present contextual factors associated with the reported incidents including where and when the event took place. This section also describes the social relationships of the priests with the alleged victims' families: their Church assignment at the time the abuse was alleged to have occurred; their relationship (if any) with the family of the child involved; and any relationship with the siblings of the alleged victim.

These variables paint a picture of the circumstances surrounding reported incidents of abuse, which may aid clinicians in their understanding of such behaviors in the population of priests who abuse children. Most importantly, however, these factors may be useful in designing policies and procedures to prevent abuse from occurring in the future. Table 4.5.1 represents the decades in which the abuse allegedly occurred, or the date it began if it occurred over multiple decades.

Table 4.5.1 ALLEGED INCIDENTS, BY DECADE

Decade	Count	Percent	Cumulative Percent
1950s	913	9.94%	9.94%
1960s	2,402	26.14%	36.08%
1970s	3,245	35.32%	71.4%
1980s	2,048	22.29%	93.69%
1990s	500	5.44%	99.13%
2000-2002	80	.87%	100%
Total	**9,188**	**100.0**	

This table summarizes the total numbers of acts alleged by the decade when they began. It is important to note that it does not include the duration of the alleged abuse if it occurred in more than one time period.

As Table 4.5.2 makes clear, the majority of priests, approximately 67%, were serving as either the pastor or associate pastor in their parish when the abuse was alleged to have occurred. A little over 10% of priests were resident priests at the time and approximately 9% were serving in the parish in some other capacity. Thus, the bulk of incidents were reported to have occurred in the context of the priest serving in leading capacity within the parish. Other roles, such as teacher in a school, were present as well but characterize far fewer incidents.

Table 4.5.2 PRIEST'S PRIMARY FUNCTION AT TIME OF ALLEGED INCIDENT

Priest's Function	Count	Percent of accused priests
Pastor	2,463	25.1%
Associate Pastor	4,150	42.3%
Resident Priest	1,023	10.4%
Teacher (grades 1-8)	55	.5%
Teacher (grades 9-12)	654	6.7%
Seminary Administrator/Faculty	184	1.8%
Chaplain	264	2.7%
Bishop, Vicar, Cardinal, Chancellor.	33	.3%
Deacon or Seminarian	77	.8%
Other Parish Roles	883	9%
Relative of alleged victim	39	.4%
Total	**9,822**	**100%**

Some priests were serving multiple functions in the community at the time allegations were made against them. This list, however, included the primary function of the priests at the time of their allegations.

Table 4.5.3 contains categories representing reported incidents of abuse, some of which were single- instances and others based upon multiple instances of abuse over a period of time. Therefore, some incidents reflect abuse in more than one location. However, the most commonly reported location where the incident took place was the priest's residence/parish residence. This was the location of at least one instance of abuse for 41% of reported allegations. Incidents were reported to have occurred in the church in approximately 16% of the cases, and in the victim's home in approximately 12% of the cases. In almost one quarter of the cases, no record of location was reported.

Table 4.5.3 LOCATION OF ABUSE

Place	Count	Percent of cases
In school	939	10.3%
In a hotel room	675	7.4%
Retreat house	133	1.5%
Priest's home / Parish residence	3730	40.9%
Vacation house	941	10.3%
Other residences (friends, family, etc.)	49	.5%
Congregate residences	51	.6%
In victim's home	1131	12.4%
Priest's office	685	7.5%
In church	1483	16.3%
In the hospital	75	.8%
In a car	897	9.8%
Outings (camp, park, pool, etc.)	757	8.3%
Other location	571	6.3%
No record of location	2109	23.1%

This is a multiple response table. The categories are not mutually exclusive since an incident of abuse may have taken place over time and in more than one place,

Table 4.5.4 shows the situations when the abuse allegedly occurred. These varied widely. Social events were the most common context (20%), followed by travel with the priest (17.8%) and visiting or working at the rectory or priest's place of residence (approximately 15%), and travel with the priest to church-related activities. It should be noted that 168 (or almost 2 percent of incidents) were alleged to have occurred during the sacrament of reconciliation. No record of the situation when abuse occurred was present in 30% of cases.

Table 4.5.4 SITUATIONS WHEN THE ABUSE ALLEGEDLY OCCURRED

	Count	Percent of cases
During a retreat	100	1.0%
Church service (before, during, after)	687	7.2%
During travel	1702	17.8%
During counseling	677	7.1%
During social event	1953	20.4%
During reconciliation	168	1.8%
During sporting event	442	4.6%
Outings	296	3.1%
School hours	492	5.1%
Church service/training	39	.4%
Priest visited home of alleged victim	394	4.1%
Hospital visit	13	.1%
Visiting/working at priest's home/rectory	1405	14.7%
Other	752	7.9%
No record of location	3035	31.8%

This is a multiple response table. The categories are not mutually exclusive, since an incident of abuse may have taken place over time and in more than one place.

Table 4.5.5 indicates the relationship between the allegedly abusive priest and the family of his alleged victim. In a little less than half of the cases, no relationship was reported, but in just over one quarter of the cases, records indicated that the priest engaged in a social relationship with the alleged victim's family.

Table 4.5.5 PRIEST/FAMILY SOCIAL RELATIONS

Did the priests socialize with the alleged victim's family?	Count	Percent
Yes	2,638	49.6%
No	2,657	50.4%
Total	5,295	100%

Table 4.5.6 describes the way in which the priests socialized with the families of their alleged victims. In cases where there was information in the records to indicate that the family of the child socialized with the priest, the majority of socializing, approximately 80%, reportedly occurred in the family's home. A little under half off the socializing was reported to have occurred at the church or in activities sponsored by the Church. Records indicated that in almost a quarter of reported incidents, families socialized with the priest in his residence. It should be noted that these were not mutually exclusive categories, so many families saw the priest socially in one of several contexts.

Table 4.5.6 TYPE OF PRIEST/FAMILY SOCIALIZING

Type of socializing	Count	Percent
In the church	702	27.5%
In his residence	620	24.3%
Vacations/social activities	436	17.1%
Church day activities	537	21.0%
In family's residence	2,031	79.6%
Other	152	6.0%

This is a multiple response table. The categories are not mutually exclusive, since priests may have socialized with the family of the alleged victim in more than one way.

Table 4.5.7 describes the number of alleged victims whose siblings were also allegedly abused. This information was available in about 60% of reported cases. In 1,842 cases, or 29% of all surveys with a response to this question, siblings of the alleged victim were also alleged to have been abused by a priest. If this number is expressed as a percentage of all incidents of abuse reported in the study, 17% of victims reported abuse of a brother or sister by a priest.

Table 4.5.7 SIBLINGS ABUSED

Were any of the alleged victim's siblings abused?	Count	Percent
Yes	1,842	29%
No	4,508	71%
Total	6,350	100.0%

THE RESPONSE FROM DIOCESES AND RELIGIOUS COMMUNITIES

5.1 INTRODUCTION TO THE REPORTING OF CHILD SEXUAL ABUSE

Every published empirical study on the disclosure of child sexual abuse indicates that a high percentage of those child sexual abuse victims who report their abuse to authorities delay disclosure of their abuse and that a significant number of children do not disclose the abuse at all[1]. The delay between the initial occurrence and the subsequent disclosure of the abuse varies, depending on a number of factors such as the abused child's age at the time of abuse, the relationship between the perpetrator and the child, the gender of the child, the severity of the abuse, developmental and cognitive variables related to the abused and the likely consequences of the disclosure.

Consequently, child sexual abuse is significantly underreported. When victims do report that they were abused, they often do so years after the abuse occurred. Adult retrospective studies of childhood sexual abuse underline the delay in disclosure. In a study of 228 adult female victims of childhood incest who were predominantly abused by males, Roesler and Weissmann-Wind found that the average age of first abuse was 6 years, and the abuse lasted on average 7.6 years. Only one-third of the subjects in this sample disclosed the abuse before the age of 18, and the average age of disclosure was 25.9.[2] Arata found that only 41% of the 204 female participants in her study, whose average age at the time of victimization was 8.5, disclosed the abuse at the time it occurred.[3] Lawson and Chaffin found that only 43% of their child subjects disclosed their abuse when they were initially interviewed.[4] Lamb and Edgar-Smith conducted a study with 45 adult female and 12 adult male victims of childhood sexual abuse, and they found that although the average age at the time of victimization was 10, 64% of the victims disclosed their abuse in adulthood.[5] In a study of childhood rape of girls, Smith, Letourneau and Saunders found that approximately half of the women waited more than eight years to disclose the abuse.[6]

If abuse is reported years after it occurred, there may be errors in the accuracy of the report due to "telescoping," or the likelihood that an individual will report the event as happening earlier or later than it actually occurred[7]. Several social science studies have tested the telescoping phenomenon. Several studies found that forward-telescoping, or recalling a past event as having occurred more recently than it actually did, is more prevalent than backward telescoping.[8] One study showed that memory disorientations, such as telescoping, occur more often in survey respondents 55 years or older than respondents less than 55 years of age.[9] Another study portrayed survey participants as showing a tendency to forward-telescope events that were prominent in their lives.[10] In other words, these survey respondents showed a higher likelihood of recalling significant life events, such as crime victimization, as occurring more recently in time than the event actually did. Yet another study examined the existence of telescoping in crime victimization surveys and found that non-reported incidents were telescoped by respondents to a slightly greater extent than incidents reported to the police.[11]

This notion reveals a propensity for crime victims to telescope forward victimizations from their past, particularly if the crime was never reported to the police or criminal justice officials. Though telescoping has consistently been an issue in temporal reporting of a variety of abuses[12], no empirical studies have examined this problem specifically with sexual abuse disclosure.

The process of disclosing childhood sexual abuse varies, though it is often described within two axes: as purposeful or accidental and as spontaneous or prompted.[13] DeVoe and Coulborn-Faller found that child subjects in their study required assistance with disclosure.[14] Sorenson and Snow noted that accidental disclosure was more common in preschool children whereas purposeful disclosure was more common in adolescents. They also found four stages of disclosure in their retrospective study of 630 subjects who were aged 3 to 17 at the time of abuse: denial, disclosure (tentative and active), recantation and reaffirmation. These researchers also found that 72% of their subjects originally denied the abuse; 78% of the subjects who tentatively revealed their abuse progressed to active disclosure; 22% recanted their reports, and of those who recanted 93% later reaffirmed the original report.[15] Lawson and Chaffin found that a significant factor in the disclosure process was the belief of the caretaker in the veracity of the disclosure.[16] Bradley and Wood's research also supported the notion that the role of the caretaker is essential. Although recantations of disclosure were rare in their sample, they found that 50% of children who recanted did so under pressure from a caretaker. [17]

One model of child sexual abuse, the Child Sexual Abuse Accommodation Syndrome, helps explain the hindrance to disclosure. This syndrome is not intended to be diagnostic, but rather it is intended as a clinical tool to assist in putting abuse victim behavior in context. It consists of five components: secrecy (the abuse occurs when the victim and perpetrator are alone, and the perpetrator encourages the victim to maintain secrecy); helplessness (children are obedient to adults and will usually obey the perpetrator who encourages secrecy); entrapment and accommodation (once the child is helplessly entrenched in the abusive situation, he or she assumes responsibility for the abuse and begins to dissociate from it); delayed disclosure (because the victims who report child sexual abuse often wait long periods of time to disclose, their disclosures are subsequently questioned); and retraction (as in the recantation stage described by Sorenson and Snow, the victims may retract their disclosures of abuse after facing disbelief and lack of support after their disclosure).[18] Of course, not all victims react in predicted ways, but some broad patterns can be discerned.

FACTORS INFLUENCING DISCLOSURE
VICTIM'S RELATIONSHIP TO THE PERPETRATOR
If the perpetrator is a relative or acquaintance, victims of child sexual abuse are less likely to report the offense, or they are likely to disclose the abuse after a delay.[19]

In Arata's study, 73% of the victims did not disclose the abuse when the perpetrator was a relative or stepparent, and 70% did not disclose when the perpetrator was an acquaintance.[20] Goodman-Brown, Edelstein, and Goodman found that those children who felt responsible for the abuse, often because the abuse occurred within the family, took longer to report the abuse.[21] Wyatt and Newcomb found that the women who did not disclose their abuse to anyone were likely to have been closely related to the perpetrator and abused in close proximity to their home.[22]

SEVERITY OF SEXUAL ABUSE

Research results vary in regard to disclosure of abuse in relation to the severity of that abuse. Arata found that child victims who experienced more severe levels of sexual abuse were less likely to disclose this type of abuse.[23] This is consistent with the findings of Gries, Goh, and Cavanaugh, who reported that fondling was reported by 80% of their subjects who disclosed.[24] In contrast, however, Hanson found that of their 341 adult females who were victims of childhood rape, the more severe assaults were likely to be reported.[25] DiPietro et al (1998) also found that contact sexual offenses were those most commonly reported in their sample of 76 children.[26]

DEVELOPMENTAL AND COGNITIVE VARIABLES

Lamb and Edgar-Smith speculate that "more astute" children may not disclose because they may "anticipate unsupportive reactions".[27] They also maintain that such children may wait until adulthood to disclose when they can choose appropriate people to tell. White, as cited in Campis, found that older victims of child sexual abuse were less likely to disclose than their younger counterparts and noted that the knowledge of social consequences was a significant hindrance to disclosure.[28] Keary and Fitzpatrick concluded that children over the age of five, who had previously disclosed sexual abuse, were more likely to disclose this information during formal assessment, but the converse was true for children under five.[29] Similarly, DiPietro found that "developmental maturation clearly facilitates" disclosure. [30]

FEAR OF NEGATIVE CONSEQUENCES

Sorenson and Snow found that fear of further harm had an impact on a child's motivation to disclose abuse and that child victims often only felt safe enough to disclose after the departure of the perpetrator.[31] Berliner and Conte also noted that the fear about perceived reactions of others prevent some children from disclosing sexual abuse.[32] Roesler and Weissmann-Wind found that 33.3% of their subjects did not disclose their abuse during childhood because they feared for their safety. They also found that 32.9% of their subjects did not report their abuse during childhood because they felt guilt or shame as a result of the abuse.[33]

GENDER DIFFERENCES

DeVoe and Coulborn-Faller; Gries, Goh, and Cavanaugh; Lamb and Edgar-Smith; and Walrath, Ybarra, and Holden all found that girls are more likely to report abuse than boys.[34] Reinhart found that sexual abuse of males was more likely to be disclosed by a third party.[35] There are no methodologically sound empirical studies that indicate that males disclose at a higher rate than females. Gender does not appear to be as important, however, as victim-perpetrator relationship in disclosure of abuse.[36]

---

[1] For a comprehensive review of the literature on disclosure of childhood sexual abuse, see Paine, M.L. and Hansen D.J. (2002) Factors influencing children to self-disclose sexual abuse. *Clinical Psychology Review*. 22: 271-295.

[2] Roesler, T.A., & Weisssmann-Wind, T.A. "Telling the Secret: Adult Women Describe Their Disclosures of Incest," *Journal of Interpersonal Violence* 9 (3, 1994): 327-338.

[3] Arata, C M. "To Tell or Not to Tell: Current Functioning of Child Sexual Abuse Survivors who Disclosed Their Victimization," *Child Maltreatment: Journal of the American Professional Society on the Abuse of Children* 3 (1, 1998): 63-71.

[4] Lawson, L., & Chaffin, M. "False Negatives in Sexual Abuse Disclosure Interviews: Incidence and Influence of Caretaker's Belief in Abuse in Cases of Accidental Abuse Discovery by Diagnosis of STD," *Journal of Interpersonal Violence* 7 (4, 1992): 532-542.

[5] Lamb, S., & Edgar-Smith, S. "Aspects of Disclosure: Mediators of Outcome of Childhood Sexual Abuse," *Journal of Interpersonal Violence* 9 (3, 1994): 307-326.

[6] Smith, D.W., Letourneau, E.J., & Saunders, B.E. "Delay in Disclosure of Childhood Rape: Results From a National Survey," *Child Abuse & Neglect* 24 (2, 2000): 273-287.

[7] Sudman & Bradburn, (1973), as cited in Schneider, Anne L. & Sumi, David. "Patterns of Forgetting and Telescoping." *Criminology.* Vol. 19, No. 3. (November 1981): p. 401.

[8] Schneider et al., (1978); NRC, (1976), as cited in Schneider, Anne L. & Sumi, David. "Patterns of Forgetting and Telescoping." *Criminology.* Vol. 19, No. 3. (November 1981): p. 401. This article discusses telescoping patterns as well as the Portland Forward Records Check.

[9] Sudman & Bradburn (1974), as cited in Gottfredson, Michael R. & Hindelang, Michael J. "A Consideration of Telescoping and Memory Decay Biases in Victimization Surveys." Journal of Criminal Justice. Vol. 5. (1977): p. 206. This article describes characteristics and tendencies of telescoping commonly found in social science research.

[10] Neter & Waksberg, (1964), as cited in Gottfredson, Michael R. & Hindelang, Michael J. "A Consideration of Telescoping and Memory Decay Biases in Victimization Surveys." Journal of Criminal Justice. Vol. 5. (1977): p. 206. This article describes characteristics and tendencies of telescoping commonly found in social science research.

[11] Schneider et al., (1978); NRC, (1976), as cited in Schneider, Anne L. & Sumi, David. "Patterns of Forgetting and Telescoping." Criminology. Vol. 19, No. 3. (November 1981): p. 409. This article discusses telescoping patterns as well as the Portland Forward Records Check.

[12] Skogan, (1975), as cited in Levine, James P. "The Potential for Crime Overreporting in Criminal Victimization Surveys." Criminology. Vol. 14, No. 3. (November 1976): p. 318; Schneider et al., (1978), as cited in Schneider, Anne L. & Sumi, David. "Patterns of Forgetting and Telescoping." Criminology. Vol. 19, No. 3. (November 1981): p. 402.

[13] Devoe, E.R., & Coulborn-Faller, K. "The Characteristics of Disclosure Among Children who May Have Been Sexually Abused," *Child Maltreatment: Journal of the American Professional Society on the Abuse of Children* 4 (3, 1999): 217-227; Reinhart, M.A. "Sexually Abused Boys," *Child Abuse & Neglect* 11 (2, 1987): 229-235; and Sorenson, T., & Snow, B. "How Children Tell: The Process of Disclosure in Child Sexual Abuse," *Child Welfare* 70 (1, 1991):

[14] Devoe & Coulborn-Faller.

[15] Sorenson and Snow, 4.

[16] Lawson and Chaffin.

[17] Bradley, A.R., & Wood, J.M. "How Do Children Tell? The Disclosure Process in Child Sexual Abuse," *Child Abuse & Neglect* 20 (9, 1996): 881-891

[18] Summit, R.C. "The Child Sexual Abuse Accommodation Syndrome," *Child Abuse & Neglect* 7 (2, 1983): 177-193.

[19] Arata, p#; Elisabeth Kahl, Desmond K. Runyan, and Doren D. Fredrickson, "Predictors of Disclosure During Medical Evaluations for Suspected Sexual Abuse," *Journal of Child Sexual Abuse* 6 (1, 2003): 133-142; Rochelle F. Hanson, Heidi S. Saunders, Benjamin E. Saunders, Dean G. Kilpatrick, and Connie Best, "Factors Related to the Reporting of Childhood Rape," *Child Abuse & Neglect* 23 (6, 1999): 559-569; Smith Letourneau and Saunders, p#; and Wyatt, G.E., & Newcomb, M.D. "Internal and External Mediators of Women's Sexual Abuse in Childhood," *Journal of Consulting & Clinical Psychology* 58 (6, 1990): 758-767.

[20] Arata.

[21] Goodman-Brown, T.B., Edelstein, R.S., & Goodman, G.S. "Why Children Tell: A Model of Children's Disclosure of Sexual Abuse," *Child Abuse & Neglect* 27 (5, 2003): 525-540.

[22] Wyatt & Newcom.

[23] Arata.

[24] Gries, L.T., Goh, D.S., & Cavanaugh, J. "Factors Associated With Disclosure During Child Sexual Abuse Assessment," *Journal of Child Sexual Abuse* 5 (3, 1996): 1-20.

[25] DiPietro.

[26] Hanson, 566

[27] Lamb & Edgar Smith, 321.

[28] Campis, L.B., Hebden-Curtis, J., & DeMaso, D.R. "Developmental Differences in Detection and Disclosure of Sexual Abuse," *Journal of the American Academy of Child & Adolescent Psychiatry* 32 (5, 1993): 920-924.

[29] Keary, K., & Fitzpatrick, C. "Children's Disclosure of Sexual Abuse During Formal Investigation," *Child Abuse & Neglect* 18 (7, 1994): 543-548.

[30] Dipietro 2003. 140

[31] Sorenson & Snow.

[32] Berliner, L., & Conte, J.R. "The Effects of Disclosure and Intervention On Sexually Abused Children," *Child Abuse & Neglect* 19 (3, 1995): 371-384.

[33] Roesler & Weissmann-Wind.

[34] Walrath, C., Ybarra, M., & Holden, E.W. "Children With Reported Histories of Sexual Abuse: Utilizing Multiple Perspectives to Understand Clinical and Psychosocial Profiles," *Child Abuse & Neglect* 27 (5, 2003): 509-524.

[35] Reinhart

[36] Paine and Hansen

5.2 REPORTING OF ALLEGATIONS OF SEXUAL ABUSE

The shape of the distribution of incidents of alleged abuse, as was shown in Figure 2.3.1 in Part Two of this report, follows a regular curve, rising steadily from 1950 to its height in the mid-1970s and then steadily decreases until the end of the study period. Although the reporting of child sexual abuse follows a completely different pattern, as is shown in Figure 5.2.1, the distribution of abuse allegations over time that are reported in the peak year 2002, are not different from the overall pattern of events. As Figure 5.2.2 shows, the distribution of incidents reported in 2002 is very similar to that shown for all allegations reported over the 52 years that is the time frame of this study.

Figure 5.2.1   YEAR OF ABUSE REPORT

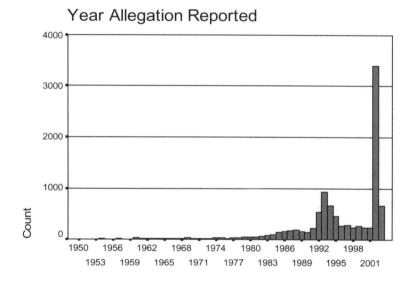

Figure 5.2.2 CASES REPORTED IN 2002, BY BEGIN DATE

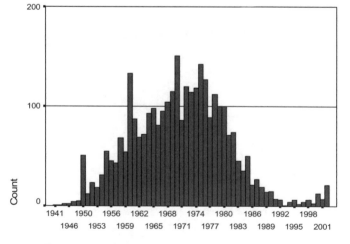

Table 5.2.1 INCIDENT BEGIN DATES REPORTED IN 2002
COMPARED TO ALL INCIDENTS

Decade	Overall Count	Percent	Percent in 2002
1950 - 1959s	939	9.7%	416 / 13.3%
1960 - 1969s	2,533	26.1%	966 / 30.7%
1970 - 1979s	3,445	35.5%	1,196 / 36%
1980s - 1989	2,074	20.6%	473 / 15%
1990s - 2003	603	6.2%	95 / 2.8%
Total	9,714		

Table 5.2.1 compares the decade by decade totals of alleged incidents for all reported incidents and for those reported in 2002. The pattern of abuse alleged in 2002 and over the entire study period is very similar.

Table 5.2.2 ABUSE REPORTS BY DECADE

Decade	Overall Count	Percent
1950s	53	.5%
1960s	190	1.8%
1970s	266	2.6%
1980s	1,146	11.2%
1990s	4,022	39.4%
2000 - 2002	4,533	44.4%
Total	10,210	100%

Table 5.2.2. shows the remarkable clustering of reports of child sexual abuse in and after the decade of the 1990s.

Figure 5.2.3 TIME FROM INCIDENT TO REPORT

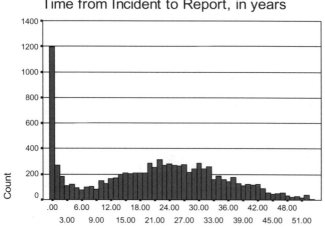

Time from Incident to Report, in years

Half of the incidents of abuse were reported by individuals who experienced the victimization. Attorneys reported one in five incidents, followed by family members, who reported approximately 17%.

Table 5.2.3 SOURCE OF ABUSE REPORT

Who reported abuse?	Count	Percent
Victim	5,327	51.6%
Teacher	36	.35%
Cleric	278	2.7%
Parent/Guardian	1,450	14.05%
Police Officer	174	1.69%
Lay Person	202	2%
Doctor	28	.3%
Attorney	2,165	21%
Self-report	174	1.7%
Other	104	1%
Siblings/Other family	328	3.2%
Anonymous	12	.1%
Counselor/Therapist	40	.4%
Total	10,318	100%

The reports of abuse came to the Church in many and varied ways. Phone calls and letters were the most commons forms of contact, followed by a legal filing by an attorney.

Table 5.2.4 FORM OF ABUSE REPORT

How was the abuse reported?	Count	Percent
Called Parish	290	2.85%
Signed letter to parish	97	.9%
Anon. letter to parish	6	.1%
In person/parish	189	1.8%
Told trusted cleric	658	6.5%
Media	114	1.1%
Called diocese	3,216	32%
Signed letter to diocese	2,433	24%
Anon. Letter to diocese	107	1%
In person/diocese	709	7%
Called P/MS	299	2.94%
Signed letter to P/MS	171	1.6%
Anon. Letter to P/MS	13	.1%
Legal filing	1,118	11%
Other	281	2.7%
Diocese contacted victim	10	.1%
Other unrelated adult	35	.35%
Cleric self-reported	86	.8%
Police/any CRJ	246	2.4%
SNAP, victim hotline	34	.3%
School representative	33	.3%
Total	10,145	100%

There was at least one effort made to follow up the initial report in half of the incidents of sexual abuse reported from the Church files for this study.

TABLE 5.2.5   FOLLOW UP EFFORTS BY ALLEGED VICTIM OF ABUSE

Second contact about incident	Count	Percent
Yes, at least one follow up effort	4,938	49.7%
No follow up	4,986	50.3%
Total	9,924	100%

5.3 RESPONSE FROM DIOCESES AND RELIGIOUS COMMUNITIES

The response to the allegations of child sexual abuse by the bishops, major superiors and other priests who were presented with the problem was first shaped by the timing of the allegation. When all allegations are considered, only one in four allegations was made within ten years of the incident that gave rise to the allegation. Half of all allegations were made between ten and thirty years after the incident and the remaining 25% were reported more than 30 years after the incident.

Study data provided the researchers with two ways to understand the responses to allegations of child sexual abuse undertaken by dioceses and religious communities—responses to the formal survey questions and the notes and explanations that were added by those who completed the incident-level Victim Surveys. The Victim Survey questions addressed investigations, the results of those investigations and the actions prompted by the results. The handwritten notes on both Cleric and Victim Surveys were recorded and coded into a credibility scale to indicate whether the Church files on an individual priest reflected a conclusion that the allegation about his actions was credible or not credible.

The actions and responses of the Church to allegations are various and multiple: an individual priest may have been counseled, evaluated, provided with treatment, suspended, or limited in his priestly capacity. These actions are present whether the allegation was found to be or not to be credible or substantiated, but with different distributions. The survey data results for actions taken as a result of the allegations of child sexual abuse include the following:

- The Diocesan and Order Profiles reported that 298 priests and deacons had been completely exonerated. No surveys were completed for priests who were exonerated, and these individuals are not included in the study statistics.
- The handwritten annotations on the surveys indicated that for 1,671 priests the allegations were thought to be credible, and not credible for 345 priests.
- 9,281 Victim Surveys had information about an investigation. In 6,696 cases, or 72%, an investigation of the allegation was carried out.
- Of the alleged incidents investigated by the dioceses and religious communities, a definitive result of the investigation was reported for 5,681 cases. Of these cases, 4,570, or 80%, were substantiated; 1,028, or 18%, were unsubstantiated; 83, or 1.5%, were found to be false. Priests were reported to deny the allegations in 56 cases. Of the investigations that did not produce a definitive result, in many cases the priest was deceased at the time of the allegation or the investigation was ongoing at the time the survey was submitted to the study.
- When all Cleric Surveys are considered, 27% of all priests subject to an allegation had their ministry restricted by a superior.

The figures that follow show the distribution of responses and actions by the Church to allegations of abuse. The percentages apply to the number of surveys within each subgroup that had a response.

ACTIONS OF DIOCESES AND RELIGIOUS COMMUNITIES

PRIESTS WITH CREDIBLE ALLEGATIONS

Of the 1,671 surveys with written support for the credibility of the allegation, notes on 525 indicated strong support.
The percentages in this figure apply to the strongly-supported cases.

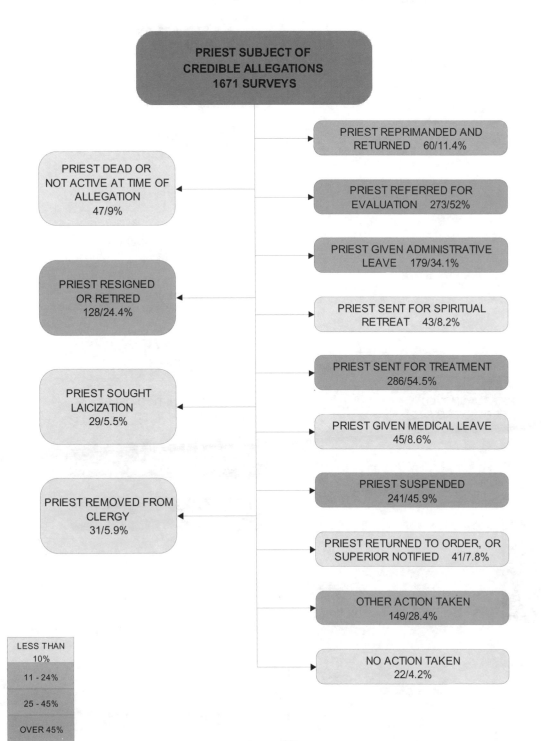

ACTIONS OF DIOCESES AND RELIGIOUS COMMUNITIES
PRIESTS WITH STRONGLY NON-CREDIBLE ACCUSATIONS
N = 215

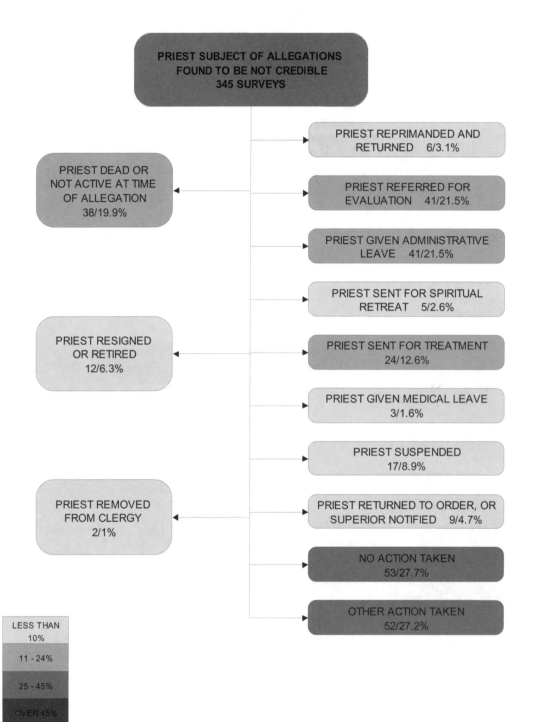

PRIEST SUBJECT OF ALLEGATIONS FOUND TO BE NOT CREDIBLE
345 SURVEYS

PRIEST DEAD OR NOT ACTIVE AT TIME OF ALLEGATION
38/19.9%

PRIEST RESIGNED OR RETIRED
12/6.3%

PRIEST REMOVED FROM CLERGY
2/1%

PRIEST REPRIMANDED AND RETURNED   6/3.1%

PRIEST REFERRED FOR EVALUATION   41/21.5%

PRIEST GIVEN ADMINISTRATIVE LEAVE   41/21.5%

PRIEST SENT FOR SPIRITUAL RETREAT   5/2.6%

PRIEST SENT FOR TREATMENT
24/12.6%

PRIEST GIVEN MEDICAL LEAVE
3/1.6%

PRIEST SUSPENDED
17/8.9%

PRIEST RETURNED TO ORDER, OR SUPERIOR NOTIFIED   9/4.7%

NO ACTION TAKEN
53/27.7%

OTHER ACTION TAKEN
52/27.2%

LESS THAN 10%
11 - 24%
25 - 45%
OVER 45%

ACTIONS OF DIOCESES AND RELIGIOUS COMMUNITIES
PRIESTS WITH SUBSTANTIATED ALLEGATIONS

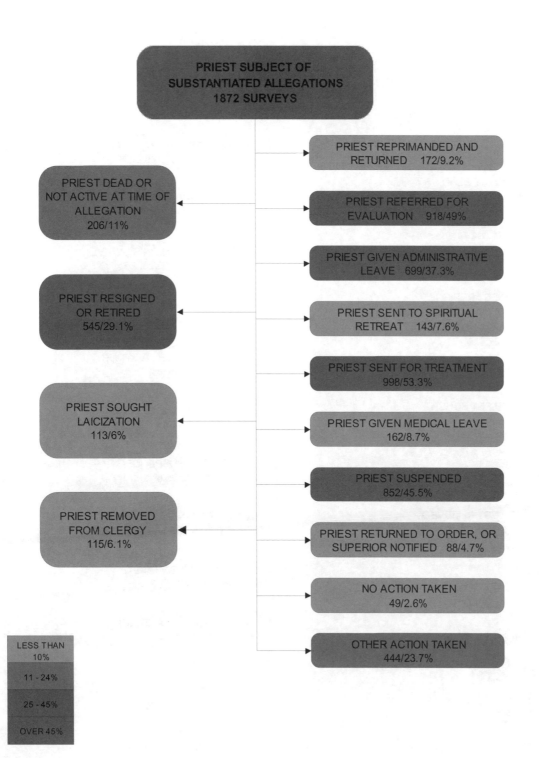

PRIEST SUBJECT OF SUBSTANTIATED ALLEGATIONS 1872 SURVEYS

PRIEST REPRIMANDED AND RETURNED   172/9.2%

PRIEST DEAD OR NOT ACTIVE AT TIME OF ALLEGATION 206/11%

PRIEST REFERRED FOR EVALUATION   918/49%

PRIEST GIVEN ADMINISTRATIVE LEAVE   699/37.3%

PRIEST RESIGNED OR RETIRED 545/29.1%

PRIEST SENT TO SPIRITUAL RETREAT   143/7.6%

PRIEST SENT FOR TREATMENT 998/53.3%

PRIEST SOUGHT LAICIZATION 113/6%

PRIEST GIVEN MEDICAL LEAVE 162/8.7%

PRIEST SUSPENDED 852/45.5%

PRIEST REMOVED FROM CLERGY 115/6.1%

PRIEST RETURNED TO ORDER, OR SUPERIOR NOTIFIED 88/4.7%

NO ACTION TAKEN 49/2.6%

OTHER ACTION TAKEN 444/23.7%

LESS THAN 10%

11 - 24%

25 - 45%

OVER 45%

ACTIONS OF DIOCESES AND RELIGIOUS COMMUNITIES
PRIESTS WITH UNSUBSTANTIATED ALLEGATIONS

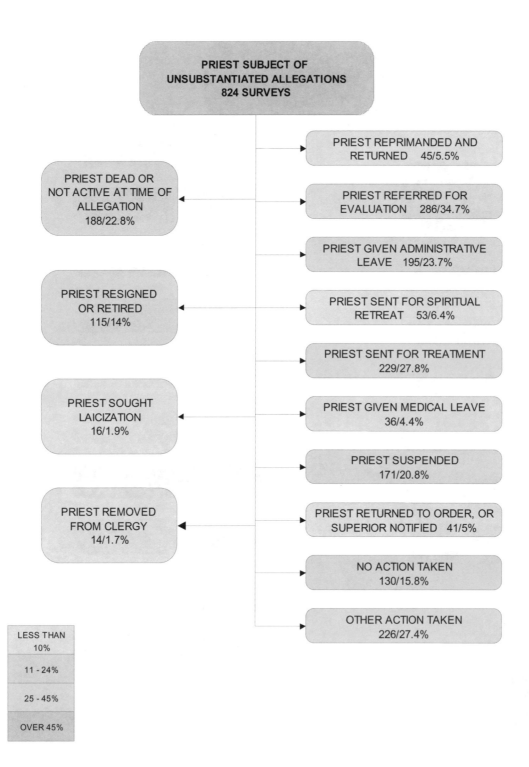

PRIEST SUBJECT OF UNSUBSTANTIATED ALLEGATIONS 824 SURVEYS

PRIEST DEAD OR NOT ACTIVE AT TIME OF ALLEGATION 188/22.8%

PRIEST RESIGNED OR RETIRED 115/14%

PRIEST SOUGHT LAICIZATION 16/1.9%

PRIEST REMOVED FROM CLERGY 14/1.7%

PRIEST REPRIMANDED AND RETURNED 45/5.5%

PRIEST REFERRED FOR EVALUATION 286/34.7%

PRIEST GIVEN ADMINISTRATIVE LEAVE 195/23.7%

PRIEST SENT FOR SPIRITUAL RETREAT 53/6.4%

PRIEST SENT FOR TREATMENT 229/27.8%

PRIEST GIVEN MEDICAL LEAVE 36/4.4%

PRIEST SUSPENDED 171/20.8%

PRIEST RETURNED TO ORDER, OR SUPERIOR NOTIFIED 41/5%

NO ACTION TAKEN 130/15.8%

OTHER ACTION TAKEN 226/27.4%

LESS THAN 10%

11 - 24%

25 - 45%

OVER 45%

5.4 SEX OFFENDER TREATMENT

Although the majority of the priests and deacons accused of child sex abuse have had only one allegation, there were two types who had inspired more concern – those priests who had multiple victims and those who abused one victim for a lengthy period of time. The aims and types of treatment for sexual offenders have changed significantly throughout the past century, which is important when understanding the types of treatment clergy have undergone since the 1950s. In the early 20th century, psychologists thought sexual offending was the result of individual psychological conflicts. As a result, many of the first treatments were psychoanalytic in nature. They were based upon a model, which implied that offending was out of the individual's control. Early psychoanalysts believed that if treatment were to occur it would have to be lengthy in order to adequately address and resolve the problem. [1]

In the 1950s, psychological methods of treatment for sexual offenders began to change.[2] Many researchers at this time believed that deviant sexual practices resulted from deviant sexual arousal, and therapeutic practices were developed to modify deviant fantasies. They took various forms, such as operant conditioning,[3] aversion therapy,[4] orgasmic reconditioning,[5] and shaping.[6] The focus was not only on modifying serious sexual fantasies, such as those about children, but also on eliminating homosexual desires.

The first behavioral treatment programs were limited in scope and concentrated upon single elements of deviant behavior. Some researchers then expanded upon these and made the programs multi-modal in nature. Through the addition of treatment components, such as social skills training, clinicians attempted to address the many factors shown by research to be associated with offending behavior. Treatment providers such as Abel recognized that sex offenders evidenced had a high prevalence of cognitive distortions, or thought processes that allowed the offenders to neutralize their feelings of guilt and shame. He and other treatment providers began to modify behavioral treatment programs so that they were cognitive-behavioral in nature in order to address these distortions.[7] In the 1980s, the cognitive behavioral treatment programs were further expanded to include the therapeutic technique of relapse prevention, which is a strategy for maintaining treatment-induced changes through self-management. This was originally developed as a model for controlling substance abuse and was later adapted by Pithers and his colleagues to address deviant sexual behavior. [8]

Relapse prevention is said to be one of the most important developments for sex offender research of that decade since offenders were finally trained to recognize and manage their own fantasies and behavior.[9] Other developments in the 1980s involved cognitive restructuring, victim empathy training, the refinement of sexual arousal monitoring, and an increased validity of phallometric testing (a measure of arousal assessment).[10] The most significant addition to treatment in the 1990s was the use of the polygraph. Though polygraph results are generally not admissible on trials of guilt or innocence, the polygraph does produce usable information about deception and gives treatment providers deeper insight into the acts committed by offenders and shows whether they are being truthful during the treatment programs.

Although it is clear that there is no cure for sex offenders, certain treatment regimes appear to be successful at reducing rates of recidivism for certain types of offenders. Unfortunately, it is not possible to present definitive statistics on the reduction of recidivism due to the numerous methodological problems associated with sex offender treatment.

The study data showed that 1,627 priests had been provided with some form of sex offender treatment, and 1,394 had been sent to a specific sex offender treatment facility at least once. Of those whose problems had prompted sex offender treatment, a substantial number, 744, or 45.7%, received more than one type of treatment. Of this group of 744 priests, a majority of 425, or 57%, participated in some form of treatment three times and 244, or 32.8%, four times. The handwritten notes on the surveys for these latter two groups of priests detailed the continuing efforts of diocesan and religious community leaders to respond constructively to sex abuse problems.

Table 5.4.1. TYPE OF SEX OFFENDER TREATMENT

Type of Treatment	Count	Percent of cases
Specialized program for clergy sex offenders	666	41%
Specialized program for sex offenders	212	13%
General treatment/program	283	17.4%
Individual psychological counseling	679	41.7%
Psychotherapy	412	25.3%
Relapse prevention program	170	10.4%
Evaluation, but not treatment	293	18%
Spiritual counseling	224	13.8%
Other	102	6.3%0

Individual priests often received multiple forms of treatment either simultaneously or consecutively. This table describes 3,041 instances of treatment or evaluation of 1,627 individual priests.

This is a multiple response table. The categories are not mutually exclusive, since a priest may have received more than one form of treatment.

Table 5.4.2. TREATMENT FACILITIES USED

Facility Name	Count	Percent of all cases
Behavioral Medicine Institute / -Atlanta, GA	8	.6%
Issac Ray Center /-Chicago, IL	50	3.6%
John Hopkins Medical Center/ Baltimore, MD	10	.7%
Progressive Clinical Services /-Cincinnati, OH	5	.4%
St. Luke Institute /-Suitland, MD	465	33.4%
Servants of the Paraclete / St. Louis, MO	115	8.2%
Shalom Center / Splendora, TX	23	1.6%
Southdown / Ontario, CANADA	113	8.1%
Servants of the Paraclete / Jemez Springs, NM	197	14.1%
Servants of the Paraclete /Albuquerque Villa, NM	36	2.6%
St. Louis Consultation Service / St. Louis, MO	61	4.4%
Institute of Living / Hartford, CT	99	7.1%
Menninger Clinic / Topeka, KS	4	.3%
New Life Center / -Middleburg, VA	8	.6%
Villa St. John Vianney /-Dowingtown, PA	138	9.9%
Other	337	24.2%

The survey respondents reported that 158 priests had been treated at a residential facility more than once.

This is a multiple response table. The categories are not mutually exclusive, since a priests may have been treated in the same facility more than once, or in more than one facility.

[1] Organic, or medical, treatments for sexual offenders surfaced in the 1940s. These treatment approaches are not discussed at length here because they have rarely been used for clergy abusers. The first hormonal treatment in the 1940s was an estrogen called, which proved to be fairly successful at reducing deviant sexual behavior. Despite its benefits, it was not widely used because of its side effects which included vomiting, nausea and feminization. The idea that sexual offending was a medical problem continued through the 1950s and the 1960s, with the introduction of medical treatments such as medroxyprogesterone acetate (MPA), which is still used today with "chemical castration" (more commonly referred to as Depo Provera).

[2] It was Eysenck's criticism of traditional psychotherapy that facilitated the move towards behavioral therapy as the preferred form of psychological treatment (Marshall et al, 1999).

[3] B.F. Skinner. *Science and Human Behavior* (New York, NY: The Free Press, 1953).

[4] R. McGuire and M. Vallance. "Aversion Therapy by Electric Shock: A Simple Technique," *British Medical Journal* 2 (1964): 594-597.

[5] John N. Marquis, "Orgasmic Reconditioning: Changing Sexual Object Choice Through Controlling Masturbation Fantasies," *Journal of Behavior Therapy & Experimental Psychiatry*, 1(1970): 263-271.

[6] John Bancroft. "The Application of Psychophysiological Measures to the Assessment and Modification of Sexual Behavior," *Behavior Research and Therapy* 9 (1971):119-130.

[7] Gene G. Abel. "Behavioral Treatment of Child Molesters," in *Eating, Sleeping, and Sex: Perspectives in Behavioral Medicine*, ed. Albert J. Stunkard and Andrew Baum (Hillsdale, NJ: Lawrence Erlbaum Associates, 1989): 223-242.

[8] Pithers note

[9] William L. Marshall, "Assessment, Treatment, and Theorizing about Sex Offenders: Developments During the Past Twenty Years and Future Directions," *Criminal Justice and Behavior* 23(1996):162-199.

COSTS TO DIOCESES AND RELIGIOUS COMMUNITIES

6.1 TOTAL COSTS

This section reports the costs to dioceses and religious communities of responding to allegations of child sexual abuse by priests between the years 1950 and 2002. Costs to dioceses are reported separately from costs to religious communities. Some dioceses and religious communities did not report cost data for certain questions because either there were no expenditures or the survey contained missing data. The data in the following tables are limited to the number of dioceses and religious communities that reported expenditures. With the exception of Table 6.1.1, which is based on reports from Diocesan/Order Profiles only, dollar amounts are based on data from the Victim Surveys.

Of all dioceses and religious communities that had submitted a Diocesan/Order Profile, approximately 80% contained a reportable figure for compensation paid to those who had alleged abuse. Total costs by type of expenditure are shown in Table 6.1.1 and the proportions of dioceses and religious communities reporting expenditure figures are shown in Table 6.1.2. The total compensation paid by dioceses to alleged victims by region of the country is shown in Table 6.1.3. The proportion of diocesan expenditures for victim compensation that was covered by insurance was about 60% (see Table 6.1.4). Nearly three-quarters of dioceses had a reportable figure for alleged victim treatment expenditures (see Table 6.1.5) but only 30% of the dioceses reported insurance coverage cost data for such treatment (see Table 6.1.6). Just over 60% of the dioceses reported cost data for priest treatment (see Table 6.1.7), and roughly 30% of the dioceses gave an insurance coverage figure for this treatment (see Table 6.1.8). Sixty-two percent of the dioceses also reported a figure for attorney fees paid for allegations of child sexual abuse by priests (see Table 6.1.9).

Of all religious communities participating in the study, approximately 60% reported a figure for total compensation for alleged victims (see Table 6.1.10) and one-quarter were able to give an insurance coverage figure (see Table 6.1.11). Nearly half of all religious communities reported cost data for victim treatment (see Table 6.1.12), but only 10% had data for insurance coverage of victim treatment (see Table 6.1.13). About 40% of the respondent religious communities had data for priest treatment costs (see Table 6.1.14), and just over 10% reported insurance coverage for this treatment (see Table 6.1.15). Half of the religious communities reported cost figures for attorney fees (see Table 6.1.16).

These cost figures have several limitations. The total compensation figures in Table 6.1.3 are not reliable since some reports include victim treatment costs in the total compensation figure (one of the survey questions asked for the approximate total compensation or payment to the victim), thereby inflating the compensation sum in these reports. Additionally, there are more than one thousand pending legal cases that have not yet reported a compensation figure for alleged victims, or resolved the amount of attorneys' fees. In cases where large-scale settlements have been made, some dioceses were unable to report a compensation figure at the victim level because the victims' attorney had not yet dispersed the money to the victims.

Similarly, some dioceses were unable to report an attorney fee at the victim level because the attorney for the diocese may have represented the diocese in cases brought by multiple victims concurrently. An additional limitation to consider regarding the reported treatment costs for priests is that many victim surveys for one particular priest also contained the same cost figure for priest treatment. The priest treatment figures, then, may be inflated due to multi-counting. A further caution about the overall costs arises because some respondents reported overall cost data on the Diocesan/Order Profile, but did not send in the Cleric and Victim Surveys providing details for how this money was spent.

Several steps were taken to assure the validity of these cost statistics All potential duplicative victim treatment costs were identified, and double counting was eliminated. Because attorney fees were reported at the victim level, those which were deemed to represent representation of a group, were divided by the number of victims that generated that attorney fee. For example, 25 Victim Surveys associated with a single priests and showing a $25 million fee would be divided by 25, resulting in a $1 million attorney fee for that survey. Most dioceses and religious communities that sent expenditure information on the Diocesan/Order Profiles provided detailed information about those costs in the Victim Surveys.

Table 6.1.1 TOTAL COSTS PAID BY DIOCESES AND RELIGIOUS COMMUNITIES, BY TYPE OF EXPENDITURE

Type of Cost	Diocese and Eparchy Costs	Religious Order and Province Costs	Sum Total Costs for Years 1950 to 2002
Alleged Victim Compensation Costs	$420,112,633.03*	$55,562,202.70	$475,674,835.73*
Compensation Costs Covered by Insurance	($182,800,358.58)	($22,765,455.82)	($205,565,814.40)
Alleged Victim Treatment Costs	$19,828,656.56	$5,148,031.36	$24,976,687.92
Alleged Victim Treatment Covered by Insurance	($5,019,729.33)	($524,994.36)	($5,544,723.69)
Priest Treatment Costs	$27,607,676.21	$5,785,963.49	$33,393,639.70
Priest Treatment Costs Covered by Insurance	($6,230,276.31)	($1,182,575.14)	($7,412,851.45)
Attorney Costs for Legal Representation	$32,033,226.55	$6,428,704.05	$38,461,930.60
Total Cost**	$499,582,192.35*	$72,924,901.60	$572,507,094.00*

*These figures do not include the highly publicized settlement figure of $85 million in the Archdiocese of Boston. No Diocesan Profile contained a data point with this specific total compensation amount.

**The total cost represents rows 1,3, 5, and 7 because insurance coverage is already included in these figures. The insurance figures are placed in parentheses to indicate that they are not additive, as they are part of the total compensation and treatment.

Table 6.1.2 NUMBER AND PERCENT OF DIOCESES AND RELIGIOUS COMMUNITES REPORTING COSTS, BY TYPE OF EXPENDITURE

Type of Cost	Diocese/Eparchy	Religious Community
Alleged Victim Compensation	193	127
	82.4%	61.4%
Compensation Costs Covered by Insurance	193	127
	58%	25.2%
Alleged Victim Treatment Costs	193	127
	74.1%	47.2%
Alleged Victim Treatment Covered by Insurance	193	127
	29%	12.6%
Priest Treatment Costs	193	127
	62.2%	40.9%
Priest Treatment Costs Covered by Insurance	193	127
	31.1%	13.2%
Attorney Costs for Legal Representation	193	127
	62.2%	51.2%

Table 6.1.3 COMPENSATION PAID BY DIOCESES TO ALLEGED VICTIMS, BY REGION

United States Dioceses/Eparchies Grouped by Catholic Region	Average Payment Made by a Diocese/Eparchy	Minimum Payment Made by a Diocese/Eparchy	Maximum Payment Made by a Diocese/Eparchy
1	$5,823,164.05	$1,600.00	$17,339,047.00*
2	$1,072,596.64	$25,000.00	$3,007,220.00
3	$1,610,752.91	$298,920.00	$5,178,605.46
4	$1,395,907.31	$900.00	$4,122,000.00
5	$4,444,040.50	$180.00	$24,719,972.19
6	$567,284.57	$500.00	$1,457,953.00
7	$1,952,707.83	$41,281.15	$15,309,988.42
8	$1,345,152.32	$90,587.00	$5,429,554.00
9	$1,010,562.26	$12,454.00	$6,169,884.00
10	$3,247,078.08	$1,200.00	$37,429,326.45
11	$3,406,149.14	$9,000.00	$9,425,000.00
12	$6,915,500.06	$25,000.00	$44,863,453.75
13	$3,885,674.12	$200.00	$28,068,887.00
14	$891,844.27	$1,395.00	$2,959,496.04

This Table does not include the highly publicized settlement figure of $85 million in the Archdiocese of Boston. No Diocesan Profile contained a data point with this specific total compensation amount. Payment figures may reflect either payment to a group or a single individual.

Table 6.1.4 VICTIM COMPENSATION PAID BY DIOCESES AND COVERED BY INSURANCE, BY REGION

United States Dioceses/Eparchies Grouped by Catholic Region	Average Payment made by an Insurance Company	Minimum Payment Made by an Insurance Company	Maximum Payment Made by an Insurance Company
1	$2,625,477.77	$651,000.00	$8,300,180.00
2	$585,489.90	$25,000.00	$2,793,462.86
3	$706,212.99	$112,500.00	$2,232,905.00
4	$1,256,124.48	$75,000.00	$2,710,500.00
5	$2,619,321.98	$5,000.00	$24,047,211.96
6	$372,204.90	$29,835.00	$1,101,248.00
7	$614,422.47	$60,000.00	$1,189,000.00
8	$957,185.94	$20,000.00	$3,637,314.00
9	$570,447.12	$400.00	$3,476,000.00
10	$1,259,092.39	$50,000.00	$8,721,612.92
11	$1,934,119.16	$45,000.00	$7,534,000.00
12	$7,817,763.40	$379,000.00	$27,151,000.00
13	$4,764,002.00	$163,800.00	$18,426,983.00
14	$422,730.80	$26,500.00	$814,000.00

In some instances the insurance carrier paid a greater sum to an alleged victim than a particular diocese. This table does not include the highly publicized settlement figure of $85 million in the Archdiocese of Boston. No Diocesan Profile contained a data point with this specific total compensation amount. Payment figures may reflect either a group's or a single individual's payment.

Table 6.1.5 VICTIM TREATMENT COSTS PAID BY DIOCESES, BY REGION

United States Dioceses/Eparchies Grouped by Catholic Region	Average Payment made by a Diocese/Eparchy	Minimum Payment Made by a Diocese/Eparchy	Maximum Payment Made by a Diocese/Eparchy
1	$91,263.17	$60.00	$482,565.63
2	$227,825.60	$4,500.00	$668,250.00
3	$249,422.65	$8,400.00	$1,038,565.00
4	$266,583.81	$900.00	$887,500.00
5	$255,220.06	$1,200.00	$1,209,519.00
6	$85,521.08	$500.00	$289,143.00
7	$252,494.98	$5,184.00	$1,110,000.00
8	$67,892.66	$7,584.68	$346,177.00
9	$71,420.28	$2,454.00	$378,200.00
10	$82,352.76	$1,000.00	$416,061.00
11	$72,945.52	$1,375.00	$226,587.00
12	$91,829.64	$10,000.00	$255,222.00
13	$176,151.28	$200.00	$944,329.00
14	$33,195.26	$1,395.00	$72,076.78

These amounts represent the combined total of victim treatment costs incurred by both dioceses and insurance companies. This Table does not include the highly publicized settlement figure of $85 million in the Archdiocese of Boston. No Diocesan Profile contained a data point with this specific total compensation amount. Payment figures may reflect either a group's or a single individual's payment.

Table 6.1.6 VICTIM TREATMENT COSTS PAID BY INSURANCE COMPANIES FOR DIOCESAN PRIESTS, BY REGION

United States Dioceses/Eparchies Grouped by Catholic Region	Average Payment Made by an Insurance Company	Minimum Payment Made by an Insurance Company	Maximum Payment Made by an Insurance Company
1	$122,347.21	$10,600.00	$234,094.40
2	$62,861.08	$1,590.00	$217,049.40
3	$181,040.82	$2,003.00	$592,961.80
4	$136,545.15	$56,000.00	$296,780.60
5	$105,739.12	$0.00	$255,758.00
6	$99,206.18	$250.00	$455,375.00
7	$38,973.84	$10,000.00	$96,000.00
8	$69,814.33	$6,644.00	$150,000.00
9	$52,054.80	$200.00	$127,124.00
10	$45,250.00	$0.00	$126,000.00
11	$45,374.89	$2,000.00	$158,450.00
12	$255,042.00	$255,042.00	$255,042.00
13	$76,520.00	$3,040.00	$150,000.00
14	$75,750.00	$26.500.00	$125,000.00

This Table does not include the highly publicized settlement figure of $85 million in the Archdiocese of Boston. No Diocesan Profile contained a data point with this specific total compensation amount. Payment figures may reflect either a group's or a single individual's payment.

Table 6.1.7 TREATMENT EXPENDITURES FOR DIOCESAN PRIESTS, BY REGION

United States Dioceses/Eparchies Grouped by Catholic Region	Average Payment Made by a Diocese/Eparchy	Minimum Payment Made by a Diocese/Eparchy	Maximum Payment Made by a Diocese/Eparchy
1	$141,091.31	$1,050.00	$527,560.40
2	$692,239.40	$3,000.00	$1,273,277.50
3	$462,503.47	$33,000.00	$1,657,907.00
4	$259,958.73	$70,000.00	$775,300.40
5	$212,753.60	$0.00	$833,500.00
6	$183,556.87	$800.00	$400,000.00
7	$301,798.08	$16,428.00	$843,851.10
8	$155,687.59	$2,259.00	$440,583.00
9	$313,554.59	$45,000.00	$1,264,444.76
10	$61,692.82	$3,853.75	$213,000.00
11	$84,493.72	$3,000.00	$253,896.00
12	$115,250.00	$15,000.00	$245,000.00
13	$54,901.80	$1,183.00	$133,000.00
14	$112,426.33	$30,000.00	$375,000.00

This Table does not include the highly publicized settlement figure of $85 million in the Archdiocese of Boston. No Diocesan Profile contained a data point with this specific total compensation amount. Payment figures may reflect either a group's or a single individual's payment.

Table 6.1.8 TREATMENT EXPENDITURES FOR DIOCESAN PRIESTS COVERED BY INSURANCE, BY REGION

United States Dioceses/Eparchies Grouped by Catholic Region	Average Payment Made by an Insurance Company	Minimum Payment Made by an Insurance Company	Maximum Payment Made by an Insurance Company
1	$268,724.90	$2,060.60	$535,389.20
2	$217,016.00	$13,500.00	$509,657.00
3	$158,159.66	$10,000.00	$370,699.00
4	$234,506.48	$35,000.00	$761,715.00
5	$55,766.97	$0.00	$133,362.00
6	$157,336.73	$800.00	$345,000.00
7	$21,153.91	$1,532.00	$87,200.00
8	$3,631.07	$1,994.27	$5,202.46
9	$34,750.00	$18,000.00	$56,000.00
10	$45,717.19	$1,194.84	$185,000.00
11	$46,852.00	$2,000.00	$86,700.00
12	$60,500.00	$20,000.00	$101,000.00
13	$0.00	$0.00	$0.00
14	$24,600.00	$3,000.00	$50,000.00

This Table does not include the highly publicized settlement figure of $85 million in the Archdiocese of Boston. No Diocesan Profile contained a data point with this specific total compensation amount. Payment figures may reflect either a group's or a single individual's payment.

Table 6.1.9 ATTORNEYS FEES PAID BY DIOCESES, BY REGION

United States Dioceses/Eparchies Grouped by Catholic Region	Average Payment Made by a Diocese/Eparchy	Minimum Payment Made by a Diocese/Eparchy	Maximum Payment Made by a Diocese/Eparchy
1	$385,369.24	$55,000.00	$890,615.05
2	$159,144.60	$31,000	$311,595.14
3	$608,074.68	$11,933.25	$4,590,039.20
4	$169,217.69	$9.00	$712,000.00
5	$217,945.44	$470.00	$1,004,607.22
6	$166,099.96	$1,744.00	$668,698.00
7	$516,807.54	$1,500.00	$2,913,626.00
8	$194,805.16	$12,000.00	$781,000.00
9	$226,719.65	$1,250.00	$1,192,258.00
10	$337,218.00	$800.00	$2,948,102.00
11	$74,947.35	$12,500.00	$165,200.00
12	$161,105.65	$10,000.00	$431,318.60
13	$83,534.30	$3,160.82	$438,000.00
14	$306,480.05	$610.00	$1,208,000.00

This Table does not include the highly publicized settlement figure of $85 million in the Archdiocese of Boston.

Table 6.1.10 VICTIM COMPENSATION PAID BY RELIGIOUS COMMUNITIES, BY SIZE OF RELIGIOUS COMMUNITY

Religious Communities Grouped by Clerical Membership	Average Payment Made by a Religious Community	Minimum Payment Made by a Religious Community	Maximum Payment Made by a Religious Community
Group 1 (1-10)	$0.00	$0.00	$0.00
Group 2 (11-20)	$54,764.17	$10,292.53	$84,000.00
Group 3 (21-30)	$121,873.75	$22,495.00	$350,000.00
Group 4 (31-40)	$160,000.00	$2,500.00	$400,000.00
Group 5 (41-75)	$593,712.31	$375.00	$5,291,300.00
Group 6 (76-110)	$2,035,110.69	$10,000.00	$6,232,500.00
Group 7 (111-150)	$683,933.75	$2,990.00	$3,000,000.00
Group 8 (151-305)	$485,296.73	$15,000.00	$2,461,308.00
Group 9 (306-540)	$1,817,300.00	$175,000.00	$7,590,500.00
Group 10 (541 and up)	$5,327,032.80	$189,110.00	$15,309,988.00

Table 6.1.11 COMPENSATION FOR ALLEGED VICTIMS COVERED BY INSURANCE, BY SIZE OF RELIGIOUS COMMUNITY

Religious Communities Grouped by Clerical Membership	Average Payment Made by an Insurance Company	Minimum Payment Made by an Insurance Company	Maximum Payment Made by an Insurance Company
Group 1 (1-10)	$0.00	$0.00	$0.00
Group 2 (11-20)	$0.00	$0.00	$0.00
Group 3 (21-30)	$75,000.00	$75,000.00	$75,000.00
Group 4 (31-40)	$12,500.00	$12,500.00	$12,500.00
Group 5 (41-75)	$1,462,710.41	$25,000.00	$4,285,000.00
Group 6 (76-110)	$715,924.99	$391,250.00	$1,256,525.00
Group 7 (111-150)	$803,333.33	$20,000.00	$3,000,000.00
Group 8 (151-305)	$183,581.53	$0.00	$507,500.00
Group 9 (306-540)	$1,456,006.25	$21,025.00	$4,951,000.00
Group 10 (541 and up)	$758,038.00	$330,000.00	$1,186,076.00

In some instances the insurance carrier paid a greater sum to an alleged victim than a particular religious community.

Table 6.1.12 TREATMENT COSTS FOR ALLEGED VICTIMS, BY SIZE OF
RELIGIOUS COMMUNITY

Religious Communities Grouped by Clerical Membership	Average Payment Made by a Religious Community	Minimum Payment Made by a Religious Community	Maximum Payment Made by a Religious Community
Group 1 (1-10)	$0.00	$0.00	$0.00
Group 2 (11-20)	$0.00	$0.00	$0.00
Group 3 (21-30)	$41,883.50	$41,883.50	$41,883.50
Group 4 (31-40)	$20,312.08	$2,500.00	$70,566.00
Group 5 (41-75)	$31,953.70	$375.00	$125,000.00
Group 6 (76-110)	$24,727.10	$2,000.00	$59,126.00
Group 7 (111-150)	$70,771.83	$2,990.00	$312,000.00
Group 8 (151-305)	$174,183.14	$500.00	$2,094,484.00
Group 9 (306-540)	$91,220.00	$6,000.00	$195,000.00
Group 10 (541 and up)	$225,502.49	$4,755.00	$521,752.50

Table 6.1.13 VICTIM TREATMENT COSTS COVERED BY INSURANCE, BY SIZE OF RELIGIOUS COMMUNITY

Religious Communities Grouped by Clerical Membership	Average Payment Made by an Insurance Company	Minimum Payment Made by an Insurance Company	Maximum Payment Made by an Insurance Company
Group 1 (1-10)	$0.00	$0.00	$0.00
Group 2 (11-20)	$0.00	$0.00	$0.00
Group 3 (21-30)	$60,000.00	$60,000.00	$60,000.00
Group 4 (31-40)	$2,519.70	$1,589.40	$3,450.00
Group 5 (41-75)	$20,625.00	$2,500.00	$50,000.00
Group 6 (76-110)	$14,729.00	$2,000.00	$27,458.00
Group 7 (111-150)	$0.00	$0.00	$0.00
Group 8 (151-305)	$48,856.70	$0.00	$200,000.00
Group 9 (306-540)	$6,000.00	$6,000.00	$6,000.00
Group 10 (541 and up)	$33,384.50	$33,384.50	$33,384.50

Table 6.1.14   TREATMENT COSTS FOR RELIGIOUS PRIESTS,
BY SIZE OF RELIGIOUS COMMUNITY

Religious Communities Grouped by Clerical Membership	Average Payment Made by a Religious Community	Minimum Payment Made by a Religious Community	Maximum Payment Made by a Religious Community
Group 1 (1-10)	$0.00	$0.00	$0.00
Group 2 (11-20)	$0.00	$0.00	$0.00
Group 3 (21-30)	$60,000.00	$60,000.00	$60,000.00
Group 4 (31-40)	$44,364.17	$10,000.00	$74,820.87
Group 5 (41-75)	$119,063.32	$3,700.00	$289,750.00
Group 6 (76-110)	$58,736.90	$2,500.00	$112,577.80
Group 7 (111-150)	$67,614.00	$16,000.00	$175,570.00
Group 8 (151-305)	$126,429.69	$0.00	$652,000.00
Group 9 (306-540)	$183,851.83	$6,700.00	$350,000.00
Group 10 (541 and up)	$446,950.57	$50,050.00	$843,851.10

Table 6.1.15 TREATMENT COSTS FOR RELIGIOUS PRIESTS COVERED BY INSURANCE, BY SIZE OF RELIGIOUS COMMUNITY

Religious Communities Grouped by Clerical Membership	Average Payment Made by an Insurance Company	Minimum Payment Made by an Insurance Company	Maximum Payment Made by an Insurance Company
Group 1 (1-10)	$0.00	$0.00	$0.00
Group 2 (11-20)	$0.00	$0.00	$0.00
Group 3 (21-30)	$50,000.00	$50,000.00	$50,000.00
Group 4 (31-40)	$38,223.18	$24,446.36	$52,000.00
Group 5 (41-75)	$249,600.00	$249,600.00	$249,600.00
Group 6 (76-110)	$33,211.39	$21,011.13	$45,411.65
Group 7 (111-150)	$25,000.00	$25,000.00	$25,000.00
Group 8 (151-305)	$51,994.44	$0.00	$187,144.00
Group 9 (306-540)	$123,578.00	$99,000.00	$148,156.00
Group 10 (541 and up)	$1,532.00	$1,532.00	$1,532.00

Table 6.1.16 ATTORNEY FEES PAID BY RELIGIOUS COMMUNITIES, BY SIZE OF RELIGIOUS COMMUNITY

Religious Communities Grouped by Clerical Membership	Average Payment Made by a Religious Community	Minimum Payment Made by a Religious Community	Maximum Payment Made by a Religious Community
Group 1 (1-10)	$0.00	$0.00	$0.00
Group 2 (11-20)	$117,646.26	$10,292.53	$225,000.00
Group 3 (21-30)	$5,049.93	$1,000.00	$10,000.00
Group 4 (31-40)	$19,600.00	$5,000.00	$32,400.00
Group 5 (41-75)	$78,150.02	$1,500.00	$578,000.00
Group 6 (76-110)	$166,164.62	$2,260.00	$775,085.50
Group 7 (111-150)	$30,286.37	$1,021.23	$85,000.00
Group 8 (151-305)	$158,291.78	$0.00	$1,309,105.00
Group 9 (306-540)	$86,200.00	$28,000.00	$230,000.00
Group 10 (541 and up)	$986,417.00	$10,625.00	$2,913,626.00

The President of John Jay College, Dr. Gerald Lynch, and members of the faculty met with Ms. McChesney and representatives of the USCCB to discuss possible approaches to the study of the nature and scope of child sexual abuse in the Church. After several weeks of discussion, Kathleen McChesney, on behalf of the USCCB, gave the John Jay College faculty group a specific set of questions to be answered, and thus defined the scope of the study. These questions were divided into four categories, as follows:

Information about the alleged offenses

- How many offenses were alleged or confirmed by conviction about any Catholic priest or deacon in the diocese?
- What was the time frame(s) of the alleged and confirmed offenses?
- Were alcohol and/or drugs used by the victim or offender at the time of the offense?
- In what location(s) did the offense occur?

Information about those who have made accusations

- The age and gender of the victims at the time of the offense.
- With whom did the victim live at the time of the offense?
- What was the relationship between the victim and the offender at the time of the offense?
- Where there any threats to the victim or grooming behavior on the part of the offender at the time of the offense?
- How long did the victim wait to report the offense?
- When was the offense reported?

Information about the accused clerics

- What diocese or religious order did the offender belong to at the time of the offense and what status did he hold in that order?
- What was the offender's job description/duties?
- If the offender was a deacon, was he married or unmarried at the time of the offense?
- What age was the offender at the time of the first and last alleged and/or confirmed offense?
- How many years was the offender ordained at the time of the first offense?
- How many alleged or confirmed victims did the offender have?
- Was there a civil or criminal action against the offender and what were the consequences?
- Was the offender a victim of any type of child sexual abuse?
- Did the offender receive any type of psychological treatment (i.e., for either psychological, sex offending, and/or substance abuse)?
- Was the offender transferred to another ministerial assignment subsequent to offending, and if so, did he re-offend?
- Did the offender have a record of having been abused by a fellow priest and/or deacon?

Information about the financial impact on the dioceses and religious community

° What was the financial cost to the Dioceses or religious community as a result of each alleged or confirmed offense?

In additional to these questions, the Board and USCCB asked for the best estimates that could be made of the extent of child sexual abuse in the United States.

DIOCESAN PROFILE: CONFIDENTIAL

FORM #1: DIOCESAN PROFILE

Please answer these ten questions to the best of your knowledge. It should include information between 1950-2002.

1. Is this institution a(n): (Please check one)
   ☐ Diocese   ☐ Eparchy   ☐ Religious Institute
   (NOTE: If a question is not applicable to your order, please write N/A.)

2. List the approximate number of active and retired Priests and Fathers in the order from 1950 (or since the establishment of the diocese) to 2002:
   a. diocesan priests: incardinated _____ extern _____
   b. religious institute priests: _____
   c. diocesan deacons   _____
   d. religious institute deacon in diocese   _____

3. What is the approximate number of Catholics in your order at this time?
   ☐ 5,000 - 45,000   ☐ 88,501 - 122,000   ☐ 239,001 - 350,700
   ☐ 45,001 - 66,000   ☐ 122,001 - 170,000   ☐ 350,701 - 475,000
   ☐ 66,001 - 88,500   ☐ 170,001 - 239,000   ☐ 475,001 - 788,700
                                                          ☐ 788,701 - 4,500,000

4. What is the approximate number of parishes operated by your order at the present time?
   ☐ 8-35   ☐ 57-71   ☐ 98-119
   ☐ 36-46   ☐ 72-84   ☐ 120-138
   ☐ 47-56   ☐ 85-97   ☐ 139-185

5. Check all regions in which the order is active.
   ☐ I   ☐ IV   ☐ VII   ☐ X   ☐ XIII
   ☐ II   ☐ V   ☐ VIII   ☐ XI   ☐ XIV
   ☐ III   ☐ VI   ☐ IX   ☐ XII

6. Based on your review of the records, indicate how many clerics have had allegations made against them while in your order.
   Number of incardinated _____   number of extern _____

7. How many clerics with allegations have been completely exonerated? _____

8. Based on your reviews of the records, please indicate the total number of victims who have made allegations against clerics in your order. _____

9. Based on your reviews of the records, please indicate the total amount of money paid out by your order to alleged victims of sexual abuse between 1950 and 2002. _____

10. For how many of the victims in Question #8 have:
    _____ all of their allegations been shown to be known false
    (# of victims)
    _____ all of their allegations been withdrawn
    (# of victims)
                    (NOTE: do not include these victims in the remainder of the survey)

ORDER PROFILE: CONFIDENTIAL

FORM #1: RELIGIOUS INSTITUTE PROFILE

Please answer these nine questions to the best of your knowledge. It should include information between 1950-2002.

1. Is this institution a: (Please check one)
   ☐ Religious Institute   ☐ Province of a Religious Institute

2. List the approximate number of active and retired clerics who have ministered in your religious institute or province from 1950 (or since the establishment of the religious institute) to 2002:
   a. religious priest members: _____
   b. permanent deacon members: _____

3. What is the approximate membership of the religious institute or province at this time?
   ☐ 1 - 10   ☐ 31 - 40   ☐ 111 – 150   ☐ 541 and up
   ☐ 11 - 20   ☐ 41 - 75   ☐ 151 - 305
   ☐ 21 - 30   ☐ 76 - 110   ☐ 306 - 540

4. What is the approximate number of priests and fathers who are now members the religious institute or province?
   ☐ 1 - 6   ☐ 22 - 35   ☐ 81 – 110   ☐ 400 and up
   ☐ 7 - 14   ☐ 36 - 57   ☐ 111 - 176
   ☐ 15 -21   ☐ 58 - 80   ☐ 177 - 399

5. Based on your review of the records, indicate how many member religious priests or permanent deacons have had allegations made against them while ministering within your province or religious institute. If any religious priests (not counted as members of your province or religious institute - but perhaps visiting from another province) were subject of such allegations while ministering in your province, please give that information on the second line in the category of "Others."

   Religious priests _____   Permanent deacons _____
   Others _____

6. How many clerics with allegations have been completely exonerated? _____

7. Based on your reviews of the records, please indicate the total number of victims who have made allegations against clerics in your province or religious institute. _____

8. Based on your reviews of the records, please indicate the total amount of money paid out by your province or religious institute to alleged victims of sexual abuse between 1950 and 2002.

   _____

9. For how many of the victims in Question #8 have:
   _____ all of their allegations been shown to be known false
   (# of victims)
   _____ all of their allegations been withdrawn
   (# of victims)

   (NOTE: do not include these victims in the remainder of the survey)

CLERIC SURVEY: CONFIDENTIAL

Please complete the following information. To ensure confidentiality, this information will be encrypted for data analysis and this page will be destroyed.

     Cleric's first initial ____

     Cleric's last initial ____

     Date of Birth __ __/__ __/__ __

REMINDER: <u>DO NOT</u> WRITE IN THE NAMES OF ANY CLERICS OR VICTIMS ANYWHERE ON THIS SURVEY. IF YOU HAVE ANY QUESTIONS AND YOU CALL THE JOHN JAY COLLEGE RESEARCH TEAM HOTLINE AT (212) 237-8539, PLEASE DO NOT SAY YOUR NAME, THE NAME OF YOUR DIOCESE, OR THE NAME OF ANY ALLEGED VICTIMS OR ABUSERS.

Please fill out this form to the best of your knowledge for every cleric against whom there are or have been allegations of sexual abuse between 1950 and 2002. Do not fill this out for clerics against whom the only allegations were known to be false. For the purpose of clarity and flow, the term "diocese" is used to refer to all diocesan, eparchial and religious orders, societies and communities.

FIRST, WE ARE GOING TO ASK YOU TO PROVIDE SOME BASIC INFORMATION ABOUT THIS PARTICULAR CLERIC.

1. Year of birth: __ __ __ __

2. At the time of the alleged offense(s), was this cleric a(n): (check as many answers if necessary if the allegations against this cleric extended over a period of time)
   - ☐ Diocesan Priest
   - ☐ Eparchian Priest
   - ☐ Extern Priest
   - ☐ Religious Priest
   - ☐ Transitional Deacon
   - ☐ Permanent Deacon
   - ☐ Eparch
   - ☐ Bishop
   - ☐ Cardinal
   - ☐ Other (specify): _____

3. If ordained, year of ordination: __ __ __ __

4. What seminary/seminaries did the cleric attend? _____

5. Was cleric married at time of alleged offense(s)?
   - ☐ Yes
   - ☐ No

6. Does the cleric have a history of being a victim of abuse?
   - ☐ Yes
   - ☐ No known abuse   (If No, skip to Question 9)

7. If yes, the type of abuse indicated in the record or known to the diocese is best described as (check all that apply)
   - ☐ Physical abuse
   - ☐ Emotional Abuse
   - ☐ Sexual Abuse
   - ☐ Verbal Abuse
   - ☐ Physical & Sexual Abuse
   - ☐ Neglect
   - ☐ Other (specify): _____

8. This abuse was allegedly committed by: (check all that apply)
   - ☐ Mother
   - ☐ Peer/acquaintance
   - ☐ Father
   - ☐ Person in a position of authority (e.g., babysitter, coach)
   - ☐ Sibling
   - ☐ Priest
   - ☐ Other family member
   - ☐ Deacon
   - ☐ Teacher
   - ☐ Other (please specify):_____

9. Are there indications in the record that the cleric had problems with alcohol or substance abuse?
   - ☐ Yes, Alcohol   ☐ Yes, Drugs   ☐ Yes, Alcohol & Drugs   ☐ No (If no, skip to question 13)

10. If you answered "Yes" to Question 9, then please indicate what action(s) was taken to address the alcohol or drug abuse problem? (check all that apply)
☐ Referral for Evaluation   ☐ Spiritual Counseling Provided
☐ Referral for Treatment   ☐ Intervention
☐ Spiritual Counseling Recommended ☐ No action taken
☐ Other action taken (describe) _____

11. If treatment was provided, where did it occur? (if none, skip to question 13)
☐ inpatient substance /alcohol abuse treatment within the diocese
☐ inpatient substance/alcohol abuse treatment outside diocese
☐ outpatient within diocese (specify type of program) _____
☐ outpatient outside of diocese (specify type of program)_____

12. During treatment for alcohol/drug abuse, did the cleric admit to sexual abuse(s) of a minor(s)?
☐ Yes   ☐ No

13. Are there other specific medical or psychological problems that raised concerns about this cleric's fitness for ministry? (if no, skip to question 18)
☐ Yes   ☐ No

14. Please describe the problem to the extent possible_____
_____

15. Was the problem recognized before any allegation of abuse?
☐ Yes   ☐ No

16. What is the approximate date the problem was recognized? _____

17. If the cleric has multiple medical or psychological problems, please specify the year each was recognized (if more than three, please continue question 16 on the back.)
Year _____   problem _____
Year _____   problem _____
Year _____   problem _____
Check here if continued on back _____

18. How many dioceses has this cleric served in? _____

19. How many times has this cleric transferred within your diocese?
Parishes _____   Congregations _____

20. Does this cleric have allegations of sexual abuse against him at any of these other dioceses in which he served?
☐ Yes   ☐ No   ☐ No information in file

21. If yes, how many victims made allegations of abuse against this cleric in each diocese, parish and congregation in which he served?
Dioceses _____   Parishes _____   Congregations_____

22. Is it known from the files, or by other means, that this cleric had behavioral/boundary problems other than allegations of sexual abuse of minors (e.g., letters of complaint from parishioners)?
☐ Yes (specify) _____
☐ No

NOW WE ARE GOING TO ASK ABOUT THIS CLERIC'S ALLEGED VICTIM(S) FROM YOUR DIOCESE

23. How many victims made allegations of sexual abuse against this cleric in your diocese? _____

24. Is there any indication that the cleric has abused more victims than there are official allegations made (e.g., victims who made a complaint claim that there are other victims who do not want to come forward)?
☐ Yes   ☐ No

25. If yes, please indicate how many other alleged victims there are who have not officially made a complaint against this cleric. _____

26. How many allegations of abuse of minors does the cleric have in each of the following age ranges and genders at your diocese? (give your best approximation of the age range based on information in the file)

# of victims under 8 years of age	_____	# male _____	# female _____
# of victims 8 - 10 years of age	_____	# male _____	# female _____
# of victims 11-14 years of age	_____	# male _____	# female _____
# of victims 15 - 17 years of age	_____	# male _____	# female _____

THE FOLLOWING QUESTIONS HAVE TO DO WITH THE INSTITUTION'S RESPONSE TO THE SEXUAL ABUSE ALLEGATIONS AGAINST THIS PARTICULAR CLERIC

27. What did the diocese do in response to the allegation(s) of sexual abuse against this cleric? (check all that apply)
☐ Cleric reprimanded, returned him to duties   ☐ Cleric referred for spiritual retreat
☐ Cleric referred for evaluation   ☐ Cleric referred for treatment
☐ Cleric given administrative leave   ☐ Cleric given medical leave
☐ Cleric resigned or retired   ☐ Cleric sought laicization
☐ Cleric reinstated   ☐ Cleric removed from clerical state
☐ Cleric suspended from ministry   ☐ Other (specify)_____
☐ No action taken

28. If the cleric was reinstated, was it:
☐ Within the diocese, same parish
☐ Within the diocese, different parish
☐ Different diocese
☐ Restricted ministry

29. What year(s) did the diocese take action against the cleric?

Year_____   Action_____
Year_____   Action_____
Year_____   Action_____

30. If the cleric participated in any type of treatment to address the sexual abuse allegations, what kind of treatment was it? (check all that apply) If no treatment, skip to question 35.

☐ Specialized sex offender treatment program specifically for clergy

☐ General treatment program not specifically for sex offenders

☐ Psychotherapist

☐ Evaluation by mental health professional or expert, but no indication of treatment

☐ Other (specify):_____

☐ Specialized sex offender treatment program for all sex offenders, not just for clergy

☐ One-on-one counseling w/ psychiatrist, psychologist, or other mental health expert

☐ Relapse prevention treatment program

☐ Spiritual counseling or direction provided by the church

31. If the cleric participated in treatment, at which facility?

☐ Behavioral Medicine Institute of Atlanta, GA

☐ Issac Ray Center, Chicago, Il

☐ Johns Hopkins Medical Institutions, Baltimore, MD

☐ Progressive Clinical Services, Cincinnati, OH

☐ St. Luke Institute, Suitland, MD

☐ Servants of the Paraclete, St. Louis, MO

☐ Shalom Center, Inc., Splendora, TX

☐ Southdown, Aurora, Ontario, CN

☐ Servants of the Paraclete, Jemez Springs, NM

☐ Servants of the Paraclete, Albuquerque Villa, NM

☐ St. Louis Consultation Service, St. Louis, MO

☐ Institute of Living, Hartford, CT

☐ Menninger Clinic, Topeka, KS

☐ New Life Center, Middleburg, VA

☐ Villa St. John Vianney, Downingtown, PA

☐ Other (specify)_____

32. How many times did the cleric participate in a sex offender treatment program? _____

33. Did the cleric complete a treatment program?
☐ Yes   ☐ No   ☐ No information in file

34. If cleric received treatment, did he re-offend after he finished treatment?
☐ Yes   ☐ No   ☐ No information in file

35. Provide additional information known or from the record that would assist in understanding the behavior of this cleric.

REMEMBER – <u>DO NOT</u> PROVIDE ANY NAMES OR OTHER IDENTIFYING INFORMATION

VICTIM SURVEY: CONFIDENTIAL

Prepare a separate profile for <u>each</u> victim who issued an allegation against this particular cleric. If a cleric had multiple allegations, prepare a separate victim profile for each victim who initiated an allegation. Please answer each of these questions to the best of your knowledge and indicate when an answer is approximate rather than specific. Remember to write the matching cleric's number in the upper right hand corner.

WE ARE NOW GOING TO ASK YOU TO PROVIDE SOME BASIC INFORMATION ABOUT EACH VICTIM WHO BROUGHT AN ALLEGATION AGAINST THIS PARTICULAR CLERIC.

1. Gender of victim (check one)
   ☐ Male   ☐ Female

2. When did the alleged abuse occur? (Be as specific about the date or range of dates as possible)
   Month __ __ Day __ __ Year __ __ __ __   OR range of dates _____

3. When was this abuse reported? (Be as specific as possible)
   Month __ __ Day __ __ Year __ __ __ __

4. Who initially made the allegation?
   ☐ The victim   ☐ The victim's parent(s) or guardian(s)
   ☐ A teacher   ☐ A police officer
   ☐ A cleric   ☐ A lay person in the Church
   ☐ Other (specify)_____   ☐ A doctor
                                             ☐ Victim's attorney

5. How was the allegation initially made?
   ☐ Called the parish   ☐ Called the diocese
   ☐ Sent a signed letter to the parish   ☐ Sent a signed letter to the diocese
   ☐ Sent an anonymous letter to parish   ☐ Sent an anonymous letter to diocese
   ☐ Went to the parish   ☐ Went to the diocese
   ☐ Told trusted priest/deacon who brought ☐ Called the Provincial or Major Superior of the
     complaint to diocese or order   order or congregation
   ☐ Information obtained through the media   ☐ Sent signed letter to the Provincial or Major
   ☐ Other (specify): _____   Superior of the order or congregation
                                             ☐ Sent anonymous letter to the Provincial or
                                               Major Superior of the order or congregation

6. Is there a record of the victim or victim's family following up on the allegation?
   ☐ No   ☐ Yes (specify method of follow up):_____

7. If the victim/victim's family did follow up, how many times? _____

8. How many times was the victim allegedly abused?
   ☐ Once   ☐ More than once (number _____) ☐ numerous (unknown number)

9. Did the victim allege abuse by more than one cleric? (If no, skip to question 12)
   ☐ Yes   ☐ No   ☐ Information not in the file

10. If yes, how many clerics allegedly abused this victim? _____

11. Did the abuse by the other cleric(s) occur before, concurrent with or after this cleric? (check all that apply)
    ☐ Before   ☐ Concurrent with   ☐ After

12. Age (in years) when alleged abuse began (or occurred, if only happened once). _____ years

13. Age (in years) when abuse ended (if occurred more than once). _____ years

14. Age (in years) when victim first told someone about the abuse. _____ years

15. Number of months/years the victim waited to report the abuse. _____

16. Where did the victim first meet the cleric?
- ☐ Mass
- ☐ Boys club/youth recreation
- ☐ Teacher in preschool, kindergarten, or elementary school (up to grade 6)
- ☐ Teacher in middle school (grades 7-8)
- ☐ Teacher in high school (grades 9-12)
- ☐ Orphanage
- ☐ Home of victim
- ☐ At a vocational inquiry
- ☐ At a social function w/ victim's family
- ☐ Other (specify)_____
- ☐ Choir
- ☐ Sunday school teacher
- ☐ At an altar service
- ☐ In the rectory
- ☐ Work in a hospital
- ☐ Seminary faculty
- ☐ In jail/prison/youth offender residence
- ☐ Home of cleric
- ☐ Seminary administrator
- ☐ While assigned to the victim's parish (e.g., as an extern priest)

17. What was the cleric's primary duty when he met the victim? (check all that apply)
- ☐ Pastor
- ☐ Resident priest
- ☐ Boys club/youth recreation
- ☐ Teacher in preschool, kindergarten, or elementary school (up to grade 6)
- ☐ Teacher in middle school (grades 7-8)
- ☐ Teacher in high school (grades 9-12)
- ☐ Seminary administrator
- ☐ Guidance counselor
- ☐ Other (specify)_____
- ☐ Associate pastor
- ☐ Seminary faculty
- ☐ Catechism teacher
- ☐ Choir
- ☐ Chaplain
- ☐ Worked in a hospital
- ☐ Saying Mass
- ☐ Bishop, Vicar, Chancellor, Cardinal
- ☐ Coach

18. Did the cleric socialize with the family of the alleged victim(s)?
- ☐ Yes ☐ No ☐ Information not in the file

19. If yes, in what way? (check all that apply)
- ☐ In the church
- ☐ Spent time with the family in his residence
- ☐ Vacations
- ☐ In church day activities (e.g., picnics)
- ☐ He spent time with the family in their residence
- ☐ Other (specify):_____

20. Type of behavior alleged by this victim (check all that apply):
- ☐ Verbal (sexual talk)
- ☐ Victim disrobed
- ☐ Cleric disrobed
- ☐ Sexual touching over clothes of victim
- ☐ Sexual touching over clothes of the cleric
- ☐ Sexual touching under clothes of victim (no penetration)
- ☐ Sexual touching under clothes of cleric (no penetration)
- ☐ Victim shown pornographic videos
- ☐ Photos taken of victim while victim was disrobed
- ☐ Masturbation in front of victim
- ☐ Mutual masturbation
- ☐ Manual (finger) penetration (of vagina or anus)
- ☐ Penetration with foreign object (e.g., sexual aid)
- ☐ Oral/genital contact where offender performed fellatio/cunnilingus
- ☐ Oral/genital contact where victim performed fellatio/cunnilingus
- ☐ Penile penetration (of anus or vagina)

CLERIC # _____

☐ Victim shown pornographic magazines/photos   ☐ Other _____

21. Was the victim threatened by the cleric in any way?
☐ Yes   ☐ No   ☐ Information not in the file

22. If yes, what type of threat?
☐ Physical threat, with weapon   ☐ Physical threat, no weapon
☐ Verbal threat (of harm to the victim)   ☐ Verbal threat (that harm will come to the cleric)
☐ Threatened family of victim   ☐ Spiritual manipulation
☐ Threatened public exposure of victim's   ☐ Other (specify):_____
    behavior to family or others

23. Where was the abuse reported to have occurred? (check all that apply)
☐ In the church   ☐ In the parish residence
☐ In the home of the victim   ☐ Cleric's office
☐ In school   ☐ In the hospital
☐ In a hotel room   ☐ In a car
☐ Retreat house   ☐ Vacation house
☐ Other (specify):_____

24. When did the abuse reportedly occur?
☐ During a retreat   ☐ During a social event
☐ During a church service   ☐ During reconciliation
☐ During travel   ☐ During a sporting event (e.g., swimming)
☐ During counseling session   ☐ During other type of travel
☐ Other (specify):_____

25. Did the victim receive any gifts from the cleric?
☐ Yes   ☐ No   ☐ Information not in the file

26. If yes, what type of gift(s)? _____

27. Were there any other enticements given to this victim?
☐ Yes   ☐ No   ☐ Information not in the file

28. If yes, what were the enticements? (check all that apply)
☐ Given money   ☐ Allowed to do special church activities (e.g., solo in the choir)
☐ Allowed to stay up late   ☐ Given alcohol or drugs
☐ Allowed to drive a car   ☐ Taken to sporting matches or other recreational activities
☐ Access to pornography, videos   ☐ Allowed to stay overnight with the cleric
☐ Other (specify) _____   ☐ Sports-related enticement (e.g., put in starting position of a
                                        team)

29. Who did the victim live with when allegedly abused (check all that apply)
☐ Mother only   ☐ Father only
☐ Both parents   ☐ Brother(s)
☐ Sister(s)   ☐ Other guardian
☐ Grandparents   ☐ Boarding school
☐ Foster parents   ☐ Orphanage
☐ With the cleric   ☐ Other (specify)_____
☐ In the rectory or church-related residence

30. Were any of victim's siblings also abused by any cleric?

☐ Yes   ☐ No   ☐ Information not in the file

31. At the time of the alleged abuse, was the victim under the influence of alcohol or drugs?
☐ Yes   ☐ No   ☐ Information not in the file

32. At the time of the alleged abuse, was the cleric under the influence of alcohol or drugs?
☐ Yes   ☐ No   ☐ Information not in the file

33. Was there a diocesan investigation? (If no, skip to Question 37)
☐ Yes   ☐ No   ☐ Information not in the file

34. If there was a diocesan investigation, what was the result? (check all that apply)
☐ Allegation substantiated   ☐ Allegation unsubstantiated
☐ Cleric admitted abuse   ☐ Allegation found to be false
☐ Other (specify) _____

35. What action was taken regarding the cleric?
☐ No action taken   ☐ Transferred cleric to another parish w/in the diocese
☐ Cleric suspended w/ treatment ordered ☐ Transferred the cleric to another diocese
☐ Cleric resigned or retired   ☐ Cleric was reinstated
☐ Cleric received treatment but   ☐ Dismissed from clerical state
   continued in ministry   ☐ Other (specify)_____

36. Was the victim or their family ever contacted regarding the results of the investigation?
☐ Yes   ☐ No   ☐ Information not in the file

37. Did the victim report the incident to the police or district attorney?
☐ Yes   ☐ No   ☐ Information not in the file

38. Was there a police investigation?
☐ Yes   ☐ No   ☐ Information not in the file

39. Was the cleric charged with a criminal offense? (If no, skip to Question 45)
☐ Yes   ☐ No   ☐ Information not in the file

40. If yes, what charge was brought?_____

41. Did the charges result in a conviction?
☐ Yes   ☐ No   ☐ Information not in the file

42. If yes, for what offense? _____

43. If there was a conviction, what was the sentence? (check all that apply)
☐ Fine   ☐ Jail
☐ Probation   ☐ Prison
☐ House arrest   ☐ Electronic monitoring
☐ Community service   ☐ Other (specify) _____

44. If there was a conviction, what was the length of the sentence imposed? _____

45. Was there any civil action taken against the cleric or the diocese for damages?
☐ Yes   ☐ No   ☐ Information not in the file

46. Was there any other form of legal action taken with respect to this cleric and this victim?
☐ Yes(specify)_____   ☐ No   ☐ Information not in the file

NOW WE ARE GOING TO ASK ABOUT FINANCIAL INFORMATION IN REGARD TO THIS VICTIM. YOU MAY NEED ASSISTANCE FROM THE ACTING BUDGET/FINANCIAL OFFICER OR ACCOUNTANT WITHIN THE DIOCESE TO ANSWER THESE QUESTIONS.

47. Was the victim given any type of compensation to settle the allegation of abuse?
☐ Yes   ☐ No   ☐ Pending   ☐ Information not in the file

48. What was the approximate total compensation or payment made to date to this victim from all sources? $ _____

49. How much of this was covered by, or derived from, insurance? $_____

50. What was the approximate payment to date for treatment for this victim? $ _____

51. How much of this was covered by or derived from insurance? $_____

52. What was the approximate payment to date for treatment for this cleric? $_____

53. How much of this was covered by or derived from insurance $_____

54. What was the approximate total payment to date made by the diocese to attorneys to represent the diocese related to this victim's allegations? $_____

WRITTEN INSTRUCTIONS

(PLEASE READ CAREFULLY AS YOU COMPLETE THE SURVEY FORMS)

SECTION 1: DIOCESAN PROFILE. Please complete this section and send it to the independent auditor no later than August 31th. The independent auditor's address is:

> Roger C. Viadero, CPA, CGFM
> Ernst & Young, LLP
> 1225 Connecticut Avenue, NW
> Washington, DC 20036

1. Institution type.
2. Number of active and retired clerics by institution type. Make sure to include all clerics from 1950-2002, to the best of your knowledge.
3. Check the box that most closely describes the number of clerics in your religious institute at this time.
4. Check the box that most closely describes the number of parishes served by your religious institute.
5. Region code: I to XIV. You can find the regional code in the Catholic directory.
6. Write in the TOTAL number of clerics with allegations of abuse in your diocese. Make sure to include all clerics with allegations from 1950-2002.
7. Write in the number of clerics who have had allegations made against them but were completely exonerated. Exonerated means that the cleric was completely cleared of the charge.
8. Write in the TOTAL number of individuals who made allegations of sexual abuse against them as children in your dioceses between 1950 and 2002. This includes all false allegations and allegations where the victim later withdrew the allegation.
9. Write in the TOTAL amount of monies paid to victims between the years 1950 and 2002. You may need the assistance of your financial/budget officer to answer this question.
10. Explain how many of the alleged victims in Question #8 made false allegations or later withdrew their allegations. The reports made by these victims will not be counted in the remainder of the survey.

SECTION 2: CLERIC AND VICTIM SURVEYS. Please complete these surveys to the best of your knowledge. Please note that for purposes of clarity and flow, when the term diocese is used in a question, it will be understood to refer to dioceses, eparchies, and religious institutes.

Before you begin to fill in this survey, please make photocopies of the survey instrument. You must make enough for each cleric with allegations of abuse against him. Once you do this, please number each of the surveys from 1 to the total number of clerics with allegations, and write that number in the upper right hand corner of the cleric survey form. You must write this number on the cleric encryption page and the four pages of the survey. The purpose of this is to link each cleric with his victim(s). You will write this same number on his victim(s)' survey forms.

Cleric Encryption. The first and last initial and birth date are converted to a unique code to provide anonymity. Please make sure that this information has been provided so that the transformation can be applied correctly.

Cleric Survey.
1. Write in the cleric's year of birth.
2. Type of cleric at time of the offense. If the cleric committed numerous offenses over a period of time, and he fulfilled multiple roles during the time he abused, please check all that apply.
3. Year ordained, if applicable.
4. Write in the name/location of the seminary that the cleric attended.
5. If a married cleric, was cleric married at the time of the alleged offense. If the cleric has multiple allegations, check yes if he was married at the time of any of these alleged offenses.
6. Any event of any types of abuse anytime in cleric's life history including the types listed in Question 7.
7. Identify all the types of abuse that the cleric is known to have experienced or is indicated in the record.
8. Identify the most likely abusing actors of the abuses identified in Question 7.
9. Identify if the cleric has abused alcohol or drugs at any time in life history.
10. Identify the action taken as a response to the drug or alcohol abuse.
11. If there was treatment for the drug or alcohol abuse, where did this treatment take place?
12. If the cleric acknowledged, during the drug or alcohol treatment program, that he abused a minor, check yes.
13. Did the cleric have any medical or psychological problems that could lead the diocese to believe he may not be fit for ministry?
14. Describe this problem. Be as specific as possible.
15. Was the problem(s) in Question 14 identified prior to the allegations of abuse?
16. What was the date this problem became known?
17. For multiple problems, identify the dates that each problem became known. If there are more than three known problems, please check the box provided and continue to identify the problems and dates on the back of the page.
18. Number of dioceses this cleric has served in, including yours.
19. Number of parishes this cleric has served in.
20. Does the cleric have any known allegations of abuse in any dioceses other than yours listed in Question 18?
21. You need to write in the total number of allegations against this cleric in all dioceses (including yours).
22. Identify any problems noted in this cleric's file other than sexual or substance abuse problems.

Information on the cleric's victim(s)
23. The total number of victims who have made allegations against this cleric in your diocese. You must fill out a victim form for each of the alleged victims in the cleric's file.

24. Does your diocese have reason to believe that there are more victims than those listed official in the cleric's file? For instance, a known victim might have reported that he/she was abused as the same time as another minor, but the other minor did not come forward and make an allegation.

25. Number of other potential victims. You do not need to fill out a victim survey for the potential victims in this question.

26. Breakdown of ages of alleged victims. Only fill this in for the victims who have made allegations, not the potential victims listed in Question 25. If the exact age of a victim cannot be determined then approximate the age based upon the information available.

Responses to Allegations Made Against Cleric

27. Identify all the specific actions taken with this cleric in response to all the abuse allegations associated with this cleric.

28. If reinstated, identify where.

29. Identify years in which action(s) was taken. If multiple actions were taken, identify all years in which those actions were taken.

30. Identify all the specific treatment strategies and protocols attempted with this cleric. Questions 31-34 address the particulars of treatment. Clerics not assigned to any treatment will have no data in Questions 31-34.

31. Identify the specific facility where the cleric participated in treatment. If the treatment center is not listed, check other and write in the proximate location of the treatment site.

32. The number of different enrollments or discrete participations in sex abuse / offender treatment programs designed or intending to achieve this type of remediation is sought.

33. Did the cleric complete the programs? If the cleric participated in more that one and completion is mixed, please characterize the completions of the treatment programs.

34. Did the cleric have allegations made against him after participating in a treatment program?

35. After you have reviewed the record of this cleric there may be facts, entries or comments that you will have found that provide added understanding concerning the cleric and responses made to the allegation of sexual abuse. Please share you insights into your reading of the record.

REMEMBER, DO NOT WRITE IN THE NAMES OF ANY CLERICS OR VICTIMS OF ABUSE!!

WRITTEN INSTRUCTIONS

Victim Survey. This must be completed for each victim of each cleric. Before you begin, photocopy the victim survey so that you have enough for all victims. If you need additional copies, you can print them out from the floppy disk. Remember to write the number of the cleric who allegedly abused this victim in the upper right hand corner of the survey instrument. Once you are finished, staple or clip together the associated cleric and victim survey instruments.

1. Gender as indicated.
2. Date alleged abuse of this victim *occurred* by this cleric. If the abuse occurred over a period of time, list the range of dates the abuse occurred. If there is no specific date(s) known, approximate the date or range of dates to the best of your knowledge based upon the files.
3. Date abuse was *reported*.
4. Person who made the allegation in Question 3.
5. How was the allegation made in Question 3.
6. Were any follow-ups made by the victim or anyone acting for the victim?
7. Number of follow-ups. Explain the method of follow up (letter, telephone, conversations).
8. Number of times this victim was abused by this cleric. If you do not know the specific number, check numerous.
9. Did other clerics allegedly abuse this victim?
   Please note the clerics identified here will have data from their files developed for this victim.
10. Total number of clerics who allegedly abused this victim.
11. If other clerics abused this victim, explain the sequential position of this cleric's alleged abuse, relative to other clerics' alleged involvement with this victim.
12. Victim's age at the time of, or beginning of, the alleged abuse.
13. Victim's age when the abuse ended, if it occurred over a period of time.
14. Age of victim at the time the first complaint or first allegation was expressed in Question 3.
15. Elapsed time between when the time of the first reported abuse and when the abuse occurred. Specify months or years.
16. Situation where cleric and victim first encountered each other. If the record is not descriptive, then identify the earliest encounter available in the record.
17. Cleric's duty or role when encountering the victim initially.
18. Did the cleric have social contact of any kind with the victim's family?
19. Type of socialization had with victim's family. Enter all the types of interactions with any of the victim's family members.
20. Identify ALL types of abuse that allegedly occurred against this victim.
21. Did cleric make any overt or implied threats directed at the victim or family members or did the victim or family members perceive that a threat was made by the cleric?
22. Nature of all threats alleged by cleric directed at victim or family members.
23. Where the alleged abuse(s) occurred.
24. When the alleged abuse(s) occurred.
25. Did the victim or family receive or have offered any type of gift, inducement, favor, benefit that had a relationship to the abuse or in response to the allegation?
26. What gift(s) was offered?
27. Were any other enticements offered to encourage the victim to participate in the abuse?
28. What were the enticements?
29. With whom did the victim live at the time of the abuse or earliest abuse in the record?
30. Did this victim have any siblings who were also allegedly abused by this cleric?
31. Was the *victim* under the influence of drugs or alcohol at any time during the abusive period?
32. Was the *cleric* under the influence of drugs or alcohol at any time during the abusive with this particular victim?
33. At any time in the association between this cleric and this victim, was there a diocesan inquiry, investigation or fact finding related to the abuse or first abuse allegation?
34. What was the result of that inquiry?

35. As a result of that inquiry, investigation or fact finding what actions were taken against the cleric? If multiple actions were taken singly or together enumerate that range of actions applied against this cleric in response to this victim's allegation(s).
36. Did the Church report its findings to the victim or victim's family?
37. Any type of complaint reported to police or governmental representative involving this cleric and this victim?
38. Was there a criminal investigation?
39. Identify any criminal charge(s) brought against this cleric as a result of the victim's allegations.
40. Specific charges brought involving this cleric and this victim. If more that once charge brought, enter all those brought.
41. Any criminal convictions, including plea agreements associated with any charges in Question 40.
42. Specify the offense for which the cleric was convicted.
43. Sentence or penalty imposed as a result of the criminal conviction(s).
44. Length of sentence imposed as a result of any criminal convictions.
45. Any civil action brought against the cleric or religious institute?
46. Other legal actions, including secular administrative remedies sought related to this cleric and this victim.

Financial information
47. Compensation (monetary or things of value in any form) made directly or indirectly to the victim, victim's family, representative, etc.
48. Total value expended for victim's compensation from all sources.
49. Identify the amount of money in Question 48 that was derived from insurance.
50. Total value expended for victim's treatment.
51. Identify the amount of money in Question 50 that was derived from insurance.
52. Total value expended for the treatment of the cleric.
53. Identify the amount of money in Question 52 that was derived from insurance.
54. Identify the total amount of monies paid to the attorneys in regard to this victim.

REMEMBER, DO NOT WRITE IN THE NAMES OF ANY CLERICS OR VICTIMS OF ABUSE!!

When you complete all the surveys, please send them to the independent auditor. The independent auditor's address is:

> **Roger C. Viadero, CPA, CGFM**
> **Ernst & Young, LLP**
> **1225 Connecticut Avenue, NW**
> **Washington, DC 20036**

Catholic Bishops' Study

RESEARCH PARTICIPATION STATEMENT

To be retained by the study participant.

This letter explains the purpose of the work you have been asked to do for the Catholic Bishops' Study, the paramount importance we give to maintaining the confidentiality of those persons you will read about in the church or diocesan files, and your right to receive counselling if, as a result of this work, you become distressed or uncomfortable. If you wish to discontinue the work, you have the right to withdraw from the project and another person will be chosen to complete the work.

Purpose

The Charter for the Protection of Children and Young People, issued by the Conference of Catholic Bishops in June of 2002, calls for the promotion of healing and reconciliation within the Catholic Church in the United States, sets out a basis for an effective response to future allegations of abuse and establishes procedures for accountability for church leaders. A significant part of this last commitment is Article 9, which reads:

> The work of the Office for Child and Youth Protection will be assisted and monitored by a Review Board, including priests, appointed by the Conference President and reporting directly to him. The Board will approve the annual report of the implementation of this Charter in each of our dioceses/eparchies, as well as any recommendations that emerge from this review, before the report is submitted to the President of the Conference and published. To understand the problem more fully and to enhance the effectiveness of our future response, the National Review Board will commission a comprehensive study of the causes and context of the current crisis. The Board will also commission a descriptive study, with the full cooperation of our diocese/eparchies, of the nature and scope of the problem within the Catholic Church in the United States, including such data as statistics on perpetrators and victims.

This project is the descriptive study, and its importance to the Catholic Church and to the larger research community cannot be overstated.

Confidentiality

All information that you report will remain completely confidential. It is of paramount importance that you not make any notation of any name or other personal information on the survey instruments as you complete them, or make any mention to anyone of any person whose name you read in a file while doing this work.

Specifically, you are asked to take particular care to ensure that:

- Any and all notes or scratch paper that you use to complete the work be destroyed at the end of each day.
- That you refrain from any discussion of the work with any person outside of the church or anyone who does not already have access to the files of alleged abusers.
- That if you call the researchers for assistance you prepare to ask your questions of them without using any names or other personal information.
- That no names are included in any material sent to the Review Board.
- That no identifying information that could link an individual to the information on a survey instrument be included when the material is sent to the Review Board.
- That completed surveys be placed first in one envelope with no external markings, then in another envelope for mailing to the Review Board.
- That you will not discuss the work you have done on this research study either during or after its completion.

Strict adherence to the principles of confidentiality will help ensure the quality of the results.

Counseling

There is a possibility that the materials you will be reviewing in the files will give rise to feelings of unhappiness, distress, embarrassment or worry. Should you find that this work becomes difficult to do or makes you sad or angry, and you wish to talk to a professional who is trained as a counsellor, you are asked to speak to the head bishop of your diocese immediately. He will remove you from this project and refer you to a counsellor to speak to about your feelings of distress.

If you ask that the responsibility for this work be given to another person, your request will be honoured.

If you understand and agree to all of the above information, please sign and date this form.

Name (written) _____

Signature _____   Date _____

Catholic Bishops' Study

AFFIRMATION

I have read the Research Participation Statement and understand each of its sections. I confirm that I understand both the purpose of and the procedures for this work

I am committed to the principles of confidentiality and the protection of human subjects and will adhere to both the spirit and the letter of what I have been asked to do to protect the privacy of the persons whose information is included in the files.

I affirm that I will seek assistance should I come to feel distressed by this work.

Print Name: _____

Signature: _____

Date: _____

DEPARTMENT OF HEALTH & HUMAN SERVICES   Public Health Service

National Institutes of Health
National Institute of Child He
and Human Development
Bethesda, Maryland 20892

November 14, 2003

Karen Terry, Ph.D.
John Jay College of Criminal Justice
Department of Law, Police Science and Criminal Justice Administration
899 Tenth Avenue
New York, NY 10019

Dear Dr. Terry:

This letter responds to your request for a certificate of confidentiality under Section 301(d) of the Public Health Service Act, 42 U.S.C. 241(d), for a project entitled "The Nature and Scope of the Problem of Sexual Abuse of Children by Catholic Priests and Deacons within the United States." The project is funded through a contract from the National Review Board of the U.S. Conference of Catholic Bishops. Thank you for the extensive information you have provided in support of this application.

Your study offers the potential for new knowledge to be developed, and it is hoped that the causes of child sexual abuse may be better understood and that future harm to children may be prevented. NIH supports these goals and applauds your initiative in undertaking this important study. However, after careful deliberation concerning the relevant facts and circumstances, we have determined that a certificate is not necessary to achieve the research objectives.

Your study plan includes multiple and wide-ranging protections for subject identifiers such that the IRB reviewing your work determined the study design to be sufficiently subject-protective that it found no more than minimal risk to the subjects and waived the requirement for informed consent under 45 C.F.R. § 46.116. The authority to issue certificates of confidentiality is an extraordinary legal power vested with the Secretary, Department of Health and Human Services and his delegates to promote the participation of subjects in sensitive research by assuring them that investigators cannot be compelled to release information that could be used to identify them. NIH issues them sparingly and generally requires that subjects be informed about the certificate.

Given your study design and other factors identified in the written application and follow-up meetings, we do not believe a certificate is necessary to achieve your research goals. Again, thank you for providing us with the extensive information on which we based this decision. I wish you every success in completing your research.

Sincerely,

Charlotte Catz, M.D.
Special Assistant for Clinical Research

CHURCH REGIONS

REGION 1
MAINE
VERMONT
NEW HAMPSHIRE
MASSACHUSETTS
CONNECTICUT
RHODE ISLAND

REGION 2
NEW YORK

REGION 3
PENNSYLVANIA
NEW JERSEY

REGION 4
DELAWARE
MARYLAND
VIRGINIA
WASHINGTON D.C.
WEST VIRGINIA

REGION 5
KENTUCKY
TENNESSEE
MISSISSIPPI
ALABAMA
LOUISIANA

REGION 6
MICHIGAN
OHIO

REGION 7
INDIANA
ILLINOIS
WISCONSIN

REGION 8
NORTH DAKOTA
SOUTH DAKOTA
MINNESOTA

REGION 9
NEBRASKA
KANSAS
IOWA
MISSOURI

REGION 10
OKLAHOMA
TEXAS
ARKANSAS

REGION 11
CALIFORNIA
NEVADA
HAWAII

REGION 12
OREGON
IDAHO
WASHINGTON
ALASKA
MONTANA

REGION 13
WYOMING
UTAH
COLORADO
ARIZONA
NEW MEXICO

REGION 14
NORTH CAROLINA
SOUTH CAROLINA
GEORGIA
FLORIDA

CHILD SEXUAL ABUSE:
A Review of the Literature

The John Jay College Research Team

KAREN J. TERRY, Ph.D.
Principal Investigator

JENNIFER TALLON
Primary Researcher

PART I – LITERATURE REVIEW

This literature review provides the reader with an overview of major academic works concerning child sexual abuse in the general population. This is a comprehensive review of the available literature, though it is not a meta-analysis (a synthesis of research results using various statistical methods to retrieve, select, and combine results from previous studies). During the course of the past thirty years, the field of sex offender research has expanded and become increasingly inter-disciplinary. It would be nearly impossible to review every piece of information relating to the topic of child sexual abuse. Instead, this is a compilation of information pertaining to theories, typologies and treatments that have attained general acceptance within the scientific community.

In reviewing the literature concerning sexual abuse within the Catholic Church, the amount of empirical research was limited, and many of the studies suffered from methodological flaws. Additionally, much of the literature consisted of either anecdotal information or impassioned arguments employed by various researchers when characterizing the responses of the church to this incendiary issue. In providing the reader with a comprehensive review, it was necessary to summarize every point of view no matter how controversial. Any of the ideas expressed in this review should not be considered indicative of the point of view of either the researchers at John Jay College of Criminal Justice, or the Catholic Church.

One aim of this literature review is to put into perspective the problem of child sexual abuse in the Catholic Church as compared to its occurrence in other institutions and organizations. However, there is little or no empirical data pertaining to the true prevalence of sexual abuse within most other organizations. For this reason, the sexual abuse of children in the Catholic Church is difficult to contextualize because there is no basis for comparison in any group, including the general population. Some journalists have conducted research on sexual abuse in particular organizations, such as the Boy Scouts. Though this work is an important step in studying the problem, it is not comprehensive in nature and more empirical work should be conducted on institutions that cater to children. Though not empirical in nature, this literature review does contain an overview of published newspaper articles on child sexual abuse in specific organizations.

ESTIMATES OF CHILD SEXUAL ABUSE

OVERVIEW

The estimation of any form of deviance in the general population is a very difficult task. It is impossible to assess the extent of sexual offending, either in general or with children as targets. Most estimates of the distribution of sexual offenders in the general population are derived from forensic sources, that is, samples of those who are arrested or convicted for sex offenses. All researchers acknowledge that those who are arrested represent only a fraction of all sexual offenders. Sexual crimes have the lowest rates of reporting for all crimes. Not all potential participants in such studies can be known or contacted, not all would use the same language to describe their experiences, and not all are willing to share information. The sexual abuse of children by Catholic priests and deacons is part of the larger problem of sexual abuse of children in the United States. This chapter is a summary of the estimates of child sexual abuse in the Catholic Church as well as the general population.

CRIMINAL JUSTICE AND SOCIAL SERVICE ESTIMATES OF CHILD SEXUAL ABUSE

Child sexual abuse data has been collected annually since 1992 through the National Child Abuse and Neglect Data System (NCANDS) of the Federal Department of Health and Human Services. These data are based on incident-level reports gathered from state child protective services and agencies and are published in an annual report. The publication *Child Maltreatment*, which is released annually, reports incident-based allegations per state along with census-based estimates of the population of children younger than 18. Child sexual abuse is defined as "maltreatment that involves the child in sexual activity to provide sexual gratification or financial benefit to the perpetrator" (Child Maltreatment, 2001). Child maltreatment reports show a decline in reported incidents from 1992 to 2001 for all reporting states. Figure 1 shows the incident data expressed as a rate per 100,000 children. Figure 2 shows the percent of the total child population who have been victims of child sexual abuse.

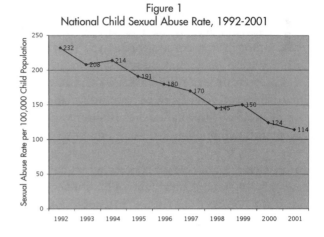

Figure 1
National Child Sexual Abuse Rate, 1992-2001

It is important to note that social service agencies and criminal justice institutions each only capture part of the picture. Incidents or events involving the sexual abuse of children may be reported directly to the police and/or may come to the attention of the staff of social service agencies. It is important to acknowledge that many such incidents may not generate any official report at all.

As a part of the work on the Study, state-level criminal justice data on the prevalence of child sexual abuse were sought from all 50 states and the District of Columbia. The agencies were asked for: 1) the number of offenders arrested for sex crimes against children for a series of years, 2) the number of child victims of sexual assault or abuse, 3) demographic information for both offenders and victims, and 4) conviction rates of those offenders arrested for child sexual abuse/assault. Of 49 states, only 13 had criminal justice system data available. Those states that have implemented the National Incident-Based Reporting System (NIBRS), which collects crime information at the incident level and includes victim age, were able to provide the requested data, if only for the most recent year. NIBRS collects data on the following types of sex crimes: forcible rape, forcible sodomy, sexual assault with an object, forcible fondling, incest and statutory rape.

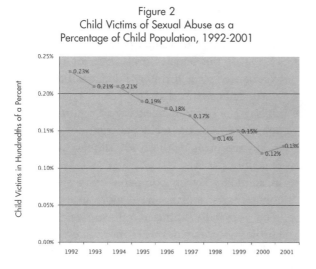

Figure 2
Child Victims of Sexual Abuse as a
Percentage of Child Population, 1992-2001

In the summaries below, this criminal justice data from NIBRS is compared to the NCANDS data. These comparisons generally show that state criminal justice systems are reporting considerably more incidents of sexual abuse than the social service agencies. The decline shown in the charts on the previous page may therefore be a result of a change in the patterns of response by victims' families, with more incidents now being reported to the police.

It should be noted that some discrepancies were found between the NCANDS data and the data obtained from the state social service agency for the same year. One explanation for this may be due to the fact that NCANDS collects data from a calendar year period and some state agencies collect data from a fiscal year period when publishing their own reports. Additionally, some data – such as that from California – are taken from the Offender Based Transaction Statistics System where only those offenders who have received a "final disposition" are included; therefore, these numbers may be substantially smaller than a count of arrests for child sexual abuse would be.

ALABAMA There were 632 child rapes reported to the Alabama state criminal justice agency in 2001, for a reported rate of 56 per 100,000 children. The NCANDS rate for all incidents of abuse is 174 per 100,000 children.

DELAWARE Delaware's criminal justice data reported 510 child victims of sexual assault crimes in 1995, for a rate of 285 per 100,000 children. This data was taken from a report requested by the Attorney General's Task Force on Child Victims and includes all known incidents of sexual assault against children where an arrest occurred. In contrast, the NCANDS report for 1995 shows only 200 incidents, for a rate of 112 per 100,000 children.

CALIFORNIA A total of 13,075 offenders were convicted of sex crimes against children in the state of California for the year 2001, for a rate of 141 sexual abuse convictions per 100,000 children. The NCANDS rate for the same year is 112 sexual abuse incidents per 100,000 children.

IDAHO NIBRS data shows that in 2001 there were 1,363 victims of child sexual abuse known to the state criminal justice system, for a rate of 363 victims per 100,000 children. The NCANDS rate is much smaller —295 known child victims, for a rate of 79 per 100,000 children.

IOWA The NIBRS data set for Iowa shows that in 2001 there were 1,454 child victims of sex crimes, for a rate of 198 victims per 100,000 children. The NCANDS data reports 1,031 victims, or a rate of 141 incidents per 100,000 children.

MICHIGAN Michigan's NIBRS data set indicates a total of 1,812 rape victims who were infants or children up to age 14, and another 1,269 rape victims who were children between 15 and 19 years old. In contrast, the 2001 NCANDS data reported 1,656 incidents of sexual abuse on children 19 and under.

SOUTH CAROLINA South Carolina's NIBRS data indicates that in 2000 there were 2,438 child victims (infants to children 16 years old) of forcible sex crimes. The NCANDS data reports 610 incidents of child sexual abuse in 2002.

SOUTH DAKOTA In South Dakota, the NIBRS data set shows 131 child victims of crimes from rape to forcible fondling, while the NCANDS data shows 169 incidents of child sexual abuse.

TENNESSEE The NIBRS system for Tennessee reports 3,488 child victims of crimes of sexual abuse for the year 2001, a rate of 248 crimes per 100,000 children. The NCANDS data reports 2,333 incidents in 2001, for a rate of 166 per 100,000 children.

RESEARCH ESTIMATES

Prevalence refers to the proportion of a population that has experienced a particular event or behavior. Since it is not known how many people in the United States experience a form of sexual abuse as children, some researchers select groups, or samples, of individuals to study and direct questions to them. If the selection of the group to be surveyed is not biased, the results of the study provide estimates of the prevalence of sexual abuse in the population from which the group is selected. In order to avoid bias in a sample, every person in the part of the population to be used as a framework for selecting the sample must have an equal chance of being asked to participate. Researchers use the data gathered from those who participate to estimate the proportion of the United States population who are sexually abused during childhood.

Studies of the incidence, as opposed to the prevalence, of sexual abuse of children concentrate on estimating the number of new cases occurring over a particular period of time and on whether the number of events or incidents is increasing or decreasing. Scholarly studies of both the incidence and the prevalence of sexual abuse of children in the United States began emerging in the 1960s and gained greater urgency after the cluster of day care center child abuse cases in the 1980s made the issue one of acute public interest. A look at victimization studies that focus on the sexual abuse of minor children suggests that the scope of this problem is extensive.

Although we do not have data reflecting the prevalence of abusers, there are data from several studies reporting the prevalence of victimization. The prevalence rates reported in these studies vary somewhat.

- 27% of the females and 16% of the males disclosed a history of childhood sexual abuse; 42% of the males were likely to never have disclosed the experience to anyone whereas 33% of the females never disclosed (Finkelhor et al., 1990).

- 12.8% of the females and 4.3% of the males reported a history of sexual abuse during childhood (MacMillan et al., 1997).

- 15.3% of the females and 5.9% of the males experienced some form of sexual assault (Moore, Nord, & Peterson, 1989).

- Only 5.7% of the incidents were reported to the police; 26% of the incidents were not disclosed to anyone prior to the study (Boney-McCoy & Finkelhor, 1995).

- In summary, when compared with their male counterparts, females were more likely to have been sexually abused during childhood. Furthermore, females were more likely than the males to disclose such information; however, disclosure rates are quite low regardless of the victim's gender.

Finkelhor and Jones (2004) have used data from NCANDS to make a national estimate of the number of sexual abuse cases substantiated by child protective service (CPS) for the period from 1992 to 2000. Using data from more than forty states they report that the number of substantiated sexual abuse cases peaked at approximately 149,800 in 1992, followed by annual declines of 2 to 11 percent per year through 2000-when the number of cases reached a low of approximately 89,355.

Professional opinion is divided about why this drop occurred and how much of the drop is real as opposed to a reflection of factors such as changes in definitions, reporting and investigation by the states (Jones and Finkelhor, 2001; Jones, Finkelhor, and Kopiec, 2001). Finkelhor and Jones (2004) examined other indicia of sex abuse rates and conclude that, taken together, they suggest that at least part of the drop in cases has resulted from a decline in sexual abuse of children. The National Crime Victimization Survey (NCVS) - which asks about rape and sexual assault for victims ages 12 and older (including acts counted within the broader definition of child sexual abuse) shows that sex offenses against children ages 12-17 declined 56 percent between 1993 and 2000. Virtually all the decline occurred in offenses committed by known perpetrators (family and acquaintances), 72 percent. Finkelhor and Jones observe that cases involving known perpetrators are the ones most likely to be categorized as sexual abuse.

Another source of self-report data on sexual abuse is the Minnesota Student Survey which has been administered to 6th, 9th, and 12th grade students in Minnesota in 1989, 1992, 1995, 1998, and 2001. Between 90 and 99 percent of Minnesota's school districts and more than 100,000 students have participated in the survey each year. The survey includes two questions about sexual abuse. Results indicate that sexual abuse by family and nonfamily perpetrators showed a slight rise between 1989 and 1992 followed by a 22-percent drop from 1992 to 2001.

At the same time reports of sexual abuse have declined, there has been a significant drop in crime rates and measures of family problems, such as violence among adult intimates, and a drop in of out-of-wedlock teenage pregnancies and live births to teenage mothers (some of which are attributable to child sexual abuse) – all of these suggest a general improvement in the well-being of children.

Additionally, Finkelhor and Jones suggest that rates of sexual abuse have perhaps been reduced as a result of increased incarceration for sexual abuse offenders. They report that surveys of state correctional facilities indicate that between 1991 and 1997, the number of individuals incarcerated in state correctional facilities for sex crimes against children rose 39 percent, from 43,500 to 60,700 (Finkelhor and Ormrod, 2001), having already more than doubled from 19,900 in 1986. They further note that these totals do not include large numbers of sexual abusers who receive sanctions that do not involve incarceration for a year or more.

Statistics from recent United States Justice Department studies of the prevalence of youth victimization confirm what other surveys have found: a startling proportion of young people experience sexual victimization (Snyder, 2000).

In a sample of 4,023 adolescents aged 12 to 17 across racial and ethnic groups, the lifetime prevalence for sexual assault is 8.1%. Seventy-four percent of these children knew their assailant well; 32.5% were friends with the abuser (Snyder, 2000). Thirty-three percent of all victims of sexual assault who reported to law enforcement agencies were aged 12 through 17 and 34% were under the age of 12 (Langan & Harlow, 1992). Juveniles were the

large majority of victims of forcible fondling (84%), forcible sodomy (79%), and sexual assault with an object (75%); of all victims of sexual assault, children below the age of 12 made up half of the victims for the above categories. The single age with the greatest proportion of sexual assault victims reported to law enforcement was age 14 (Langan & Harlow, 1992)

One meta-analysis of the various studies on victim prevalence found that the overall prevalence of male children who are sexually abused is 13 percent, whereas the prevalence of female children who are sexually abused is 30 to 40 percent (Bolen & Scannapieco, 1999). This study also identified three significant explanations as to why there is such a wide range in childhood sexual victimization rates, including the number of screen questions used to identify abuse victims, the size of the sample, and the years in which the studies were conducted.

As will be illustrated in the subsequent sections, the prevalence and nature of sexual abuse within specific social organizations varies. However, these variations can be attributed to the inaccuracy typically associated with reporting crimes.

REPORTING CHILD SEXUAL ABUSE

Every published empirical study on the disclosure of child sexual abuse indicates that a high percentage of those child sexual abuse victims who report their abuse to authorities delay disclosure of their abuse, and that a significant number of children do not disclose the abuse at all. The delay between the initial occurrence and the subsequent disclosure of the abuse varies, depending on a number of factors such as the abused's age at the time of the events, the relationship between the perpetrator and the abused, the gender of the abused, the severity of the abuse, developmental and cognitive variables related to the abused, and the likely consequences of the disclosure.

Consequently, child sexual abuse is significantly underreported. When victims do report that they were abused, they often do so years after the abuse occurred. Adult retrospective studies of childhood sexual abuse underline the delay in disclosure. In a study of 228 adult female victims of childhood incest who were predominantly abused by males, Roesler and Weissmann-Wind (1994) found that the average age of first abuse was 6 years, and the abuse lasted on average 7.6 years. Only one-third of the subjects in this sample disclosed the abuse before the age of 18, and the average age of disclosure was 25.9. Arata (1998) found that only 41% of the 204 female participants in her study, whose average age at the time of victimization was 8.5, disclosed the abuse at the time it occurred. Lawson and Chaffin (1992) found that only 43% of their child subjects disclosed their abuse when they were initially interviewed. Lamb and Edgar-Smith (1994) conducted a study with 45 adult female and 12 adult male victims of childhood sexual abuse, and they found that although the average age at the time of victimization was 10, 64% of the victims disclosed their abuse in adulthood. In a study of childhood rape of girls, Smith, Letourneau, and Saunders (2000) found that approximately half of the women waited more than eight years to disclose the abuse.

The process of disclosing childhood sexual abuse varies, though it is often described within two axes: as purposeful or accidental; and as spontaneous or prompted. DeVoe and Coulborn-Faller (1999) found that child subjects in their study required assistance with disclosure. Sorenson and Snow (1991) noted that accidental disclosure was more common in preschool children, whereas purposeful disclosure was more common in adolescents. They also found four stages of disclosure in their retrospective study of 630 subjects who were aged three to 17 at the time of abuse: denial, disclosure (tentative and active), recantation and reaffirmation. These researchers also found that 72% of their subjects originally denied the abuse; 78% of the subjects who tentatively revealed their abuse progressed to active disclosure; 22% recanted their reports, and of those who recanted 93% later reaffirmed the original report. Lawson and Chaffin (1992) found that a significant factor in the disclosure process was the belief of the caretaker in the veracity of the disclosure. Bradley and Wood's (1996) research also supported the notion that the role of the caretaker is essential. Although recantations of disclosure were rare in their sample, they found that 50% of children who recanted did so under pressure from a caretaker.

Summit's (1983) model of child sexual abuse, the Child Sexual Abuse Accommodation Syndrome, explains the hindrance to disclosure. This syndrome consists of five components: secrecy (the abuse occurs when the victim and perpetrator are alone, and the perpetrator encourages the victim to maintain secrecy); helplessness (children are obedient to adults and will usually obey the perpetrator who encourages secrecy); entrapment and accommodation (once the child is helplessly entrenched in the abusive situation, he or she assumes responsibility for the abuse and begins to dissociate from it); delayed disclosure (because the victims who report child sexual abuse often wait long periods of time to disclose, their disclosures are subsequently questioned); and retraction (as in the recantation stage described by Sorenson and Snow, the victims may retract their disclosures of abuse after facing disbelief and lack of support after their disclosure).

VICTIM'S RELATIONSHIP TO THE PERPETRATOR
If the perpetrator is a relative or acquaintance, victims of child sexual abuse are less likely to report the offense, or they are likely to disclose the abuse after a delay (Arata, 1998; DiPetro, 2003; Hanson et al, 1999; Smith et al, 2000; Wyatt and Newcomb, 1990).

In Arata's study, 73% of the victims did not disclose the abuse when the perpetrator was a relative or stepparent, and 70% did not disclose when the perpetrator was an acquaintance. Goodman-Brown, Edelstein, and Goodman found that those children who felt responsible for the abuse, often because the abuse occurred within the family, took longer to report the abuse. Wyatt and Newcomb found that the women who did not disclose their abuse to anyone were likely to have been closely related to the perpetrator and abused in close proximity to their home.

SEVERITY OF SEXUAL ABUSE
Research results vary in regard to disclosure of abuse in relation to the severity of that abuse. Arata (1998) found that child victims who experienced more severe levels of sexual abuse were less likely to disclose this type of abuse. This is consistent with the findings of Gries, Goh, and Cavanaugh (1996), who reported that fondling was reported by 80% of their subjects who disclosed. In contrast, however, Hanson et al. (1999) found that of their 341 adult

females who were victims of childhood rape, the more severe assaults were likely to be reported. DiPietro et al. (1998) also found that contact sexual offenses were those most commonly reported in their sample of 76 children.

DEVELOPMENTAL AND COGNITIVE VARIABLES

Lamb and Edgar-Smith (1994) speculate that "more astute" children may not disclose because they may "anticipate unsupportive reactions." They also maintain that such children may wait until adulthood to disclose when they can choose appropriate people to tell. White et al. (1986), as cited in Campis et al. (1993), found that older victims of child sexual abuse were less likely to disclose than their younger counterparts and noted that the knowledge of social consequences was a significant hindrance to disclosure. Keary and Fitzpatrick (1994) concluded that children over the age of five, who had previously disclosed sexual abuse, were more likely to disclose this information during formal assessment, but the converse was true for children under five. Similarly, DiPietro (2003) found that "developmental maturation clearly facilitates" disclosure (p. 140).

FEAR OF NEGATIVE CONSEQUENCES

Sorenson and Snow (1991) found that fear of further harm had an impact on a child's motivation to disclose abuse and that the child victims often only felt safe enough to disclose after the departure of the perpetrator. Berliner and Conte (1995) also noted that the fear about perceived reactions of others prevents some children from disclosing sexual abuse. Roesler and Weissmann-Wind (1994) found that 33.3% of their subjects did not disclose their abuse during childhood because they feared for their safety. They also found that 32.9% of their subjects did not report their abuse during childhood because they felt guilt or shame as a result of the abuse.

GENDER DIFFERENCES

DeVoe and Coulborn-Faller; Gries, Goh, and Cavanaugh; Lamb and Edgar-Smith; and Walrath, Ybarra, and Holden all found that girls are more likely to report abuse than boys. Reinhart found that sexual abuse of males was more likely to be disclosed by a third party. There are no methodologically sound empirical studies that indicate that males disclose at a higher rate than females. Gender

does not appear to be as important, however, as victim-perpetrator relationship in disclosure of abuse (Paine and Hanson, 2002).

CHILD SEXUAL ABUSE WITHIN SPECIFIC SOCIAL ORGANIZATIONS

BOY SCOUTS OF AMERICA

In 1991, journalist Patrick Boyle investigated the confidential files of the Boy Scouts and reported his findings in a five-part series in *The Washington Times* during the week of May 20-24, 1991. The results of his investigation are also included in his 1994 book, *Scout's Honor: Sexual Abuse in America's Most Trusted Institution*. In the first article of the series, Boyle outlined the statistics of abuse in this organization. According to the Boy Scout records, 416 male Scout employees were banned between the periods of 1971 to 1989 as a result of sexual misconduct. Boyle stated that there were 1,151 reported cases of sexual abuse within this time period. The Boy Scouts had one million adult volunteers and four million Scouts (including Cub Scouts, Boy Scouts, etc.) during this time period. The majority of the victims were believed to have been Boy Scouts, who typically range in age from 11 to 17. Boyle found that Scoutmasters perpetrated the majority of the abuse, but Assistant Scoutmasters, of which there were roughly 147,000, were also responsible. It also appears that most of the abuse occurred during camping trips. The Scouts claimed that sexual abuse in this organization was not a major crisis, but Boyle argued that sexual abuse is more common in Scouting than accidental deaths or serious injuries combined.

The four other parts in this series focused on various topics through case study illustration. The articles assert that the organization let known child molesters slip through the system and that this information was covered up in a manner that would protect the image of the Boy Scouts. When a Scoutmaster was reported to local Scout officials, Boyle stated that they often made deals in order to ensure that the scandal would remain a secret. If the Scoutmaster agreed to leave, then there would be no police involvement. What the Scouts did not realize is that the offenders were moving away and joining new troops where they continued to offend.

Even those offenders who were reported to the Scouts National Headquarters purportedly managed to evade the system and continued to act as Scoutmasters.

Boyle also discussed the impact of the abuse on the boys through individual narratives. Since the information in the confidential files is limited, the effects of the abuse on the children are unknown. However, Boyle asserts that out of the approximately 400 abuse cases he investigated, four victims attempted suicide and at least three leaders who were charged with abuse also made suicide attempts.

As public awareness concerning the abuse grew, the Boy Scouts recognized the need to combat this problem. Boyle claims that the organization has paid at least fifteen million dollars in order to settle cases out of court, with payments ranging from $12,000 to $1.5 million. In cooperation with experts in the field of sexual abuse, the Scouts have developed an extensive training program, which is meant to raise the awareness of both children and Scoutmasters. It has recently become a requirement that all employees must pass a background check in order to work for the Boy Scouts. They have also instituted policies prohibiting homosexual Scout leaders, which have come under the scrutiny of various civil rights organizations.

While there are not any empirical studies devoted to understanding the prevalence of sexual abuse in the Boy Scouts, the work of Patrick Boyle is the most comprehensive, albeit dated, information available. A database search of major newspapers illustrates that between 1970 and 2003, 22 incidents have been reported in major newspapers. The majority of the cases fit Boyle's findings in that the perpetrators used various "grooming" tactics in order to coerce the victim into sexual acts. The number of known victims for each offender ranged from one to 20, with some victims not coming forward until adulthood. In many cases, the Scoutmaster knew the child's parents, and the offenses ranged from inappropriate touching to intercourse. While the majority of the information presented in these articles is scarce, the information indicates that some of the perpetrators also worked as teachers and Catholic priests.

BIG BROTHER ORGANIZATION

The purpose of the Big Brother organization is to provide a mentor for economically or situationally disadvantaged youths between the ages of seven and thirteen. As with the Boy Scouts, the Big Brother/Sister organization has also experienced incidents of sexual abuse. No empirical data exist, but a database search of major newspapers revealed six published incidents between 1973 and 2001. As with the Boy Scouts, the offenders hailed from a variety of professions, including a school principal and naval officer.

As cited in Boyle (1994), Donald Wolff reviewed 100 allegations of sexual abuse in the Big Brother Organization and determined that, much like Scouting, the majority of offenders were single and came from various professions. These results were based upon an unpublished study commissioned by the Big Brother Organization that was subsequently presented at an inter-organizational conference. The sexual abuse progressed from inappropriate touching to other sexual acts, and the most common situations in which the abuse occurred were camping trips and visits to the perpetrator's house. These offenders also appeared to target emotionally vulnerable children. However, unlike the Boy Scouts or Catholic Church, once criminal charges were filed, Wolff found that they often led to confessions or convictions. The review also showed that many of the perpetrators were also involved in educating and counseling children other than the Boy Scouts. In light of these findings, the Big Brothers have instituted a strict screening process, which involves a criminal background check for all volunteers.

YOUNG MEN'S CHRISTIAN ASSOCIATION (YMCA)

There is no record of any empirical data or official reports outlining the prevalence of sexual abuse in the YMCA, but journalistic reports provide some insight. There are eight major news articles that deal directly with YMCA volunteers molesting children. The perpetrators worked for the organization in various capacities, including camp counselors and sports coaches. The offenders targeted both girls and boys, and many of the articles illustrated that the perpetrator in question was a habitual offender. One offender claimed he had targeted 20 victims while another had been charged with 75 counts of sexual abuse, including 10 counts of rape.

Some of the perpetrators had prior records for sexual abuse, and some were employed in schools.

ATHLETIC ORGANIZATIONS

There is no empirical data indicating the prevalence of sexual abuse within sporting organizations. However, a review of journalistic reports yielded the largest findings out of any other youth organization. Forty-five articles were devoted to sexual abuse cases in a variety of sports including swimming, basketball, baseball, track and field, football, soccer, hockey and gymnastics. The majority of the cases illustrate that the perpetrator was somehow involved with a school, either as a teacher or principal. Many of the perpetrators appeared to have multiple victims. The offenders also appeared to groom their victims over a period of time. One case involved a coach who was charged with 400 counts of sexual abuse, though most perpetrators had approximately 10 to 12 alleged victims, and the offending behaviors ranged from touching to rape. The perpetrators also "groomed" the victims' families, socializing with them in order to gain their trust and access to the victim. The cases occurred in North America, the United Kingdom and Ireland, and a few included prominent figures in their respective sport. In many of the cases, the coaches were suspended from the organization or were subjected to criminal charges. The victims ranged in age; however, a majority of them appeared to be in their teens.

CHILD CAREGIVERS

Finkelhor et al. (1988) conducted an empirical study that evaluated substantiated claims of sexual abuse from center-based and family-based day care institutions. In order to be included in this study, the facility had to cater to children six years of age or younger; 270 institutions were so identified. Substantiation was based upon the investigations of local agencies including child protection, licensing, and police agencies. The study yielded 1,639 victims (484 girls, 269 boys, and 859 victims for which gender was not unidentified) and 382 perpetrators (222 males, 147 females, and 13 whose gender was not identified) over the time period of 1983-1985. The authors urge that the data be interpreted with caution due to the fact that some government agencies did not cooperate with the researchers' requests and that the information sought was not always kept in one location and not uniformly organized.

Despite these cautions, the researchers were able to estimate the following statistics: 30.7 of every 10,000 centers and 15.3 of every 10,000 families have cases of reported child sexual abuse; 5.5 out of every 10,000 children enrolled in day-care centers and 8.9 children out of every 10,000 children in families are reported to be sexually abused. The researchers concluded that while a day-care center is more likely to be reported for sexual abuse, the risk of a child being abused is actually lower when enrolled in a center than in their own home due to the presence of more children. In evaluating the perpetrators, the following relationships were revealed: 16% of perpetrators were directors/owners; 30% were teachers; 15% were nonprofessional child caretakers; 8% were in a non-child care capacity; 25% were family members of the staff; and 5% were outsiders. There also appeared to be a rather high number of female perpetrators involved in day care abuse, including 44% of child care workers, 6% of family members, and 6% of multiple perpetrators.

CATHOLIC CHURCH

The prevalence of sexual misconduct within the Catholic Church has been estimated by a number of social scientists. In an empirical investigation of treatment efficacy, Loftus and Camargo (1993) concluded that in their clinical sample of 1,322 priests and brothers, 27.8% reported having engaged in a sexual relationship with an adult woman while 8.4% reported sexual misconduct with a minor. Another researcher, Anthony Sipe (1990), showed that 2% of priests engage in pedophiliac behavior while an additional 4% of priests are sexually preoccupied with adolescent boys or girls. Sipe also concluded that 20% to 40% of priests engage in sexual misconduct with adults. However, these figures must be interpreted with caution due to the fact that they are based upon the authors' clinical experiences and not empirical evidence. Fones et al. (1999) found that in a sample of 19 clergymen (17 of which were Roman Catholic priests), 39% of the sample had offended against adolescents and 52% characterized the nature of their sexual behavior as deliberate. Like most studies conducted on this population, these results should be cautiously interpreted since the small sample size makes them unlikely to be generalizable.

While the social sciences have grappled with the establishment of a methodologically sound prevalence rate, journalists throughout the nation have also posed various figures. Jason Berry (1992) claims there are 400 priests and brothers who have sexually abused children. These figures are based upon Berry's coverage of the sexual abuse cases in Louisiana between 1984 and 1992. During this time period, Berry estimates that the Catholic Church spent nearly $400 million in legal, medical, and psychological expenses. A recent archival investigation conducted by New York Times reporter Laurie Goodstein (2003) postulates that by the end of 2002, more than 1,205 clerics had been named either publicly or privately by 4,268 victims. Forty-three percent of clerics are said to have offended against children younger than age 12, and the majority of abusive acts were focused upon boys (80%). The alleged abuse is postulated to have occurred most frequently during the 1970's and 1980's. Goodstein reports that the abuse is purported to have occurred most frequently during the 1970's and 1980's. Half of the investigated clerics have been listed as having multiple victims, and 16% accounted for having five or more victims.

While these studies might begin to shed some light upon the true state of affairs within the Catholic Church, they are not sound enough to utilize in drawing conclusions. This presents a very interesting conundrum in which lack of information and institutional secrecy leads to sensationalism. According to Jenkins (1995), the emphasis upon sexual abuse committed by the clergy is a result of a shift in media coverage beginning during the 1980s. As a result, the image of the "pedophile priest" (Jenkins, 1996) was created and endorsed by the media and special interest groups in order to further their causes. While the media has portrayed this "crisis" as being centered solely in the Catholic Church, Jenkins offers evidence through the citation of liability insurance that illustrates that there were several hundred cases of sexual abuse involving non-Catholic clergy.

In response to this apparent lack of knowledge, various theological scholars within the Catholic Church have undertaken the task of assessing the true extent of the abuse. Plante (2003) extrapolated from data presented by the St. Luke's Institute to conclude that during the past 50 years sexual offenses have been committed by an estimated 3,000 clerics, thus resulting in 24,000 victims. However, Plante noted that this figure may be comprised of men from various religions, and therefore it cannot be concluded that all of the offenders are Catholic priests. In a literature review conducted by The Catholic League for Religious and Civil Rights (2004), the figure for abusive clerics cited in the media ranged anywhere from 1 to 1.8 percent.

The primary problem with these studies is that they are based upon speculation about the true nature and scope of child sexual abuse in the Catholic Church. Researchers from John Jay College of Criminal Justice (2004) conducted a descriptive study of the nature and scope of the problem, seeking information from all dioceses and religious communities in the United States. They found that 4,392 priests and deacons had allegations of child sexual abuse from 1950-2002 against 10,667 children, representing approximately 4% of all priests in the United States in that time period.

A recent attempt to place the issue of sexual abuse and the clergy into a proper perspective was undertaken by Kafka (2004) at the behest of the Vatican. Through a critical review of the available literature, Kafka stated that the typical child sexual abuser in the Catholic Church is a diocesan priest who is an ephebophile. Though primary knowledge is from clinical samples, clergy offenders seem to differ from offenders in the general population. Studies that have examined clergy with co-occurring problems have found them to exhibit fewer psychological problems than other sex offenders. However, methodological limitations preclude firm conclusions about groups of clergy who offend.

THEORIES AND ETIOLOGY OF
CHILD SEXUAL ABUSE BY MALES

Why men sexually abuse children has been one of the foremost questions guiding research on sexually deviant behavior in the twentieth century. As with most forms of deviant behavior, there are various explanations as to the etiology and maintenance of sexual offending. Within the specialist literature, biological, psychological and sociological theories have been designed to explain the onset of deviant sexual fantasies and behavior. However, owing to the heterogeneity of the perpetrators of such abuse and the complex nature of this behavior, no one theory adequately explains: (a) the motivating factors that lead an adult male to have sexual relations with a child and (b) the sustaining factors that contribute to the continuance of such relations (Bickley & Beech, 2001). Nonetheless, understanding the etiology and maintenance of sexual offending is important in order to implement policies that are appropriate for all types of sexual offenders. Table 1 at the end of this section summarizes the theories on deviant sexual behavior.

BIOLOGICAL THEORY

Biological theorists are concerned with organic explanations of human behavior. Therefore, when it comes to sexual behavior, these theorists postulate that physiological factors, such as hormone levels and chromosomal makeup, have an effect on the behavior (Berlin, 1983; Marshall & Barbaree, 1990). Androgens, which are male sex hormones, promote sexual arousal, orgasm, and ejaculation, as well as regulate sexuality, aggression, cognition, emotion and personality (Rösler & Witztum, 2000; Marques et al., 2002). As a result, biological theories about deviant sexual behavior usually pertain to rape because it is considered an act of violence, and researchers have long hypothesized that there is a correlation between aggression and high testosterone levels (Money, 1970; Rada, Laws and Kellner, 1976). The theories that address pedophilia most often look at abnormal hormonal and androgenic levels in the brain.

Biological theories of deviant sexual behavior are particularly concerned with the role of androgens and androgen-releasing hormones, which are known to be related to physical changes in the male. The secretion of androgens is controlled by the hypothalamus and the pituitary, and hormones are carried from the anterior lobe of the pituitary to the testes. The testes are an important contributor to the body's output of testosterone, which, once released, circulates in the blood. When not bound to proteins, the testosterone is metabolically active; if bound, androgens can only become active when in contact with receptors for testosterone. It is at this time that physical changes, such as increases in body hair, muscle mass and penis enlargement, are caused through androgenic effects (Hucker and Bain, 1990).

When males reach puberty, there is a major increase in testosterone levels in the testes. Because sex drive increases dramatically at this time, there is generally believed to be a correlation between testosterone levels and sex drive, with testosterone being the primary biological factor responsible for normal and abnormal sexual behavior. Levels of plasma testosterone increase with erotic activity, which has been measured in males before, during and after they view erotic films (Pirke, Kockott and Dittmar, 1974). Although a review of biological studies shows conflicting results about the correlation between rising hormonal levels and sexual activity, Bancroft (1978) stated that the results imply that hormone levels are affected by erotic stimulus.

From a chromosomal perspective, Berlin (1983) discusses the possibility of a biological condition, such as Klinefelter's Syndrome, predisposing a male towards sexually abusive behavior. Klinefelter's Syndrome is a condition wherein males appear to be essentially normal boys until puberty. At puberty, 80% of males with this syndrome display both the physical characteristics and hormonal profiles of women. Berlin proposes that males with Klinefelter's Syndrome may experience problems with regard to both their sexual orientation and the nature of their erotic desires. A review of the literature suggests that the prevalence of sexual deviation among individuals who are diagnosed with Klinefelter's Syndrome may be higher than it is among individuals who have not been diagnosed with Klinefelter's Syndrome. Although Berlin cautions against making causal inferences between sexual deviation and Klinefelter's Syndrome, he attempts to support his theory by citing evidence presented by Baker and Stroller (1968). Over 100 articles regarding Klinefelter's Syndrome were reviewed, and Berlin's conclusion was in concordance with Baker and Stroller's findings.

PSYCHODYNAMIC THEORY

Psychoanalytic explanations of deviant sexual behavior were initially attributed to Freud, who proposed four states of childhood development: oral, anal, phallic and genital. He viewed sexual deviance as an expression of the unresolved problems experienced during the stages of development. These unresolved problems brought about fixations or hindrances during stages of development, with consequent distortion of a sexual object or a sexual aim (Schwartz, 1995). For example, psychoanalytic theory proposes that boys experience what is termed "the oedipal conflict" during the phallic stage of development. The oedipal conflict is characterized by competition between father and son for the mother's affection. At the same time, boys discover the differences between themselves and girls and conclude girls are actually boys whose jealous fathers have cut off their penises (Schwartz, 1995). Schwartz (1995) states that castration anxiety leads to the oedipal conflict, which is when boys no longer compete with their fathers for their mother's affections. However, if a boy fails to resolve the oedipal conflict, he may develop a permanent aversion to females as an adult if their appearance brings back this fear of castration.

Psychodynamic theory also asserts that the human psyche is composed of three primary elements: the id, the ego and the superego. In order to understand how all three elements interact, Freud proposed that all human behavior is motivated by wishes that often exist at a preconscious level (Holmes & Holmes, 2002).

The id is the unconscious domain from which all the instinctual human drives originate (i.e., hunger, sex, aggression, etc.). The id is ruled by the pleasure principle that demands instant gratification of these urges. The second part of Freud's model, the ego, is the conscious part of the human psyche that serves as the mediator between the id and the external environment. This element is primarily conscious and is ruled by the reality principle that accepts that there is a time and a place for everything (Holmes & Holmes, 2002). It is this aspect of the psyche that interacts with the external environment in order to ensure survival. The final element, the superego, is more commonly referred to as the conscience. This aspect of the psyche has both conscious and unconscious aspects and, as Holmes and Holmes state, "most lessons about the consequences of behavior stem from experience and not perceptions of how the self would look relative to its environment" (Holmes & Holmes, 2002, p. 30). Thus, the superego is bolstered by past experiences that clearly define the behaviors that warrant punishment and reward. These notions are then internalized in such a manner as to allow for the development of a system of morals.

In summary, Freudian theory portrays the human psyche as being in a constant struggle to fulfill the primal desires of the id and the moral authority of the superego. This theory assumes that sexual aggressors are lacking in a strong superego and have become overwhelmed by their primal id. While psychologists generally once accepted this explanation, it has fallen out of favor due to its lack of empirical evidence in favor of more testable theories, such as cognitive behavioral and integrated theories.

BEHAVIORAL THEORY

Behavioral theorists explain deviant sexual behavior as a learned condition. Laws and Marshall (1990) presented a theoretical model of sexually deviant behavior that describes how sexually deviant interests may be learned through the same mechanisms by which conventional sexuality is learned. The model is divided into two parts: the acquisition processes and the maintenance processes. There are six basic conditioning principles (Pavlovian Conditioning, Operant

Conditioning, Extinction, Punishment, Differential Consequences and the Chaining of Behavior); two social learning influences (General Social Learning Influences and Self-Labeling Influences); and three maintenance processes (Specific Autoerotic Influences, Specific Social Learning Influences and Intermittent Reinforcement). The model adopts the position that maladaptive behavior can result from quantitative and qualitative combinations of processes that are intrinsically orderly, strictly determined and normal in origin. Thus, deviant sexual preferences and cognitions are acquired by the same mechanisms by which other individuals learn more conventionally accepted modes of sexual expression.

ATTACHMENT THEORY

According to attachment theory, humans have a propensity to establish strong emotional bonds with others, and when individuals have some loss or emotional distress, they act out as a result of their loneliness and isolation.

As Marshall and Barbaree (1976) point out, the period surrounding pubescence and early adolescence is critical in the development of both sexuality and social competence. With adequate parenting up to this point in development, boys should have by now acquired appropriate inhibitory controls over sexual and aggressive behavior and, thus, the transition to adult functioning, with both social constraints against aggression and the skills necessary to develop effective relationships with age appropriate partners, should not be compromised. Parents also fulfill the role of instilling a sense of self-confidence in the developing boy as well as a strong emotional attachment to others.

Research indicates that there is a relationship between poor quality attachments and sexual offending. Marshall (1989) found that men who sexually abuse children often have not developed the social skills and self-confidence necessary for them to form effective intimate relations with peers. This failure causes frustration in these men that may cause them to continue to seek intimacy with under-aged partners. Seidman et al. (1994) conducted two studies aimed at examining intimacy

problems and the experience of loneliness among sex offenders. According to these studies, sex offenders have deficiencies in social skills (i.e., problems in accurately perceiving social cues, problems in deciding on appropriate behavior and deficiencies in the skills essential to enact effective behavior) that seriously restrict the possibility of attaining intimacy. The evidence suggests that deficiencies in intimacy are a distinctive and important feature of sex offenders. The rapists and non-familial child molesters in the sample appeared to be the most deficient in intimacy. Loneliness was also a significantly distinguishable variable in differentiating the sex offenders from controls and wife batterers.

Mulloy and Marshall (1999) outlined Bartholomew's four-category model of attachment and make the following observations. A secure attachment style is characterized by the individual having a positive concept of both himself and others. He is confident about his ability to make friends and interacts well with others. An individual utilizing a preoccupied attachment style has a negative self-concept but a positive concept of others. He does not feel confident about his ability to deal with problems without the help of others. The fearful attachment style, wherein the individual has a negative concept of himself and others, finds that the individual is likely to blame himself for problems in his life and finds it frightening to go to others for help and to trust people around him. Those engaging in a dismissing attachment style have a positive self-concept and a strong sense of self-confidence. However, this individual has a negative concept of others and does not seek out others for help or support. This individual is likely to say that he does not care what others think of him and rarely has a strong emotional involvement in relationships. Marshall and Marshall (2002) cited Ward et al.'s (1995) proposition that sexual offenders who have a preoccupied insecure attachment style will characteristically "court" the child and treats him or her as a lover.

COGNITIVE-BEHAVIORAL THEORY

When individuals commit deviant sexual acts, they often try to diminish their feelings of guilt and shame through "neutralizations." These neutralizations generally take the forms of excuses and justifications, with the offenders rationalizing their behavior (Scott and Lyman, 1968; Scully, 1990; Sykes and Matza, 1957). These neutralizations are cognitive distortions (CDs), or distorted thinking patterns that allow the offenders to remove from themselves any responsibility, shame or guilt for their actions (Abel et al., 1984). These rationalizations protect the offenders from self-blame and allow them to validate their behavior through cognitive defenses. Cognitive-behaviorists explore how offenders' thoughts affect their behavior.

CDs are not unique to sex offenders, only the content of the distortions (Marshall et al., 1999:60). All individuals have distorted thoughts, and in most situations CDs are relatively harmless (e.g., a motorist rationalizes that speeding on the highway is acceptable since there is little traffic). However, sex offenders' CDs are likely to lead to victimization (e.g., she didn't fight with me so she must have wanted sex). Though sex offenders do not form a homogeneous group of individuals, they show strikingly similar CDs about their victims, their offenses and their responsibility for the offenses.

It is unclear as to whether CDs are conscious distortions or whether offenders genuinely believe these altered perceptions of reality. Some researchers suggest that CDs are self-serving, and thus, the offender consciously distorts thoughts initially (Abel et al., 1984). However, it is also suggested that the offenders eventually believe the distortions as they become more entrenched in their behavior (Marshal et al., 1999). Regardless, CDs are considered crucial to the maintenance of offending behavior for both rapists and child molesters because they serve the needs of the offenders to continue their behavior without feeling guilt for their actions.

There are many ways in which distortions manifest themselves in sex offenders. Sykes and Matza (1957) list five primary neutralization techniques, including the denial of responsibility, the denial of injury, the denial of the victim, the condemnation of the accusers, and the appeal to higher loyalties. Cognitive-behavioral theorists have explained these techniques in terms of CDs, the most common of which are minimization and/or denial of the offense and justification of the offense. Additionally, sex offenders often lack victim empathy and show an inability to recognize the level of planning that went into their offenses (including grooming of the victims). Some researchers also label sexual entitlement as a specific CD, resulting from the narcissistic attitudes of offenders who seek only to fulfill their own desires (Hanson, Gizzarelli and Scott, 1998, p. 197). However broadly or specifically the CDs are defined, these distorted thoughts are conducive towards the maintenance of deviant sexual practices.

Most sex offenders minimize or deny their offenses, including the damage caused to the victim, the violence used, their responsibility for the offense, the planning of the offense and the lasting effects as a result of the offense. Several researchers have categorized types of minimization and denial (Haywood et al., 1994; Marshall et al., 1999), and these include: complete or partial denial of the offense, minimization of the offense, minimization of their own responsibility, denial or minimization of harm to the victim, denial or minimization of planning, denial or minimization of deviant fantasies and denial of their personal problems that led to the deviant behavior.

Some sex offenders deny all or part of their offenses. They may completely deny that they committed the offense – claiming, for instance, that the victim made up the story or they cannot remember what happened – or they may not admit to aggravating factors of the offense. Partial denial, as described by Marshall et al. (1999), includes refutation of a problem (e.g., I am not a sex offender) or the refusal to accept that an act was sexual abuse (e.g., the victim consented). Though some researchers claim that denial is not an accurate predictor variable for recidivism (Hanson and Bussiere, 1998), there is a substantial body of literature that claims the opposite (Marques, Day et al., 1994; Simkins, Ward, Bowman and Rinck, 1989.) Few therapists allow deniers to participate in treatment until they at least admit that they committed the offense (Marques, Day et al., 1994).

In addition to minimizing or denying their offenses, sex offenders make excuses as to why they committed the deviant acts. By justifying their actions, offenders acknowledge their guilt in the acts, but they do not take responsibility for them. Commonly, they blame the victims for their offenses or justify their offenses through the victims' actions.

Justification is common in the vast majority of sex offenders since it assists in allaying remorse and guilt for the acts committed. Scully and Marolla (1984), who interviewed 114 incarcerated rapists, explain five ways in which rapists commonly justify their behavior. They claim that the victim is a seductress, and she provoked the rape; women mean yes when they say no, or the victim did not resist enough to really mean no; most women relax and enjoy it, and they are actually fulfilling the woman's desires; nice girls do not get raped, and prostitutes, hitchhikers and promiscuous women get what they deserve; and the rape was only a minor wrongdoing, so the perpetrator is not really an "offender." Though these researchers focused on the excuses and justifications of rapists, many of their findings are also evident in child sexual abusers, who also justify their actions by neutralizing their guilt.

Child molesters justify their actions in many ways. Common justifications include claims that they are helping the child to learn about sex, that sexual education is good for the child, that the child enjoys it, that there is no harm being done to the child, that the child initiated the sexual contact and that the child acts older than he or she is. Like offenders with adult victims, child molesters often assert that the child did not resist and must have therefore wanted the sexual interaction. They fail to recognize any other explanations as to why the child might not have resisted, such as fear, uncertainty about what was happening or the idea that the perpetrator is someone they knew and trusted.

Ward and Keenan (1999) claim that the cognitive distortions of child sexual offenders emerge from five underlying implicit theories that they have about themselves, their victims and their environment. These implicit theories consider the following factors:
- Children as sexual objects. Children, like adults, are motivated by a desire for pleasure and are capable of enjoying and desiring sex.
- Entitlement. The desires and beliefs of the abuser are paramount and those of the victim are either ignored or viewed as only of secondary importance.

- Dangerous world. The abuser views other adults as being abusive and/or unreliable and perceives that they will reject him in promotion of their own needs.
- Uncontrollability. The abuser perceives his environment as uncontrollable wherein people are not able to exert any major influence over their personal behavior and/or the world around them.
- Nature of harm. The abuser considers the degree of harm to his victim and perceives sexual activity as beneficial and unlikely to harm a person.

Offenders rarely modify these implicit theories even when faced with evidence (behavior) to the contrary. Instead, the offender may simply reinterpret or reject it. For example, a child's friendly behavior might be evidence to the offender that the child wants to have sex with him.

Similar to Ward and Keenan's idea that the distortions of sexual offenders reflect their more general implicit theories about their victims, Marshall et al. (1999) stress that "the distorting process thought to be characteristic of sexual offenders does not differentiate them from the rest of us; it is the content of their distortions, and the goals manifested by their behaviors, that differentiates them."

All sex offenders have a tendency to misread social cues by others and are poor at identifying emotions such as anger or fear in their victims. Both rapists and child molesters often perceive their victims as initiating sexual contact, and see their victims' actions as sexually provocative. Child molesters misread cues from children in several ways, and the better they know the victim the more likely this is to happen. Children are naturally affectionate towards adults, particularly those whom they know well. Child molesters view these naturally affectionate actions – such as sitting on an adult's lap—as sexual in nature and perceive the children as initiating sexual contact. They also perceive any sexual curiosity displayed by the child as a desire to know about sex, and they want to "teach" the child through sexual experiences. These misperceptions reinforce the offenders' narcissistic beliefs and detract from the ability for an offender to feel any empathy for his victims.

INTEGRATED THEORY

Finkelhor (1984) is one of the leading theorists on child sexual abuse. He proposed a four-factor model of the preconditions to child sexual abuse, which integrate the various theories about why individuals begin to participate in sexually deviant behavior. This organizational framework addresses the full complexity of child sexual abusers, from the motivation to offend (etiology of offending behavior) to the rationalization of this behavior (maintenance of behavior). The primary focus of Finkelhor's model is on the internal barriers, or "self talk," comments and observations of sex offenders about the world around them. This self talk allows offenders to break through barriers which, until this time, had prevented them from acting out their feelings about perceptions of injustice, loneliness and other such stressors. Once these barriers are diminished, this mistaken thinking can lead to actions, which are the result of normal internal barriers being absent.

In order to better explain this process, Finkelhor constructed an organizational framework consisting of four separate underlying factors that explain not only why offenders abuse, but also why the abuse continues. These factors include: (1) emotional congruence, (2) sexual arousal, (3) blockage and (4) disinhibition.

Finkelhor coined the term "emotional congruence" to convey the relationship between the adult abuser's emotional needs and the child's characteristics. For example, if an abuser's self-perception is child-like (i.e., he has childish emotional needs), he may wish to relate to other children. Similarly, if an abuser suffers from low self-esteem and a low sense of efficacy in social relationships, he may be more comfortable relating to a child due to the sense of power and control.

Sexual arousal, the second component of Finkelhor's theory, evaluates the reasons why children would elicit sexual arousal in an adult. Finkelhor looks to social learning theory in order to explain this phenomenon. One explanation is that the child sexual abuser was molested when he was a child. Through conditioning and imprinting, he comes to find children arousing later in adulthood.

An alternate explanation is that the child sexual abuser's experience of being victimized as a child is not conditioned, but modeled by someone (i.e., his abuser) who finds children sexually stimulating.

Blockage essentially deals with the abuser's ability to have his sexual and emotional needs met in adult relationships. Finkelhor looks to both psychoanalytic theory and attachment theory to explain this component. As stated previously, psychoanalytic theory describes child molesters as having intense conflicts about their mothers or "castration anxiety" that makes it difficult or impossible to relate to adult women. With regard to adult attachments, child molesters have failed to develop the appropriate social skills and self-confidence necessary to form effective intimate relations with adults. Finkelhor further breaks down the theory of blockage to incorporate what he calls developmental blockages and situational blockages. Developmental blockages once again refer to psychoanalytic theory wherein an individual is psychologically prevented from moving into the adult sexual stage of development. Situational blockage refers to the event wherein an individual, who has apparent adult sexual interests, is blocked from normal sexual expression owing to the loss of a relationship or some other transitory crises.

The final component, disinhibition, refers to the factors that help a child molester overcome his inhibitions so that he allows himself to molest a child. Finkelhor looks to cognitive-behavioral theories to explain this component. Specifically, he considers the influence of cognitive distortion in the facilitation of child molesting behavior. Further, personality factors, such as substance abuse and stress, are viewed as entities that contribute to the lowering of inhibitions.

Overall, this organizational framework describes who is at risk to offend. It is likely that individuals who offend have been able to cope with many of the above problems (e.g., developmental blockage) and opportunities (e.g., access to children) at different times. However, it is the combination of these problems, in addition to some type of demand on their coping system that contributes towards an attitude supportive of sexual offending, thereby establishing a risk to offend. That risk increases the likelihood that a person may act out in a sexual fashion because his or her belief system has filtered out the normal inhibitions towards sexual offending. Unfortunately, the relief that is associated with sexual offending is reinforcing because it provides an emotional and physical response to coping in a way in which the offenders feel they have control, unlike much of the other parts of their lives.

THEORIES OF OFFENDING BY CLERGY

There is no clear consensus as to why some priests molest children and others do not. Hands (2002) has proposed a psychodynamic model in which experiences of shame interact with unrealistic, moral expectations conveyed through Church teachings that have been internalized. The result of this process is the creation of a shame cycle, which stunts the individual's psychosexual development and contributes to sexual misconduct. The internalization of Church doctrine concerning celibacy/chastity reinforces many cognitive distortions, which allows the abuse to persist. Hands also hypothesizes that the steps the Church has taken to discourage the formation of close friendships between priests, under the pretense that it may lead to homosexual behavior, have also played a role in the creation of a pro-offending environment. With this increased social isolation comes a greater alienation from the body. Therefore, sexuality is repressed only to later emerge as an obsession. Hands cites the work of Sullivan, who theorizes that the result of this repression is the development of "primary genital phobia." Central to this theory is the notion that when the individual experiences any sexual feelings, thoughts, or emotions, they are ignored only to later manifest themselves as obsessions unless they are directly addressed.

Sipe (1995) has proposed a model of clergy offending which consists of four specific categories. Those in Sipe's Genetic Lock find that their sexual attraction is inherently determined. The Psychodynamic Lock consists of priests who, as a result of their childhood experiences, have been locked at a level of psychosexual development that makes them prone to offending. Sipe hypothesizes that combina-

tions of genetic and psychodynamic factors contribute to one another and interact with cognitive factors. All of these variables combine in such a manner as to influence the priests to sexually abuse a child. In the Social/Situational Lock, the priest is otherwise healthy, but the experience of celibacy suspends psychosexual development. Similar to the theory of primary genital phobia, sex is externally denied, but internally explored. Sipe concludes that offending behavior in this model is of a developmental nature and can be resolved once the offender psychologically matures. The Moral Lock displays no clear explanation for the offending behavior other than the individuals in this model make a conscious choice to commit sexual abuse.

In his 1990 book, *A Secret World: Sexuality and the Search for Celibacy*, Sipe theorized that a history of childhood sexual abuse might contribute to sexual offending as an adult. In discussing the causes of pedophilia, Sipes noted that a large number of sexually abusive clerics had been victimized as youths. While this is not applicable to every case, sexual victimization as a child may lead the individual to seek refuge in the clergy as a way of denying the reality of life. Sipe contends that the experience of celibacy interacts with these past traumas and can either enhance the memory or stunt the priest's psychosexual development at a preadolescent/ adolescent stage, leading to sexual misconduct.

In contrast to the psychodynamic approach adopted by Sipe, Krebs (1998) claims that the institutional hierarchy of the Catholic Church contributes to the creation of a pro-offending environment. In concordance with the theories of Andrew Shupe, institutional religion is based upon "hierarchies of unequal power," which span both spiritual and organizational dimensions. Those in elite positions within the institution have moral authority over the masses, which allows them to control privileges and ostracize individuals. The Church also engages in neutralization tactics in order to protect these offending priests and the image of the institution. In turn, this gives the pedophile approval from superiors to continue offending and establishes an environment in which the behavior can persist.

Table 1. Summary of theories explaining child sexual abuse

THEORY	DESCRIPTION OF THEORY
BIOLOGICAL THEORY	Concerned with organic explanations of human behavior; physiological factors (e.g., hormone levels, chromosomal makeup) have an effect of sexual behavior; androgens promote sexual arousal, orgasm, and ejaculation, as well as regulate sexuality, aggression, cognition, emotion and personality; abnormal levels of androgens lead to aggressive sexual behavior.
PSYCHODYNAMIC THEORY	Sexual deviance is an expression of the unresolved problems experienced during the stages of development; the human psyche is composed of three primary elements: the id, the ego and the superego; sexual deviancy occurs when the id (pleasure principle) is overactive.
BEHAVIORAL THEORY	Deviant sexual behavior is a learned condition, acquired through the same mechanisms by which conventional sexuality is learned; it is acquired and maintained through basic conditioning principles.
ATTACHMENT THEORY	Humans have a propensity to establish strong emotional bonds with others, and when individuals have some loss or emotional distress, they act out as a result of their loneliness and isolation.
COGNITIVE-BEHAVIORAL THEORY	Addresses the way in which offenders' thoughts affect their behavior; focuses on the way in which sex offenders diminish their feelings of guilt and shame by rationalizing it through excuses and justifications.
INTEGRATED THEORY	There are preconditions to child sexual abuse, which integrate the various theories about why individuals begin to participate in sexually deviant behavior; addresses the motivation to offend and the rationalization of the behavior; focus is on the inhibitions of the offenders (internal barriers) and how when these barriers are diminished, distorted thoughts can lead to deviant actions.
THEORIES ON ABUSE BY CLERGY	No clear consensus as to why some priests molest children and others do not, though many theories address the stunted psychosexual development of the priest; the psychodynamic model addresses the way in which the experiences of shame interact with unrealistic, moral expectations conveyed through church teachings that have been internalized, resulting in the creation of a shame cycle that stunts the individual's psychosexual development and contributes to sexual misconduct; experience of celibacy interacts with past traumas (e.g., childhood sexual abuse) and may stunt the priest's psychosexual development at a preadolescent/adolescent stage leading to sexual misconduct.

THE OFFENSE CYCLE

When sexually abusing a child, the abuser must make a series of decisions prior to committing the deviant act. These decisions may be made over a period of time or on the spur of the moment if the opportunity to abuse presents itself. In order to understand a child molester's behavior, it is necessary to evaluate the antecedent conditions that allow for a pro-offending environment and how these antecedents vary amongst offenders. Though discussed at a greater length in the next section of this paper, a brief explanation is necessary here of two types of child molesters: the fixated offender and the regressed offender.

Fixated, or preferential, child molesters are exclusively attracted to children. They are likely to have many victims as a result of their failure to have developed a sexual attraction to their age mates. In contrast, the regressed offender is sexually attracted to age mates, but the abuse is triggered by some type of stressor in the environment. These offenders are less likely than fixated offenders to have multiple victims since the abuse serves almost as a means of them coping with the stressful situation. Regressed offenders display greater guilt and shame and exhibit a positive treatment prognosis.

Since regressed offenders are influenced by external stressors in the environment, it is possible to teach them to identify their high-risk situations. Most importantly, it is possible to identify a series of Seemingly Unimportant Decisions (SUDs). These decisions place the offenders in a position where they are likely to reoffend. An example of this would be a child molester who starts to walk by the playground on his way home from work. Through the utilization of cognitive distortions, it appears to him as if he is just taking a new route home. However, this SUD places him in an environment in which he has access to victims. If the process is not stopped, he is likely to progress until the antecedent conditions create an environment in which reoffending is inevitable.

The key feature of the offense cycle involves the interaction of thoughts, feelings and behaviors. Essentially, negative thoughts will cause the offender to experience negative feelings, prompting the use of certain behavioral measures to combat these feelings. There are multiple determinants involved in this cycle, but the core point is that sexual abuse is not a random act. These determinants may include situational factors (i.e., the opportunity to offend), affective states (depression, anger, isolation), past learning, biological influences and prevailing contingencies of reinforcement (current, unforeseen support or back up). As mentioned earlier, the regressed offender is susceptible to external stressors and utilizes the abuse as a means of coping. This cycle is most applicable to these offenders as it illustrates the interaction of the external world and individual perception.

There are several steps involved in the offense chain. The offender will first have negative thoughts. Thoughts may be characterized by themes such as "Nobody likes me" or "I'm no good." These thoughts then lead to feelings such as anger, frustration, sadness and inadequacy. The thoughts and feelings then interact in such a manner as to influence the offender's behavior. It is at this point that the offender begins to make poor decisions (SUDS) and withdraws from people around him. Isolation results in a lack of communication that causes the thoughts and feelings mentioned earlier to go unresolved.

The pro-offending thinking then causes the offender to progress to the point where he starts to experience deviant sexual fantasies also referred to as lapse fantasies. These fantasies lead to masturbation, and the offender begins to feel better about the negative thoughts and feelings experienced earlier in the cycle. Through fantasizing and orgasm, the offender has now found a way to tame the painful feelings, but he is placing himself into more dangerous situations. It is not uncommon at this point for the offender to take steps short of committing a sexual offense such as targeting a victim and engaging in a fantasy rehearsal of the future abuse.

Once the offender has engaged in the fantasy rehearsal, he reaches a point in the cycle where he decides to give up. In a sense, he is saying to himself, "Why not? I've already gone this far. I may as well do it." It is at this point when the offender begins to "groom" his victim (see next section) and plan the abusive act. This planning causes the offender to experience a sense of excitement that further motivates him until he is at the point of committing the offense.

After adequate grooming has taken place, the offender sexually abuses the victim. The act itself serves as a reinforcement of the original fantasy. However, once the act has occurred, there exist new anxiety provoking thoughts. Examples of some of the thoughts the offender may be contemplating include, "What have I done? I might get caught." These thoughts lead to new feelings of guilt and fear despite the release of tension achieved through the recent abusive act. These feelings of guilt, fear and remorse cause the cycle to come to a stop during which the offender tries to regain a sense of normality. By refusing to acknowledge the thoughts and feelings associated with the abuse, the cycle begins once more since the original issues had never been addressed.

GROOMING

Those offenders who take time to plan the deviant act are known to indulge in what is termed "grooming" behavior. Grooming is a pre-meditated behavior intended to manipulate the potential victim into complying with the sexual abuse. Based on a survey of tactics used by abusers to groom their victims, Pryor (1996) describes several methods by which offenders approach and initiate sex with their victims. These methods include verbal and/or physical intimidation, seduction or the use of enticements such as candy, money or other gifts. The tactics used by offenders depend somewhat on the potential victim's response to the tactic. If an offender encounters little to no resistance from the potential victim, he will continue to use the same tactic repeatedly. If, however, some resistance is encountered, the offender may either change the tactic and/or become more forceful in his endeavor. One common tactic noted by Pryor is the seduction and testing of a child. This tactic is used when there is an existing relationship with a child and the child is accustomed to the affectionate expression of the offender. The offender gradually extends the affectionate touching to include sexual behavior, all the while "testing" the child's response. If no overt resistance is observed, the sexual abuse continues.

A less frequent tactic that is mentioned by Pryor entails the offender catching the victim by surprise. In this instance, the offender may orchestrate a situation to distract the victim or seize the opportunity to abuse when it arises. The latter is most common and is usually a result of the offender's frustration from waiting for the right time to initiate contact. A third and more intimidating tactic used by offenders entails garnering victim compliance through the use of either verbal or physical force. In this situation, the offender either commands the victim to perform sexual acts and/or physically forces the victim to engage in sexual acts. This tactic is more common in more serious, repeat offenders. Pryor found that emotional manipulation and verbal coercion were the most common tactics used by offenders to groom their victims. This occurs in various ways, such as doing favors for the victim in exchange for sex and/or emotionally blackmailing the victim into compliance. Even though it may appear that there is room for negotiation on the part of the victim, the outcome always favors the offender. Offenders who have ongoing contact with their victims often utilize this tactic (i.e., incest offenders).

Another tactic used by offenders in order to groom their victims entails disguising sexual advances in the context of playing a game. For example, the offender will begin by tickling the victim and gradually progress to fondling. While this approach may appear spontaneous, it has been well planned by the offender, yet orchestrated in a rather surreptitious manner.

The most methodical and deliberate tactic of engaging a victim in sex involves a process of initially introducing the victim to the idea of sex and then gradually engaging them in sexual activity. Pryor describes this tactic as turning the victim out. For example, the offender will begin by displaying himself in the nude or introducing the victim to pornography. Then there is a period of rationalizing that sex is okay. This may be followed by fondling the victim or having the victim fondle him, all the while rationalizing that sex is okay and possibly verbally praising the victim for his/her efforts. This exchange slowly builds up to more serious sexual acts and possibly to the point where the victim is being rewarded with gifts for his/her participation.

Over time, the victim becomes groomed to the point that engaging in sex with the offender is more or less automatic. While most grooming tactics are premeditated, this tactic is more methodically planned and the offender is willing to wait months or possibly years to accomplish his task.

When offenders set out to groom a victim, they will usually use tactics that have previously proved successful in gaining their victim's compliance. However, given that offenders attend to their victim's response, they are open to changing their tactics if an approach proves unsuccessful.

TYPOLOGIES OF CHILD SEXUAL ABUSERS

I n the ongoing effort to develop an understanding of characteristics that would allow for classification of sex offenders into specific groups, many researchers have proposed typologies of offenders. These typologies, or classification schemes, utilize offender characteristics and/or victim-choice information, including interpersonal and situational characteristics, to outline a framework for analysis (e.g. Knight & Prentky, 1990; Simon et al., 1992; Schwartz, 1995).

THE FIXATED/REGRESSED TYPOLOGY

In the 1970s, researchers began to classify offenders based upon their motivation for committing sexually deviant behavior. One of the most basic classification schemes was proposed by Groth et al. (1982), who considered two issues: the degree to which the deviant sexual behavior is entrenched and the basis for psychological needs. With regard to the first issue, Groth proposed the fixated-regressed dichotomy of sex offending. This is not simply a dichotomous distinction, but rather exists on a continuum, as shown in Figure 1.

The fixated offender is characterized as having a persistent, continual and compulsive attraction to children. They are usually diagnosed with pedophilia, or recurrent, intense, sexually arousing fantasies of at least six months in duration involving pre-pubescent children (American Psychiatric Association, 1999). Finkelhor (1984) classifies these offenders as exclusively involved with children and points out that they are usually not related to their victims and are attracted to children from adolescence. According to Holmes and Holmes (2002), the offender has not fully developed and shows characteristics of a child. In particular, fixated offenders do not develop past the point where they find children attractive and desirable. The fixated offender's actions are typically premeditated in nature and do not result from any perceived stress. In addition, this type of offender is often unable to attain any degree of psychosexual maturity and, during adulthood, has had virtually no age-appropriate sexual relationships. The fixated offender is more likely to choose victims who are male and not related to him (Abel and Rouleau, 1990; Simon et al., 1992; West, 1987).

It is the fixated offenders who are most dangerous to society, constituting "a public health problem" (Abel, Lawry, Kalstrom et al., 1994) as well as a "criminal problem" (Freeman-Longo, 1996). These offenders develop relationships with vulnerable children (vulnerable in either an emotional or situational sense), and they typically recruit, groom and maintain the children for a continuing sexual relationship (Conte, 1991). The offenders delude themselves into believing they have established a caring, supportive role with the child and that the child is able to derive pleasure and educational experience from the interaction (Abel and Rouleau, 1995; Marshall and Barbaree, 1990b).

Fixated offenders are particularly dangerous because their offenses often go unreported, and subsequently, many have been convicted of far fewer offenses than they actually committed (Abel and Rouleau, 1990; Abel et al., 1994; Elliot, Browne and Kilcoyne, 1995). Offenders who abuse young boys are at the highest risk of recidivating and are also likely to commit the most offenses (Marques, Day, et al., 1994; Marques, Nelson et al., 1994). Abel and Rouleau's (1990) study of 561 male offenders who voluntarily sought treatment showed that the non-incestuous offenders in the sample who assaulted young boys averaged 281 offenses with an average of 150 victims. It is the strongly fixated offenders who have the most victims and the highest rate of recidivism and should consequently be considered the highest risk to the community.

The regressed offenders' behavior, on the other hand, usually emerges in adulthood and tends to be precipitated by external stressors. Gebhard et al. (1965) touched upon the role of external stressors as precursors to sexual offending. In this early classification system, the authors state that sexual offending is the product of environmental stressors and disordered childhood relationships. These two variables intersect in such a manner as to render the offender powerless to control his behavior, thus culminating in an offensive act. At the time of the creation of this classification system, the authors were unable to specify childhood precursors to offending; however, there has been extensive research evaluating the nature of stressors. These stressors can be situational, such as unemployment, marital problems and substance abuse, or can related to negative affective states such as loneliness, stress, isolation or anxiety. These stressors, according to Schwartz (1995), often lead to poor self-confidence and low self-esteem, thereby undermining the abusers confidence in themselves as men. Sexual involvement with children is not fixed, but is instead often a temporary departure from the offender's attraction to adults (Simon et al., 1992). This type of offender is more likely to choose victims who are female.

Regressed offenders tend to victimize children to whom they have easy access, and as such, they often victimize their own children. It is difficult to establish accurate patterns of arousal for regressed offenders, and researchers (Freund, McKnight, Langevin et al., 1972; Quinsey, Steinman, Bergerson et al., 1975) have found that they have similar arousal patterns to "normal" men. Arousal is generally measured through a penile plethysmograph (PPG) as the male is shown erotic material. The control group generally shows some level of arousal to photos of young children in erotic poses, and it is therefore difficult to differentiate between the two groups. This indicates that, as with rapists, the offender is not necessarily motivated by sexual needs alone.

A distinction is made between a sex-pressure offense and a sex-force offense. In a sex-pressure offense, the offender either entices or entraps his victim. In his pursuit for sexual gratification, the offender would prefer his victim to cooperate. However, should his victim resist, the offender usually will not follow through with the sexually abusive behavior.

In contrast, a sex-force offense is one wherein the offender uses either intimidation or physical aggression. When intimidation is used, the offender may be drawn to his victim primarily because the victim is easily overpowered and may present less resistance than an adult. The offender is using his victim purely as a means of sexual release. Those offenders who use physical aggression to overpower their victim, commonly known as "sadistic" offenders, must inflict pain in order to achieve sexual gratification. Fortunately, this type of offender is the rarest.

Figure 3. The fixated and regressed offender continuum, showing that fixation is continuous, not dichotomous.

Table 2. Characteristics of fixated and regressed offenders.

	MOTIVATION	PRIMARY VICTIM PREFERENCE	RISK OF REOFFENDING
FIXATED OFFENDER	• Having never developed an attraction to age-appropriate partners, the fixated offender has a persistent, continual, and compulsive attraction to children. • Behavior emerges in adolescence. • Offenses are premeditated in nature and do not stem from stressors. • Most likely to be diagnosed/characterized with pedophila/ephebophilia.	• Extrafamilial • Female (prepubescent), male (pubescent/adolescent) • Typically recruits vulnerable children and engages in extensive grooming in order to ensure the continuation of the abuse	• Very high risk of recidivism • The risk of recidivism increases according to the number of victims.
REGRESSED OFFENDER	• Offending stems from stressors in the individuals environment which undermine self esteem and confidence. • Behavior emerges in adulthood. • Offending is a departure from the offender's attraction to adults. • Similar to rapists, the offender is not necessarily motivated by sexual needs alone.	• Intrafamilial, acquaintance • Gender varies, depending on who is accessible. • Tend to victimize children to whom they have easy access	• Since they are not sexually fixated on children, they are at a lower risk of reoffending if treated. • Capable of feeling remorse for their actions

Simon et al. (1992) attempted to empirically validate the fixated-regressed typology. They sampled 136 consecutive cases of convicted offenders over a two-year period. They reviewed pre-sentence data that comprised a case history, MMPI results, pre-sentence reports and police report data. Application of the criteria defining fixated versus regressed status yielded a unimodal and continuous distribution of offenders rather than the bimodal (fixated/regressed) distribution predicted by Groth's theory. Based on the results of this study, Simon et al. suggested that Groth's fixated/regressed dichotomy was unable to account for all child sexual abusers and recommended using a modification of Groth's

approach. This modification would entail the use of Groth's criteria along a continuum and rejecting the original dichotomy. The findings of Simon et al. identify a potentially causal link between general criminality, anti-social behavior and child molestation. These variables have been typically ignored by theories such as Groth's. A further contrast between Groth's classification system and Simon et al. is the suggested existence of at least three different age groups of child molesters (not two). The presence of these age clusters suggests that situational opportunities (i.e., marital discord and availability of a young, potential victim) may interact with the "stable" tendency of an individual with a past history of antisocial acts. This leads to a potential increase in the risk of child sexual abuse. Thus, molesters of different age groups may differ in terms of the predisposition to molest as well as opportunity.

THE FBI TYPOLOGIES

The FBI also expanded on Groth's typologies to include seven subgroups of offenders: regressed, morally indiscriminate, sexually indiscriminate, inadequate (these are situational offenders); seductive, fixated and sadistic (these are preferential). Four of these subgroups (regressed, morally indiscriminate, sexually indiscriminate and inadequate) correspond to regressed offenders as described by

Groth and three subgroups (seduction, introverted and sadistic) correspond to Groth's description of fixated child molesters. The morally indiscriminate offender chooses his victim based on accessibility, whereas the sexually indiscriminate offender is driven by his desire to experiment with almost any type of sexual behavior. The inadequate offender chooses his victim because he is socially inept and likely to perceive his victim as a vulnerable object through which he may satisfy his sexual curiosity. Those offenders who utilize seduction will groom their victim. However, the introverted offender does not have the social skills necessary to seduce a victim, thus they molest very young children. Table 3 summarizes the characteristics of these offender types.

Table 3. The FBI typologies of situational and preferential offenders and their seven subgroups.

TYPE OF OFFENDER	CHARACTERISTICS OF OFFENDERS
Situational offenders	
REGRESSED	Offenders have poor coping skills, target victims who are easily accessible, abuse children as a substitute for adult relationships.
MORALLY INDISCRIMINATE	Offenders do not prefer children over adults and tend to use children (or anyone accessible) for their own interests (sexual and otherwise).
SEXUALLY INDISCRIMINATE	Offenders are mainly interested in sexual experimentation, and abuse children out of boredom.
INADEQUATE	Offenders are social misfits who are insecure, have low self-esteem, and see relationships with children as their only sexual outlet.
Preferential offenders	
SEDUCTIVE	Offenders "court" children and give them much affection, love, gifts, and enticements in order to carry on a "relationship."
FIXATED	Offenders have poor psychosexual development, desire affection from children, and are compulsively attracted to children.
SADISTIC	Offenders are aggressive, sexually excited by violence, target stranger victims, and are extremely dangerous.

Source: Holmes and Holmes (1996)

THE MTC:CM3 TYPOLOGY

In their attempt to classify child molesters, Knight and Prentky (1990) employed deductive-rational and inductive-empirical research strategies (simultaneously) to develop multidimensional typologies of offenders on two axes. Axis I addresses the degree to which an offender is fixated with children and is further broken down to consider the offender's level of social competence. Axis II evaluates the amount of contact an offender has with children and is analyzed according to the meaning (interpersonal or sexual) of that contact. This axis further evaluates the amount and type of physical injury involved in the contact. Through this system, which is known as the Massachusetts Treatment Center: Child Molester Typology, versions 3 [MTC:CM3], each offender is assigned a separate Axis I and Axis II typology. Knight and Prentky state that this classification system has already demonstrated reasonable reliability and consistent ties to distinctive developmental antecedents. In addition, the preliminary results of a 25-year recidivism study of offenders conducted by the authors indicate that aspects of this system have important prognostic implications.

In 2001, Looman et al. attempted to replicate Knight and Prentky's research strategies with 109 child molesters in Canada. These child molesters were classified in accordance with the MTC:CM3 typology. Groups of molesters were compared on a number of meaningful variables, such as number of victims and sexual deviance. Results showed that it is possible to apply the MTC:CM3 child molester typology in a population outside of Massachusetts. All molesters, with the exception of the sadistic types, were classified into all subgroups with an acceptable level of reliability. The authors claim that this exception may be due to the low number of offenders who fell into these subgroups rather than difficulties with the classification system. Differences were found between groups on the phallometric assessments, with the high fixation-low social competence group having highest levels of deviance on the slide assessment for Axis I. Interestingly, the average deviance indices for all four levels of Axis I indicated at least a failure to differentiate appropriate from inappropriate stimuli in terms of sexual responding; however, the high fixation-low social competence group was the only one that demonstrated a clear sexual preference for children. The high fixation-low social competence group was also distinguished by their preferences for male victims and their higher levels of self-reported childhood sexual abuse. On Axis II, the low contact-high injury offenders displayed more deviant arousal on the female's sexual violence assessment than other groups. These offenders were also more intrusive in their offending and were more likely to use physical force. Although most Axis II groupings were equally likely to choose male as well as female victims, the exploitative group had a clear preference for female victims. Differences were not found for groups when rates of sexual and violent recidivism were examined although it was revealed that sadistic offenders committed a great number of violent offenses. Preferential child molesters (i.e., those in high fixation and high contact categories) were found to be more likely to exhibit deviant arousal, to have greater numbers of victims and to cause little physical harm. They were also more likely to commit new sexual offenses although this difference was not significant. Given that deviant sexual arousal is one of the best predictors of sexual recidivism, these individuals present as being higher risk and having higher treatment needs. Low contact-high injury offenders also had a greater number of victims and were more likely to display deviant arousal. They were more likely to target strangers, were more intrusive in their offending and were more likely to cause serious physical harm to their victims. With regard to implications for risk assessment, sadistic offenders had a greater number of violent offenses, indicating that these offenders may be at higher risk for violent nonsexual offenses. Also, low social competence offenders were more likely to reoffend in a nonsexual, nonviolent manner.

Table 4. MTC: CM3 classification of child molesters.

AXIS	DESCRIPTION OF AXIS MEASUREMENT
Axis I	• Assesses the extent to which the offender is fixated with children (on a continuum) • Measures the level of social competence of the offender
Axis II	• Assesses the amount of contact the offender has with children (e.g., exclusively involved with extrafamilial children, abuses own children) • Meaning of the contact (sexual and interpersonal) • Amount and type of physical injury involved in the contact (including threats and use of force)

OTHER TYPOLOGIES

Other researchers have used various forms of data in their attempt to differentiate types of child molesters. Baxter et al. (1984) evaluated the criminal records, personal histories, social-sexual competence and physiological responses to erotic stimuli of incarcerated pedophiles, ephebophiles (those individuals with recurrent, intense, sexually arousing fantasies about adolescents) and rapists. Results indicated that there were significant differences among the groups in criminal and personal background. Pedophiles tended to be older, more poorly educated, more likely to be unmarried and less frequently involved in nonsexual crime. Social and social-sexual inadequacy was common to all groups as reflected by under-assertiveness, low self-esteem and negative attitudes.

Baxter et al.'s data provide a degree of support for the view of the pedophile as a sexual deviate. Pedophiles were somewhat older than other subjects and were more likely to be repetitive sexual offenders, with less nonsexual criminal involvement than rapists or ephebophiles. They were more likely to exhibit deviant sexual arousal, inasmuch as they responded much more to children than non-pedophilic subjects. However, the pedophiles did not so much show an erotic preference for children as display a failure to either inhibit responding to children or to show a clear erotic preference for adults. Non-pedophilic subjects showed an attenuated response to children relative to adults while pedophiles did not. Although the findings of the present study are consistent with earlier reports that many pedophiles are married and have children of their own, they conflict with the reports indicating that pedophiles tend to exhibit strong sexual preferences for children. The authors suggest that this may be a result of the rather small sample from which the present data were obtained. Overall, choice of victim was clearly related only to sexual response patterns, and then only in the case of a prepubescent victim. Pedophiles and homosexual offenders responded more to male children than did heterosexual offenders.

Simkins (1993) conducted an exploratory investigation, the purpose of which was to compare sexually repressed and non-repressed child molesters on therapy progress and on a battery of personality and research instruments. From information obtained on psychosexual histories, 68 child molesters were categorized as repressed, non-repressed or exploitive. Results indicated that significantly larger portions of therapy failures were sexually repressed. There were also significant differences between repressed and non-repressed offenders on some of the special research scales of the MMPI, the Burt Rape Myth Scales, some of the Multiphasic Sexual Inventory Scales and Mosher's Sex Guilt Scale. Differences on these measures are consistent with the characteristics of intrafamilial child molesters reported in the clinical and research literature. The results of this investigation are, however, quite speculative due to the small sample size of the repressed group. It is also conceivable that differences in treatment effectiveness between repressed and non-repressed groups may be attributed to differences in social skills rather than to sexual repression.

Danni et al. (2002) conducted a study for the purpose of differentiating three types of child sexual offenders–pedophiles, ephebophiles and incest offenders. In this study, 168 convicted sex offenders participated. Data was gathered from the pre-sentence investigation reports, which were used by the court for sentencing proceedings. Eight independent variables were found to significantly discriminate among the three types of sex offenders almost 90% of the time. These variables were: sexually victimized as a child, pre-pubertal victim, seduction motive, age-appropriate relationships, stress, own child as victim, social facade and anger. Based on these results, the authors concluded that pedophiles are more likely to have experienced sexual victimization as a child, to prefer pre-pubertal sex partners and to be motivated to seduce their victims than non-pedophiles. The findings also illustrate that ephebophiles are more likely to have experienced external stress than non-ephebophiles, while incest offenders are more likely to have a higher level of perceived entitlement than non-incest offenders. Ephebophiles were correctly classified in 92.86% of the cases and incest offenders were classified correctly in 100% of the cases. However, pedophiles were the most difficult to correctly classify (84.06%). The authors attribute this phenomenon to the fact that pedophiles' victims are typically young and are not always able to effectively verbalize or convey the things that happen to them. The forms of seduction utilized by the offender may confuse the victims. The authors conclude that the primary characteristic of pedophilia is the offender's own childhood sexual victimization. The unwillingness to disclose that information makes it less likely that a pedophile will be discovered. They purport that this manipulative behavior is harder to detect.

Laws et al. (2000) conducted a study that examined the extent to which the use of multiple measures of pedophilic interest improved on the diagnostic accuracy of any single measure. One hundred twenty-four males voluntarily consented to participate in an outpatient evaluation and treatment program for child molesters. Of these, 56% were referred from the Florida Department of Corrections, 31% were referred from private prac-

titioners, mental health clinics or other professionals (i.e., attorneys), and 13% were self-reported. All participants admitted to either a sexual attraction to children or to some inappropriate sexual activity with a child. The average age of the participants was 36.08 years (range = 18-74). Eighty-seven percent were Caucasian, 8% were African American and 5% were Hispanic. About 26% were married or involved in a common-law relationship, 28% were separated or divorced and 46% had never married. Socioeconomic status based on annual income showed that 14% were middle class, 20% were lower middle class and 66% were lower class. Fifty-two men did not participate in the research due to various reasons, including a) bisexual child molesters were excluded, b) anyone who did not complete all three measures were excluded and c) the attrition rate for the outpatient treatment project was quite high. The remaining 72 child molesters completed a self-report card-sort measure of sexual interest, as well as direct monitoring of penile response (using the PPG) when presented with erotic slides or audio material. The reliability of all measures was high. All three measures used to assess pedophilic interest (i.e., card-sort, PPG slides, PPG audio) significantly differentiated boy-object and girl-object child molesters. The card-sort measure showed the greatest classification accuracy and was the only measure to significantly improve accuracy once the other two modalities were considered. Consideration of all three measures proved classification accuracy (91.7%) greater than any single measure.

CHARACTERISTICS OF CLERGY OFFENDERS

Some researchers claim that clergy offenders are truly unique in comparison to offenders within the general population (Kafka, 2004). This is a theory that has been illustrated by a number of researchers. Camargo (1997) concluded that clergy offenders were unique based upon their status as Diocesan priests and the combination of passivity (with the absence of overt hostility), test-taking styles which present the self as being free of major symptoms, low anxiety and high relative gregariousness. Haywood et al. (1996) found that non-cleric offenders reported more psychopathology as measured by the MMPI-1 and that, contrary to expectations, there were no differences concerning a history of childhood sexual abuse between clergy and non-clergy offenders. These findings contrast with those of Langevin et al. (2000) who concluded that while the clergy offenders in their sample were similar to the matched group of non-clergy offenders, 70.8% were sexually deviant and characterized as homosexual pedophiles with courtship disorder. Few of the participants in either group had been sexually abused as children. None of the clergy participants were diagnosed with antisocial personality disorder, but they did exhibit symptoms of substance abuse.

Certain personality characteristics have also been shown to be unique to clergy offenders. Fones et al. (1999) studied the sexual struggles of 19 clergymen and found that they grappled with loneliness, masturbation conflicts, and a wish to be known beyond their role by others. Through a review of the available literature, Plante (1996) maintains that clergy offenders display shyness, loneliness, and passivity. Their MMPI scores illustrate the presence of depression, authority concerns, and addiction problems while Rorschach results indicated greater affect constriction than normal. Plante, et al. (1996) found that the presence of over-controlled hostility differentiated clergy offenders from non-offending priests. The authors found that the sexually abusive clergy tended to have higher verbal IQ scores than the control group. While this finding showed slight significance, it was nullified when age was taken into account. It is postulated that those priests who sexually offend may in fact be acting out their chronically over-controlled anger and aggression. Ruzicka (1997) studied 10 convicted clergy offenders (seven of which were either Catholic priests or religious brothers) and concluded that the subjects were well educated, of average to above-average intelligence, and had a limited history of substance abuse. Irons and Laaser (1994) studied a sample of 25 male clergy who had been referred for sexual misconduct, primarily with adults. They came from

backgrounds "characterized by rigidity and dysfunction with themes of abuse, had little insight into these areas, had insufficient training in the issue of transference/counter transference, had virtually no training or education concerning sexual abuse, domestic violence, addictive disease, or healthy professional boundaries, and failed to appreciate how their history of trauma affected their professional life." Most of the individuals in the sample met the diagnosis for personality disorders with features of antisocial/psychopathic traits or paranoid, sadistic, or schizoid features. The results also illustrate that narcissistic and dependant traits clustered and modeled together in an exploitive manner.

What is interesting to note is the personality functioning of non-offending priests. In a review of research conducted after *Vatican II*, Doyle (2003) cites the unpublished work of Baars and Terruwe (1971), which reveals that 20-25% of the priests had serious psychiatric difficulties while 60-70% suffered from emotional immaturity. The authors assert that some of the priests experienced psychological disturbances developed in childhood whereas others developed difficulties while in the seminary. These results are consistent with the findings of Kennedy (1972), who concluded that 6% of priests were psychologically and emotionally developed, 29% were still developing, 57% were underdeveloped, and 8% were maldeveloped. Those who were underdeveloped were more comfortable with teenagers, had few friends their own age, and used intellectualization as a coping device. As cited by Scheper-Hughes (1998), Kennedy ascertains that "The vows of poverty and obedience infantilize the adult male, making him dependant on a series of father figures at a time when they should be in control of their own lives and responsible for the lives of children and young people. The vow of celibacy takes from the adult a main vehicle for the expression of intimate social relations. The end result is chronic infantilization."

THE EVALUATION OF TREATMENT NEEDS
OF SEXUAL OFFENDERS

In order to determine the treatment needs of an individual, an exhaustive assessment must first take place. During the assessment, clinicians will examine a broad range of variables in order to identify the factors that place an individual at risk of committing sexual abuse. While there is no universally accepted assessment paradigm, mental health professionals are likely to assess risk through actuarial and clinical means.

Actuarial assessments seek to evaluate an individual through interpretation of standardized scores on various risk assessment instruments whereas clinical assessments are based upon the mental health professional's personal judgment and knowledge. Grubin (1997) argues that actuarial instruments provide little information pertaining to the causation and management of sexual offending and say nothing about the individual. While clinical assessments can provide greater detail, Grubin provides evidence that it is a paradigm essentially based upon "untested and unsound theoretical foundations." The available literature suggests that one possible solution to the shortcomings of these models is to utilize a hybrid of the two in order to render a comprehensive report.

When interpreting risk factors, it is imperative that the mental health professional specifies both the static and dynamic factors applicable to the individual. Static factors involve variables that are stable over time whereas dynamic variables are subject to change. While numerous studies have evaluated static risk factors, the literature is practically void of studies devoted to the evaluation of dynamic factors (Hanson, 1998). Hanson and Harris (2000) addressed this issue by providing evidence that dynamic factors can be broken down further into stable dynamic risk factors (those expected to remain unchanged for a substantial period of time) and acute dynamic risk factors (factors that change rapidly). In their study of 208 sexual offense recidivists and 201 non-recidivist sex offenders, the authors concluded that stable dynamic risk factors showed the greatest potential in differentiating the recidivists from the non-recidivists. Criminal lifestyle variables were found to be the strongest predictors of recidivism. However, these results must be interpreted with caution due to methodological limitations.

Once the differentiation has been made between static and dynamic factors, research has illustrated that specific factors contribute to offending behavior. Browne et al. (1998) found that in a sample of 98 sex offenders, treatment drop out was best predicted by having spent time in prison, having committed a violence-related index offense, having committed non-contact offenses, unemployment, substance abuse and delinquent/disruptive behavior during treatment. Hanson and Harris (2000) concluded that recidivists had poor social support, attitudes tolerant of sexual assault, antisocial lifestyles, poor self-management strategies and difficulties complying with supervision. The recidivists showed similarities with the non-recidivists concerning general mood, but the recidivists displayed more anger and subjective distress before reoffending. Prentky et al. (1997) provided evidence illustrating that the strongest predictors of sexual offense recidivism include the degree of sexual preoccupation with children, presence of paraphilias and the number of prior sexual offenses. The meta-analysis conducted by Hanson and Bussière (1998) illustrated that the best predictors of recidivism were sexual deviancy as measured by PPG, history of sex crimes, psychological characteristics, negative relationship with mother, failure to complete treatment and the presence of depression and anxiety.

In recent years, a variety of evaluative instruments have been developed in order to assess the risk of sex offender recidivism. Some of these instruments include the Sex Offender Risk Appraisal Guide (SORAG), Rapid Risk Assessment of Sexual Offense Recidivism (RRASOR), Static-99 and the Minnesota Sex Offender Screening Tool-Revised (MnSOSTR). General recidivism tools such as the Violence Risk Appraisal Guide (VRAG) and the Psychopathy Checklist-Revised (PCL-R) have also shown promise in determining sex offender recidivism. Barbaree et al. (2001) concluded that when these instruments were cross-validated on a sample of 215 sex offenders, the VRAG, SORAG, RRASOR and Static-99 were capable of predicting general, violent and sexual recidivism. MNSOST-R scores and guided clinical interviews were able to indicate general recidivism, but showed little sensitivity in discerning between serious or sexual reoffending. Out of all of these measures, the PCL-R, when used alone, was sensitive in predicting general and serious recidivism but was unable to predict sexual recidivism.

According to Abel et al. (1994), screening tests for pedophilia have existed in various forms for a number of years. These screening tools have included interviews, questionnaires, home visits and police reports. Institutional policies have also been developed in the hopes of managing child molestation (education/training, elimination of individual staff-child interactions), yet all of these methods suffer from various limitations. The Abel Screening Tool (1994) entails a questionnaire and slides depicting children, adolescents and adults. The individual then rates these images based upon on how sexually arousing they are. A psychophysiological hand monitor then records physiological responses. The efficacy of the instrument was established by comparing the responses of a self-selecting sample of "normal" participants to that of pedophiles that had molested pubescent males and prepubescent males/females. The Abel Screen displays high specificity (77%-98%), sensitivity (76%-91%) and efficiency (77.5%-96.9%) when applied in a setting that assumes a 5% prevalence rate of child molestation. The volumetric phallometer (sensitivity 86.7%; specificity 95%; and efficiency 94.6%) and circumferential plethysmograph (sensitivity 47.5%; specificity 100%; efficiency 97.4%) also display respectable sensitivity, specificity and efficiency, but evidence suggests that these instruments are much more intrusive, expensive and problematic than the Abel Screen.

The Violence Risk Appraisal Guide (VRAG) and the Sex Offender Risk Appraisal Guide (SORAG) are very similar in their content. Rice and Harris (1997) utilized the VRAG on a sample of 159 sex offenders in order to determine its predictive accuracy in assessing sexual recidivism. The results support use of the VRAG in predicting violence among high-risk offenders, and it performed well upon cross-validation and follow-up when the two samples were combined. The authors claim that from a practical standpoint, the focus should be placed upon predictions of future violence, not necessarily a differentiation between sexual and nonsexual violence. Nunes et al. (2002) compared the predictive accuracy of the SORAG to the revised Static-99. When the instruments were evaluated independently of one another, evidence suggests that they did not provide any unique contributions and may be redundant. However, when phallometric scores were computed in conjunction with Static-99 scores, accuracy increased. The authors propose that this effect was not observed in the use of the SORAG because it targets only general deviant arousal.

Static-99, one of the most recent and promising risk assessment instruments, consists of only static risk factors taken from the RRASOR and the Structured Anchored Clinical Judgment (SACJ). Hanson and Thornton (2000) combined the two scales in order to determine whether or not a hybrid would display greater predictive accuracy than the individual scales. These instruments were applied across four data sets, and it was concluded that while the RRASOR and the SACJ were nearly equivalent in their predictive accuracy of sexual recidivism, Static-99 showed the greatest accuracy. However, Sjöestedt and Långström (2001) provide evidence illustrating that the RRASOR and Static-99 should not be used as the only determinants of risk. Cross-validation of these two instruments on a sample of 1,400 Swedish sex offenders illustrated that both instruments displayed moderate predictive accuracy regarding short-term sexual recidivism. However, Static-99 was found to have greater predictive accuracy when it came to assessing violent recidivism, not sexual recidivism.

Social scientists have undertaken the task of developing a risk assessment instrument to screen for the presence of ephebophiles within the clergy. Musser et al. (1995) found that the Millon Clinical Multiaxial Inventory (MCMI-II) was incapable of differentiating cleric sex offenders from mentally ill clerics. Cimbolic et al. (1999) attempted to create an ephebophile scale by combining 11 items from the MCMI-II with 16 items from the MMPI-2. When tested on a sample of 165 Catholic priests undergoing treatment, the authors concluded that a combination of the two scales displayed greater accuracy and increased the internal consistency of the MCMI-II items. However, the combined scale failed to identify many of the ephebophiles in the sample. The individual scales were capable of differentiating sexually abusive clerics from mentally ill clerics, but the authors urge that a multidimensional approach be utilized when evaluating sex offenders.

MODELS OF TREATMENT FOR OFFENDERS
WHO ABUSE CHILDREN

OVERVIEW

Treatment for sexual offenders has changed drastically over the past half-century (Laws and Marshall, 2003). Even though earlier non-behavioral treatment approaches were important in establishing that child sex offenders could be engaged in treatment, John B. Watson and Alfred Kinsey were prominent in the development of behavioral treatment approaches in the early to mid-20th century. Kurt Freund developed penile plethysmography (PPG) in 1957 in response to the sexual preference hypothesis. Despite many criticisms of the PPG, it remains popular and continues to be widely used.

The earliest behavioral approaches to treatment reflected the view that deviant sexual behavior was a distorted manifestation for pedophilia and other paraphilias. Exhibitionists and child molesters were treated with electrical aversion; the modification of sexual fantasies was the target of efforts applied to sadists and voyeurs. However, limited information existed about the long-term effects on overt behavior of these techniques.

A combination of behavioral and cognitive behavioral treatments began to emerge in the late 1960s. This decade is also noted for the further development of phallometric evaluations in assessment and the associated focus on modifying sexual preferences, introduction of cognitive processes and the first description of more comprehensive treatment programs. In the early 1970s, cognitive psychology began to penetrate the field of treating child sex offenders – social skills training, assertiveness, sexual dysfunctions and gender role behavior. The first conference, at which sexual offender issues were discussed from a behavioral or cognitive behavioral perspective, was in 1975-this subsequently became known as the Association for the Treatment of Sexual Abuse (ATSA). The most significant innovation of the 1980s was the adaptation of the relapse prevention model from an addictions perspective, as well as formulating social learning theories of sexual offending behavior. Further, a wide variety of programs described targets such as sexual preferences, sex education, victim empathy, social skills, self-esteem, substance abuse, anger management and relapse prevention.

Contemporary sex offender treatment programs (both in the U.S. and internationally) employ a multidimensional approach that includes cognitive-behavioral techniques, relapse prevention strategies and psychopharmacology to treat child sex offenders. Although there is no "cure" for individuals who sexually molest children, the above treatment approaches appear to be successful with regard to reducing recidivism rates (Barbaree & Marshall, 1991; Eccles & Walker, 1998; Fisher & Beech, 1999; Wood et al., 2000; Aytes et al., 2001).

COGNITIVE-BEHAVIORAL TREATMENT AND RELAPSE PREVENTION

Cognitive-behavioral treatment has emerged as the principal type of treatment used to modify deviant sexual arousal, increase appropriate sexual desires, modify cognitive distortions and improve interpersonal coping skills. As a comprehensive structured treatment approach, cognitive-behavioral treatment integrates cognitive restructuring methods and behavioral techniques. According to Nicholaichuk and Yates (2002), this treatment approach is based on the premise that "cognitive and affective processes and behavior are linked, and that cognitions, affect, and behavior are mutually influential." Therefore, treatment typically includes targeting the following: (1) deviant sexual behavior and interests, (2) a wide range of social skills/relational deficits and (3) cognitive distortions, which permit the offender to justify, rationalize and/or minimize the offending behavior (Marshall & Barbaree, 1990; McGrath et al., 1998).

DEVIANT SEXUAL BEHAVIOR AND INTERESTS

Combinations of behavioral approaches are frequently used in an attempt to address deviant sexual behavior/interests. These approaches include covert sensitization, aversion therapy and masturbatory satiation. The objective of these approaches is to reduce deviant sexual behavior/fantasy while maintaining and/or increasing sexual arousal to appropriate stimuli (Abel et al, 1992; Becker, 1994; Marshall & Barbaree, 1990; Quinsey & Earls, 1990; McGrath et al., 1998).

Covert sensitization involves the pairing of a negative consequence (aversive event) with the sexual arousal stimulus. An example of this technique would consist of having the offender imagine a paraphilic event in order to elicit arousal, and at that point, imagine the humiliation of getting arrested for the event while at work or at home with his family.

Aversion therapy is similar to covert sensitization; however, the sexual arousal stimulus is paired with an aversive event (i.e., mild electric shock, sniffing a noxious odor such as ammonia, sniffing rotting meat or tissue or boredom/fatigue). The goal of both of these approaches is to teach the offender to associate negative consequences/events with sexually deviant arousal/thoughts.

Masturbatory satiation requires the offender to masturbate to ejaculation while verbalizing an appropriate sexual fantasy. The offender then continues to masturbate for 50-120 minutes while verbalizing deviant sexual fantasies. Since masturbation is unlikely to result in orgasm during the given time period, it is hoped that the offender will learn to associate deviant fantasy with unsatisfactory sexual activity. Furthermore, sexual gratification becomes associated with appropriate sexual behavior.

SOCIAL SKILLS/RELATIONAL DEFICITS

Cognitive-behavioral treatment seeks to enhance the offender's interpersonal functioning, which includes enhancing relationship skills, appropriate social interaction and empathy (Marshall, 1989; McFall, 1990; Seidman et al., 1994; Marshall et al., 1999). Social problem solving, conversational skills, managing social anxiety, assertiveness, conflict reso-

lution, empathy and intimacy, anger management, self-confidence and the use of intoxicants are targeted (Laws & Marshall, 2003). Educational modules, which include role-playing of specific types of social interactions, behavioral assignments and presentations on various aspects of social skills are the techniques utilized to address these social difficulties.

The inclusion of empathy-enhancement in treatment is based on the belief that the attitudes of sexual offenders toward their victims will change if they understand how the victim feels. The subsequent development of empathy will inhibit future sexual abuse since empathy is something that people learn, rather than an instinct. This is achieved in treatment through utilization of audiovisual methods and materials to demonstrate the pain associated with victimization. These methods include writing assignments, wherein the offender describes his sexual assault from the victim's view point, and the use of role-play wherein the offender plays the role of himself confronted by a peer as well as the role of his victim, respectively (Mulloy & Marshall, 1999).

COGNITIVE DISTORTIONS

Cognitive restructuring is an integral part of cognitive-behavioral treatment. As mentioned previously, child sex offenders construct internal rationalizations, excuses and cognitive distortions in order to maintain their sexually deviant behavior. Therefore, it is paramount that an offender's cognitive distortions are challenged so that he can comprehend his faulty thinking and recognize its distorted, self-serving nature (Marshall & Barbaree, 1990). Additionally, the clinician will present more socially appropriate and adaptive views, and the benefits of accepting such views are identified. This is achieved by examining the role of rationalizations, excuses and cognitive distortions from a non-sexual approach in the lives of average people, thereby normalizing the process while showing its hazards. Role-play is also utilized in which the therapist plays the role of the offender, elaborating on the cognitive distortions elicited throughout the offense process, while the offender plays various roles, including that of a victim's parent and/or an old friend, who supports his taking responsibility for his behavior and admitting his distortions.

THE RELAPSE PROCESS

The classical relapse prevention treatment approach was initially developed in response to the clinical difficulties associated with the treatment of addictive behaviors, such as alcoholism and drug dependency. This approach was subsequently altered for use in the treatment of sex offenders (Eccles & Marshall, 1999; Laws, 1999; Laws et al., 2000). In the classical model of relapse prevention, a lapse, which is perceived as a momentary indulgence but not a relapse, involved an actual reindulgence in the problem behavior (i.e., drinking). However, in the sex offender model of relapse prevention, a lapse is defined as "offense precursor activities such as deviant fantasies, purchasing pornography or cruising for potential victims," and perceived as a relapse (Laws et al., 2000). Therefore, in the treatment of sex offenders, the relapse prevention approach pays considerable attention to behaviors that might lead to sex offending as opposed to the actual reindulgence in the aberrant behavior. Relapses are regarded as the culmination of a series of events and situations through which the offender proceeds prior to offending (Eccles & Marshall, 1999).

The relapse process (sometimes called a cycle or a chain) is based on the offender's capacity to cope with high-risk situations. These situations are defined as a set of circumstances that threaten the offender's sense of self-control. In treatment, the relapse process begins with the offender declaring his intent to abstain from the deviant behavior. Self-management skills and the anticipation of adaptive coping mechanisms are reinforced. As the offender encounters high-risk situations, his self-management skills and coping mechanisms are challenged. Should the offender successfully cope with this situation, his sense of self-management survives and abstinence remains intact. Conversely, should the offender fail to successfully cope with the situation, his sense of self-management decreases, and a tendency to passively yield to the temptation of the next high-risk situation ensues. Each time the offender fails to cope with a high-risk situation, he will engage in one of the behaviors involved in his relapse process (i.e., deviant fantasy, the purchase of pornography). However, at this stage, these behaviors are considered lapses as opposed to a relapse. Several factors, subsumed by a concept referred to as the "Abstinence Violation Effect" (AVE), determine whether a lapse becomes a relapse. A major aspect of the AVE is a conflict between the offender's definition of himself as an abstainer and his recent indulgence in a behavior that is part of his relapse process (e.g., self-deprecation, the expectation to fail, his need for immediate gratification). At this stage, if the offender does not use treatment effectively to cope with his beliefs and/or urges, and to regain his confidence in self-management, a relapse is inevitable (Pithers et al., 1983; Pithers et al., 1983; Pithers, 1990; Eccles & Marshall, 1999; Marques et al., 2000; Launay, 2001). Ward and Hudson's (2000) self-regulation model expanded the original relapse prevention process to incorporate more comprehensive cognitive, affective and behavioral factors. Further, within Ward and Hudson's model, post offense factors are considered.

The self-regulation model of relapse prevention contains nine phases (life event, desire for deviant sex or activity, offense-related goals established, strategy selected, high-risk situation entered, lapse, sexual offense, post offense evaluation and attitude toward future offending) and four pathways (avoidant-passive, avoidant-active, approach-automatic and approach-explicit). According to Ward and Hudson, an important aspect of this model is that the offender can "exit the relapse process at any time by implementing appropriate coping strategies . . . move back and forth between different points in the offense chain. . . [and] remain at specific phases for a relatively long time before moving on to the next phase."

In 2002, Bickley and Beech evaluated the ability of the self-regulation model to classify sexual offenders. The sample consisted of 87 child abusers who ranged in age from 21 to 75. The majority of the participants (62%) had offended outside the family, 15% had offended inside the family, and 23% had offended both inside and outside the family. Of the participants, 36% had offended against boys, 33% against girls, and 31% had offended against both sexes. Fifty-three percent of the sample had a previous conviction for a sexual offense. The participants were classified as belonging to one of the four pathway groups identified by Ward and Hudson's self-regulation model of sexual offense process.

Results indicated that the profile of the "fixated" child molester is consistent with the self-regulation model's description of an approach pathway. In contrast, the "regressed" offender is consistent with Ward and Hudson's description of an avoidant pathway. Bickley and Beech concluded that the self-regulation model could be reliably employed in the classification of child molesters, with inter-rater agreement found in more than 80% of the sample. Furthermore, differences across the two group distinctions (i.e., avoidant vs. approach, active vs. passive) in both the psychometric and offense demographic data provided objective support for the validity of the framework.

TREATMENT EFFICACY STUDIES

Most studies conducted on treatment efficacy focus on the rate of recidivism among offenders. In studying recidivism rates, researchers compare sex offenders who have participated in treatment to those who have not. Further, they consider specific variables such as the type of treatment implemented and whether or not an offender completed the treatment process.

In a follow-up study conducted on 89 sex offenders in Ontario, Looman et al. (2000) found that those offenders who participated in treatment had a sexual recidivism rate of 23.6%, whereas the those offenders who did not participate in treatment had a sexual recidivism rate of 51.7%. Similarly, when 296 treated and 283 untreated offenders were followed for a six-year period, Nicholaichuk et al. (2002) found that convictions for new sexual offenses among treated sex offenders were 14.5% versus 33.2% for untreated offenders. Further, during the follow-up period, 48% of treated offenders remained out of prison as compared to 28.3% of untreated offenders. Time series comparisons of treated offenders and comparison samples also showed that treated offenders reoffended at significantly lower rates after ten years.

In reviewing studies pertaining to the efficacy of a particular type of treatment, there is significant evidence that cognitive-behavioral treatment has emerged as the principle type of sex offender treatment targeting deviant arousal, increasing appro-

priate sexual desires, modifying distorted thinking and improving interpersonal coping skills (Marshall & Barbaree, 1990; Marshall & Eccles, 1999; Marshall & Pithers, 1994; Becker, 1994; Hall, 1995; Abracen & Looman, 2001; Burdon et al., 2002; Nicholaichuk et al., 2002; Craig, 2003). Further, Marshall and Anderson (2000) found that cognitive-behavioral treatment programs that have an internal self-management relapse prevention component appear to be the most successful in reducing recidivism rates.

Studies of the effects of treatment completion on recidivism have also supported the effectiveness of treatment (Hall, 1995; Hanson & Bussière; Hanson, 2002). A retrospective study, conducted by McGrath et al. (2003), found that the reduction in the sexual recidivism rate among those offenders who participated in treatment was statistically, as well as clinically, significant. Treatment completers were almost six times less likely to be charged with a new sexual offense than were offenders who refused, dropped out or were terminated from treatment.

PHARMACOLOGICAL INTERVENTIONS

Physiologically, the androgen (hormone) testosterone is the major activator element of sexual desire, fantasies and behavior, and basically controls the frequency, duration and magnitude of spontaneous erections. Given this, medications used to treat deviant sexual behavior are aimed at the reduction of testosterone and/or totally suppressing testosterone action at the levels of the receptor (Rösler & Witztum, 2000). These medications include antiandrogens such as Cyproterone Acetate (CPA), Medroxyprogesterone (MPA or Depo-Provera) and Long-Acting Analogues of Gonadotropin-Releasing Hormone (GnRH) (Berlin, 1983; Bradford, 1990; Grubin, 2000; Rösler & Witztum, 2000).

Further, given the compulsive nature of pedophilic behavior, benefits with regard to the containment of such behavior have been seen through treatment with selective serotonin reuptake inhibitors (SSRIs) such as Sertraline, Fluoxetine, Fluvoxamine, Desipramine and Clomipramine.

Even though there are a number of studies on the efficacy of the above medications with regard to the treatment of sexually deviant behavior, most studies conclude that a combination of medical and psychological treatment has proven to be the most beneficial.

SEX OFFENDER TREATMENT FOR PREISTS

In 1993, Loftus and Camargo published a study evaluating their Southdown Treatment Center for clergy offenders. They found that the majority of the patients were diocesan priests; between the ages of 49 and 60 when they were first referred for treatment; ministered in parishes and educational settings; had no criminal or psychiatric history; and had no history of substance abuse. The offense data illustrates that the abuse occurred frequently (four or more times) and the ages of the victims varied. In evaluating their treatment, the authors urge that clerics should be treated no differently from other sex offenders. There has been some evidence in favor of the utilization of non-verbal psychotherapies because the patients provided evidence that there appears to be a sense of alienation from the body. Recidivism is discussed with caution since only 40 out of the 111 men in the sample are accounted for in the study. With that issue taken into account, there appears to be a recidivism rate of 10%.

The 1996 article by Warberg, Abel, and Osborn explored the uses of cognitive behavioral therapy with clergy through analyzation of case studies. Through various measures, therapists are able to teach clergy that the behavior is anything but impulsive and can be interrupted early in the process. Failure to appreciate the power differentiation between minister and parishioner, naivety about sexual issues/minimal training in transference/counter transference, and desensitization of the intimacy of the minister/laity relationship all combine to affect victim empathy. Paraphilias must also be evaluated when assessing treatment needs in order to render a comprehensive plan. The authors assert that 20% of professional sexual misconduct cases were found to have a history of prior paraphilias. It is stressed that interpersonal and emotional factors (anxiety, stress, depression, deficits in social/assertive skills, alcohol/drug abuse, personality disorders/intrapsychic conflicts) play a role in the development of professional sexual misconduct. In order to ensure the safety of the minister and congregation, those who have engaged in sexual misconduct must be thoroughly evaluated and placed under constant surveillance by staff members.

VICTIMS OF CHILD SEXUAL ABUSE BY PRIESTS

When an individual is victimized by a priest, they are not only harmed physically and emotionally, but spiritually as well. Bland (2002) illustrated that when an individual was sexually abused by a priest they displayed greater symptoms of grief, anger, a sense of meaninglessness, feelings that God had treated them unfairly, dissociation, depression, sexual problems, sleep disturbances, higher scores on the sexual abuse trauma index and higher scores on the trauma symptom checklist. Fater and Mullaney (2000) conducted a phenomenological study of seven adult male survivors of clergy abuse. The survivors experienced a bifurcated rage (self directed and outwardly directed) and spiritual distress that pervaded every aspect of their life. McLaughlin (1994) found that those abused by clergy distanced themselves from the church in order to avoid re-victimization. While it was clearly illustrated that clerical sexual abuse affected church attendance and participation, the results are inconclusive pertaining to the affect on the victim's relationship with God. These findings are also consistent with those of Rossetti (1995), who further found that female victims of sexual abuse displayed a decline in their trust of God, but the male victims did not.

The parish also experiences the ramifications of the abuse. Rossetti (1997) divided his sample into three groups: those who had no awareness of charges of sexual abuse within their parish, those who were aware that a priest in their diocese had been accused and those whose own parish priest had been charged. The results illustrated that while trust in the priesthood and church declined across the three groups, trust in God remained consistent. The study also illustrated that parishioners were more likely to distrust the Church's handling of sexual misconduct and less likely to accept Church doctrine on sexuality and morals. Rossetti concluded that North American Catholics viewed new priests in the parish with suspicion, were less willing to allow offending priests back into the parish and are less likely to believe that the modern Church is better than the Church in the past. In evaluating the effects of the sexual abuse cases in Newfoundland, Nason-Clark (1998), interviewed 24 Roman Catholic women to assess their reaction to the scandal. Each woman in the sample could remember where she was when she first heard about the story, and all recall having initially reacted to the news with disbelief and, later, with anger (19 out of the 24 participants). The anger was targeted at the offending priests, bishop, other Catholic priests, and the Church hierarchy while some were angry with the Catholics who lived in the parish where the priests were charged. They also experienced a sense of betrayal and guilt that caused them to alter their relationship with the Church. Four years after the initial interview, the author conducted a follow-up study and found that some women had made their way back to the Church while others had decided to stay away. Participants believed that the Church in Newfoundland had not recovered from the scandal, and that they will never regard priests in the same manner again.

BIBLIOGRAPHY

Abel, G.G., Becker, J.V., & Cunningham-Rathner, J. (1984). Complications, consent, and cognitions in sex between children and adults. International Journal of Law & Psychiatry, 7, 89-103.

Abel, G.G., Osborn, C., Anthony, D., & Gardos, P. (1992). Current treatments of paraphiliacs. Annual Review of Sex Research, 3, 225-290.

Abel, G.G., Lawry, S.S., Karlstrom, E., Osborn, C.A., & Gillespie, C.F. (1994). Screening tests for pedophilia. Criminal Justice and Behavior, 21, 115-131.

Abel, G.G., & Rouleau, J.L. (1990). The nature and extent of sexual assault. In W.L. Marshall, & D.R. Laws (Eds.). Handbook of Sexual Assault: Issues, Theories, and Treatment Of The Offender (pp. 9-21). New York, NY: Plenum Press.

Abel, G.G., & Rouleau, J.L. (1995). Sexual abuses. Psychiatric Clinics of North America, 18, 139-153.

Abracen, J., & Looman, J. (2001). Issues in the treatment of sexual offenders: Recent developments and directions for future research. Aggression and Violent Behavior, 1, 1-19.

Agency of Human Services—Social and Rehabilitation Services. (2003). Abuse and neglect statistics. Retrieved March 29, 2003 from http://www.state.vt.us/srs/abuse.htm.

American Psychiatric Association. Diagnostic and Statistical Manual of Mental Disorders: DSM-IV-TR. Washington, DC: American Psychiatric Association.

Arata, C. M. (1998). To tell or not to tell: Current functioning of child sexual abuse survivors who disclosed their victimization. Child Maltreatment: Journal of the American Professional Society on the Abuse of Children, 3, 63-71.

Arizona's Child Abuse InfoCeter. (2003). Child Abuse Statistics. Retrieved March 26, 2003, from http://www.ahsc.arizona.edu/ACAInfo/statistics/factsheet.htm.

Arkansas Commission on Child Abuse. (2002). Fact Sheet About Child Abuse in Arkansas. Retrieved March 26, 2003 from www.accardv.uams.edu/facts.htm.

Aytes, K.E., Olsen, S.S., Zakrajsek, T., Murray, P., Ireson, R. (2001). Cognitive/ behavioral treatment for sexual offenders: An examination of recidivism. Sexual Abuse: A Journal of Research and Treatment, 13, 223-231.

Baker, H.J., & Stoller, R.J. (1968). Sexual psychopathology in the hypogondal male. Archives of General Psychiatry, 18, 631-634.

Bancroft, J. (1978). The relationship between hormones and sexual behavior in humans. In J. Hutchinson (Ed.). The Biological Determinants of Sexual Behavior. Chichester: Wiley.

Barbaree, H.E., & Marshall, W.L. (1991). Treatment of the adult male child molester. In C.R.Bagley, & R.J. Thomlison (Eds.). Child Sexual Abuse: Critical Perspectives on Prevention, Intervention, and Treatment (pp. 217-256). Middletown, Ohio: Wall & Emerson.

Barbaree, H.E., Peacock, E.J., Cortoni, F., Marshall, W.L., & Seto, M. (1998). Ontario penitentiaries' program. In W.L. Marshall (Ed.). Sourcebook of Treatment Programs for Sexual Offenders (pp. 59-77). New York: Plenum Press.

Barbaree, H.E., Seto, M.C., Langton, C.M., & Peacock, E.J. (2001). Evaluating the predictive accuracy of six risk assessment instruments for adult sex offenders. Criminal Justice & Behavior, 28, 490-521.

Baxter, D.J., Marshall, W.L., Barbaree, H.E., Davidson, P.R., & Malcolm, P.B. (1984). Deviant sexual behavior: Differentiating sex offenders by criminal and personal history, psychometric measures, and sexual response. Criminal Justice and Behavior, 11, 477-501.

Becker, J.R. (1994). Offenders: Characteristics and treatment. The Future of Children: Sexual Abuse of Children, 4, 176-197.

Beckett, R. (1998). Community treatment in the United Kingdom. In W.L. Marshall (Ed.). Sourcebook of Treatment Programs for Sexual Offenders (pp. 133-152). New York: Plenum Press.

Beech, A.R. (1998). A psychometric typology of child abusers. International Journal of Offender Therapy and Comparative Criminology, 43, 319-339.

Beech, A., & Fisher, D. (2000). Maintaining relapse prevention skill and strategies in treated child abusers. In D. R. Laws (Ed.). Remaking Relapse Prevention with Sex Offenders (pp. 455-465). California: Sage Publications.

Benson, G.L. (1994). Sexual behavior by male clergy with adult female counselees: Systematic and situational themes. Sexual Addiction & Compulsivity, 1, 103-118.

Berlin, F.S. (1983). Sex offenders: A biomedical perspective and a status report on biomedical treatment. In J.G. Greer (Ed.). The Sexual Aggressor: Current Perspectives on Treatment (pp. 83-123). New York: Van Nostrand Reinhold.

Berliner, L., & Conte, J.R. (1995). The effects of disclosure and intervention on sexually abused children. Child Abuse & Neglect, 19, 371-384.

Berry, J. (1992). Lead Us Not Into Temptation: Catholic Priests and Sexual Abuse of Children. New York, NY: Image Books.

Bickley, J.A., Beech, A.R. (2002). An investigation of the Ward and Hudson pathways model of the sexual offense process with child abusers. Journal of Interpersonal Violence, 17, 372-393.

Bickley, J., Beech, A.R. (2001). Classifying child abusers: Its relevance to theory and clinical practice. Journal of Offender Therapy and Comparative Criminology, 45, 51-69.

Blanchard, G.T. (1991). Sexually abusive clergymen: A conceptual framework for intervention and recovery. Pastoral Psychology, 39, 237-245.

Bland, M.J. (2002). The psychological and spiritual effects of child sexual abuse when the perpetrator is a Catholic priest. Dissertation Abstracts International, 63 (4-A), P.1253.

Bolen, R., & Scannapieco, M. (1999). Prevalence of child sexual abuse: A corrective metanalysis. Social Service Review, 73, 281-313.

Boney-McCoy, S., & Finkelhor, D. (1995). Psychosocial sequelae of violent victimization in a national youth sample. Journal of Consulting and Clinical Psychology, 63, 726-736.

Bowlby, J. (1976). Human personality development in an ethological light. In G. Serban, & A. Kling (Eds.). Animal Models In Human Psychobiology (pp. 27-36). New York, NY: Plenum Press.

Boyle, P. (1991, May 20). Scouts honor: Scouting's sex abuse trail leads to 50 states. Washington Times, p. A1.

Boyle, P. (1991, May 21). Scout's honor part 2: Pedophilic preference is in a class all its own. Washington Times, p. B5.

Boyle, P. (1994). Scout's Honor: Sexual Abuse in America's Most Trusted Institution. Rocklin, CA; Prima Publishing.

Bradford, J.M.W., (1990). The antiandrogen and hormonal treatment of sex offenders. In W.L. Marshall (Ed.). Handbook of Sexual Assault: Issues, Theories, and Treatment of the Offender (pp. 297-310). New York: Plenum Press.

Bradley, A.R., & Wood, J.M. (1996). How do children tell? The disclosure process in child sexual abuse. Child Abuse & Neglect, 20, 881-891.

Brewster, A.B. (1996). Clergy sexual misconduct: The affair everyone remembers. Pastoral Psychology, 44, 353-362.

Browne, K.D., Foreman, L., & Middleton, D. (1998). Predicting treatment drop-out in sex offenders. Child Abuse Review, 7, 402-419.

Bryant, C. (1999). Psychological treatment of priest sex offenders. In T.G. Plante (Ed.). Bless Me Father For I Have Sinned: Perspectives on Sexual Abuse Committed by Roman Catholic Priests (pp. 87-110). Westport, CT: Praeger Publishers.

Burdon, W.M., & Gallagher, C.A. (2002). Coercion and sex offenders: Controlling sex-offending behavior through incapacitation and treatment. Criminal Justice and Behavior, 29, 87-109.

Burkett, E. & Brunie, F. (1993). A Gospel of Shame: Children, Sexual Abuse, and the Catholic Church. New York, NY: Penguin Books.

Camargo, R.J. (1997). Factor, cluster, and discriminant analyses of data on sexually active clergy: The molesters of youth identified. American Journal of Forensic Psychology, 15, 5-24.

Campis, L.B., Hebden-Curtis, J., & DeMaso, D.R. (1993). Developmental differences in detection and disclosure of sexual abuse. Journal of the American Academy of Child & Adolescent Psychiatry, 32, 920-924.

CANTS Allegation. (1998). Child Abuse and Neglect Statistics Annual Report—Fiscal Year 1997. Retrieved April 15, 2003 from http://www.state.il.us/dcfs/cants97_fig4.shtml.

Cardock, C. & Gardner, J.R. (1990). Psychological intervention for parishes following accusations of child sexual abuse. In S.J. Rossetti (Ed.). Slayer of the Soul: Child Sexual Abuse and the Catholic Church (pp. 123-142). Mystic, CT: Twenty-Third Publications.

Catholic League for Religious and Civil Rights. (2004). Catholic Clergy and Other Professionals.

Child Maltreatment Report. (2001). Washington DC. Published by Children's Bureau, Administration on Children, Youth and Families.

Child Protect: The Montgomery Area Children's Advocacy Center (1999). Child Abuse Statistics. Retrieved March 26, 2003, from http://www.childprotect.org/statistics.htm.

Child sexual abuse: Kentucky abuse numbers have tripled in ten years. (1997, March 24). Sex Weekly. Retrieved March 30, 2003, from Lexis-Nexis.

Child Welfare League of America. (2001) Idaho's children 2001: Child abuse and neglect. Retrieved March 26, 2003, from http://www.cwla.org/advocacy/statefactsheets/2001/idaho.htm. Child Welfare League of America. (2002). District of Columbia's children 2002: Child abuse and neglect. Retrieved March 26, 2003, from http://www.cwla.org/advocacy/statefactsheets/2002/dc.htm.

Child Welfare League of America. (2003). Hawaii's children 2003. Retrieved March 29, 2003 from http://www.cwla.org/advocacy/statefactsheets/2003/hawaii.pdf.

Child Welfare League of America. (2003). Illinois's children 2003. Retrieved March 29, 2003 from http://www.cwla.org/advocacy/statefactssheets/illinois.pdf.

Child Welfare League of America. (2003). Iowa's Children 2003. Retrieved March 29, 2003 from http://www.cwla.org/advocacy/statefactssheets/iowa.pdf.

Child Welfare League of America. (2003). Maine's Children 2003. Retrieved March 30, 2003 from http://www.cwla.org/advocacy/statefactsheets/maine.pdf.

Child Welfare League of America. (2003). Delaware's children 2003. Retrieved March 29, 2003 from http://www.cwla.org.

Child Welfare League of America. (n.d.). New Jersey's Children. Retrieved May 20, 2003 from http://www.cwla.org/advocacy/statefact sheets/2003/newjersey.pdf.

Child Welfare League of America. (2000). Connecticut's children 2001: Child abuse and neglect. Retrieved March 26, 2003, from http://www.cwla.org/advocacy/statefact sheets/2001/connecticut.htm.

Child Welfare League of America. (2001) Alabama's Children 2001. Retrieved March 26, 2003, from http://www.cwla.org/advocacy/state factsheets/2001/alabama.htm.

Children Now. (2001). California report card 2001: Factors for School Success. Retrieved from http://www.childrennow.org/california/rc-2001/reportcard-2001.htm.

Children's Action Alliance (2002). Arizona's abused and neglected children: Child Protective Services (CPS) reports and response. Retrieved March 26, 2003, from http://www.azchildren.org/caa/mainpages/FactSheets&Links/facts_aboutabuse_andneglect.asp.

Cimbolic, P., Wise, R.A., Rossetti, S., & Safer, M. (1999). Development of a combined objective ephebophile scale. Sexual Addiction & Compulsivity, 6, 253-266.

Colorado Coalition Against Sexual Assault. (2003). Toward Healing and Justice: A Handbook for Survivors of Sexual Assault. Denver, CO: Colorado Coalition Against Sexual Assault.

Conte, J.R. (1991). The nature of sexual offenses against children. In C.R. Hollin, & K. Howells (Eds.). Clinical Approaches to Sex Offenders and Their Victims (pp. 11-34). Oxford, England: John Wiley & Sons.

CPS Watch (2001). Florida foster care statistics. Retrieved March 26, 2003, from http://www.cpswatch.com/oldsite/stats/states/FL.htm.

CPS Watch. (n.d.) Kansas foster care statistics. Retrieved April 2003 from http://www.cpswatch.com/oldsite/stats/states/ KS.htm.

CPS Watch. (n.d.). Idaho foster care statistics. Retrieved March 26, 2003, from http://www.cpswatch.com/oldsite/stats/states/ID.htm.

Craig, L.A., Browne, K.D., Stringer, I. (2003). Treatment and sexual offense recidivism. Trauma, Violence, & Abuse, 4, 70-89.

Danni, K.A., Hampe, G.D. (2002). An analysis of predictors of child sex offender types using pre-sentence investigation reports. International Journal of Offender Therapy and Comparative Criminology, 44, 490-504.

De Fuentes, N. (1999). Hear our cries: Victim-survivors of clergy sexual misconduct. In T.G. Plante (Ed.). Bless Me Father For I Have Sinned: Perspectives on Sexual Abuse Committed by Roman Catholic Priests (pp. 135-167). Westport, CT: Praeger Publishers.

Department of Health and Human Services, Division of Family and Youth Services. (1994). Fiscal Year 1993 Annual Report. Division of Family and Youth Services.

Department of Health and Human Services—Division of Family and Youth Services. (1996). Fiscal Year 1993 Annual Report. Division of Family and Youth Services.

Devoe, E.R., & Coulborn-Faller, K. (1999). The characteristics of disclosure among children who may have been sexually abused. Child Maltreatment: Journal of the American Professional Society on the Abuse of Children, 4, 217-227.

Doyle, T.P. (2003). Roman Catholic clericalism, religious duress, and clergy sexual abuse. Pastoral Psychology, 51, 189-231.

Drake, Brett. (1996). Predictors of preventive services provisions among unsubstantiated cases. Child Maltreatment, 1, 168-175.

Dunebrook. (2000). Child abuse statistics. Retrieved April, 2003 from http://www.dune brook.org/stats.html. Eccles, A., & Marshall, W.L. (1999). Relapse prevention. In W.L. Marshall (Ed.). The Development of Cognitive Behavioral Treatment of Sex Offenders (pp. 127-146). England: John Wiley & Sons, Ltd.

Eccles, A., & Walker, W. (1998). Community-based treatment with sex offenders. In W.L. Marshall (Ed.). Sourcebook of Treatment Programs for Sexual Offenders (pp. 93-103). New York: Plenum Press.

Elliott, M., Browne, K., & Kilcoyne, J. (1995). Child sexual abuse prevention: What offenders tell us. Child Abuse & Neglect, 19, 579-594.

Fater, K. & Mullaney, J. (2000). The lived experiences of adult male survivors who allege childhood sexual abuse by clergy. Issues in Mental Health Nursing, 21, 281-295.

Ferder, F. & Heagle, J. (1995). Clergy pedophiles and ministry: Another perspective. America, 173, 6-11.

Fernandez, Y.M., & Marshall, W.L. (2000). Contextual issues in relapse prevention treatment. In D.R. Laws (Ed.). Remaking Relapse Prevention with Sex Offenders (pp. 225-235). California: Sage Publications.

Finkelhor, D. (1984). Child Sexual Abuse: New Theory and Research. New York: The Free Press.

Finkelhor, D., Hotaling, G., Lewis, I.A., & Smith, C., (1990). Sexual abuse in a national survey of adult men and women: prevalence, characteristics, and risk factors. Child Abuse & Neglect, 14, 19-28.

Finkelhor, D. & Ormrod, R. (2001). Crimes against children by babysitters. Juvenile Justice Bulletin, September 2001.

Finkelhor, D., Williams, L.M., & Burns, N. (1988). Nursery Crimes: Sexual Abuse in Day Care. Newbury Park, CA; Sage Publication.

Fisher, D., & Beech, A.R. (1999). Current practice in Britain with sexual offenders. Journal of Interpersonal Violence, 14, 240-256.

Flakenhain, M.A. et al. (1999). Cluster analysis of child sexual offenders: A validation with Roman Catholic priests and Brothers. Sexual Addiction & Compulsivity, 6, 317-336.

Fones, C.S.L., Levine, S.B., Althof, S.E., & Risen, C.B. (1999). The sexual struggles of 23 clergymen: A follow-up study. Journal of Sex & Marital Therapy, 25, 183-195.

Fordham Institute for Innovation in Social Policy. (1999). Social state of Connecticut '99: Part III a Closer Look: A Social Profile of Connecticut. Retrieved March 26, 2003, from http://www. cga.state.ct.us/coc/soc_index00/part_III.html.

Francis, P.C. & Turner, N.R. (1995). Sexual misconduct within the Christian Church: Who are the perpetrators and those they victimize? Counseling & Values, 39, 218-228.

Freeman-Longo, R.E. (1996). Feel good legislation: Prevention or calamity. Child Abuse & Neglect, 20, 95-101.

Freund, K., McKnight, K., Langevin, R., Cibiri, S. (1972). The female child as surrogate object. Archives of Sexual Behavior, 2, 119–133.

Gebhard, P.H., & Gagnon, J.H. (1964). Male sex offenders against very young children. American Journal of Psychiatry, 121, 576-579.

Goetz, D. (1992). Is the pastor's family safe at home? Leadership, 13, 38-44.

Gonsiorek, J.C. (1999). Forensic psychological evaluations in clergy abuse. In T.G. Plante (Ed.). Bless Me Father For I Have Sinned: Perspectives on Sexual Abuse Committed by Roman Catholic Priests (pp. 27-57). Westport, CT: Praeger Publishers.

Goodman-Brown, T.B., Edelstein, R.S., & Goodman, G.S. (2003). Why children tell: A model of children's disclosure of sexual abuse. Child Abuse & Neglect, 27, 525-540.

Goodstein, L. (2003, January). Decades of damage; Trail of pain in Church crisis leads to nearly every diocese. New York Times, p.1.

Gordon, A., & Hover, G. (1998). The Twin Rivers Sex Offender Treatment Program. In W.L. Marshall (Ed.). Sourcebook of Treatment Programs for Sexual Offenders (pp. 3-15). New York: Plenum Press.

Gries, L.T., Goh, D.S., & Cavanaugh, J. (1996). Factors associated with disclosure during child sexual abuse assessment. Journal of Child Sexual Abuse, 5, 1-20.

Groth, A.N., Hobson, W.F. and Gary, T.S. (1982). The child molester: Clinical observations. In J. Conte and D.A. Shore (Eds.). Social Work and Child Sexual Abuse. New York; Haworth.

Grubin, D. (1997). Inferring predictors of risk: Sex offenders. International Review of Psychiatry, 9, 225-231.

Grubin, D. (1999). Actuarial and clinical assessment of risk in sex offenders. Journal of Interpersonal Violence, 14, 331-343.

Grubin, D. (2000). Complementing relapse prevention with medical intervention. In D.R. Laws (Ed.). Remaking Relapse Prevention with Sex Offenders (pp. 201-212). California: Sage Publications.

Hall, G.C.N. (1995). Sexual offender recidivism revisited: A meta-analysis of recent treatment studies. Journal of Consulting and Clinical Psychology, 63, 802-809.

Hands, D.R. (2002). Beyond the cloister- Shamed sexuality in the formation of the sex-offending clergy. In B.K. Schwartz & H.R. Cellini (Eds.). The Sex Offender (pp. 29-1-29-8). Kingston, NJ: Civic Research Institute.

Hanson, R.F., Saunders, H.S., Saunders, B.E., Kilpatrick, D.G., & Best, C. (1999). Factors related to the reporting of childhood rape. Child Abuse & Neglect, 23, 559-569.

Hanson, R.K. (1998). What do we know about sex offender risk assessment? Psychology, Public Policy, & Law, 4, 50-72.

Hanson, R.K. (2000). What is so special about relapse prevention? In D.R. Laws (Ed.), Remaking Relapse Prevention with Sex Offenders (pp. 27-38). California: Sage Publications.

Hanson, R.K., Gizzarelli, R., & Scott, H. (1994). The attitudes of incest offenders: Sexual entitlement and acceptance of sex with children. Criminal Justice & Behavior, 21, 187-202.

Hanson, R.K., Gordon, A., Harris, A.J.R., Marques, J.K., Murphy, W., Quinsey, V.L., Seto, M.C. (2002). First report of the collaborative outcome data project on the effectiveness of psychological treatment for sex offenders. Sexual Abuse: A Journal of Research and Treatment, 14, 169-194.

Hanson, R. K., & Bussière, M.T. (1998). Predicting relapse: A meta-analysis of sexual offender recidivism studies. Journal of Consulting and Clinical Psychology, 66, 348-362.

Hanson, R. K., Steffy, R. A., & Gauthier, R. (1993). Long-term recidivism of child molesters. Journal of Consulting and Clinical Psychology, 61.

Hanson, R.K. & Harris, A.J.R. (2000). Where should we intervene? Dynamic predictors of sexual offense recidivism. Criminal Justice and Behavior, 27, 6-35.

Hanson, R.K. & Harris, A.J.R. (2001). A structures approach to evaluating change among sexual offenders. Sexual Abuse: A Journal of Research and Treatment, 13, 105-122.

Hanson, R.K. & Thornton, D. (2000). Improving risk assessments for sex offenders: A comparison of three actuarial scales. Law and Human Behavior, 24, 119-136.

Hanson, R.K., Scott, H., Steffy, R.A. (1995). A comparison of child molesters and nonsexual criminals: Risk predictors and long-term recidivism. Journal of Research in Crime and Delinquency, 32, 325-337.

Haywood, T.W., Grossman, L.S., & Kravitz, H.M. (1994). Profiling psychological distortions in alleged child molesters. Psychological Reports, 75, 915-927.

Haywood T.W., Kravitz, H.M., Grossman, L.S., Wasyliw, O.E., & Hardy, D.W. (1996). Psychological aspects of sexual functioning among cleric and noncleric alleged sex offenders. Child Abuse & Neglect, 20, 527-536.

Haywood, T.W. & Green, J. (2000). Cleric serial offenders: Clinical characteristics and treatment approaches. In L.B. Schlesinger (Ed.). Serial Offenders: Current Thoughts, Recent Findings (pp. 247-262). Boca Raton, FL: CRC Press.

Haywood, T.W., Kravitz, H.M., Wasyliw, O.E., Goldberg, J., & Cavanaugh, J.L. (1996). Cycle of abuse and psychopathology in cleric and noncleric molesters of children and adolescents. Child Abuse & Neglect, 20, 1233-1243.

Health and Human Services. (2003). Retrieved March 29, 2003 from http://www.acf.hhs.gov/programs/cb/publications/cwo99/state data.htm.

Holmes, R.M. and Holmes, S.T. (1996). Profiling Violent Crimes: An Investigative Tool. Thousand Oaks, CA; Sage Publications.

Holmes, S.T. & Holmes, R.M. (2002). Sex Crimes: Pattern and Behavior. California: Sage Publications, Inc.

Hopkins, N.M. (1991). Congregational intervention when the pastor has committed sexual misconduct. Pastoral Psychology, 39, 247-255.

Hucker, S.J., & Bain, J. (1990). Androgenic hormones and sexual assault. In W.L. Marshall (Ed.). Handbook of Sexual Assault: Issues, Theories, and Treatment of the Offender (pp. 93-102). New York: Plenum Press.

Hudson, P.E. (1997). Spirituality as a component in a treatment program for sexually addicted Roman Catholic clergy. Counseling & Values, 41, 174-183.

Hudson, S.M., & Ward, T. (2000). Relapse prevention: Assessment and treatment implications. In D.R. Laws (Ed.). Remaking Relapse Prevention with Sex Offenders (pp. 102-121). California: Sage Publications.

Hudson, S.M., Wales, D.S., & Ward, T. (1998). Kia Marama: A Treatment Program for Child Molesters in New Zealand. In W.L. Marshall (Ed.). Sourcebook of Treatment Programs for Sexual Offenders (pp. 17-28). New York: Plenum Press.

Hughes, A.A. (1996). Sexual abuse: Helping the Church recognize and respond to victims. Pastoral Psychology, 45, 119-127.

Irons, R. & Laaser, M. (1994). The abduction of fidelity: Sexual exploitation by clergy-Experience with inpatient assessment. Sexual Addiction & Compulsivity, 1, 119-129.

Isley, P.J. & Isley, P. (1990). The sexual abuse of male children by Church personnel: Intervention and prevention. Pastoral Psychology, 39, 85-99.

Isley, P.J. (1997). Child sexual abuse and the Catholic Church: An historical and contemporary review. Pastoral Psychology, 45, 277-299.

Jenkins, P. (1995). Clergy sexual abuse: The symbolic politics of a social problem. In J. Best (Ed.). Images of Issues (pp. 105-130, second edition). New York, NY: Aldine De Gruyter.

Jenkins, P. (1996). Pedophiles and Priests: Anatomy of a Contemporary Crisis. Bridgewater, NJ: Replica Books.

Jenkins, P. (1998). Creating a culture of clergy deviance. In A. Shupe (Ed.). Wolves within the Fold: Religious Leadership and Abuses of Power (pp. 118-132). New Brunswick, NJ: Rutgers University Press.

John Jay College (2004). The Nature and Scope of Sexual Abuse of Minors by Catholic Priests and Deacons in the United States, 1950-2002. Washington, DC; United States Conference of Catholic Bishops.

Kahl, E., Runyan, D.K., & Fredrickson, D.D. (2003). Predictors of disclosure during medical evaluations for suspected sexual abuse. Journal of Child Sexual Abuse, 6, 133-142.

Kear-Colwell, J., & Boer, D. P. (2000). The treatment of pedophiles: Clinical experience and the implications of recent research. International Journal of Offender Therapy and Comparative Criminology, 44, 593-605.

Keary, K., & Fitzpatrick, C. (1994). Children's disclosure of sexual abuse during formal investigation. Child Abuse & Neglect, 18, 543-548.

Kelly, A.F. (1998). Clergy offenders. In W.L. Marshall (Ed.). Sourcebook of Treatment Programs for Sexual Offenders (pp. 303-318). New York, NY: Plenum Press.

Kennedy, E.C., Heckler, V.J., & Kobler, F.J. (1977). Clinical assessment of a profession: Roman Catholic clergymen. Journal of Clinical Psychology, 33, 120-128.

Knight, R.A., & Prentky, R.A. (1990). Classifying sexual offenders: The development and corroboration of taxonomic models. In W. L. Marshall (Ed.). Handbook of Sexual Assault: Issues, Theories, and Treatment of the Offender (pp. 23-52). New York: Plenum Press.

Knight, R. A., Carter, D. L., Prentky, R. A. (1989). A system for the classification of child molesters: Reliability and application. Journal of Interpersonal Violence, 4, 3-22.

Krebs, T. (1998). Church structures that facilitate pedophilia among Roman Catholic clergy. In A. Shupe (Ed.). Wolves Within the Fold: Religious Leadership and Abuses of Power (pp. 67-84). New Brunswick, NJ: Rutgers University Press.

Laaser, M.R. (1991). Sexual addiction and the clergy. Pastoral Psychology, 39, 213-235.

Lamb, S., & Edgar-Smith, S. (1994). Aspects of disclosure: Mediators of outcome of childhood sexual abuse. Journal of Interpersonal Violence, 9, 307-326.

Langan, P. A, & Harlow, C. W. (1992). Child Rape Victims, 1992. Washington, DC: U.S. Department of Justice, Office of Justice Programs, Bureau of Justice Statistics.

Langevin, R., Curnoe, S., & Bain, J. (2000). A study of clerics who commit sexual offenses: Are they different from other sex offenders? Child Abuse & Neglect, 24, 535-545.

Launay, G. (2001). Relapse prevention with sex offenders: practice, theory and research. Criminal Behavior and Mental Health, 11, 38-54.

Laws, D.R. (1999). Relapse prevention: The state of the art. Journal of Interpersonal Violence, 14, 285-302.

Laws, D.R., & Marshall, W.L. (1990). A conditioning theory of the etiology and maintenance of deviant sexual preference and behavior. In W.L. Marshall (Ed.). Handbook of Sexual Assault: Issues, Theories, and Treatment of the Offender (pp. 209-229). New York: Plenum Press.

Laws, D.R., Hanson, R.K., Osborn, C.A., & Greenbaum, P.E. (2000). Classification of child molesters by plethysmographic assessment of sexual arousal and a self-report measure of sexual preference. Journal of Interpersonal Violence, 15, 1297-1312.

Laws, D.R., Hudson, S.M., & Ward (2000). The original model of relapse prevention with sex offenders: Promises unfulfilled. In D.R. Laws (Ed.). Remaking Relapse Prevention with Sex Offenders (pp. 3-24). California: Sage Publications.

Laws, D.R., Marshall, W.L, (2003). A brief history of behavioral and cognitive behavioral approaches to sex offenders: Part 1. Early developments. Sexual Abuse: A Journal of Research and Treatment, 15, 75-92.

Laws, D.R., Marshall, W.L, (2003). A brief history of behavioral and cognitive behavioral approaches to sex offenders: Part 2. The modern era. Sexual Abuse: A Journal of Research and Treatment, 15, 93-120.

Lawson, L., & Chaffin, M. (1992). False negatives in sexual abuse disclosure interviews: Incidence and influence of caretaker's belief in abuse in cases of accidental abuse discovery by diagnosis of STD. Journal of Interpersonal Violence, 7, 532-542.

Lin, J.M., Maxwell, S.R., & Barclay, A.M. (2000). The proportions of different types of sex offenders and the degree of difficulty in treating them: A comparison of perceptions by clinicians in Taiwan and in Michigan. International Journal of Offender Therapy and Comparative Criminology, 44, 222-231.

Loftus, J.A. & Camargo, R.J. (1993). Treating the clergy. Annals of Sex Research, 6, 287-303.

Longo, R.E. (2002). A holistic/integrated approach to treating sex offenders. In B. Schwartz (Ed.). The Sex Offender: Current Treatment Modalities and Systems Issues, Vol. IV (2). New Jersey: Civic Research Institute, Inc.

Looman, J., Abracen, J., & Nicholaichuk, T.P. (2000). Recidivism among treated sexual offenders and matched controls: data from the Regional Treatment Centre (Ontario). Journal of Interpersonal Violence, 15, 279-290.

Looman, J., Gauthier, C., Boer, D. (2001). Replication of the Massachusetts Treatment Center child molester typology in a Canadian sample. Journal of Interpersonal Violence, 16, 753-767.

Lothstein, L. (1999). Neuropsychological findings in clergy who sexually abuse. In T.G. Plante (Ed.). Bless Me Father For I Have Sinned: Perspectives on Sexual Abuse Committed by Roman Catholic Priests (pp. 59-85). Westport, CT: Praeger Publishers.

Louisiana Children's Trust Fund. (n.d.). What is child abuse and neglect? Retrieved April 2003 from http://www.lctf.org/abuse%20and%20 neglect%20in%20louisiana.htm.

Luepker, E.T. (1999). Effects of practitioners' sexual misconduct: a follow-up study. Journal of the American Academy of Psychiatry & the Law, 27, 51-63.

MacMillan H.L., Fleming J.E., Trocmé N., Boyle M.H., Wong M., Racine Y.A., et al. (1997). Prevalence of child physical and sexual abuse in the community: results from the Ontario Health Supplement. JAMA, 278, 131-5.

Maletzky, B.M. (2002). A 25-year follow-up of cognitive-behavioral therapy with 7,275 sexual offenders. Behavior Modification, 26, 123-148.

Mann, R.E., & Thornton, D. (1998). The evolution of a multisite sexual offender treatment program. In Marshall, W.L. (Ed.). Sourcebook of Treatment Programs for Sexual Offenders (pp. 47-57). New York: Plenum Press.

Manuel, G. (1999). Beginning an intervention in clergy sexual abuse. In T.G. Plante (Ed). Bless Me Father For I Have Sinned: Perspectives on Sexual Abuse Committed by Roman Catholic Priests (pp. 22-26). Westport, CT: Praeger Publishers.

Marques, J.K. (1999). How to answer the question "Does sex offender treatment work?" Journal of Interpersonal Violence, 14, 437-451.

Marques, J.K., Day, D.M., & Nelson, C. (1994). Effects of cognitive-behavioral treatment on sex offender recidivism: Preliminary results of a longitudinal study. Criminal Justice & Behavior, 21, 28-54.

Marques, J.K., Nelson, C., Alarcon, J.M., & Day, D.M. (2000). Prevention relapse in sex offenders: what we learned from SOTEP's experimental treatment program. In D.R. Laws (Ed.). Remaking Relapse Prevention with Sex Offenders (pp. 321-340). California: Sage Publications.

Marques, J., Nelson, C., & West, M.A. (1994). The relationship between treatment goals and recidivism among child molesters. Behavior Research & Therapy, 32, 577-588.

Marshall, W.L. (1989). Intimacy, loneliness and sexual offenders. Behavior Research Therapy, 27, 491-503.

Marshall, W.L. (1999). Current status of North American assessment and treatment programs for sexual offenders. Journal of Interpersonal Violence, 14, 221-239.

Marshall, W.L. (1996). Assessment, treatment, and theorizing about sex offenders: Developments during the past twenty years and future directions. Criminal Justice and Behavior, 23, 162-199.

Marshall, W.L. (1993). The treatment of sex offenders: What does the outcome data tell us? A reply to Quinsey, Harris, Rice and Lalumiere. Journal of Interpersonal Violence, 8, 524-530.

Marshall, W.L., Anderson, D., & Fernandez, Y. (1999). Cognitive Behavioral Treatment of Sexual Offenders. England: John Wiley & Sons, Ltd.

Marshall, W.L., & Anderson, D. (2000). Do relapse prevention components enhance treatment effectiveness? In D. R. Laws (Ed.). Remaking Relapse Prevention with Sex Offenders (pp. 39-55). California: Sage Publications.

Marshall, W.L., & Barbaree, H.E. (1990). An integrated theory of the etiology of sexual offending. In W.L. Marshall (Ed.). Handbook of Sexual Assault: Issues, Theories, and Treatment of the Offender (pp. 257-275). New York: Plenum Press.

Marshall, W.L., & Barbaree, H.E. (1990). Outcome of comprehensive cognitive-behavioral treatment programs. In W.L. Marshall (Eds.). Handbook of Sexual Assault: Issues, Theories, and Treatment of the Offender (pp. 363-385). New York: Plenum Press.

Marshall, W.L., Barbaree, H.E., & Eccles, A. (1991). Early onset and deviant sexuality in child molesters. Journal of Interpersonal Violence, 6, 323-336.

Marshall, W.L., & Christie, M.M. (1981). Pedophilia and aggression. Criminal Justice and Behavior, 8, 145-158.

Marshall, W.L., & Eccles, A. (1991). Issues in clinical practice with sex offenders. Journal of Interpersonal Violence, 6, 68-93.

Marshall, W.L., & Eccles, A. (1996). Cognitive-behavioral treatment of sex offenders. In V.B. Van Hasselt, & M. Hersen (Eds.). Sourcebook of Psychological Treatment Manuals for Adult Disorders (pp. 295-332).

Marshall, L.E. & Marshall, W.L. (2002). The role of attachment in sexual offending: An examination of preoccupied-attachment-style offending behavior. In B. Schwartz (Ed.). The Sex Offender: Current Treatment Modalities and Systems Issues (pp. 1-7).

Marshall, W.L., Jones, R., Ward, T., Johnston, P., & Barbaree, H. (1991). Treatment outcome with sex offenders. Clinical Psychology Review, 11, 465-485.

Marshall, W.L., & Pithers, W.D. (1994). A Reconsideration of treatment outcome with sex offenders. Criminal Justice and Behavior, 21, 10-27.

Matson, S. (2002). Sex offender treatment: a critical management tool. Corrections Today, 64, 114-118.

McCall, D. (2002). Sex and the clergy. Sexual Addiction & Compulsivity, 9, 89-95.

McFall, R. (1990). The enhancement of social skills. In W. L. Marshall (Ed.), Handbook of Sexual Assault: Issues, Theories, and Treatment of the Offender (pp. 311-327). New York: Plenum Press.

McGlone, G.J. (2001). Sexually offending and non-offending Roman Catholic priests: Characterization and analysis. Dissertation Abstracts International, 62 (1-B), pp. 557.

McGrath, R.J., Cumming, G., Livingston, J. A., & Hoke, S. E. (2003). Outcome of a treatment program for adult sex offenders: From prison to community. Journal of Interpersonal Violence, 18, 3-17.

McGrath, R.J., Hoke, S.E., Vojtisek, J.E. (1998). Cognitive-behavioral treatment of sex offenders: A treatment comparison and long-term follow-up study. Criminal Justice and Behavior, 25, 203-225.

McLaughlin, B.R. (1994). Devastated spirituality: The impact of clergy sexual abuse on the survivor's relationship with God and the Church. Sexual Addiction & Compulsivity, 1, 145-158.

Minnesota Student Survey 1991: A Report on Special Populations. (1991). St. Paul: Minnesota Department of Education.

Money, J. (1970). Use of an androgen-depleting hormone in the treatment of male sex offenders. Journal of Sex Research, 6, 165-172.

Moore, K.A., Nord, C.W., & Peterson, J.L. (1989). Nonvoluntary sexual activity among adolescents. Family Planning Perspectives, 21, 110-114.

Mulloy, R. & Marshall, W.L. (1999). Social Functioning. In W.L. Marshall, D. Anderson, & Y. Fernandez (Eds.). Cognitive Behavioral Treatment of Sexual Offenders (pp. 93-110). England: John Wiley & Sons, Ltd.

Musser, P., Cimbolic, P., & Rossetti, S. (1995). Ephebophilia and the MCMI-II. Sexual Addiction & Compulsivity, 2, 214-222.

Myer Hopkins, N. (1999). The use and limitations of various models for understanding clergy sexual misconduct: The impact on the congregation. Journal of Sex Education and Therapy, 24, 268-276.

Nason-Clark, N. (1998). The impact of abuses of clergy trust on female congregants' faith and practice. In A. Shupe (Ed.). Wolves Within the Fold: Religious Leadership and Abuses of Power (pp.85-100). New Brunswick, NJ: Rutgers University Press.

Nicholaichuk, T., Gordon, A., Gu, D., Wong, S. (2002). Outcome of an institutional sexual offender treatment program: A comparison between treated and matched untreated offenders. Sexual Abuse: A Journal of Research and Treatment, 12, 139-153.

Nicholaichuk, T., & Yates, P. (2002). Treatment efficacy: outcomes of the clearwater sex offender program. In B. Schwartz (Ed.). The Sex Offender: Current Treatment Modalities and Systems Issues (Vol. 4). New Jersey: Civic Research Institute, Inc.

Nunes et al. (2002). A comparison of modified versions of the Static-99 and the Sex Offender Risk Appraisal Guide. Sexual Abuse: A Journal of Research and Treatment, 14, 253-269.

Oates, R. Kim. (2000). Erroneous concerns about child sexual abuse. Child Abuse and Neglect, 24, 149-157.

Pennsylvania Department of Public Welfare. (n.d.). Office of children, youth and families. Retrieved May 21, 2003 from www.dpw.state.pa.us/ocyf/ocyfca.asp.

Pirke, K.M., Kockott, G., & Dittmar, F. (1974). Psychosexual stimulation and plasma testosterone in man. Archives of Sexual Behavior, 3, 577-584.

Pithers, W.D. (1990). Relapse prevention with sexual aggressors: A method for maintaining therapeutic gain and enhancing external supervision. In W.L. Marshall (Ed.). Handbook of Sexual Assault: Issues, Theories, and Treatment of the Offender (pp. 343-361). New York: Plenum Press.

Pithers, W.D., Kashima, K.M., Cumming, G.F., Beal, L.S., Buell, M.M. (1988). Relapse prevention of sexual aggression. Annals of the New York Academy of Sciences, 528, 244-260.

Pithers, W.D., Marques, J.K., Gibat, C.C., Marlatt, G.A. (1983). Relapse prevention with sexual aggressives: A self-control model of treatment and maintenance change. In J.G. Greer (Eds.). The Sexual Aggressor: Current Perspectives on Treatment (pp. 214-239). New York: Van Nostrand Reinhold.

Placa, A.J. (1990). Legal aspects of the sexual abuse of children. In S.J. Rossetti (Ed.). Slayer of the Soul: Child Sexual Abuse and the Catholic Church (pp. 149-173). Mystic, CT: Twenty-Third Publications.

Plante, T.G. (1996). Catholic Priests who sexually abuse minors: Why do we hear so much yet know so little? Pastoral Psychology, 44, 305-310.

Plante, T.G. (2003). After the earthquake. America, p. 11.

Plante, T.G., Manuel, G., & Bryant, C. (1996). Personality and cognitive functioning among hospitalized sexual offending Roman Catholic priests. Pastoral Psychology, 45, 129-139.

Polizzi, D.M., MacKenzie, D.L., & Hickman, L.J. (1999). What works in adult sex offender treatment? A review of prison-and non prison-based treatment programs. International Journal of Offender Therapy and Comparative Criminology, 43, 357-374.

Prentky, R.A., Knight, R.A., Lee, A.F. (1997). Child sexual molestation: Research issues. National Institute of Justice Research Report (June). U.S. Department of Justice.

Prentky, R.A., Knight, R.A., & Lees, A.F. (1997). Risk factors associated with recidivism among extrafamilial child molesters. Journal of Consulting and Clinical Psychology, 65, 141-149.

Prentky, R.A., Lee, A.F.S, Knight, R.A., & Cerce, D. (1997). Recidivism rates among child molesters and rapists: A methodological analysis. Law and Human Behavior, 31, 635-659.

Prevent Child Abuse Georgia. (n.d.). Statistics. Retrieved March 26, 2003, from http://www.preventchildabusega.org/html/statistics.html.

Prevent Child Abuse. (2003). Wisconsin - Prevalence of Child Abuse. Retrieved March 29, 2003 from http://www.preventchildabusewi.org/prevalence.htm.

Proulx, J., Tardif, M., Lamoureux, B., Lussier, P., (2000). How does recidivism risk assessment predict survival? In D.R. Laws, S.M. Hudson, & T. Ward (Eds.). Remaking Relapse Prevention With Sex Offenders: A Sourcebook (pp. 466-484). Thousand Oaks, CA; Sage Publications, Inc.

Pryor, D.W. (1996). Unspeakable Acts: Why Men Sexually Abuse Children. New York: New York University Press.

Pullen, E. (1998). An advocacy group for victims of clerical sexual abuse. In A. Shupe (Ed.). Wolves within the Fold: Religious Leadership and Abuses of Power (pp. 67-84). New Brunswick, NJ: Rutgers University Press.

Quinsey, V.L., & Earls, C.M. (1990). The modification of sexual preferences. In W.L. Marshall (Ed.). Handbook of Sexual Assault: Issues, Theories, and Treatment of the Offender (pp. 279-293). New York: Plenum Press.

Quinsey, V.L., Harris, G.T., Rice, M.E., & Lalumiere, M.L., (1993). Assessing treatment efficacy in outcome studies of sex offenders. Journal of Interpersonal Violence, 8, 512-523.

Quinsey, V.L., Khanna, A., Malcolm, P.B. (1998). A retrospective evaluation of the regional treatment centre sex offender treatment program. Journal of Interpersonal Violence, 13, 621-644.

Quinsey, V.L., Steinman, C.M., & Bergersen, S.G. (1975). Penile circumference, skin conductance, and ranking responses of child molesters and "normals" to sexual and nonsexual visual stimuli. Behavior Therapy, 6, 213-219.

Rada, R.T., Laws, D.R., & Kellner, R. (1976). Plasma testosterone levels in the rapist. Psychosomatic Medicine, 38, 257-268.

Reinhart, M.A. (1987). Sexually abused boys. Child Abuse & Neglect, 11, 229-235.

Rice, M.E. & Harris, G.T. (1997). Cross-validation and extension of the Violence Risk Appraisal Guide for child molesters and rapists. Law and Human Behavior, 21, 231-241.

Rice, M.E., Quinsey, V.L., Harris, G.T. (1991). Sexual recidivism among child molesters released from a maximum-security psychiatric institution. Journal of Consulting and Clinical Psychology, 59, 381-386.

RID Alaska. (2000). Family Service Child Reports of Harm by Region, Fiscal Year 2000. Retrieved March 1, 2003 from www.alaska.net/~rosenbau/Stat.html.

Rigali, N.J. (1994). Church responses to pedophilia. Theological Studies, 55, 124-140.

Roberts, C.F., Doren, D.M., & Thornton, D. (2002). Dimensions associated with assessments of sex offender recidivism risk. Criminal Justice & Behavior, 29, 569-589.

Roesler, T.A., & Weissmann-Wind, T.A. (1994). Telling the secret: adult women describe their disclosures of incest. Journal of Interpersonal Violence, 9, 327-338.

Rösler, A., & Witztum, E. (2000). Pharmacotherapy of Paraphilias in the Next Millennium. Behavioral Sciences and the Law, 18, 43-56.

Rossetti, S.J. (1995). The impact of child sexual abuse on attitudes toward God and the Catholic Church. Child Abuse & Neglect, 19, 1469-1481.

Rossetti, S.J. (1995). The mark of Cain: Reintegrating pedophiles. America, 173, 9-18.

Rossetti, S.J. (1996). A Tragic Grace: The Catholic Church and Child Sexual Abuse. Collegeville, MN: The Liturgical Press.

Rossetti, S.J. (1997). The effects of priest-perpetration of child sexual abuse on the trust of Catholics in priesthood, Church, and God. Journal of Psychology and Christianity, 16, 197-209.

Rossetti, S.J. (2002). The Catholic Church and child sexual abuse. America, 186, 8-16.

Ruzicka, M.F. (1997). Predictor variables of clergy pedophiles. Psychological Reports, 80, 589-590.

Sapp, Allen D. & Carter, David L. (1978). A Descriptive Study of Texas Residents' Attitudes. Huntsville, TX: Sam Houston State University.

Scheper-Hughes, N. (1998). Institutionalized sex abuse and the Catholic Church. In N. Scheper-Hughes & C. Sargent (Eds.). Small Wars: The Cultural Politics of Childhood (pp. 295-317). Berkeley, CA: University of California Press.

Schwartz, B.K. (1995). Characteristics and Typologies of Sex Offenders. In B. Schwartz (Ed.). The Sex Offender: Corrections, Treatment and Legal Practice (Vol. 2). New Jersey: Civic Research Institute, Inc.

Schwartz, B.K. (1995). Characteristics and Typologies of Sex Offenders. In B. Schwartz (Ed.). The Sex Offender: Corrections, Treatment and Legal Practice (Vol. 3). New Jersey: Civic Research Institute, Inc.

Scott, M.B., & Lyman, S.M. (1968). Paranoia, homosexuality, and game theory. Journal of Health & Social Behavior, 9, 179-187.

Scully, D., & Marolla, J. (1990). Convicted rapists' vocabulary of motive: Excuses and justifications. In D. Brissett, & C. Edgley (Eds.). Life as Theater: A Dramaturgical Sourcebook (pp. 261-280, second edition). Hawthorne, NY: Aldine de Gruyter.

Seidman, B.T., Marshall, W.L., Hudson, S.M., Robertson, P.J. (1994). An examination of intimacy and loneliness in sex offenders. Journal of Interpersonal Violence, 9, 518-534.

Sexual Assaults in Wisconsin 1995. (1996). Madison, Wisconsin: Wisconsin Office of Justice Assistance, Statistical Analysis Center.

Sexual Assaults in Wisconsin 1998. (1999). Madison, Wisconsin: Wisconsin Office of Justice Assistance, Statistical Analysis Center.

Simon, L.M.J., Sales, B., Kaskniak, A., & Kahn, M. (1992). Characteristics of child molesters: Implications for the fixated-regressed dichotomy. Journal of Interpersonal Violence, 7, 211-225.

Simkins, L. (1993). Characteristics of sexually repressed child molesters. Journal of Interpersonal Violence, 8, 3-17.

Simkins, L., Ward, W., & Bowman, S. (1989). The Multiphasic Sex Inventory: Diagnosis and prediction of treatment response in child sexual abusers. Annals of Sex Research, 2, 205-226.

Sipe, A.R. (1999). The problem of prevention in clergy sexual abuse. In T.G. Plante (Ed.). Bless Me Father For I Have Sinned: Perspectives on Sexual Abuse Committed by Roman Catholic Priests. (pp. 111-134). Westport, CT: Praeger Publishers.

Sipe, A.W.R (1995). Sex, Priests, and Power: Anatomy of a Crisis. New York, NY: Brunner/Mazel, Inc.

Sipe, A.W.R. (1990). A Secret World: Sexuality and the Search for Celibacy. New York, NY: Brunner/Mazel, Inc.

Sipe, A.W.R. (1998). Clergy abuse in Ireland. In A. Shupe (Ed.). Wolves Within the Fold: Religious Leadership and Abuses of Power (pp. 133-151). New Brunswick, NJ: Rutgers University Press.

Sjöestedt, G. & Långström, N. (2001). Actuarial assessment of sex offender recidivism risk: A cross-validation of the RRASOR and the Static-99 in Sweden. Law and Human Behavior, 25, 629-645.

Smith, L.M. (1994). Lifting the veil of secrecy: Mandatory child abuse reporting statutes may encourage the Catholic Church to report priests who molest children. Law & Psychology Review, 18, 409-421.

Smith, D.W., Letourneau, E.J., & Saunders, B.E. (2000). Delay in disclosure of childhood rape: Results from a national survey. Child Abuse & Neglect, 24, 273-287.

Snyder, H. N. (2000). Sexual Assault of Young Children as Reported to Law Enforcement: Victim, Incident, and Offender Characteristics, NIBRS Statistical Report. Washington, DC: U.S. Department of Justice, Office of Justice Programs Bureau of Justice Statistics.

Sorenson, T., & Snow, B. (1991) How children tell: The process of disclosure in child sexual abuse. Child Welfare, 70, 3-15.

Spencer, A. (1998). Peterhead Prison Program. In W.L. Marshall (Ed.). Sourcebook of Treatment Programs for Sexual Offenders (pp. 29-46). New York: Plenum Press.

Stanton, C. (1990). Officially responding to an accusation of sexual abuse: Reflections of a Diocesan communications director. In S.J. Rossetti (Ed.). Slayer of the Soul: Child Sexual Abuse and the Catholic Church (pp. 143-148). Mystic, CT: Twenty-Third Publications.

Steinhauser, K. (1993). Legal issues in sexual abuse and domestic violence. Pastoral Psychology, 41, 321-336.

Stoner, S.A., & George, W.H. (2000). Relapse prevention with harm reduction: Areas of overlap. In D. R. Laws (Ed.). Remaking Relapse Prevention with Sex Offenders (pp. 56-75). California: Sage Publications.

Summit, R.C. (1983). The child sexual abuse accommodation syndrome. Child Abuse & Neglect, 7, 177-193.

Swaffer, T., Hollin, C., Beech, A., Beckett, R., & Fisher, D. (2000). An exploration of child sexual abusers' sexual fantasies before and after treatment. Sexual Abuse: A Journal of Research and Treatment, 12, 61-68.

Sykes, G.M., & Matza, D. (1957). Techniques of neutralization: A theory of delinquency. Sociological Review,22, 664-670.

Tauteoli, Kelly & Lewis, Robert. (1992). Child sexual abuse: Statistics, trends, and case outcomes. Retrieved April 10, 2003 from http://www.jrsa.org/pubs/forum/archives/Mar92.html.

The Effectiveness of Treatment of Sexual Offenders: Report of the Association for the Treatment of Sexual Abusers, Collaborative Data Research Committee, November 3, 2000.

The Gallup Organization. (1995). Disciplining Children in America: A Gallup Poll Report. Princeton, N.J.: The Gallup Organization.

Thompson, K.M, S.A. Wonderlich, R.D. Crosby & J.E. Mitchell. (2001). sexual victimization and adolescent weight regulation practices: A test across three community based samples. Child Abuse and Neglect, 25, 291-305.

Thomson, J.G., Marolla, J.A., & Bromley, D.G. (1998). Disclaimers and accounts in cases of Catholic priests accused of pedophilia. In A. Shupe (Ed.). Wolves Within the Fold: Religious Leadership and Abuses of Power (pp. 175-189). New Brunswick, NJ: Rutgers University Press.

University of Nevada, Reno. (n.d.). Reporting child abuse and neglect. Retrieved May 2003 from www.unce.unr.edu/publications/FS01/FS0140.htm.

U.S. Dept. of Health and Human Services, Children's Bureau. (2001). Child Maltreatment 2001. Washington, DC: U.S. Government Printing Office.

Valcour, F. (1990). The treatment of child sexual abusers in the Church. In S.J. Rossetti (Ed.). Slayer of the Soul: Child Sexual Abuse and the Catholic Church (pp. 45-66). Mystic, CT: Twenty-Third Publications.

Walrath, C., Ybarra, M., & Holden, E.W. (2003). Children with reported histories of sexual abuse: Utilizing multiple perspectives to understand clinical and psychosocial profiles. Child Abuse & Neglect, 27, 509-524.

Wang, C.T. & Daro, D. (1998). Current Trends in Child Abuse Reporting And Fatalities: The Results of the 1997 Annual Fifty State Survey. The Center on Child Abuse Prevention Research. Chicago, IL: National Committee to Prevent Child Abuse.

Warberg, B.W., Abel, G.G., Osborn, C. (1996). Cognitive-behavioral treatment for professional sexual misconduct among the clergy. Pastoral Psychology, 45, 49-63.

Ward, T., & Hudson, S.M. (1998). The construction and development of theory in the sexual offending area: A metatheoretical framework. Sexual Abuse: A Journal of Research & Treatment, 10, 47-63.

Ward, T., & Hudson, S.M. (2000). A self-regulation model of relapse prevention. In D.R. Laws (Ed.). Remaking Relapse Prevention with Sex Offenders (pp. 79-101). California: Sage Publications.

Ward, T., & Keenan, T. (1999). Child Molesters' Implicit Theories. Journal of Interpersonal Violence, 14, 821-838.

Washington State Institute for Public Policy. (1998, August). Sex Offenses in Washington State: 1998 Update. Olympia, WA: WSIPP.

Wasyliw, O.E., Benn, A.F., Grossman, L.S., & Haywood, T.W. (1998). Detection of minimization of psychopathology on the Rorschach in cleric and noncleric alleged sex offenders. Assessment, 5, 389-397.

Way, I., Chung, S., Jonson-Reid, M., & Drake, B. (2001). Maltreatment perpetrators: A 54-month analysis of recidivism. Child Abuse and Neglect, 25, 1093-1108.

Weiss, P. (1999). Assessment and Treatment of Sex Offenders in the Czech Republic and in Eastern Europe. Journal of Interpersonal Violence, 14, 411-421.

West, D.J. (1987). Sexual Crimes and Confrontations: A Study of Victims and Offenders. Aldershot: Gower.

Whetsell-Mitchell, J. (1995). Rape of The Innocent: Understanding and Preventing Child Sexual Abuse. Washington: Taylor & Francis Ltd.

Wood, M.R., Grossman, L.S., & Fichtner, C.G. (2000). Psychological assessment, treatment, and outcome with sex offenders. Behavioral Sciences and the Law, 18, 23-41.

Wyatt, G.E., & Newcomb, M.D. (1990). Internal and external mediators of women's sexual abuse in childhood. Journal of Consulting & Clinical Psychology, 58, 758-767.

Young, J.L. & Griffith, E.E.H. (1995). Regulating pastoral counseling practice: The problem of sexual misconduct. Bulletin of the American Academy of Psychiatry and Law, 23, 421-432.

Young, J.L. & Griffith, E.E.H. (1998). Reconsideration of sexual misconduct by clergy counselors: The case of F.G. v. MacDonell. Journal of the American Academy of Psychiatry & the Law, 26, 289-293.

Young, J.L. & Griffith, E.E.H. (1999). Developments in clergy malpractice: The case of Sanders v. Casa View Baptist Church. Journal of the American Academy of Psychiatry & the Law, 27, 143-147.

PART II – ANNOTATED BIBLIOGRAPHY

T his annotated bibliography is a compilation of previously published empirical or descriptive research on child sexual abuse. The academic studies described herein have been published in a variety of scholarly and professional journals and books.

Prior to beginning an empirical study, it is necessary to understand the literature already published on that topic. There are three methods by which a body of literature can be presented: in a summary, in a synthesis or in a critical format. An annotated bibliography is a summary of the literature. It presents an abstract of the information from each article or book. This information will later be the basis of a literature review, providing a synthesis of the information by topic rather than by book or article. Additionally, we will provide an analysis of the studies included in this bibliography, including a critique of current research and an analysis of studies that are most useful in regard to the current project.

This annotated bibliography is separated into seven sections covering the following topics: prevalence of child sexual abuse, theories of sexual offending, typologies of sexual offenders, evaluation of sexual offenders, treatment of sexual offenders, assessment of treatment efficacy, and institutional response to sexual abuse by clergy. It is organized so that the reader can look through the Table of Contents and easily identify an area of interest and review the literature published on a particular topic. The scope of this annotated bibliography is not exhaustive (e.g., it does not include every article published on child sexual abuse). However, we believe that it does provide an extensive overview of each topic.

ESTIMATING THE PREVALENCE OF CHILD SEXUAL ABUSE

NATIONAL STATISTICS

THE GALLUP ORGANIZATION. (1995). *DISCIPLINING CHILDREN IN AMERICA: A GALLUP POLL REPORT.* PRINCETON, NJ: THE GALLUP ORGANIZATION.

This 1995 telephone survey, conducted by the *Gallup Poll*, indicated that as many as 19 per 1,000 children have suffered sexual abuse. The results indicate that more children are abused (all types of abuse) and neglected than are found in Child Protective Services reports.

WANG, C. & DARO, D. (1998). *CURRENT TRENDS IN CHILD ABUSE REPORTING AND FATALITIES: THE RESULTS OF THE 1997 ANNUAL FIFTY STATE SURVEY.* THE CENTER ON CHILD ABUSE PREVENTION RESEARCH. CHICAGO, IL: NATIONAL COMMITTEE TO PREVENT CHILD ABUSE.

In 1998 a survey was sent to the "federally appointed liaisons for child abuse and neglect" in each of the fifty states and the District of Columbia. Information presented in this 1997 report included (but is not limited to) the following: the number of reported and substantiated victims of child maltreatment during 1995, 1996, and 1997; a breakdown by type of maltreatment; and the number of confirmed fatalities resulting from child abuse. Child sexual abuse constituted 7% of reported cases and 8% of substantiated cases. However, not all states responded to the survey.

STATEWIDE STATISTICS

Only 30 States and the District of Columbia published empirical studies concerning sexual abuse statistics.

ALABAMA

CHILD PROTECT: THE MONTGOMERY AREA CHILDREN'S ADVOCACY CENTER (1999). *CHILD ABUSE STATISTICS.* RETRIEVED MARCH 26, 2003, FROM *HTTP://WWW.CHILDPROTECT.ORG/STATISTICS.HTM*

In 1999, the child advocacy group Child Protect amassed the following figures regarding child sexual abuse within Alabama: a total of 763 cases of child abuse and neglect were reported and 566 of these cases were indicated; 54% of the cases involved neglect, 25% involved physical abuse, 12% involved sexual abuse, and 9% were unspecified. This data is based upon figures derived from the counties of Montgomery, Autauga, Chilton, Elmore, and Lowndes.

CHILD WELFARE LEAGUE OF AMERICA (2001). *ALABAMA'S CHILDREN 2001.* RETRIEVED MARCH 26, 2003, FROM *HTTP://WWW.CWLA.ORG/ADVOCACY/ STATEFACTSHEETS/2001/ALABAMA.HTM*

During 1998, a total of 16,668 cases of child abuse and neglect were reported. It was computed 15.4 per 1,000 children were abused. When the types of abuse are specified, 7.1 were neglected, 6.1 were physically abused, and 3.3 were sexually abused (per 1,000 children).

ALASKA

DEPARTMENT OF HEALTH AND HUMAN SERVICES, DIVISION OF FAMILY AND YOUTH SERVICES. (1994). *FISCAL YEAR 1993 ANNUAL REPORT.* DIVISION OF FAMILY AND YOUTH SERVICES.

The rate of child sexual abuse in Alaska is six times the national average. This figure is based upon the following data: Child Protective Services received 1,431 reports of sexual abuse in 1989 (out of 7,786 reports total), 1,556 in 1990 (out of 9,021 reports total), 1,681 in 1991 (out of 10,283 reports total), 2,039 in 1992 (out of 12,386 reports total), and 2,249 in 1993 (out of 14,617 reports total).

DEPARTMENT OF HEALTH AND HUMAN SERVICES—DIVISION OF FAMILY AND YOUTH SERVICES. (1996). *FISCAL YEAR 1993 ANNUAL REPORT*. DIVISION OF FAMILY AND YOUTH SERVICES.

Child Protective Services received 2,421 reports of child sexual abuse in 1994, and 2,031 reports of child sexual abuse in 1995. The total number of maltreatment reports was 15,465 in 1994 and 15,706 in 1995. The at-risk population is listed as 186,271 in 1994 and 187,351 in 1995.

RID ALASKA. (2000). *FAMILY SERVICE CHILD REPORTS OF HARM BY REGION, FISCAL YEAR 2000*. RETRIEVED MARCH 1, 2003 FROM *HTTP://WWW.ALASKA.NET/~ROSENBAU/ STAT.HTML*

This report divided Alaska into four regions: Northern Region, Southcentral Region, Southeast Region, and Anchorage Region. The total number of child sexual abuse cases (reported), for all regions, was 1,869 (11.5% of abuse statistics). Statistics are also included on a breakdown of felony and misdemeanor cases by city court site.

ARKANSAS

ARKANSAS COMMISSION ON CHILD ABUSE. (2002). *FACT SHEET ABOUT CHILD ABUSE IN ARKANSAS*. RETRIEVED MARCH 26, 2003 FROM *WWW.ACCARDV.UAMS.EDU/ FACTS.HTM*

The source of this information gathered by the Arkansas Commission is the US Department of Health and Human Services—Administration for Children and Families (April 2000). This fact sheet provides statistics on general information about child abuse in Arkansas. The types of abuse are not differentiated. In 1998, based upon a child population of 653,721, 13.1 per 1,000 children were victims of abuse, compared to 12.9 for the nation. The fact sheet also states that nearly 12% of child abuse victims were sexually abused.

ARIZONA

ARIZONA'S CHILD ABUSE INFOCENTER. (2003). *CHILD ABUSE STATISTICS*. RETRIEVED MARCH 26, 2003, FROM *HTTP://WWW.AHSC.ARIZONA.EDU/ ACAINFO/STATISTICS/FACT SHEET.HTM*

The Arizona Child Abuse InfoCenter reported that out of 17,104 cases of abuse, 60% involved alleged neglect, 32% physical abuse, 6% sexual abuse, and 2% emotional abuse. These figures are based upon the Semi-annual Report; Arizona Department of Economic Security; Division of Children, Youth and Families from April 1st, 2002 until September 30, 2002.

CHILDREN'S ACTION ALLIANCE (2002). *ARIZONA'S ABUSED AND NEGLECTED CHILDREN: CHILD PROTECTIVE SERVICES (CPS) REPORTS AND RESPONSE*. RETRIEVED MARCH 26, 2003, FROM *HTTP://WWW.AZCHILDREN.ORG/CAA/_MAIN PAGES/FACT_SHEETS_&_LINKS/FACTS_ABOUT_ABUSE_ AND_NEGLECT.ASP*

Based upon the Arizona Children Organization, 6% of abuse reports were related to alleged sexual abuse. The majority of the cases are related to situations of alleged neglect (60%) and physical abuse (32%) while allegations of emotional abuse are the least reported (2%). When these reports are further evaluated, 13% are classified as high risk, 27% as moderate risk, 40% as low risk, and 20% as potential abuse and neglect.

CALIFORNIA

CHILDREN NOW. (2001). *CALIFORNIA REPORT CARD 2001: FACTORS FOR SCHOOL SUCCESS*. RETRIEVED FROM *HTTP://WWW.CHILDRENNOW.ORG/CALIFORNIA /RC-2001/REPORTCARD-2001.HTM*

The Children Now Organization has concluded that over 660,000 children were abused in 2000. However, there is no differentiation between the types of abuse reported. In 1996, 78 per 1,000 reports were filed whereas in 2000, there was a decrease to 68 reports per 1,000 children. When the data is evaluated by region, there appears to be an increase in Glenn, Inyo and Tehama counties while Lassen, Solano and Yuba counties have displayed a decline.

COLORADO

COLORADO COALITION AGAINST SEXUAL ASSAULT. (2003). *TOWARD HEALING AND JUSTICE: A HANDBOOK FOR SURVIVORS OF SEXUAL ASSAULT.* DENVER, CO: COLORADO COALITION AGAINST SEXUAL ASSAULT.

This resource for survivors of sexual assault includes information on the definitions of sexual violence and assault, health and medical concerns, various agency responses to the problem, contacts for survivors, and some basic statistics. In Colorado, one in four women suffered an attempted or completed sexual assault in her life-time, whereas one in seventeen men experienced the same. Sixty-one percent of rape cases occurred before the victim was eighteen.

OATES, R. KIM. (2000). ERRONEOUS CONCERNS ABOUT CHILD SEXUAL ABUSE. *CHILD ABUSE AND NEGLECT, 24* (1), 149-157.

The aim of the author was to assess the incidence of child sexual abuse, with a focus on false reporting (what Oates classifies as "erroneous concerns"). Case records of reported child sexual abuse, from January 1st, 1992 to December 31st, 1992, were evaluated; the cases had been investigated by the Denver Department of Social Services. In total, 551 cases were reviewed. Of those, 43% were substantiated, 31% were inconclusive, and 34% were not considered cases of abuse.

CONNECTICUT

CHILD WELFARE LEAGUE OF AMERICA. (2000). *CONNECTICUT'S CHILDREN 2001: CHILD ABUSE AND NEGLECT.* RETRIEVED MARCH 26, 2003, FROM HTTP://WWW.CWLA.ORG/ADVOCACY/STATEFACT SHEETS/2001/CONNECTICUT.HTM.

Based upon figures from the Child Welfare League of America (CWLA) in 1998, Connecticut had 16,923 reports of child abuse and neglect. This indicates that abuse occurred at a rate of 21.4 per 1,000 children in the population. When the type of abuse is examined, 18.5 children were neglected, 3.5 were physically abused, and 0.9 were sexually abused.

FORDHAM INSTITUTE FOR INNOVATION IN SOCIAL POLICY. (1999). *SOCIAL STATE OF CONNECTICUT '99: PART III A CLOSER LOOK: A SOCIAL PROFILE OF CONNECTICUT.* RETRIEVED MARCH 26, 2003, FROM HTTP://WWW.CGA.STATE.CT.US/COC/SOC_INDEX00/PART_III.HTML

Based upon data from 1997, 36,638 cases of child abuse were filed. The abuse occurred at a rate of 45.7 per 1,000 children and there were more than 1,000 reported cases of child sexual abuse. This appears to be a slight improvement when compared to previous years; however, the authors contend that it is still higher than any year prior to 1995.

DELAWARE

CHILD WELFARE LEAGUE OF AMERICA. (2003). *DELAWARE'S CHILDREN 2003.* RETRIEVED MARCH 29, 2003, FROM HTTP://WWW.CWLA.ORG

Based on annual statistics of child abuse and neglect for the year 2000, this agency reports a rate of 0.9 per 1,000 children in Delaware as being sexually abused.

HEALTH AND HUMAN SERVICES. (2003). RETRIEVED MARCH 29, 2003 FROM HTTP://WWW.ACF.HHS.GOV/PROGRAMS/CB/PUBLICATIONS/CWO99/STATEDATA.HTM

In 1998, 8.6% of substantiated child abuse reports were sexual in nature compared to 1999, when 11.1% of substantiated cases were related to sexual abuse.

DISTRICT OF COLUMBIA

CHILD WELFARE LEAGUE OF AMERICA (2002). *DISTRICT OF COLUMBIA'S CHILDREN 2002: CHILD ABUSE AND NEGLECT.* RETRIEVED MARCH 26, 2003, FROM HTTP://WWW.CWLA.ORG/ADVOCACY/STATEFACT SHEETS/2002/DC.HTM.

The Child Welfare League of America, an advocacy organization, concluded that 2,308 cases of child abuse were reported in the District of Columbia during 1999. This is a rate of 24.2 children per 1,000 that were abused. When this figure is examined on the basis of types of abuse, 17.4 were neglected, 3.5 were physically abused, and 0.4 were sexually abused. These figures are encouraging as there is a reported decline of 113% from 1998.

FLORIDA

CPS WATCH (2001). *FLORIDA FOSTER CARE STATISTICS.* RETRIEVED MARCH 26, 2003, FROM *HTTP://WWW.CPSWATCH.COM/OLDSITE/STATS/STATES/ FL.HTM*

Based upon data gathered from the Florida Department of Children and Families, CPS Watch has compiled figures concerning child abuse and neglect. While the date of when these figures were compiled is unclear, the 2001 publication shows that 6,011 cases of child sexual abuse were reported, accounting for 7.32% of all types of maltreatment.

GEORGIA

PREVENT CHILD ABUSE GEORGIA. (N.D.). *STATISTICS.* RETRIEVED MARCH 26, 2003, FROM *HTTP://WWW.PRE VENTCHILDABUSEGA.ORG/HTML/STATISTICS.HTML*

Based upon official reports of child abuse, an examination of the data illustrates that from 1998 to 2000, there was an increase in reports of child abuse and neglect. There were 2,050 reports of sexual abuse in 1998, 2,265 reports in 1999, and 2,354 in 2000. This indicates that there was a change of + 4% during the three years. Note that "Other" includes drug exposure, addiction at birth, gunshot wounds, medical care needed and child fatalities, among others.

HAWAII

CHILD WELFARE LEAGUE OF AMERICA. (2003). *HAWAII'S CHILDREN 2003.* RETRIEVED MARCH 29, 2003 FROM *HTTP://WWW.CWLA.ORG/ADVOCACY/ STATEFACT SHEETS/2003/HAWAII.PDF*

In 2000, there were 295,767 estimated children under the age of 18 in Hawaii. Of every 1,000 children, 0.8 were sexually abused (based on official statistics).

IDAHO

CHILD WELFARE LEAGUE OF AMERICA. (2001). *IDAHO'S CHILDREN 2001: CHILD ABUSE AND NEGLECT.* RETRIEVED MARCH 26, 2003, FROM *HTTP://WWW.CWLA.ORG/ADVO CACY/STATEFACT-SHEETS /2001/IDAHO.HTM*

In 1998, the CWLA reports that there were 7,936 cases of child abuse and neglect in Idaho. This is an abuse rate of 2.6 per 1,000 children in which 10.7 were neglected, 7 were physically abused, and 3.7 were sexually abused.

CPS WATCH. (N.D.). *IDAHO FOSTER CARE STATISTICS.* RETRIEVED MARCH 26, 2003, FROM *HTTP://WWW. CPSWATCH.COM/OLDSITE/STATS/STATES/ID.HTM*

Based upon data collected by the Idaho Department of Health and Welfare, Division of Family and Community Services, CPS Watch has listed the prevalence of child abuse and neglect. While the date of when these figures were compiled is unclear, there were 1,290 cases of child sexual abuse reported, accounting for 47.54% of all types of child maltreatment.

ILLINOIS

CANTS ALLEGATION. (1998). *CHILD ABUSE AND NEGLECT STATISTICS ANNUAL REPORT—FISCAL YEAR 1997.* RETRIEVED APRIL 15, 2003, FROM *HTTP://WWW. STATE.IL.US/DCFS/CANTS97_FIG4.SHTML*

Based on government statistics this organization concluded that 7.58% of abuse allegations received by DCFS concerned sexual abuse and 10.25% of all abuse allegations were sexual in nature.

CHILD WELFARE LEAGUE OF AMERICA. (2003). *ILLINOIS'S CHILDREN 2003.* RETRIEVED MARCH 29, 2003, FROM *HTTP://WWW.CWLA.ORG/ADVOCACY/ STATEFACTSSHEETS/ILLINOIS.PDF*

According to statistics for 2000, 1.0 out of every 1,000 children was sexually abused in Illinois. This is based upon an estimated population of 3,245,451 children under the age of 18.

INDIANA

DUNEBROOK. (2000). *CHILD ABUSE STATISTICS.* RETRIEVED APRIL, 2003, FROM *HTTP://WWW.DUNE BROOK.ORG/STATS.HTML.*

Based upon official figures collected by Child Protective Services, 42,979 reports were filed concerning child abuse and neglect during 2000. When the types of abuse are examined, 63% involved neglect, 19% involved physical abuse, 10% involved sexual abuse, and 8% involved sexual maltreatment. When sexual abuse was examined, a rate of 1.7 victims per 1,000 female children and 0.4 victims per 1,000 male children was established.

IOWA

CHILD WELFARE LEAGUE OF AMERICA. (2003). *IOWA'S CHILDREN 2003.* RETRIEVED MARCH 29, 2003, FROM *HTTP://WWW.CWLA.ORG/ADVOCACY/STATE FACTSSHEETS/IOWA.PDF*

In 2000, based upon official statistics, 1.3 out of every 1,000 children was sexually abused. There were an estimated 733,638 children under the age of 18 in 2000.

KANSAS

CPS WATCH. (N.D.). *KANSAS FOSTER CARE STATISTICS.* RETRIEVED APRIL, 2003, FROM *HTTP://WWW. CPSWATCH.COM/OLDSITE/STATS/STATES/KS.HTM*

CPS Watch collected statistics from the Kansas Department of Social and Rehabilitation Services based upon a child population of 697,452, of which 8,488 are in the care of the state. While the date of when these figures were compiled is unclear, there were 1,023 cases involving sexual abuse.

KENTUCKY

CHILD SEXUAL ABUSE: KENTUCKY ABUSE NUMBERS HAVE TRIPLED IN TEN YEARS. (1997, MARCH 24). *SEX WEEKLY.* RETRIEVED MARCH 30, 2003, FROM LEXIS-NEXIS.

In 1996, the rape crisis centers in Kentucky reported 5,800 cases of sexual abuse/assault. This is triple the amount from one decade ago. Of the 5,800 recorded cases, 34% involved children ages seventeen and under.

RECORD NUMBER OF CHILD ABUSERS PROSECUTED. (1997, JULY 7). *SEX WEEKLY.* RETRIEVED MARCH 30, 2003, FROM LEXIS-NEXIS.

This report evaluates cases between the years of 1994 and 1996 in Kentucky. Statewide, 10,610 incidents of child abuse were reported and of those cases, 4,624 were substantiated by social workers. The news article focuses upon the subject of child sexual abuse, but the numbers are not distributed according to specific types of abuse. It appears as if the phrases "child sexual abuse" and "child abuse" are used interchangeably.

LOUISIANA

LOUISIANA CHILDREN'S TRUST FUND. (N.D.). *WHAT IS CHILD ABUSE AND NEGLECT?* RETRIEVED APRIL, 2003, FROM *HTTP://WWW.LCTF.ORG/ABUSE%20 AND%20NEGLECT %20IN%20LOUISIANA.HTM*

As based upon official reports in 1999, 31,699 reports were filed concerning child abuse and neglect resulting in the investigation of 23,921 cases. The investigations yielded 7,664 valid cases (32%) involving 12,813 children.

MAINE

CHILD WELFARE LEAGUE OF AMERICA. (2003). *MAINE'S CHILDREN 2003.* RETRIEVED MARCH 30, 2003, FROM *HTTP://WWW.CWLA.ORG/ADVOCACY/ STATEFACTSHEETS/MAINE.PDF*

Based upon statistics for the year 2000, 3.2 out of every 1,000 children were sexually abused. The estimated child population in 2000 was 301,238.

MINNESOTA

MINNESOTA STUDENT SURVEY 1991: A REPORT ON SPECIAL POPULATIONS. (1991). ST. PAUL: MINNESOTA DEPARTMENT OF EDUCATION.

The original Minnesota survey was conducted in order to ascertain a portrait of adolescent life.

However, the authors of this piece felt that the portrait was inaccurate, because at-risk adolescents were excluded due to the design of the study (i.e., it was given to students at public schools to fill out, thus neglecting adolescents in custody or alternative schools). A slightly revised edition of the 1989 study was administered in 1991 to a sample of 3,573 students in Minnesota alternative schools, area learning centers, residential treatment centers, and Corrections/Detention centers. The data collected from this group was then compared to the 91,175 students who participated in the original 1989 Minnesota Student Survey. For alternative schools there were 2,425 completed surveys that included students ages 12 to 21. The results are as follows: 16% of females and 2% of males reported intrafamilial sexual abuse (compared to 8% of females and 2% of males in regular schools); 35% of females and 5% of males reported extrafamilial abuse (compared to 17% and 3% respectively); and, 38% of females and 5% of males reported either/both types of sexual abuse (compared to 20% and 4% respectively). Four hundred and sixty-one surveys were collected from Corrections/Detention centers. These results illustrate that 17% of females and 9% of males reported intrafamilial sexual abuse (compared to 5% and 2% respectively); 45% of females and 15% of males reported extrafamilial sexual abuse (compared to 17% and 2% respectively); and 48% of females and 17% of males reported either/both types of sexual abuse (compared to 18% and 3% respectively). Males greatly outnumbered females in this sample. Three hundred and forty-eight surveys were returned from adolescents in Residential Treatment Centers. Forty-one percent of females and 8% of males reported intrafamilial abuse (compared to 10% and 2% respectively); 54% of females and 16% of males reported extrafamilial abuse (compared to 16% and 3% respectively); and 63% of females and 18% of males reported either/both types of sexual abuse (compared to 19% and 3% respectively).

MISSOURI

DRAKE, B. (1996). PREDICTORS OF PREVENTIVE SERVICES PROVISIONS AMONG UNSUBSTANTIATED CASES. CHILD MALTREATMENT, 1, 168-175.

This article evaluates unsubstantiated child maltreatment reports where voluntary preventive services were provided by the state. Data is also presented on substantiated cases in order to see how the services offered varied when based upon substantiation. The initial data consisted of all child abuse and neglect cases reported to the Missouri Department of Family Services (N = 48,415) during the 1992 calendar year. Of the 48,415 cases in the database, 35,014 were unsubstantiated cases. Of these, 28,039 cases (80%) were free of missing data. Among these cases, 2,674 were reports of sexual abuse. Sexual abuse cases showed statistically significant differences between the preventive services group and the control group.

Way, I., Chung, S., Jonson-Reid, M., & Drake, B. (2001). Maltreatment perpetrators: A 54-month analysis of recidivism. *Child Abuse and Neglect, 25*, 1093-1108.

This study looks at recidivism rates for alleged child abuse perpetrators. A comparison is made between those whose initial reports were substantiated and those whose initial report was not substantiated in order to determine if one groups recidivates at a higher rate than the other. This sample included 31,531 perpetrators who committed intrafamilial maltreatment. The cases that were examined came from the Missouri Department of Family Services. Abuse is broken down into three types: sexual abuse, physical abuse, and neglect. In the sample, 1,321 (or 4.2%) of the index cases were sexual abuse. Overall, the recidivism rate was 42.4%; for sexual abuse it was 4%. The primary finding of this study was that perpetrators whose index event was unsubstantiated returned to the system at a higher rate. In conclusion, the authors state that there needs to be a way to determine which individuals with unsubstantiated cases of abuse are likely to be at risk of recidivating.

NEVADA

UNIVERSITY OF NEVADA, RENO. (N.D.). REPORTING CHILD ABUSE AND NEGLECT. RETRIEVED MAY, 2003, FROM HTTP://WWW.UNCE.UNR.EDU/PUBLICATIONS/ FS01/FS0140.HTM

According to the *Nevada Child Abuse & Neglect Statistics (2000),* compiled by the State of Nevada Division of Child and Family Services, a total of 6,976 cases of child abuse and neglect were reported in 2000. Of these cases, 254 involved sexual abuse/exploitation.

NEW JERSEY

CHILD WELFARE LEAGUE OF AMERICA. (N.D.). *NEW JERSEY'S CHILDREN.* RETRIEVED MAY 20, 2003, FROM *HTTP://WWW.CWLA.ORG/ADVOCACY/STATEFACT SHEETS/2003/NEWJERSEY.PDF*

During 2000, 38,330 reported cases of child abuse and neglect were filed with child protective services at a rate of 18.4 children per 1,000. Of these cases, 8,727 were substantiated creating a rate of 4.2 per 1,000 children.

NORTH DAKOTA

THOMPSON, K.M, WONDERLICH, S.A., CROSBY, R.D., & MITCHELL, J.E. (2001). SEXUAL VICTIMIZATION AND ADOLESCENT WEIGHT REGULATION PRACTICES: A TEST ACROSS THREE COMMUNITY BASED SAMPLES. *CHILD ABUSE AND NEGLECT 25,* 291-305.

In a statewide survey of 966 children, prevalence of sexual abuse was found to be 12.4%. In an urban sample in which a different survey was utilized, a prevalence rate of 20.6% was found within the sample of 2,086. In a rural sample, which utilized a different survey, a prevalence rate of 13.7% prevalence was found in a sample of 2,629.

PENNSYLVANIA

PENNSYLVANIA DEPARTMENT OF PUBLIC WELFARE. (N.D.). *OFFICE OF CHILDREN, YOUTH AND FAMILIES.* RETRIEVED MAY 21, 2003, FROM *HTTP://WWW.DPW. STATE.PA. US/OCYF/OCYFCA.ASP*

During 2000, 22,809 cases of child abuse were filed with official organizations. Of these cases, 5,002 were substantiated (21.9%) and 50% of the substantiated cases involved allegations of sexual abuse.

TEXAS

SAPP, A.D. & CARTER, D.L. (1978). *A DESCRIPTIVE STUDY OF TEXAS RESIDENTS' ATTITUDES.* HUNTSVILLE, TX: SAM HOUSTON STATE UNIVERSITY.

This study evaluated the opinions of Texas residents on issues of child abuse. Additionally, the researchers attempted to determine the extent of child abuse in the state and public awareness of the issue. The researchers randomly selected 2000 Texas residents from 178 counties to receive a mail survey. Of the 2000 surveys, 1,339 were returned with usable data. The authors found that 8.5% of respondents reported that their children had been abused and 37.5% of these cases involved sexual abuse.

UTAH

TAUTEOLI, K. & LEWIS, R. (1992). *CHILD SEXUAL ABUSE: STATISTICS, TRENDS, AND CASE OUTCOMES.* RETRIEVED APRIL 10, 2003, FROM *HTTP://WWW.JRSA. ORG/PUBS/FORUM/ARCHIVES/MAR92.HTML.*

This article discusses awareness of child sexual abuse in the state of Utah. In the 1980's, a series of child abductions that resulted in murders led to the formation of a statewide taskforce that sought to determine the incidence of child sexual abuse in Utah. The main aim was to determine if child sexual abuse was increasing or decreasing. The authors took information from the 1990 Annual Report of the Central Register for Child Abuse and Neglect.

VERMONT

AGENCY OF HUMAN SERVICES—SOCIAL AND REHABILITATION SERVICES. (2003). *ABUSE AND NEGLECT STATISTICS.* RETRIEVED MARCH 29, 2003, FROM *HTTP://WWW.STATE.VT.US/SRS/ABUSE.HTM*

Data reported by this agency found that in 1999, 436 (49% substantiated) children were sexually abused. During 2000, 471 (45% substantiated) were sexually abused and in 2001, 424 (38% substantiated) children were sexually abused. The highest number was reported in 1992, in which 811 children were sexually abused.

STATE SEES DROP IN CASES OVER SIX YEARS. (1997, AUGUST 4). *SEX WEEKLY.* RETRIEVED MARCH 30, 2003, FROM LEXIS-NEXIS.

This article reports that Vermont has a "higher rate of child sexual abuse than the rest of the nation." In 1990, there were 77 child victims of sexual abuse from ranging in age from infancy to age 3. In 1996, the number decreased to 21. There were no figures provided for other age groups and the source of this data is unclear.

WASHINGTON

WASHINGTON STATE INSTITUTE FOR PUBLIC POLICY. (1998, AUGUST). *SEX OFFENSES IN WASHINGTON STATE: 1998 UPDATE.* OLYMPIA, WA: WSIPP.

This report presents government statistics on the prevalence of child sexual abuse based upon cases accepted for investigation by DSHS. In 1985, about 10% of the cases accepted involved sexual abuse; in 1990, just over 10%; in 1995, about 7%; and in 1997, about 7.5%. The report also assesses the recidivism rates for Washington State sex offenders from 1985 to 1991.

WISCONSIN

PREVENT CHILD ABUSE. (2003). *WISCONSIN—PREVALENCE OF CHILD ABUSE.* RETRIEVED MARCH 29, 2003, FROM *HTTP://WWW.PREVENTCHILDABUSEWI.ORG/PREVALENCE.HTM*

Based on data from the Department of Health and Human Services, in 2001 there were 4,606 cases of substantiated child sexual abuse in Wisconsin.

SEXUAL ASSAULTS IN WISCONSIN 1995. (1996). MADISON, WISCONSIN: WISCONSIN OFFICE OF JUSTICE ASSISTANCE, STATISTICAL ANALYSIS CENTER.

These statistics are based on official data (those reported to law enforcement agencies). In 1995, 6,101 estimated sexual assaults were reported to law enforcement agencies in the state. Seventy-five percent of the victims were juveniles and over 68% were 15 years of age or younger. These numbers are broken down further by age group and assault "type": 218 (17.2%) of children ages 1-12 and 222 (17.5%) of juveniles ages 13-15 reported having experienced forcible rape; 134 (10.6%) of teens ages 16-17 reported forcible rape and 163 (12.9%) of individu-

als age 18-20 reported experiencing a forcible rape. Two hundred and seventy five (53.8%) children ages 1-12 experienced forcible sodomy compared to 103 (20.2%) individuals ages 13-15. Thirty-seven (7.2%) individuals ages 16-17 and 25 (5.0%) individuals ages 18-20 also experienced forcible sodomy. One hundred and eighteen (60.2%) children ages 1-12 experienced assault with an object compared to 25 (12.8%) cases reported by individuals ages 13-15 and 7 (3.6%) individuals ages 16-17 and, 9 (4.6%) cases for individuals 18-20. In total, 1438 cases of forcible fondling were reported for children ages 1-12, 727 cases for children ages 13-15, 225 cases for individuals ages 16-17, and 161 cases for individuals ages 18-20.

SEXUAL ASSAULTS IN WISCONSIN 1998. (1999). MADISON, WISCONSIN: WISCONSIN OFFICE OF JUSTICE ASSISTANCE, STATISTICAL ANALYSIS CENTER.

This is official data based upon cases reported to law enforcement agencies in the state of Wisconsin during the year 1998. An estimated 6,056 individuals were victims of sexual abuse. This is a 3.0% increase from 1997. Seventy-eight percent of the victims were juveniles and over 70% were 15 years of age or younger. The average age of all sexual assault victims was 15 and the median was 14. Sexual assault was broken down into several categories: forcible rape (N=1,135), forcible sodomy (N=467), assault with an object (N=187), forcible fondling (N=2,658), statutory rape (N=1,257), and ejaculate/excrete upon victim (N=28). The categories of assault can be broken down by age group: ages 1-12 experienced 193 (17%) cases of forcible rape; 251 (53.7%) forcible sodomy; 87 (46.8%) assault with an object; 1,216 forcible fondling. Ages 13-15 experienced 207 (18.3%) forcible rape; 101 (21.6%) forcible sodomy; 43 (23.1%) assault with an object; 671 forcible fondling. For ages 16-17, 155 (13.7%) experienced forcible rape; 26 (5.6%) experienced forcible sodomy; and, 12 (6.5%) experienced assault with an object; 211 forcible fondling. Of those ages 18-20, 160 (14.1%) experienced forcible rape; 20 (4.3%) experienced forcible sodomy; 9 (4.8%) experienced assault with an object; 165 experienced forcible fondling. The average age of victims who were either ejaculated or excreted upon was 13.

ESTIMATES OF ABUSE WITHIN SPECIFIC SOCIAL ORGANIZATIONS

CATHOLIC CHURCH

BERRY, J. (1992). *LEAD US NOT INTO TEMPTATION: CATHOLIC PRIESTS AND SEXUAL ABUSE OF CHILDREN.* NEW YORK, NY: IMAGE BOOKS.

This popular press book written by a journalist provides a detailed account of the "scandal" surrounding the sexual abuse of children in Louisiana between 1984 and 1992. Berry claims there are 400 priests and brothers who have molested minors and estimates that the Church has spent $400 million in legal, medical, and psychological expenses. The book is divided into three parts. Part one explores the issue of child sexual abuse by clergy in Louisiana and its impact; part two examines the issue of celibacy and hetero/homosexual tension in cleric culture; and the third section illustrates the responses of the Church and the victim rights movement.

JENKINS, P. (1995). CLERGY SEXUAL ABUSE: THE SYMBOLIC POLITICS OF A SOCIAL PROBLEM. IN J. BEST (ED.), *IMAGES OF ISSUES* (PP. 105-130, SECOND EDITION). NEW YORK, NY: ALDINE DE GRUYTER.

This book attempts to examine the reasons why clergy sexual abuse within the Catholic Church has become such a major issue in recent years. However, the author does not provide any empirical data to support his opinion. Jenkins contends that even though this issue has existed for years, it was not until the mid-1980's that it received public attention. This is a result of a shift in the nature of media coverage. An emphasis on "tabloid" reporting and true-crime stories has drawn greater attention to sexual abuse. While the media portrays this "crisis" as being centered on the Catholic Church, Jenkins offered evidence through the citation of liability insurance, which illustrated that there were several hundred cases of sexual abuse involving non-Catholic clergy. He claimed that the view of this issue as a crisis was a result of the publicity allotted to the sensational cases of Gilbert Gauthe and the Mount Cashel orphanage. In conjunction with other highly publicized cases, the media began

to present high estimates concerning the prevalence of abuse, which affected public opinion of the Catholic Church. Professional interest groups have played a part in shaping the image of Catholic clergy abuse as a problem, most notably legal and mental health professionals. Lawyers have encouraged victims to pursue civil suits. This has created a snowball effect in which past victims have now come forward to stake their claim. The Catholic Church is an appealing target because it is a lucrative institution. Thus, it would be more beneficial to sue the Catholic Church, which has a strong economic enterprise, as opposed to a smaller church. Mental health professionals have promoted negative views concerning clergy abuse. The expert witness and victim's self-help groups have increased the notoriety concerning the Catholic Church, which has lead to the creation of stereotypes and expectations. These stereotypes influence juries and make it more likely that they will be prepared to find against the Church. Jenkins asserted that special interest groups such as gay rights and feminists have targeted the Catholic Church because of its doctrine. While social ideas concerning women's rights have changed, the Catholic Church has remained adamant in its views concerning divorce, abortion, contraception, women's ordination, homosexuality, and celibacy. These special interest groups shifted the attention from the individual priests to the hypocrisy of the Church and its hierarchy. Thus, the Catholic Church provided these groups with a platform from which they can voice their opinions.

SIPE, A.W.R. (1990). *A SECRET WORLD: SEXUALITY AND THE SEARCH FOR CELIBACY,* 8, 159-187, NEW YORK, NY: BRUNNER/MAZEL, INC.

Chapter 8 of this book, entitled "Priests and Children," discusses pedophilia in the Church based upon the author's experiences as a clinician. In a study, the author found that 2% of Catholic priests could be considered pedophiles, which supports earlier research findings. In addition to that figure, 4% of priests are sexually preoccupied with adolescent boys or girls during at least one point in their lives. Sipe described the behavior as being either occasional, compulsive, or developmental. When the incident occurs in a developmental sense, the priest acts out once with a child as part of his own developmental experimentation, which has been stunted in some way. Homosexual and heterosexual offenses are evenly distributed, but Sipe contends that the homosexual contact is four times more likely to come to the public's attention. Sipe also asserted that these pedophiles have an attraction to children prior to ordination, but rarely act out extensively prior to entering the priesthood. The chapter also includes a discussion of the legal ramifications of sexual abuse and contends that it is unclear as to who should be held accountable for the misconduct. He notes that at the time of this book's publication, the Church had avoided addressing the sexuality of the clergy and that this in turn has hindered moral development. In addressing the psychological evaluation of sexually offending clergy, Sipe stresses that the following questions must be asked: Is the behavior homosexual or heterosexual; is it compulsive; is it an isolated incident or part of a pattern; and is it fixated or regressed? In discussing the theories of pedophilia, it is noted that a large number of sexually abusive clerics had been victimized as youths. While this is not applicable in every case, sexual victimization as a child may lead the individual to seek refuge in the clergy as a way of denying the reality of life. Sipe contends that the experience of celibacy interacts with these past traumas and can either enhance the memory or stunt the priest's psychosexual development at a preadolescent/adolescent stage, which leads to sexual misconduct. Victim access is discussed and the avenues that may be pursued include selection from schools, altar boys, family, friends, and the congregation. In addition to displaying pedophiliac behavior and cognitive distortions, these priests also demonstrated exhibitionistic behavior that was directly linked to their level of psychosexual development (the more immature they are, the more likely they are to engage in this behavior). The effects of sexual abuse on the victims vary, but the impact is long lasting and may result in sexual depersonalization, depression, sexually acting out, and suicide. When a child has been victimized by a priest, the impact of the abuse effects how the child perceives God, the Church,

and the clergy. The abuse also raises the question as to how these institutions will view the victim. This chapter also provides a brief overview of the various therapeutic measures used to treat sexually offending clerics including psychotherapy, behavioral therapy, surgery, and medication. In discussing the reasons why the Church has not openly discussed the issue of sexually abusive priests, Sipe contends that it is because there is a lack of information on pedophilia. This lack of information is intertwined with the Church's system of secrecy concerning sexual matters. The Church managed sexual abuse through the reassignnment of priests, sending them on a retreat to repent for their sins, or sending them to a psychiatric institution run by the Church. These measures show a lack of understanding concerning pedophilia and a desire to keep the scandal a secret. In discussing the future of the Catholic Church, Sipe asserted that there are four factors that will continue to affect the problem of pedophilia in the Church. These factors are as follows: the lack of education concerning sexuality and celibacy creates a situation in which adolescence is prolonged/postponed and celibacy becomes a way of hiding from one's problems; the structure of the Church and the seminary tolerates and sometimes encourages sexual regression and fixation; the emphasis upon secrecy hinders accountability; and the lack of sexual education in the Church fosters defenses such as denial, rationalization, and splitting.

OTHER RELIGIOUS ORGANIZATIONS

There have not been any empirical studies devoted to ascertaining the prevalence of sexual abuse within other religions. While little has been revealed concerning sexual abuse within the Jewish faith, The Awareness Center is a victim's rights organization for survivors of sexual abuse. On their website (*http://www.theawarenesscenter.org*), these survivors have listed the cases of 40 Rabbis accused of sexual misconduct with adults and children. A search of major U.S. news sources also yielded few results, and articles found are either not empirical or lack specific prevalence details.

BOY SCOUTS OF AMERICA

While there are not any empirical studies devoted to understanding the prevalence of sexual abuse in the Boy Scouts, the work of Patrick Boyle is the most comprehensive, albeit dated, information available. A database search of major newspapers illustrates that between 1970 and 2003, 22 incidents have been discussed in various articles. The majority of the cases fit Boyle's findings in that the perpetrators used various grooming tactics in order to coerce the child into sexual acts. The number of known victims for each offender ranged from one to 20, with some victims not coming forward until adulthood. In many cases, the Scoutmaster knew the child's parents and the offenses ranged from inappropriate touching to intercourse. While the majority of the information presented in these articles is scarce, the information indicated that some of the perpetrators also worked as teachers and Catholic priests.

BOYLE, P. (1991, MAY 20). SCOUT'S HONOR: SCOUTING'S SEX ABUSE TRAIL LEADS TO 50 STATES. *THE WASHINGTON TIMES*, P. A1.

In a five-part series, journalist Patrick Boyle explored the prevalence of sexual abuse in scouting through evaluating the confidential files of the organization in 1991. The results of his investigation are also included in his 1994 book, *Scout's Honor: Sexual Abuse in America's Most Trusted Institution*. Between the period of 1971 to 1989, 416 male Scout employees were banned as a result of sexual misconduct. There have been 1,151 known cases of sexual abuse within scouting. Boyle argued that sexual abuse is more common in scouting than accidental deaths or serious injuries combined. During this time, the Scouts claimed that the sexual abuse was not a major crisis. The Boy Scouts had one million adult volunteers and four million Scouts. Boyle found that Scoutmasters perpetrated the majority of the abuse, but assistant Scoutmasters, of which there are about 147,000, were also responsible. All of the victims appeared to come from the Boy Scouts, who range in age from 11 to 17 and numbered 959,000 at the time of this article's publication. It also appears as if the majority of the abuse occurred during camping trips. The four other parts in this series that were reported

during the week of 5/20/91 to 5/24/91 focused on various topics through case study illustration. The stories illustrated how the organization let known child molesters slip through the system and how the information was covered up in a manner that would protect the image of the Boy Scouts. Boyle also discusses the impact of the abuse on the boys through individual narratives. While the information in the confidential files is limited, the effects of the abuse on the children are unknown. However, Boyle asserts that out of the 400 abuse cases he investigated, four Scouts attempted suicide and at least three leaders who were charged with abuse also made suicide attempts. When a Scoutmaster was reported to local Scout officials, they oftentimes made deals in order to ensure that the scandal would remain a secret. If the Scoutmaster agreed to leave, there would be no police involvement. What the Scouts did not realize is that the offenders were moving away and joining new troops where they continued to offend. Even those offenders who were reported to the Scouts' National Headquarters managed to evade the system and continued to act as Scoutmasters. As public awareness concerning the abuse grew, the Boy Scouts realized the need to combat this problem. Boyle claims that the organization has paid at least fifteen million dollars in order to settle cases out of court, with payments ranging from $12,000 to $1.5 million. In cooperation with experts in the field of sexual abuse, the Scouts have developed an extensive training program, which is meant to raise the awareness of both children and Scoutmasters. It has recently become a requirement that all employees must pass a background check in order to work for the Boy Scouts. They have also instituted policies prohibiting homosexual scout leaders, which have come under the scrutiny of various civil rights organizations.

BOYLE, P. (1991, MAY 21). SCOUT'S HONOR PART 2: PEDOPHILIC PREFERENCE IS IN A CLASS ALL ITS OWN. *THE WASHINGTON TIMES*, P. B5.

This part of the series on child abuse in the Boy Scouts focuses on the offender. Boyle argued that for the most part, scouting leaders have tried to protect boys by excluding homosexuals. However, a review of the organization's confidential files revealed that out of 200 cases, 64 offenders were married/engaged and 18 were divorced. Some of the offenders were involved with the victim's mother at the time of the abuse. Many scout leaders also professed that they had no clear reason to believe that these offenders were homosexual. The author also discusses the process involved in selecting new Scoutmasters, which in the past involved a simple check of references. The methods of seduction are also discussed and include the use of campouts, games, abuse of loyalty and authority, initiation rites, trips alone, physical exams, sleepovers, and awards.

BIG BROTHER ORGANIZATION

The purpose of the Big Brother organization is to provide disadvantaged youths between the ages of seven and 13 with a mentor. Similar to the Boy Scouts, the Big Brother/Sister organization has also experienced incidents of sexual abuse. No official data exists, but a database search of major newspapers revealed six published incidents between 1973 and 2001. As with the Boy Scouts, the offenders hailed from a variety of professions and included a school principal and a naval officer.

BOYLE, P. (1994). *SCOUT'S HONOR: SEXUAL ABUSE IN AMERICA'S MOST TRUSTED INSTITUTION*. ROCKLIN, CA; PRIMA PUBLISHING.

In his book, *Scout's Honor*, Patrick Boyle briefly reviews the work conducted by Donald Wolff. In reviewing nearly 100 cases of sexual abuse in the Big Brother and Sister organization, the largest area of concern rested with the Big Brother organization, in which the majority of the abuse stemmed from the Big Brother-Little Brother relationship. Much like the abuse reported in scouting, the majority of offenders were single and came from various professions. The sexual abuse progressed from inappropriate touching to other sexual acts and the most common situations in which the abuse occurred were camp trips and the trips to the perpetrator's house. These perpetrators also appeared to target emotionally vulnerable children. However, unlike the Boy Scouts or Catholic Church, once criminal charges were filed Wolff found that they often led to confessions or convictions. The review also revealed that many of the perpetrators were

also involved in educating and counseling children as well as scouting. In light of these findings, the Big Brothers have instituted a strict screening process, which involves a criminal background check for all volunteers.

YOUNG MEN'S CHRISTIAN ASSOCIATION (YMCA)

There is no record of any empirical data or official reports outlining the prevalence of sexual abuse in the YMCA. Eight articles were found that deal directly with YMCA volunteers molesting children. The perpetrators worked for the organization in various capacities including camp counselors and sports coaches. The offenders targeted both girls and boys and some had a multitude of victims, with one offender claiming he had targeted 20 victims while another had been charged with 75 counts of sexual abuse, including 10 counts of rape. Some of the perpetrators had prior records for sexual abuse and some were employed in schools.

ATHLETIC ORGANIZATIONS

There is no empirical data indicating the prevalence of sexual abuse within sporting organizations. Through a database search of major U.S. newspapers, youth sports teams returned the largest results out of any youth organization. Forty-five articles were devoted to sexual abuse cases in a variety of sports including swimming, basketball, baseball, track and field, football, soccer, hockey, and gymnastics. The majority of the cases illustrated that the perpetrator was somehow involved with a school either as a teacher or principal. Many of the perpetrators appeared to have multiple victims. The offenders also appeared to groom their victims over a period of time. One case involved a coach who was charged with 400 counts of sexual abuse, whereas some of the other perpetrators reportedly had 10 or 12 victims and the behaviors ranged from touching to rape. The victim's families were also charmed in some instances so that the perpetrator could gain their trust and access to the victim. The perpetrators hailed from North America, the UK, and Ireland and a few had been prominent figures in their respective sport. In many of the cases, the coaches were suspended from the organization or were subjected to criminal charges. The victims ranged in age; however, a majority of them appeared to be in their teens.

CHILD CAREGIVERS

FINKELHOR, D. & ORMROD, R. (2001). CRIMES AGAINST CHILDREN BY BABYSITTERS. *JUVENILE JUSTICE BULLETIN*, SEPTEMBER 2001.

In evaluating the FBI's National Incident-Based Reporting System, the authors examined the prevalence of sexual abuse by babysitters. Babysitters are responsible for 4.2% of all reported offenses for children under the age of six, but sexual abuse outnumbered physical abuse by two to one. Those who are at a high risk of sexual abuse fall within the age range of three to five. Those babysitters reported to the police were predominantly male (77%) and 48% of the offenders were juveniles. The sexual acts committed include forcible fondling (42%), forcible sodomy (11%), forcible rape (8%) and sexual assault with an object (3%). Male perpetrators were more likely to target female victims. The female perpetrators were often juvenile offenders and were more likely to be reported for physical abuse.

FINKELHOR, D., WILLIAMS, L.M., & BURNS, N. (1988). *NURSERY CRIMES: SEXUAL ABUSE IN DAY CARE*. NEWBURY PARK, CA; SAGE PUBLICATION.

This study evaluated substantiated claims of sexual abuse from center-based and family-based day care institutions. In order to be included in this study, the facility had to cater to children six years of age or younger, of which 270 institutions were identified. Substantiation was based upon the investigations of local agencies including child protection, licensing, and police agencies. The 270 cases illustrated 1,639 victims (484 girls and 269 boys) and 382 perpetrators (222 males, 147 females, and 13 whose gender could not be identified) over the time period of 1983-1985. The authors urge that the data be interpreted with caution due to the fact that some government agencies did not cooperate with the researchers' requests and that the information sought was not always kept in one location and not uniformly organized. However, the researchers were able to estimate the following statistics: 30.7 of every 10,000 centers and 15.3 of every 10,000 families have cases of reported child sexual abuse, 5.5 out of every 10,000 children enrolled in day-care centers and 8.9 children out of every 10,000 children in families are reported to be sexually abused. The researchers concluded that while a day-care center is more likely to be reported for sexual abuse, the risk of a child being abused is actually lower when enrolled in a center than in their own home due to the presence of more children. In evaluating the perpetrators the following relationships were revealed: 16% were directors/owners, 30% were teachers, 15% were nonprofessional child caretakers, 8% were in a non-child care capacity, 25% were family members of the staff, and 5% were outsiders. There also appeared to be a rather high number of female perpetrators involved in day care abuse with 44% of child care workers, 6% of family members, and 6% of multiple perpetrators being female.

THEORIES OF SEXUAL OFFENDING

GENERAL THEORIES

LAWS, D.R., & MARSHALL, W.L. (1990). A CONDITIONING THEORY OF THE ETIOLOGY AND MAINTENANCE OF DEVIANT SEXUAL PREFERENCE AND BEHAVIOR. IN W. L. MARSHALL (EDS.), *HANDBOOK OF SEXUAL ASSAULT: ISSUES, THEORIES, AND TREATMENT OF THE OFFENDER, 13, 209-229.* NEW YORK: PLENUM PRESS.

This article presented a theoretical model of sexually deviant interests that described how they may be learned through the same mechanisms by which conventional sexuality is learned. The model is divided into two parts: acquisition processes and maintenance processes. The authors noted that the model adopts the position that maladaptive behavior can result from quantitative and qualitative combinations of processes that are themselves intrinsically orderly, strictly determined, and normal in origin. This conditioning and social learning model stated that deviant sexual preferences and cognitions are acquired through the same mechanisms by which other persons learn more conventionally accepted modes of sexual expression. The model is presented as a set of 13 general principles and 14 propositions that are derived from the 13 principles. There are six basic conditioning principles (Pavlovian Conditioning, Operant Conditioning, Extinction, Punishment, Differential Consequences, and the Chaining of Behavior); two social learning influences (General Social Learning Influences and Self-Labeling Influences); and three maintenance processes (Specific Autoerotic Influences, Specific Social Learning Influences, and Intermittent Reinforcement). In addition, the authors discuss the treatment application of the theoretical model.

MARSHALL, W.L., & BARBAREE, H.E. (1990). AN INTEGRATED THEORY OF THE ETIOLOGY OF SEXUAL OFFENDING. IN W. L. MARSHALL (EDS.), *HANDBOOK OF SEXUAL ASSAULT: ISSUES, THEORIES, AND TREATMENT OF THE OFFENDER, 15, 257-275.* NEW YORK: PLENUM PRESS.

This article represented an attempt to integrate a widely disparate literature concerning factors that play a role in the etiology of sexual offending and lead to its persistence. In order to achieve their goal, the authors discuss biological influences, childhood experiences, general cultural features, availability of pornography, and transitory situational factors. In conclusion, the authors stated that all of these factors must be taken into account when planning the treatment of sex offenders.

SCHWARTZ, B.K. (1995). CHARACTERISTICS AND TYPOLOGIES OF SEX OFFENDERS. IN B. SCHWARTZ (EDS.). *THE SEX OFFENDER: CORRECTIONS, TREATMENT AND LEGAL PRACTICE, 2.* NEW JERSEY: CIVIC RESEARCH INSTITUTE, INC.

Outlined theoretical explanations for sexually deviant behavior, including: psychoanalytic theory, ego psychology theory, neurosis theory, Jungian theory, relational theories, behavioral theories, cognitive-behavioral theories, addictions theory, anthropological theories, family theories, societal theories, political theory, the integrated theory of child abuse, and the integrated theory of deviancy. Further, it reviewed causative factors and methods of treatment.

WARD, T., & KEENAN, T. (1999). CHILD MOLESTERS' IMPLICIT THEORIES. *JOURNAL OF INTERPERSONAL VIOLENCE, 14* (8), 821-838.

The authors argued that child molesters' cognitive distortions are generated by maladaptive implicit theories concerning the nature of victims, the offender, and the world. An examination of a number of scales used to measure distortions and several articles describing offenders' cognitive distortions resulted in the formulation of five implicit theories —Children as Sexual Objects; Entitlement; Dangerous World; Uncontrollability; and Nature of Harm—each capable of generating a number of maladaptive thoughts. Implicit theories were used to explain, understand, and predict the behavior of victims and aid in the planning and execution of sexual offenses. They typically were not consciously articulated and facilitated the processing of offense-related information. According to the authors, there was ample evidence from developmental, social, cognitive, and personality psychology to support the influential role of implicit theories in individuals' understanding of themselves and the social world. It is therefore reasonable to assume that the multitude of distorted beliefs and attitudes exhibited in child molesters are the product of a small number of theories. The authors suggested that effective treatment is likely to require the challenging and restructuring of these core theories. Finally, the authors argued that it is possible to develop an integrated account of child molesters' cognitive distortions by focusing on the role of implicit theories in offense-related behavior. This perspective linked research and theory in a number of diverse areas of psychology and attempted to create a common framework for understanding the relationship between cognition and behavior.

WARD, T., & HUDSON, S.M. (1998). THE CONSTRUCTION AND DEVELOPMENT OF THEORY IN THE SEXUAL OFFENDING AREA: A META-THEORETICAL FRAMEWORK. *SEXUAL ABUSE: A JOURNAL OF RESEARCH & TREATMENT, 10,* 1.

The authors outlined a meta-theoretical framework, or a multi-theory approach to sexual abuse, that took into account a number of different levels of theory, such as comprehensive, middle, and micro-levels, and stresses the importance of distinguishing between different types of causal factors. Further, the authors illustrated the utility of the described meta-theory and demonstrated how different theories of sexual offending can be meaningfully integrated within this framework.

THEORIES OF OFFENDING BY CLERGY

HANDS, D.R. (2002). BEYOND THE CLOISTER-SHAMED SEXUALITY IN THE FORMATION OF THE SEX-OFFENDING CLERGY. IN B.K. SCHWARTZ & H.R. CELLINI (EDS.), *THE SEX OFFENDER* (PP. 29-1-29-8). KINGSTON, NJ: CIVIC RESEARCH INSTITUTE.

This chapter presented a brief overview of the influence that Church doctrine has had on sexually abusive clerics. Hands argued that the experience of shame interacts with unrealistic, moral expectations that have been internalized. The result of this process is a shame cycle, which stunts the individual's psychosexual development and contributes to sexual misconduct. The internalization of Church doctrine concerning celibacy/chastity reinforces many cognitive distortions, which allow the cycle of abuse to persist. The Church's interpretation of sexual misconduct as a personal sin directly contrasts with the view held by the criminal justice system. The Church has also discouraged the formation of close friendships among the clergy for fear that it might lead to homosexuality. With increased social isolation comes increased alienation from the body. Thus sexuality is repressed only to later emerge as an obsession. According to Sullivan, "primary genital phobia" is a result of this repression. When the individual experiences any sexual feelings, thoughts, or emotions they are reflexively ignored. The obsession occurs because these feelings are never directly addressed or managed in a productive manner.

JENKINS, P. (1996). *PEDOPHILES AND PRIESTS: ANATOMY OF A CONTEMPORARY CRISIS.* BRIDGEWATER, NJ: REPLICA BOOKS.

CHAPTER 1: THE CONSTRUCTION OF PROBLEMS AND PANICS
This chapter provided an overview of the format of the book and the issue of child sexual abuse in the Church. While it has been acknowledged that the abuse occurs, Jenkins contends that not much else is known about this issue. The author summarized the construction of the problem as going through the following stages: (1) many clergy are active in the sexual abuse of children; (2) many Catholic priests are active in sexual abuse; and (3) the structure of Catholicism makes priests more likely to abuse children. The Catholic Church is likely to be targeted due to its size and centralized hierarchy. The media's interpretation of cases of sexual abuse and litigation make it impossible to compare the prevalence of abuse across denominations.

CHAPTER 2: THE ANTI-CATHOLIC TRADITION
In this chapter, Jenkins provided a historical overview of anti-clericalism and anti-Catholicism. While it is believed that anti-Catholicism ceased

during the 1930s to 1980s, Jenkins argued that the emergence of books such as *Lead Us Not into Temptation* and *A Gospel of Shame* facilitated these ideas. Anti-Catholicism has also been integrated into culture through development of Catholic stereotypes and humor. It is argued that the idea of the predatory priest has always existed in a subcultural setting only to emerge into mainstream culture when the time was right.

CHAPTER 3: THE DISCOVERY OF CLERGY SEX ABUSE

Jenkins claimed that during the 1980's, allegations of sexual abuse committed by priests became prevalent. Two views about this phenomenon exist. One argument theorized that the abuse has been around for years but that it has only emerged during the last decade. Accepting this argument would mean that the crisis began in the 1960's, perhaps as a result of relaxed sexual discipline. The second argument posited that the abuse is a result of the liberal reforms of *Vatican-II*. Jenkins provided an overview of the publicized cases and included a timeline of major events. He hypothesized that the major scandal in the Louisiana diocese created a "snowball effect" in which the media increased their coverage of the issue and became more aggressive in pursuing such stories. This placed pressure upon the Church, which had to react quickly by implementing new policies in order to handle the problem. As a result of the media portraying the abuse as "a Catholic problem," they have neglected to evaluate the prevalence of abuse in other denominations.

CHAPTER 4: THE MEDIA AND THE CRISIS

This chapter discussed the media coverage of sexual abuse in the Catholic Church in both national and local publications. These publications portrayed the problem as being a crisis and scandal, requiring swift intervention. The news media also utilized images unique to the Catholic Church, which further characterized the crisis as being solely a Catholic phenomenon. Jenkins drew a contrast between these images and the more wholesome portrayal of the Catholic Church in films made between 1938 and 1944. Changing media values are one possible reason for this occurrence as the emphasis shifted towards tabloid reporting and sensationalism. In constructing the abuse "crisis," the media turned to Jason Berry and Andrew Greeley as experts. Soon, other authorities on the topic began

to emerge and each had their own agenda. Since these cases were widely publicized, public awareness of the issue of child sexual abuse also increased. Jenkins posits that these reports facilitated the investigation and prosecution of new cases as well as the creation of the image of the pedophile priest.

CHAPTER 5: PEDOPHILIA AND CHILD ABUSE

This chapter sought to evaluate three specific areas of child sexual abuse by clergy: defining the abuse in question, assessing the number of perpetrators, and establishing a historical context in which the allegations were made. In defining the problem, Jenkins drew attention to the differences between pedophilia and ephebophilia. While there were cases that involve extensive abuse, not all of them were severe. The media's reliance upon the image of the pedophile priest thus distorted the true nature of the problem. In citing a study conducted by the Chicago Diocese, Jenkins ascertained that the prevalence rate amongst priests is less than two percent. In establishing an historical context, the author illustrated how social feelings concerning sex offenders have cycled through the years. During the 1980's the effects of abuse on the victims began to receive attention that raised public awareness concerning sex offenders. The McMartin abuse scandal influenced ideas about clergy abuse by illustrating that sexual abuse could occur anywhere, leading to heightened suspicion. A discussion concerning the treatment of clergy offenders is included. Due to the dwindling number of priests in the seminary, the Church was willing to shift attention away from punitive measures to treatment needs in order to preserve its numbers. Treatment programs were created in the belief that the offender could be cured and reinstated into the ministry. While experts in the field attacked this point of view, it was still followed by the Church.

CHAPTER 6: CONFLICT IN THE CHURCHES

In evaluating the cases of sexual abuse in the Church, various themes began to emerge. Jenkins asserted that "the authoritarian nature of the Church and its hierarchy, the special privileges accorded to priests, the apparent neglect of the interests of women and children, and an ambiguous and hypocritical attitude towards sexuality" are notions that have existed for years. This battle between liberals and conservatives in the Church was sparked by the reforms of *Vatican-II* and a dwindling priesthood. Church doctrine concerning sexuality came under fire from Catholic traditionalists who felt that the reforms of *Vatican-II* were too liberal and facilitated an environment in which abuse was allowed to exist. The liberals were concerned about reforms to the patriarchal Church hierarchy, which displayed little consideration for the laity. The clergy abuse scandal provided a platform for reformists to point out the apparent hypocritical nature of various Church doctrines.

CHAPTER 7: "SINS OF THE FATHERS"; THE FEMINIST RESPONSE

This chapter discussed the role of the feminist movement in the exposure of sexual abuse in the general population and clergy. Church doctrine concerning abortion and birth control came under criticism as a result of the movement. Feminists argued that sexual violence is a result of patriarchal culture, which is influenced by social institutions such as the Catholic Church. When the allegations of abuse began to emerge, feminists integrated them as evidence in favor of their argument. The definition of clergy sexual abuse was broadened to incorporate heterosexual relations between the priest and adult women. Jenkins argued that feminist rhetoric benefited from a social environment already ripe with discontent and an ever-changing legal interpretation of the problem.

CHAPTER 8: THE LEGAL ENVIRONMENT

During the 1980's the civil system saw the growth of torts concerning child sexual abuse. This was due to the claims of child maltreatment in nursery schools across the nation as well as new research concerning the credibility of child witnesses and recovered memories. This was also the first time that mandatory child abuse reporting statutes were passed throughout the nation. The Church is a billion-dollar industry, which makes it an appealing target for civil litigants. Litigation was pursued even when the evidence was not very strong and based upon retrospective data. Due to the statute of limitations, criminal prosecution was not an option for many victims. When the Church tried to defend itself against these excessive civil suits, various organizations claimed that hypocrisy and selfishness were inherent in the Church hierarchy. Jenkins argued that juries are more likely to be sympathetic towards victims, thereby creating an environment in which clergy litigation is an appealing choice.

CHAPTER 9: DEFENDING THERAPY

Jenkins posits that mental health professionals also have an interest in clergy litigation, as they would be called for treatment and their expert opinion. As the definition of child abuse changed in the 1970's, children were viewed as honest witnesses. This was impacted by a variety of research that evaluated the child's capability as a witness and the validity of memories. During the 1980's, allegations of ritual sexual abuse swept the nation and created a modern day witch-hunt. This chapter included a brief overview of the recovered memory phenomenon, media attention allotted the topic, and its impact on allegations of sexual abuse. Clergy abuse served to reinforce therapeutic assumptions whereas the ideas concerning ritual abuse reinforce the idea of the pedophile priest. As the validity of recovered memories and ritual abuse allegations were exposed, a backlash occurred where the topic lost any momentum it may have had.

JENKINS, P. (1998). CREATING A CULTURE OF CLERGY DEVIANCE. IN A. SHUPE (ED.) *WOLVES WITHIN THE FOLD: RELIGIOUS LEADERSHIP AND ABUSES OF POWER* (PP. 118-132). NEW BRUNSWICK, NJ: RUTGERS UNIVERSITY PRESS.

Clergy deviance is explained through the impact the media has had in publicizing "scandals" and the reactions of Catholics to this news. Jenkins asserted that there were no scandals prior to the 1970's. This meant that the Church was protected from media scrutiny and that the pattern of multiple offenses committed by "pedophile priests" could not be followed. The media blackout promoted an environment in which those few priests who were inclined to engage in malfeasance experienced a sense of invulnerability because there was no possibility of incurring sanctions. The internal structure of the Church and the shortage of priests caused many Bishops to ignore discrepancies in order to preserve the clergy. Jenkins provided an overview of the relationship between the Catholic Church and media dating back to the 1920's. In the media's zeal to expose scandals in the Catholic Church, the Church utilized its power to boycott such publications. This ploy proved effective in controlling potential scandals. During the 1970's, films and novels depicted the secret sexual lives of priests, which is in stark contrast to the wholesome films of the 1950's. Jenkins posits that the Watergate scandal played a role in encouraging exposé journalism. This coupled with changing demographics and a split in the Church concerning the revisions of *Vatican II*, all played a role in creating an environment in which sexual abuse scandals were exposed by the media. According to Jenkins, "Media attitudes therefore helped create an absolute criminogenic social environment," and the extent to which this environment has been exploited remains unclear.

KREBS, T. (1998). CHURCH STRUCTURES THAT FACILITATE PEDOPHILIA AMONG ROMAN CATHOLIC CLERGY. IN A. SHUPE (ED.) *WOLVES WITHIN THE FOLD: RELIGIOUS LEADERSHIP AND ABUSES OF POWER* (PP. 67-84). NEW BRUNSWICK, NJ: RUTGERS UNIVERSITY PRESS.

Krebs argued that the structure of the Church and its hierarchy facilitate sexual abuse. Anonymity was granted to pedophiliac priests due to the Church's international nature, organizational hierarchy, and internal polity. The organizational hierarchy was discussed in relation to the work of Andrew Shupe, who observed five unique characteristics. Institutional religion is based on what Shupe called "hierarchies of unequal power," which span different dimensions including the spiritual and organizational. Those in elite positions have moral authority, which allows them to control privileges as well as shun and excommunicate. Third, the Catholic Church is what Shupe referred to as a "trusted hierarchy," which influenced parental socialization of children to believe and trust in Church officials. Clergy malfeasance occurs in trusted hierarchies. Fourth, the structure of the Church provided "opportunity structure" and "protected places" that allow for deviancy. The Church also engaged in neutralization to protect these offending priests. In turn, this gives the pedophile approval from superiors to continue offending. Shupe contends that by taking any neutralizing action, the problem can occur once more. These priests can be reassigned to new parishes and diocese where only a few members of the hierarchy may know their history. Krebs also argued that newly implemented structures continued to facilitate pedophilia in the Church. One such structure is the study group comprised of the entire Church community, which seeks to find a solution to this problem. Krebs asserted that the focus of these groups has been to ascertain that while sexual abuse occurs in the Catholic Church, it is more prevalent in other institutions. The reason why sexual abuse in the Church is a major issue is because the offenders are ordained priests who took a vow of celibacy.

LOFTUS, J.A. (1999). SEXUALITY IN PRIESTHOOD: NOLI ME TANGERE. IN T.G. PLANTE (ED.) *BLESS ME FATHER FOR I HAVE SINNED: PERSPECTIVES ON SEXUAL ABUSE COMMITTED BY ROMAN CATHOLIC PRIESTS* (PP. 7-19). WESTPORT, CT: PRAEGER PUBLISHERS.

Loftus provided an historical overview of sexuality in the priesthood. He explained that a focus of priestly teachings concerning celibacy is characterized by the phrase "if no one touches me, I will not experience sexual desire, or at least not sexual temptation." The work of Sipe is discussed in examining the issue of celibacy. The author contends that there is no simple way to define celibacy and that it is a complex and dynamic issue. There is also a public relations issue related to the fact that many parishioners believe that priests are indeed celibate and always have been. The work of Loftus & Camargo (1993) is discussed and the author posits that the question should not be what an acceptable definition of celibacy is, but rather how sexuality is experienced within this population. Research is hindered because there is no access to data concerning sexuality in the "normal" priest population.

LOTHSTEIN, L. (1999). NEUROPSYCHOLOGICAL FINDINGS IN CLERGY WHO SEXUALLY ABUSE. IN T.G. PLANTE (ED.) *BLESS ME FATHER FOR I HAVE SINNED: PERSPECTIVES ON SEXUAL ABUSE COMMITTED BY ROMAN CATHOLIC PRIESTS* (PP. 59-85). WESTPORT, CT: PRAEGER PUBLISHERS.

This chapter presented a review of the literature concerning neuropsychology and sexual offending. Studies have shown that there appear to be abnormalities located in the fronto-temporal region of the brain of sex offenders. However, these studies suffer from methodological flaws and the results are typically confounded by substance abuse. The Institute for Living clergy study is discussed, in which 400 clerics have been evaluated for paraphiliac and non-paraphiliac sexual behavior. The findings supported the theory that sex offenders, from the general and cleric population, appear to have an abnormality in the fronto-temporal region of their brains. While the abnormalities are similar there are differences between the cleric and non-cleric offenders. The author warned against inferring a causal link between brain dysfunction and paraphiliac behavior. It was recommended when assessing clerics that those who have a history of hard neurological signs (massive head trauma, seizures, history of unconsciousness, etc.) should be considered as being at a high risk for sexual disinhibition. Those who have a history of soft neurological signs (impulsivity, anxiety, etc.) must also be thoroughly evaluated.

PALLONE, N.J. (2002). SIN, CRIME, ARROGANCE, BETRAYAL: A PSYCHODYNAMIC PERSPECTIVE ON THE CRISIS IN AMERICAN CATHOLICISM. *BRIEF TREATMENT AND CRISIS INTERVENTION, 2* (4), 341-372.

In this article Pallone states that the crisis of sexual misconduct in the Roman Catholic Church is in fact homosexual statutory rape. Along this line, Pallone also states that a majority of the victims were not of "pre-pubescent age" as specified in the DSM IV; therefore the offenders cannot be considered pedophiles. It is a new disorder, considered ephebophilia, and he presents an in-depth explanation of the disorder based on "Fenichel's (1945) speculations about the genesis of psychosexual pathology among (sexually inexperienced but palpably) narcissistic adult males and incorporating the contribution of Catholic doctrine on the Virgin birth" (p. 366). The disorder is not yet recognized by the DSM IV; however, there is a danger in creating a new category of mental disorder whose behavior has been deemed criminal.

The offenders consist of a relatively small number of priests. Few clerics were being prosecuted, and only seemed to face arrest and prosecution after the press had learned of the civil liability payments made to the victims. In most situations, responsibility is not admitted by the diocese, while the victims are paid to keep silent. The press focuses only on current cases while those that occurred more than a month ago is considered ancient history. Pallone points out that this is not an isolated American phenomenon, but is also occurring in countries such as Ireland, Canada, Australia, England, Poland, and Africa.

SCHEPER-HUGHES, N. (1998). INSTITUTIONALIZED SEX ABUSE AND THE CATHOLIC CHURCH. IN N. SCHEPER-HUGHES & C. SARGENT (EDS.) *SMALL WARS: THE CULTURAL POLITICS OF CHILDHOOD* (PP. 295-317). BERKELEY, CA: UNIVERSITY OF CALIFORNIA PRESS.

The author presented a response to the theories proposed by the Winter Commission in Newfoundland. In posing this argument, it was urged that the Church look even deeper into the institutional and structural roots of sexual abuse within institutions. According to ethnographic data, sexual abuse is not endemic or universal. Scheper-Hughes argued that "social isolation, arbitrary parental authority over children, patriarchal values, single-parent households, and negative images of the social worth of children all promote and exacerbate child sexual abuse." A brief discussion concerning clergy abuse in Ireland is included. The author cited the work of Kennedy (1972) who found that 8% of priests were maldeveloped, 57% were underdeveloped, 29% were developing, and only 6% were developed. In a personal interview with the author he ascertained that "The vows of poverty and obedience infantalize the adult male, making him dependant on a series of father figures at a time when they should be in control of their own lives and responsible for the lives of children and young people. The vow of celibacy takes from the adult a main vehicle for the expression of intimate social relations. The end result is chronic infantilization." However, the Winter Commission was silent on the topic of celibacy. The author draws parallels between corporal punishment, with its erotic undertones, to that of clergy abuse. Corporal punishment was said to have created a sexualized environment, which may have provided the antecedent conditions for sexual offending.

SIPE, A.W.R. (1995). *SEX, PRIESTS, AND POWER: ANATOMY OF A CRISIS, 1,* 3-23, NEW YORK, NY: BRUNNER/MAZEL, INC.

Sipe extrapolated upon the findings of his 1990 book, *A Secret World: Sexuality and the Search for Celibacy.* In studying the celibacy patterns of Catholic priests, the author postulated that 20% have engaged in heterosexual relationships and behaviors, 10% have engaged in homosexual behavior, 4% have had adolescent partners and 2% are pedophiles. Sipe asserted that child molestation is a result of the flawed celibate/sexual system of the Church. Since the Church has not developed a clear understanding of human sexuality in general, they were unable to formulate a response to this issue. This is coupled with the fact that the teachings of the Church were not always followed by those in power.

After having reviewed the histories of 473 abusive priests, it was found that 70-80% of priests were sexually abused as children and 10% were approached by a priest while studying in the seminary. The author has developed four specific categories to explain sexual abuse in the clergy. Those in Sipes' Genetic Lock find that their sexual attraction is inherently determined. The Psychodynamic Lock consists of priests who, as a result of their childhood experiences, have been locked into one level of psychosexual development, rendering them prone to offending behavior. Sipe hypothesized that a combination of genetic and psychodynamic factors interacts with cognitive factors. All of these variables combine in such a manner as to influence the priest to sexually abuse a child. In the Social/Situational Lock, the priest is otherwise healthy but the experience of celibacy suspends their psychosexual development. Similar to the theory of primary genital phobia, sex is externally denied but internally explored. Sipe concluded that the offending behavior is of a developmental nature, which could be resolved, once the offender matured. The Moral Lock provided no clear explanation for the offending behavior. According to Sipe, these individuals are cold and calculating and make a conscience choice to sexually abuse children just because they desire the experience.

Sipe, A.W.R. (1995). *Sex, priests, and power: Anatomy of a crisis*, 2, 24-43, New York, NY: Brunner/Mazel, Inc.

This chapter evaluated Sipe's estimation that 6% of priests have sexually abused minors. It is argued that the evidence presented by the victim's rights movement have supported this estimate. Survivors do not pursue lawsuits solely to gain monetary restitution. Their motivation is to gain the assurance that no other children will be victimized. Thus, there is a conflict with the responsibilities allotted to the Bishops, who seek to protect the Church's holdings and power. Among the factors that must be examined when evaluating clergy offenders are the age and gender of the child, whether the incident is isolated or of a serial nature, whether the offender is fixated or regressed, whether the behavior is compulsive or addictive, and determining what exactly the abuse entailed. A discussion of treatment elaborated upon the idea that one of the difficulties in treating these offenders is that the abuse is viewed as a sin that may be resolved through confession and penance. During the course of treatment, the Church should monitor the offender for a period of about five years.

Sipe, A.W.R. (1998). *Clergy abuse in Ireland*. In A. Shupe (Ed.) *Wolves within the fold: Religious leadership and abuses of power* (pp. 133-151). New Brunswick, NJ: Rutgers University Press.

This chapter provided an overview of clergy abuse in Ireland. What made the abuse in Ireland so unique is the integration of Church and State, which has existed since the country's emancipation from the UK. Through the years, various reforms have occurred including the legalization of divorce and the Abortion Information Bill, which allowed certain medical centers to provide information pertaining to the operation. These reforms did not occur until the mid-1990s. In 1996, the Irish hierarchy pledged full cooperation with the authorities in addressing the issue of cleric abuse. Sipe contends that all of the accounts of sexual abuse in Ireland have in fact been well known and recorded accurately albeit censored. This abuse has been known as a characteristic of the Church in Ireland for years. The relation between the Irish Church and that of the American Church illustrated an interesting connection in supporting Sipe's thesis. Seventeen percent of the US population during the period of 1960-1970 was Irish American. However, 54% of priests were Irish Americans or Irish and 85% of archbishops and 75% of Bishops were Irish American. This connection has led Sipe to raise the following questions: (1) Is there a correlation between ethnic origin and clergy abuse; (2) What is the rate of sexual abuse/activity by priests in Ireland versus the US; (3) How many sexually abusive priests in the US, England, and elsewhere were born or educated in Ireland; (4) Is the proportion of known sexually abusive Irish-born or Irish educated priests greater or less than their representation in the indigenous clergy pool? Sipe contends that cleric abuse revealed a structure of systematic abuse of children handed down through the ages and shaped by priests and nuns. This structure developed during the Potato Famine, which produced the severe social and economic ramifications: survivor guilt and the experience of fear, bankruptcy of various institutions other than the Catholic Church, consolidation of Church power, and the effect of emigration on the population.

TYPOLOGIES OF THE SEXUAL OFFENDER

TYPOLOGIES OF OFFENDERS WHO ABUSE CHILDREN

BAXTER, D.J., MARSHALL, W.L., BARBAREE, H.E., DAVIDSON, P.R., & MALCOLM, P.B. (1984). DEVIANT SEXUAL BEHAVIOR: DIFFERENTIATING SEX OFFENDERS BY CRIMINAL AND PERSONAL HISTORY, PSYCHOMETRIC MEASURES, AND SEXUAL RESPONSE. *CRIMINAL JUSTICE AND BEHAVIOR, 11* (4), 477-501.

The authors examined criminal records, personal history, social-sexual competence, and physiological responses to erotic stimuli in incarcerated pedophiles, ephebophiles, and rapists. There were significant differences among groups in criminal and personal background. In particular, pedophiles tended to be older, more poorly educated, more likely to be unmarried, and less frequently involved in nonsexual crime. Social and social-sexual inadequacies were common to all groups, as reflected in under-assertiveness, low self-esteem and negative attitudes. The data provided a degree of support for the popular view of the pedophile as a sexual deviant. Pedophiles were somewhat older than other subjects, were more likely to be repetitive sexual offenders, with less nonsexual criminal involvement than rapists or ephebophiles. They also were more likely to exhibit deviant sexual arousal, inasmuch as they responded much more to children than non-pedophilic subjects. However, the pedophiles did not so much show an erotic preference for children as show a failure to either inhibit responding to children or to show a clear erotic preference for adults. Non-pedophilic subjects showed an attenuated response to children relative to adults whereas pedophiles did not. Although the findings of the present study were consistent with earlier reports that many pedophiles are married and have children of their own, they conflict with those reports indicating that pedophiles tended to exhibit strong sexual preferences for children. The authors suggested that this may be a result of the rather small sample from which the present data were obtained. Overall, choice of victim was clearly related only to sexual response patterns, and then only in the case of a prepubescent victim. Pedophiles and homosexual offenders responded more to male children than did heterosexual offenders. Beyond this, there appeared to be little to differentiate between the offender who attacks young pubescent victims and the offender who chooses only mature adult victims.

BEECH, A.R. (1998). A PSYCHOMETRIC TYPOLOGY OF CHILD ABUSERS. *INTERNATIONAL JOURNAL OF OFFENDER THERAPY AND COMPARATIVE CRIMINOLOGY, 43* (4) 319-339.

A psychometric battery of measures, assessing a range of problem areas, was completed by 140 convicted untreated child abusers. Measures were adjusted for social desirability. Cluster analysis of the data identified men on the basis of deviance (levels of pro-offending attitudes and social inadequacy) and denial (self-reported levels of offending behaviors). Examination of offense histories found that high-deviancy men, compared to low-deviancy men, were more likely to have been convicted of a previous sexual offense; to have committed offenses against boys, or both boys and girls; to have committed extrafamilial, or both extra-and-intrafamilial, offenses; and to have had many victims. A method of identifying deviancy, which showed strong cross-validation, also was derived. Although low-deviancy men were much more likely to be incest offenders than were high-deviancy men, nearly 40% of high-deviancy men were found to be intrafamilial offenders, suggesting that identifying deviancy level may be a useful adjunct to any risk assessment.

BICKLEY, J.A., BEECH, A.R. (2002). AN INVESTIGATION OF THE WARD AND HUDSON PATHWAYS MODEL OF THE SEXUAL OFFENSE PROCESS WITH CHILD ABUSERS. *JOURNAL OF INTERPERSONAL VIOLENCE, 17* (4), 372-393.

This article discussed a study wherein the authors sought to evaluate the Ward and Hudson pathways model for classifying child abusers. Eighty-seven child abusers participated in the study. The participants ranged in age from 21 to 75. The majority of the participants (62%) had offended outside the family, 15% had offended inside the family, and 23% had offended both inside and outside the family. Of the participants, 36% had offended against boys, 33% against girls, and 31% had offended against both genders. Fifty-three percent of the sample had a previous conviction for a sexual offense. All participants attended The Lucy Faithful Foundation residential assessment and treatment program for sexual offenders (Wolvercote Unit), based in the United Kingdom. The participants were classified as belonging to one of the four pathway groups identified by Ward and Hudson's self-regulation model of sexual offense process. The model distinguishes between offenders who have approach or avoidant goals and between their uses of active or passive strategies. The article stated that the profile of the "preferential" child molester is consistent with Ward and Hudson's description of an approach pathway. In contrast, the "situational" offender is consistent with Ward and Hudson's description of an avoidant pathway. The authors concluded that the study was able to demonstrate that the self-regulation model (Ward and Hudson) could be reliably employed in the classification of child molesters, with interrater agreement found in more than 80% of the sample. Furthermore, differences across the two group distinctions (i.e., avoidant vs. approach, active vs. passive) in both the psychometric and offense demographic data provided objective support for the validity of the framework. The article also discussed the treatment implications of the self-regulation model.

BICKLEY, J., BEECH, A.R. (2001). CLASSIFYING CHILD ABUSERS: ITS RELEVANCE TO THEORY AND CLINICAL PRACTICE. *JOURNAL OF OFFENDER THERAPY AND COMPARATIVE CRIMINOLOGY*, 45 (1), 51-69.

This article aimed to critically review some of the classification approaches that have been adopted in an attempt to provide a reliable and valid classification system for child molesters and to consider the impact that such systems have had on the structuring of interventions to meet the differing needs of this client group. Classification systems were viewed in terms of their reliability of criteria, consistency and ease of usage, pertinence to a large number of individuals, valid distinction between types, relevance to treatment, and theoretical relevance to explanation and prediction. The article concluded that although a number of approaches have been adopted in order to reduce the heterogeneity of child molesters, none of the systems to date had adequately met the criteria outlined above. Definitional limitations, sampling differences, low base rates of convictions for sexual offences, and socially desirable responding greatly limit the reliability, validity, and coverage of many of the current classification systems. Furthermore, the statistically significant differences found between the groups bear little relationship to the clinical relevance of such distinctions. The suggested profile for group membership is found only in a small percentage of offenders, and there is often extensive overlap between these groups. Consequently, no one standardized method is universally applied in the classification of child molesters, and therefore, comparison between the various studies remains problematic.

DANNI, K.A. & HAMPE, G.D. (2002). AN ANALYSIS OF PREDICTORS OF CHILD SEX OFFENDER TYPES USING PRE-SENTENCE INVESTIGATION REPORTS. *INTERNATIONAL JOURNAL OF OFFENDER THERAPY AND COMPARATIVE CRIMINOLOGY*, 44 (4), 490-504.

The purpose of this study was to differentiate three types of child sexual offenders – pedophiles, ephebophiles, and incest offenders. The sample consisted of 168 convicted sex offenders. The data for the study was gathered from pre-sentence investigation reports used by the court for sentencing proceedings. Using multiple discriminate analyses, eight independent variables were found to significantly discriminate between the three types of sex offenders almost 90% of the time. These variables were: sexual victimization as a child, pre-pubertal victim, seduction motive, age-appropriate relationships, stress, own child as victim, social façade, and anger. The authors hypothesized that (1) Pedophiles are more likely to have experienced sexual victimization as a child, to prefer pre-pubertal sex partners, and to be motivated to seduce their victims more than non-pedophiles; (2) Ephebophiles are more likely to have experienced external stress than non-ephebophiles; and (3) Incest offenders are more likely to have a higher level of perceived entitlement than non-incest offenders. All three hypotheses were accepted. The child sex offenders most difficult to correctly classify were the pedophiles (84.06%). The authors attributed this phenomenon to the fact that pedophiles' victims are typically young and are not always able to effectively verbalize or convey the things that happen to them; pedophiles are characterized as trying to please the victims by using forms of seduction (i.e., gifts). In addition, according to the authors, the primary characteristic of pedophilia is the offender's own childhood sexual victimization. The unwillingness to disclose this information makes it less likely a pedophile will be discovered. The authors purported that it is for these reasons this manipulative behavior is harder to detect. Ephebophiles were correctly classified in 92.86% if the cases. Incest offenders were classified correctly in 100% of the cases.

KNIGHT, R.A., & PRENTKY, R.A. (1990). CLASSIFYING SEXUAL OFFENDERS: THE DEVELOPMENT AND CORROBORATION OF TAXONOMIC MODELS. IN W. L. MARSHALL (EDS.). HANDBOOK OF SEXUAL ASSAULT: ISSUES, THEORIES, AND TREATMENT OF THE OFFENDER, 3, 23-52. NEW YORK: PLENUM PRESS.

This article provided a detailed description of how the methodology for generating and testing schemes in deviant populations could be applied to the study of sex offenders. Based on research conducted by the authors during the 1980s at the Massachusetts Treatment Center, the article discussed how the authors employed both deductive-rational and inductive-empirical research strategies simultaneously to determine whether reliable and valid typologies could be created for rapists and child molesters. The authors concluded that their application of a programmatic approach to typology construction and validation has produced taxonomic systems for both child molesters and rapists. The taxonomic system for child molesters has already demonstrated reasonable reliability and consistent ties to distinctive developmental antecedents. In addition, the preliminary results of a 25 year recidivism study of child molesters conducted by the authors indicated that aspects of the model have important prognostic implications. The authors argued that the data presented on the child molester typology strongly support the subdivision of these offenders and indicate that considerable explanatory power will be sacrificed if child molesters are considered a homogeneous group.

KNIGHT, R.A., CARTER, D.L., & PRENTKY, R.A. (1989). A SYSTEM FOR THE CLASSIFICATION OF CHILD MOLESTERS: RELIABILITY AND APPLICATION. JOURNAL OF INTERPERSONAL VIOLENCE, 4 (1) 3-22.

The authors began this article by outlining the benefits of establishing adequate typologies to moderate clinical and administrative decisions and for providing guidance in studying the etiology of sexual abuse. The article then presented the criteria for this typology (Massachusetts Treatment Center: Child Molester Typology, version 3 [MTC:CM3]) and reported data on its interrater reliability. The sample consisted of 177 child molesters. The study indicated that the major decisions in MTC:CM3 have reasonable reliability and reported that the structural changes introduced into the system have also shown substantial concurrent validity, and its components appear to tap stable traits with distinguishable developmental roots. In an appendix to the article, the authors outlined Inclusionary and Exclusionary Criteria.

LAWS, D.R., HANSON, R.K., OSBORN, C.A., & GREENBAUM, P.E. (2000). CLASSIFICATION OF CHILD MOLESTERS BY PLETHYSMOGRAPHIC ASSESSMENT OF SEXUAL AROUSAL AND A SELF-REPORT MEASURE OF SEXUAL PREFERENCE. JOURNAL OF INTERPERSONAL VIOLENCE, 15 (12), 1297-1312.

This study examined the extent to which the use of multiple measures of pedophilic interest improved on the diagnostic accuracy of any single measure. One hundred and twenty-four males voluntarily consented to participate in an outpatient evaluation and treatment program for child molesters. Of these, 56% were referred from the Florida Department of Corrections, 31% were referred from private practitioners, mental health clinics, or other professionals (i.e., attorneys), and 13% were self-reported. All participants admitted to either a sexual attraction to children or to some inappropriate sexual activity with a child. The average age of the participants was 36.08 yrs (range=18-74). Eighty-seven percent were Caucasian, 8% were AfricanAmerican, and 5% were Hispanic. About 26% were married or common-law, 28% were separated or divorced, and 46% had never married. Socioeconomic status based on annual income showed that 14% were middle class, 20% were lower middle class, and 66% were lower class. Fifty-two men did not participate in the research due to the exclusion of both bisexual child molesters and those who did not complete all three measures. In addition to the exclusion criteria, the attrition rate for the outpatient treatment project was quite high. The remaining 72 child molesters completed a self-report card-sort measure of sexual interest, as well as direct monitoring of penile response through penile plethysmograph (PPG) when presented with erotic slides or audio material. The reliability of all measures was high (alpha .91-.96). All three measures of pedophilic interest (i.e., card sort, PPG slides, PPG audio) significantly differentiated boy-object (n=20) and girl-object child molesters (n=52). The card-sort measure displayed the greatest classification accuracy and was the only measure to significantly improve accuracy, once the other two modalities were considered. Consideration of all three modalities proved classification accuracy (91.7%) greater than any single measure.

LIN, J. M., MAXWELL, S. R., & BARCLAY, A. M. (2000). THE PROPORTIONS OF DIFFERENT TYPES OF SEX OFFENDERS AND THE DEGREE OF DIFFICULTY IN TREATING THEM: A COMPARISON OF PERCEPTIONS BY CLINICIANS IN TAIWAN AND IN MICHIGAN. INTERNATIONAL JOURNAL OF OFFENDER THERAPY AND COMPARATIVE CRIMINOLOGY, 44 (2), 222-231.

This study compared the perceptions of clinicians in Taiwan and in Michigan concerning the types of sex offenders they were serving and the difficulties involved in treating these sex offenders. The Groth typology of sex offenders was used as the baseline typology. Results show significant difference in proportions of rapists and child molesters between Taiwan and Michigan, but no significant differences were found in other types. The rankings by clinicians of the degree of difficulty in treating different types of sex offenders were identical in both areas, although the clinical experiences of clinicians between the two areas were different. The results showed that the proportion of child molesters among overall sex offenders is higher in Michigan compared to that in Taiwan. The authors noted that cognitive-behavioral and relapse prevention treatment are the two prevalent therapies in North America, but whether such therapies are effective in Taiwan is still unknown.

LOOMAN, J., GAUTHIER, C., BOER, D. (2001). REPLICATION OF THE MASSACHUSETTS TREATMENT CENTER CHILD MOLESTER TYPOLOGY IN A CANADIAN SAMPLE. JOURNAL OF INTERPERSONAL VIOLENCE, 16 (8), 753-767.

One hundred and nine child molesters who were assessed or treated at the Regional Treatment Centre (Ontario) were classified according to the MTC child molester typology. Interrater reliabilities were obtained for 20 participants and ranged from .90 to .40, which were comparable to those obtained in the MTC sample. Groups were compared on a number of meaningful variables, such as number of victims and sexual deviance. Results illustrated that it is possible to apply the MTC child molester typology in a population outside the MTC. Offenders were classified into all subgroups with an acceptable level of reliability, with the exception of the sadistic types. However, this exception may be due to the low number of offenders who fell into these subgroups rather than difficulties with the classification system. The authors recommended that future research will have to utilize a larger sample in order to address this concern. Differences were found between groups on the phallometric assessments, with the high fixation-low social competence group having highest levels of deviance on the slide assessment for Axis I. Interestingly, the average deviance indices for all four levels of Axis I indicated at least a failure to differentiate appropriation from inappropriate stimuli in terms of sexual responding. However, the high fixation-low social competence group was the only group that demonstrated a clear sexual preference for children. The high fixation-low social competence group was also distinguished by their preferences for male victims and their higher levels of self-reported childhood sexual abuse. On Axis II, the low contact-high injury offenders displayed more deviant arousal on the female's sexual violence assessment than other groups. These offenders were also more intrusive in their offending and were more likely to use physical force. Although most Axis II groupings were equally likely to choose victims of both genders, the exploitative group had a clear preference for female victims. Differences were not found for groups when rates of sexual and violent recidivism were examined, although it was found that sadistic offenders committed a great number of violent offenses. With regard to the implications for treatment, the findings of this study are consistent with expectations based on descriptions of the categories. However, the phallometric data suggest additional treatment implications than can be derived from the MTC typology alone. For example, preferential child molesters (i.e., those in high fixation and high contact categories) were more likely to exhibit deviant arousal, to have greater numbers of victims, and to cause little physical harm. They were also more likely to commit new sexual offenses, although this difference was not significant. Given that deviant sexual arousal is one of the best predictors of sexual recidivism, these individuals presented as being higher risk and having higher treatment needs. Low contact-high injury offenders also had a greater number of victims and were more likely to display deviant arousal. They were more likely to target strangers, were more intrusive in their offending, and were more likely to cause serious physical harm to their victims. With regard to implications for risk assessment, sadistic offenders had a greater number of violent offenses, indicating that these offenders may be at higher risk for violent nonsexual offenses. Also, low social competence offenders were more likely to re-offend in a nonsexual, nonviolent manner.

MARSHALL, W.L., BARBAREE, H.E., & ECCLES, A. (1991). EARLY ONSET AND DEVIANT SEXUALITY IN CHILD MOLESTERS. *JOURNAL OF INTERPERSONAL VIOLENCE*, 6 (3), 323-336.

One hundred and twenty-nine outpatient child molesters (91 nonfamilial and 38 father/daughter offenders) were assessed and interviewed regarding various aspects of their deviant sexuality. Of the total sample, 29% reported having deviant fantasies prior to age 20. This was most pronounced (41.1%) among those who molested the extrafamilial boys. Fourteen percent of the nonfamilial offenders against boys, 11.8% of the nonfamilial offenders against girls, and 7.9% of the incest offenders had one or more paraphilia in addition to their index offense. Only three participants in the total sample reported more than two additional paraphilias. These results support the research that a substantial proportion of adult sex offenders develop their deviant behaviors during adolescence. Of particular interest for conditioning theories of

the etiology of sexual offending is the observation that only 21.7% of the total sample said that they recalled having deviant sexual fantasies prior to their first actual offense.

PRENTKY, R.A., KNIGHT, R.A., LEE, A.F. (1997). CHILD SEXUAL MOLESTATION: RESEARCH ISSUES. *NATIONAL INSTITUTE OF JUSTICE RESEARCH REPORT (JUNE)*. U.S. DEPARTMENT OF JUSTICE.

Section one of this article discussed the frequency of child sexual abuse, characteristics of the offender, and the factors that lead to sexual deviancy. Section two included classification models for typing and diagnosing child molesters and describes treatment approaches and strategies for community-based maintenance and control. Section three talked about re-offense risk as it relates to criminal justice decisions and discusses predictors of sexual recidivism. To illustrate the variability of recidivism among child molesters, section four presented the findings of a 25-year follow-up study of 115 released offenders. Finally, some of the shortcomings of current approaches to reduce child molester re-offense risk are touched upon, and an argument was made for post-release treatment and aftercare programs. The authors formulated a number of conclusions that all indicate that there is no single "profile" that accurately describes or accounts for all child molesters. They concluded that sexual focus in child molesters has two independent dimension: intensity of pedophilic interest and exclusivity of the sexual preference for children; in contrast to popular belief, most victims of child abuse do not go on to become child molesters; a history of impulsive, antisocial behavior is a well-documented risk factor for certain predatory, extrafamilial child molesters and offenders who have this background and who began their offending careers in adolescence have also evidenced higher degrees of nonsexual targets; early childhood experiences, such as high turnover in primary caregivers may interfere with the development of viable, age-appropriate adult relationships, making it more likely that children are selected as sexual targets; physiological arousal to children often accompanies a sexual interest in them. Phallometric assessment of sexual arousal in response to depictions of children can differentiate child molesters from non-molesters, same-sex molesters from opposite-sex molesters, and extrafamilial molesters from incest molesters; studies support the reliability and validity of MTC:CM3 classification system; recidivism rates across studies are confounded by differences in legal guidelines and statutes among states, length of exposure time (i.e., time in the community, where the opportunity exists to re-offend), offender characteristics, treatment-related variables (including differential attrition rates, amount of treatment, and integrity of treatment program), and amount and quality of post-treatment supervision; a 25-year follow-up study of 111 extrafamilial child molesters included extensive data from criminal justice records and rationally derived composites of variables. The study demonstrated an ability to discriminate among offenders who committed sexual crimes involving physical contact with a victim, non-sexual crimes involving physical contact with a victim, and non-sexual crimes in which no physical contact with a victim occurred. The results also indicated that the authors were able to predict re-offense probabilities with reasonable accuracy. If these results can be replicated in studies of other offenders, use of a scale based on archival records may represent an easy, cost-effective, and reliable substitute for intrusive and time-consuming physiological assessment. It was also noted that cognitive-behavior therapy and, when appropriate, antidepressant and antiandrogen medication has reduced recidivism among child molesters.

SCHWARTZ, B.K. (1995). CHARACTERISTICS AND TYPOLOGIES OF SEX OFFENDERS. IN B. SCHWARTZ (ED.). *THE SEX OFFENDER: CORRECTIONS, TREATMENT AND LEGAL PRACTICE, 3.* NEW JERSEY: CIVIC RESEARCH INSTITUTE, INC.

This chapter described epidemiology and demographic statistics on sex offender characteristics and typologies. Characteristics reviewed include: factors related to age, race/ethnic origin, cognitive skills, lifestyle, marital status/sexuality, mental illness/alcoholism and personality disorders, sexual abuse, and parental relationships. Typologies reviewed include: Groth's, the FBI's, Knight and Prentky's, and Meiselman's.

SIMKINS, L. (1993). CHARACTERISTICS OF SEXUALLY REPRESSED CHILD MOLESTERS. *JOURNAL OF INTERPERSONAL VIOLENCE, 8* (1), 3-17.

This was an exploratory investigation, the purpose of which was to compare sexually repressed and non-repressed child abuse offenders on therapy progress and on a battery of personality and research instruments. From information obtained on psychosexual histories, 68 child molesters were categorized as repressed, non-repressed or exploitive. Results indicated that a significantly larger portion of therapy failures were offenders who were sexually repressed. There were also significant differences between repressed and non-repressed offenders on some of the special research scales of the MMPI, the Burt Rape Myth Scales, some of the Multiphasic Sexual Inventory Scales and the Mosher's Sex Guilt Scale. Differences on these measures were consistent with the characteristics of intrafamilial child molesters reported in the clinical and research literature. The results of this investigation were, however, quite speculative due to the small sample size of the repressed group. It was also conceivable that differences in treatment effectiveness between repressed and non-repressed groups may be attributed to differences in social skills rather than to sexual repression.

SIMON, L.M.J., SALES, B., KASKNIAK, A., & KAHN, M. (1992). CHARACTERISTICS OF CHILD MOLESTERS: IMPLICATIONS FOR THE FIXATED-REGRESSED DICHOTOMY. *JOURNAL OF INTERPERSONAL VIOLENCE, 7* (2), 211-225.

This study attempted to empirically validate the fixated-regressed typology. The sample consisted of 136 consecutive cases of convicted child molesters tried in Pima County, Arizona, over a two-year period (1984-1985) for whom case history, MMPI, pre-sentence reports, and police report data were collected prior to sentencing. Application of the criteria defining fixated versus regressed status yielded a unimodal and continuous distribution of child molesters rather than the bimodal distribution predicted by Groth's theory. This raised questions concerning the clinical utility of describing individual offenders dichotomously or of using such descriptions to make legal or therapeutic decisions. It suggested that Groth's dichotomy is unable to account for all child sexual abuses and recommends using a modification of Groth's approach that would involve using his criteria along a continuum and rejecting the dichotomous assumption. Further, the results suggested that these offenders also engaged in general criminal and antisocial behavior. It indicated that these criminal tendencies may be causally related to child molestation but are typically ignored by theories like Groth's that focus exclusively on psychological and psychosexual development. The study also found that the prevalence of alcohol and drug abuse among child molesters was similar to the alcohol and drug abuse that prevails in other types of criminal offenders. Finally, contrary to Groth's theory, the results suggested the existence of at least three different age groups of child molesters (not two). The presence of these age clusters, however, suggested that situational opportunities, such as marital discord and availability of a young, potential victim, may interact with a "stable" tendency of an individual with a past history of antisocial acts to increase the likelihood of child sexual abuse. Thus, molesters of different age groups may differ in terms of a predisposition to molest as well as the opportunity to do so.

CHARACTERISTICS OF CLERGY OFFENDERS

BENSON, G.L. (1994). SEXUAL BEHAVIOR BY MALE CLERGY WITH ADULT FEMALE COUNSELEES: SYSTEMATIC AND SITUATIONAL THEMES. SEXUAL ADDICTION & COMPULSIVITY, 1 (2), 103-118.

Through analysis of structured interviews with five Protestant clerics and four Roman Catholic clerics, Benson attempted to understand the situational themes present in cases of clergy sexual misconduct. All of the clerics had engaged in several sexual relationships with adult women. The following systemic themes appeared in the narratives: chronic and pervasive lack of intimacy; abused, abandoned, or exploited by a parent; and grandiose care taking in which the cleric described "taking care" of others as a crucial aspect of their identity. The situational themes included poor control of sexual impulse, recent significant narcissistic injury, and chronic pervasive feelings of shame.

BIRCHARD, T. (2000). CLERGY SEXUAL MISCONDUCT: FREQUENCY AND CAUSATION. SEXUAL RELATIONSHIP THERAPY, 15 (2), 127-139.

This article explored the causes of cleric sexual misconduct with adult women. Birchard found that three main issues in cleric misconduct were boundary ambiguity, institutional inattentiveness (both variables ranked equally high on the list of causes), and personal needs. Other variables found to have an impact were societal and outside factors. Limitations of the study included the issue of gender bias, subjective methodology, the researcher's insider knowledge, and methodological issues surrounding the surveying instrument.

BREWSTER, A.B. (1996). CLERGY SEXUAL MISCONDUCT: THE AFFAIR EVERYONE REMEMBERS. PASTORAL PSYCHOLOGY, 44 (6), 353-362.

This article provided a very brief overview of the issues surrounding clergy sexual misconduct. The perpetrator was discussed in the context of being personality disordered or committing an act of boundary violation in response to a crisis in their lives. Those who have personality disorders were concerned about attaining power while those who act out of desperation feel a great deal of remorse after the act. The effect on the adult victims involved with the cleric may vary. Some women may walk away from the relationship feeling exploited while others may feel that they were genuinely cared for. The author posited that the congregation requires intervention after the misconduct is known because it will affect congregational life. It is important that those who are dissatisfied have a chance to voice their opinion in order for healing to begin.

CAMARGO, R.J. (1997). FACTOR, CLUSTER, AND DISCRIMINANT ANALYSES OF DATA ON SEXUALLY ACTIVE CLERGY: THE MOLESTERS OF YOUTH IDENTIFIED. AMERICAN JOURNAL OF FORENSIC PSYCHOLOGY, 15 (2), 5-24.

This retrospective study grew out of a larger study examining the factors related to sexual object choice and molestation. The author evaluated the records of 1,322 male cleric sex offenders in a residential treatment center and divided the population according to offense type. It was postulated that the cleric child molesters would display factor scores, which would differentiate them from other offenders. It was found that the combination of passivity (with the absence of overt hostility), test-taking styles that present the self as being free of major symptoms, low anxiety and high relative gregariousness, and Diocesan priest status made the group distinctive. It was also hypothesized that these offenders could be statistically identified through scores on the MMPI and WAIS, which was also confirmed in this study and was concurrent with past research. The author also examined whether significant cluster groups could be established through factor analysis of MMPI scores. Elevation on MMPI scales 2, 4, 7, and 8 was found to be a cluster of small significance.

FLAKENHAIN, M.A., ET AL. (1999). CLUSTER ANALYSIS OF CHILD SEXUAL OFFENDERS: A VALIDATION WITH ROMAN CATHOLIC PRIESTS AND BROTHERS. *SEXUAL ADDICTION & COMPULSIVITY, 6*, 317-336.

This study tested 97 Roman Catholic priests with the MMPI-2 in order to replicate clusters found in previous sex offender research, but through utilization of a more restrictive sample of sex offenders. This was proven to be true as four clusters were found to be significant: sexually and emotionally underdeveloped, significantly psychiatrically disturbed, undefended characterological, and defended characterological. These clusters were validated through use of the MCMI-II and NEO-PI-R. The authors contend that their findings illustrate that these subgroups have stability and meaningfulness since they were replicated on a restricted population.

FRANCIS, P.C. & TURNER, N.R. (1995). SEXUAL MISCONDUCT WITHIN THE CHRISTIAN CHURCH: WHO ARE THE PERPETRATORS AND THOSE THEY VICTIMIZE? *COUNSELING & VALUES, 39* (3), 218-228.

This article reviewed the problem of clergy misconduct and examined the characteristics of the priests, women who get involved with members of the clergy, the repercussions, and the steps being taken by two churches (Evangelical Lutheran Church and the Disciples of Christ) to rectify the situation. Characteristics of those clerics involved in misconduct included "the naive" (those who fail to establish boundaries and have a desire to not be set apart from others), those with serious personality disorders (narcissism), and those with sexual addictions.

Profiles of the abused women included the "Advice Seeker, Fragile Lover, Overly Affectionate Parishioner," and those with personality disorders (histrionic & borderline) or a history of sexual abuse. The repercussions for these women included the normal feelings associated with sexual victimization as well as the threat of being vilified and ostracized by the parish. This in turn tainted their feelings for the clergy, church, and God. The policies enacted by the Evangelical Lutheran Church and the Disciples of Christ include placing an emphasis on investigating all allegations of misconduct in the hopes of discouraging false claims and reducing the secrecy concerning sexual misconduct in the Church.

HAYWOOD, T.W., KRAVITZ, H.M., GROSSMAN, L.S., WASYLIW, O.E., & HARDY, D.W. (1996). PSYCHOLOGICAL ASPECTS OF SEXUAL FUNCTIONING AMONG CLERIC AND NON-CLERIC ALLEGED SEX OFFENDERS. *CHILD ABUSE & NEGLECT, 20* (6), 527-536.

The authors postulated that cleric offenders would differ from non-cleric offenders and a normal control group in reported sexual functioning as measured by the Derogatis Sexual Functioning Inventory (DSFI). Their sample consisted of 30 Roman Catholic child molesters, 39 non-cleric child molesters, and 38 normal control subjects. The findings of this study suggested that cleric offenders were more likely to report fewer victims, had offenses directed towards older male victims, and displayed fewer paraphilias than non-cleric offenders. The data also illustrated that cleric offenders appeared to experience less psychological disturbance than non-cleric offenders and they had lower scores on the DSFI when compared to the entire sample. The authors suggested that the low DSFI scores may be a result of their training and socialization in the seminary. It is also suggested that differences on the DSFI may be attributed to the issue that the offenders in the sample admitted to having committed an offense. While they found no difference between admitters versus deniers in the cleric and non-cleric samples, it is a consideration for future research to examine the effect of cognitive distortions on self-reported sexual functioning.

HAYWOOD, T.W., KRAVITZ, H.M., WASYLIW, O.E., GOLDBERG, J., & CAVANAUGH, J.L. (1996). CYCLE OF ABUSE AND PSYCHOPATHOLOGY IN CLERIC AND NON-CLERIC MOLESTERS OF CHILDREN ANDADOLESCENTS. *CHILD ABUSE & NEGLECT, 20* (12), 1233-1243.

A sample including 45 non-cleric admitted child molesters, 40 non-cleric normal control subjects, 24 cleric admitted child molesters, and 48 cleric normal control subjects were evaluated for childhood sexual abuse and present psychopathology. The first hypothesis was confirmed that childhood sexual abuse was linked with becoming a child molester in adulthood. However, contrary to the expectations of the authors, there was no difference between cleric and non-cleric offenders. Non-cleric offenders reported more psychopathology than cleric offenders as measured by the MMPI-1. Psychopathology, lower education, non-cleric status, and history of childhood sexual abuse were shown to be strong variables in the prediction of sexual offending in adulthood. The authors suggested that these results be interpreted with caution because the cleric offenders and cleric normal control samples were not similar. The offender group was comprised of celibate priests while the control group was comprised of Protestant ministers, who are allowed to marry. Limitations of the study included the reliance upon self-reports, which inhibited data collection regarding detailed accounts of childhood sexual abuse. The use of the MMPI to assess psychopathology may have affected results because previous research (Loftus & Camargo, 1993) has illustrated that the MMPI may not be sensitive enough to detect the psychological aspects of offending in clerics.

LAASER, M.R. (1991). SEXUAL ADDICTION AND THE CLERGY. *PASTORAL PSYCHOLOGY, 39* (4), 213-235.

Laaser discussed the role of sexual addiction in clergy misconduct. He asserted that sexual addiction and the role of pastor interact in such a way as to form the new identity of sexually addicted clergy. Rape and child molestation are discussed in terms of "authority rape," in which the individual in power initiates the activity and the victim is unable to resist because they regard their victimizer as being powerful and knowledgeable. Laaser claimed that the victim wants to be a part of that power in

order to be nurtured by the authoritative figure and thus will do anything in order to attain this. These feelings are transferred onto the authority figure, possibly assuming the role of a parent. In the author's attempt to apply what is known about sexual addiction to the clergy several characteristics emerged. Sexually addicted clergy were likely to engage in the following: ordination used as a way of reducing the shame experienced as a result of their addiction, co-dependency and enabling, denial, withdrawal, blackouts, rigidity, blaming, reaction formation, loss of personal values, the maintenance of the myth that there is a perfect person out there who will understand and nurture them, anger, and entitlement.

LANGEVIN, R., CURNOE, S., & BAIN, J. (2000). A STUDY OF CLERICS WHO COMMIT SEXUAL OFFENSES: ARE THEY DIFFERENT FROM OTHER SEX OFFENDERS? *CHILD ABUSE & NEGLECT, 24* (4), 535-545.

This article compared 24 cleric offenders with 24 non-cleric sex offenders for differences on the basis of sexual history and preference, substance abuse, mental illness and personality, history of crime and violence, neuropsychological impairments, and endocrine abnormalities. The offenders were matched according to offense type, age, education, and marital status and then compared to a control sample of 2,125 sex offenders matched only according to offense type. The findings suggested that cleric sex offenders did not significantly differ from the matched non-cleric sex offenders. While the cleric offenders were similar to the matched group, 70.8% of the clerics were sexually deviant and were characterized as being homosexual pedophiles with courtship disorder. Cleric offenders were older at the time of the first reported offense and better educated than the non-cleric offenders. Few participants in the cleric and non-cleric groups had been sexually abused as children. None of the clergy participants were diagnosed with antisocial personality disorder, but some displayed signs of substance abuse. The authors concluded that the same assessment techniques (most notably phallometric testing) used for the general population of sex offenders should be utilized for cleric offenders. Limitations of the study included the fact that the participants were older than sex offenders in general and they were not matched on the basis of religion.

MCGLONE, G.J. (2001). SEXUALLY OFFENDING AND NON-OFFENDING ROMAN CATHOLIC PRIESTS: CHARACTERIZATION AND ANALYSIS. *DISSERTATION ABSTRACTS INTERNATIONAL, 62* (1-B), PP. 557.

This study utilized archival data on 158 sexually offending Roman Catholic priests (pedophiles and ephebophiles) and compared them to a matched group of non-offending clerics. Comparison of MCMI-II and Rorschach scores illustrated that the majority of pedophiles had more dependent and schizoid features than the ephebophile group. The ephebophiles showed differences on the following Rorschach variables: human representation variable, reflections, texture, responses, the number of responses, and Lambda. The MCMI-II data did not illustrate any higher than normal levels of narcissism or levels of dependency.

PLANTE, T.G. (1996). CATHOLIC PRIESTS WHO SEXUALLY ABUSE MINORS: WHY DO WE HEAR SO MUCH YET KNOW SO LITTLE? *PASTORAL PSYCHOLOGY, 44* (5), 305-310.

This article provided a brief overview of the literature regarding clergy offenders and their victims. The author pointed out that while there were numerous literatures devoted to sexual abuse in general, there were very few pertaining to clergy abuse. Plante posits that one reason why much is unknown about the topic is because it is a contradiction. Society regards priests as being holy and God-like, not predatory and abusive. In establishing personality profiles of those individuals called to the clergy, the article cited the MMPI data gathered by Dunn (1999) that found that they were perfectionistic, worrisome, introversive, socially inept, isolated, and withdrawn. Barry & Bordin (1967) found that they came from homes where the mother was perceived as being dominant and guilt was often used as a tool of discipline. Keddy, et al. (1990) found that priests displayed more defensiveness in their MMPI scores. Plante then went on to articulate that it was not until the mid-1980's that these cases garnered public attention, but the true extent of the crisis is unknown. The literature also illustrated that most Catholic priests believed to be pedophiles are in fact ephebophiles who have a preference for boys. A review of the literature showed that personality variables found to be linked to clergy offenders included shyness, loneliness, and passivity. Clerics have also displayed elevated MMPI scores in the areas of depression, authority concerns, and addiction problems. Rorschach results indicated a greater affect constriction than normal. The author called for further research to better understand the etiology of abuse.

PLANTE, T.G., MANUEL, G., & BRYANT, C. (1996). PERSONALITY AND COGNITIVE FUNCTIONING AMONG HOSPITALIZED SEXUAL OFFENDING ROMAN CATHOLIC PRIESTS. *PASTORAL PSYCHOLOGY, 45* (2), 129-139.

This study sought to understand the personality and cognitive characteristics of sexually abusive clerics in a sample of 160 Roman Catholic priests (80 sexual abusers and 80 controls). Researchers administered the MMPI-2 (to evaluate defensive coping styles on scales L, K, O-H, and R), WAIS-R, and Halstead-Reitan measurements. Overcontrolled hostility was found to be the only variable that differentiated the sex offenders from the control group. The cognitive measures did not differentiate the two groups; the authors found that the sexually abusive clergy tended to have higher verbal IQ scores than the control group. While this finding showed slight significance, it was nullified when age was accounted for as a variable. It is postulated that those priests who sexually offend may in fact be acting out their chronically overcontrolled anger and aggression. The authors warned that while these results show promise, the study was hindered by a number of methodological flaws. The control group was comprised only of hospitalized clergy as opposed to a normal group. The researchers only used the selected personality and cognitive measures, data was not collected from patient's history, details of the offense were not disclosed, and the significant differences found may not have shown clinical significance.

RUZICKA, M.F. (1997). PREDICTOR VARIABLES OF CLERGY PEDOPHILES. *PSYCHOLOGICAL REPORTS, 80,* 589-590.

Data was collected from 10 convicted cleric offenders in order to isolate variables, which may serve as screening tools. The variables evaluated in the pilot included familial traits, past sexual experience as a victim, etc. The sample consisted of five Catholic priests, two Catholic religious brothers, a Baptist, a Methodist, and a Protestant minister. Findings illustrated that the subjects were well educated, of average to above average intelligence, and had a limited history of substance abuse. Eight out of the 10 perpetrators reported having a prior psychiatric history and one had a criminal record. Three of the subjects asserted that they were heterosexual while the rest of the sample identified themselves as homosexual or bisexual. Every subject in the sample had more than one victim (age range from six to 18 years old) and the duration of the abuse ranged from five weeks to five years. Eight out of the 10 perpetrators reported a preference for boys.

THOMSON, J.G., MAROLLA, J.A., & BROMLEY, D.G. (1998). DISCLAIMERS AND ACCOUNTS IN CASES OF CATHOLIC PRIESTS ACCUSED OF PEDOPHILIA. IN A. SHUPE (ED.). *WOLVES WITHIN THE FOLD: RELIGIOUS LEADERSHIP AND ABUSES OF POWER* (PP. 175-189). NEW BRUNSWICK, NJ: RUTGERS UNIVERSITY PRESS.

This chapter examined the narratives priests used to initiate sexual abuse of children and how they explained their actions. The narratives were gathered from four books and 257 press reports. Narratives are divided into two sections, disclaimers and accounts. Disclaimers are prospective interpretations, which are developed in the victim-perpetrator relationship and are concealed. The authors asserted that, "Disclaimers are offered to cushion an anticipated reaction when some behavior is about to be discovered." Five types of disclaimers exist. Hedging disclaimers are used when the individual is considering a line of behavior but they are willing to consider alternatives. Credentialing occurs when a person is committed to a behavior they know will be discrediting and thus they offer evidence to legitimize the action. Sin license is similar to credentialing but the individual tries to depict the situation in a manner where general rules of conduct may be suspended. Cognitive disclaimers are utilized when an individual believes that a situation is not likely to be viewed in a similar manner by others and they need to reassure

these individuals. Appeals for the suspension of judgment are utilized when the individual expects the behavior to result in a negative emotional response. The authors found that the majority of the priests' disclaimers were credentialing in which they utilized the explanation of divine approval. This strategy gives the priest a sense of power and provides a basis for the abuse to be concealed. Accounts are retrospective interpretations publicly offered to explain the behavior and may be divided into excuses and justifications. Excuses are designed to mitigate the individual's responsibility while justifications are meant to normalize the behavior. Justifications consist of denial of injury, denial of victim, condemnation of condemners, appeal to loyalties, sad tale, and self-fulfillment. In evaluating the clergy narratives the authors found that almost every example involved denial of injury accounts. This is done in a variety of ways including the claim that the sex was consensual. The work of the clergy is emphasized in order to assert that it should not be compromised by a behavioral lapse. The abuse may be minimized and isolated in order to legitimize acceptable and unacceptable traits of sexuality. Excuses consist of four types: accident accounts, defeasibility accounts, biological drive accounts, and scapegoating accounts. The authors found that accident accounts were usually articulated by Church officials and serve to assert that the individual could not control environmental variables, thus mitigating responsibility. Scapegoating accounts were utilized by Church officials to shift responsibility for the behavior to the actions of another individual. This is evident in officials' asserting that various interest groups were utilizing the scandal for their own political agenda. Defeasibility was also utilized in order to explain impaired mental capacity as a result of mental disorder, intoxication/addiction, or psychological duress. This excuse is utilized most often at the individual priest's level while Church officials use the other two strategies. The authors concluded that narratives should be interpreted as a sequence rather than individual events. These narratives must also be evaluated through their social context as well.

THE EVALUATION OF SEXUAL OFFENDERS

RISK FACTORS

Browne, K.D., Foreman, L., & Middleton, D. (1998). Predicting treatment drop-out in sex offenders. Child Abuse Review, 7, 402-419.

Researchers attempted to evaluate the impact of 30 risk factors upon treatment drop out in a sample of 96 sex offenders. Of these factors, nine showed significance in discerning those offenders who would comply with treatment from offenders who would drop out. These factors were organized in a manner that allowed them to address criminal history, present situation, history, psychological problems, and responsiveness to treatment. Among the factors that showed significance included having spent time in prison, having a violence-related index offense, non-contact offenses, unemployment, substance abuse, and delinquent/disruptive behavior during treatment. However, the authors found that a history of sexual offending or childhood victimization did not affect treatment outcome.

Grubin, D. (1999). Actuarial and clinical assessment of risk in sex offenders. Journal of Interpersonal Violence, 14 (3), 331-343.

In this article, the author reviewed clinical and actuarial methods of risk assessment and discussed the impact of fantasy on offending behavior. Grubin posited that neither are capable of providing reliable results when used on their own due to the heterogeneity of the population and the low base rate of incidence. However, when used in conjunction they may prove to be more reliable. The literature review concerning actuarial assessments included a discussion of studies conducted by Marshall (1994), Thornton and Travers (1991), and Quinsey, Rice, & Harris (1995). The article then went on to evaluate clinical assessments and posited that a problem with this technique is that clinicians arrive at their conclusions through an inductive manner, which is based primarily upon their experiences with a few offenders. The author then discussed the role of fantasy in violent crimes and the risk attributed to

them. Through citation of a study conducted by Prentky et al. (1989) in which it was found that fantasy was related to offending in serial killers, Grubin argued that while fantasy is a risk factor it is not clear why certain people act upon them and others do not. This point is supported by discussion of the study conducted by Gosselin and Wilson (1980) in which it was found that sadistic fantasy was incredibly common but it does not always lead to sexual offending. In order to understand the impact fantasy has on behavior, clinicians must evaluate other risk factors. Grubin claimed that the presence of personality disorders, pervasive inadequacy, historical/behavioral variables, isolation, and empathy may play a role in facilitating that link. There was a discussion of the studies conducted by Grubin (1994) and Grubin & Gunn (1991) in which the sexual murderers in their sample differed from the rapists in the degree of social and emotional isolation they experienced. The author urged that this variable be examined in conjunction with other variables contributing to risk and serve as an indicator of underlying disorder, particularly in regards to empathy. In essence, a hybrid of actuarial and clinical assessment would be necessary in order to evaluate the importance of social and emotional isolation.

Hanson, R.K. & Harris, A.J.R. (2000). Where should we intervene? Dynamic predictors of sexual offense recidivism. Criminal Justice and Behavior, 27 (1), 6-35.

This study attempted to evaluate the uses of dynamic factors in assessing risk. The authors differentiated between stable dynamic risk factors (those expected to remain unchanged for a substantial period of time) and acute dynamic risk factors (factors that change rapidly). The sample consisted of 208 sexual offense recidivists and 201 non-recidivist sex offenders classified as being rapist, boy-child molester, or girl-child molester. The study was retrospective in nature and focused on those offenders who recidivated while under surveillance and those who did not. Information was collected through interviews with parole officers and analysis of files at two points (six months and one month before recidivism occurred). Risk of recidivism was then gauged through use of the SIR, Psychopathy Checklist-Revised (PCL-R), Violence Risk Appraisal Guide (VRAG), and the Rapid Risk Assessment for Sexual Offense Recidivism (RRA-SOR) on the data available in the files. The researchers also coded for sexual offense history, sexual deviancy, treatment history, antisocial personality disorder, and miscellaneous variables. During the interviews with supervisors the variables evaluated were social influences and any problems during supervision. It was found that the recidivists had poor social support, attitudes tolerant of sexual assault, antisocial lifestyles, poor self-management strategies, and difficulties complying with supervision. The recidivists showed similarities with the non-recidivists concerning general mood, but the recidivists showed more anger and subjective distress before re-offending. The authors noted their concern over the influence of retrospective recall bias and rater bias on the results. The authors concluded that the stable dynamic risk factors showed the greatest potential in differentiating the recidivists from the non-recidivists and that criminal lifestyle variables were the strongest predictors of recidivism. An interesting observation was the finding that all of the offenders in this sample who were subjected to hormonal therapy as a requirement of their community supervision recidivated.

PRENTKY, R.A., KNIGHT, R.A., & LEES, A.F.S. (1997). RISK FACTORS ASSOCIATED WITH RECIDIVISM AMONG EXTRAFAMILIAL CHILD MOLESTERS. *JOURNAL OF CONSULTING AND CLINICAL PSYCHOLOGY,* 65 (1),141-149.

The researchers attempted to evaluate the predictive accuracy of ten specific risk factors for child molesters. The risk factors examined were: amount of contact with children, degree of sexual preoccupation with children, impulsivity, juvenile and adult antisocial behavior, frequency of prior sexual offenses, paraphilias, history of alcohol use, social competence, and victim gender. Researchers analyzed the files of 111 child molesters released from the Massachusetts Treatment Center between 1960 and 1984. They determined that the degree of sexual preoccupation with children, paraphilias, and number of prior sexual offenses were the strongest predictors of sexual recidivism. In examining the risk factors associated with violent recidivism/victim-involved recidivism, juvenile and adult antisocial behavior coupled with paraphilia and a low amount of contact with children showed significance.

PROULX, J., TARDIF, M., LAMOUREUX, B., LUSSIER, P. (2000). HOW DOES RECIDIVISM RISK ASSESSMENT PREDICT SURVIVAL? IN LAWS, D.R., HUDSON, S.M., & WARD, T. (EDS.). *REMAKING RELAPSE PREVENTION WITH SEX OFFENDERS: A SOURCEBOOK* (PP. 466-484). THOUSAND OAKS, CA; SAGE PUBLICATIONS, INC.

This chapter provided a brief overview of what constitutes recidivism as well as the static and dynamic predictors of sexual recidivism. The overview paid particular attention to the meta-analysis compiled by Hanson & Bussière (1998) that determined that the best predictors were sexual deviancy as measured by penile phallometer (PPG), history of sex crimes, psychological characteristics, negative relationship with mother, failure to complete treatment, and the presence of depression and anxiety. These findings were similar to the findings of the Quinsey, Khanna & Malcolm (1998) study of 483 sexual offenders. However, both studies only focused upon mixed groups of offenders and not specific types of sexual offenders that the chapter attempted to address by reviewing the literature pertaining to sexual aggression towards women and children. The overview then addressed the pros and cons of actuarial and acute dynamic predictors of sexual recidivism. These predictors were then placed within the context of the relapse prevention model and management in the community.

EVALUATIVE PARADIGMS

GRUBIN, D. (1997). INFERRING PREDICTORS OF RISK: SEX OFFENDERS. *INTERNATIONAL REVIEW OF PSYCHIATRY,* 9 (2-3), 225-231.

This article addressed the value of actuarial risk assessment instruments. The low base rate of sexual offending, diversity of the offender population, and probabilistic confusion hinder these instruments. Grubin suggested that actuarial instruments provide little information pertaining to causation/

management and say nothing about the individual. The article addressed various risk factors associated with sexual recidivism and referred to the meta-analysis conducted by Hanson & Bussière (1998) in which the majority of the risk factors found to be significant were static in nature. While clinical assessments paint a more conclusive picture of the individual, it is a technique essentially based upon "untested and unsound theoretical foundations." Clinical risk factors are idiographic in nature, sensitive to environmental and time factors, and do not exist in isolation. The use of deductive and inductive processes was recommended when assessing an individual's risk of recidivism (i.e., rapist typologies developed by Knight & Prentky, 1990 or the longitudinal research conducted by Malmuth [1986, 1991] on non-offender males).

HANSON, R.K. (1998). WHAT DO WE KNOW ABOUT SEX OFFENDER RISK ASSESSMENT? *PSYCHOLOGY, PUBLIC POLICY, & LAW, 4* (1-2), 50-72.

This article described different approaches to risk assessment (guided clinical, pure actuarial, and adjusted actuarial), summarized the literature concerning risk factors, and reviewed recent attempts to create actuarial instruments to assess sex offender recidivism. The article raised the issues that while numerous studies have evaluated the static (stable) risk factors, the literature is practically void of studies devoted to the evaluation of dynamic (changeable) risk factors. Hanson postulated that the research is more useful for identifying high-risk offenders than determining release.

EVALUATIVE INSTRUMENTS

BARBAREE, H.E., SETO, M.C., LANGTON, C.M., & PEACOCK, E.J. (2001). EVALUATING THE PREDICTIVE ACCURACY OF SIX RISK ASSESSMENT INSTRUMENTS FOR ADULT SEX OFFENDERS. *CRIMINAL JUSTICE & BEHAVIOR, 28* (4), 490-521.

This article compared the efficacy of the Violence Risk Appraisal Guide (VRAG), Sex Offender Risk Appraisal Guide (SORAG), Rapid Risk Assessment of Sexual Offense Recidivism (RRASOR), Static-99, Minnesota Sex Offender Screening Tool-Revised (MnSOSTR), Psychopathy Checklist-Revised (PCL-R), and the uses of guided clinical assessments in determining recidivism. The sample consisted of 215 sex offenders who had been released between the years of 1989 and 1996. Half of the offenders committed crimes against females 14 or older while the other half offended against male or female children younger than fourteen. Recidivism rates were followed for 4.5 years during which 38% reoffended (24% serious reoffenses and 9% for sexual reoffenses). The authors concluded that the VRAG, SORAG, RRASOR, and Static-99 predicted general, violent, and sexual recidivism. MNSOST-R scores and guided clinical interviews were able to indicate general recidivism, but showed little sensitivity in discerning between serious or sexual reoffending. Out of all of these measures, the PCL-R when used alone was sensitive to predicting general and serious recidivism but was unable to predict sexual recidivism.

ROBERTS, C.F., DOREN, D.M., & THORNTON, D. (2002). DIMENSIONS ASSOCIATED WITH ASSESSMENTS OF SEX OFFENDER RECIDIVISM RISK. *CRIMINAL JUSTICE & BEHAVIOR, 29* (5), 569-589.

The authors conducted two studies in order to explore the different dimensions of actuarial risk assessment. The first study explored the structure underlying the interrelationships between actuarial instruments on a sample of 103 male sexual offenders being evaluated for civil commitment in Wisconsin. Examiners were told to score the entire case record using the PCL-R, RRASOR, Static-99, MnSOST-R, VRAG, and diagnostic information from *DSM-IV*. It was found that: (1) the PCL-R, MnSOST-R, VRAG, and Static-99 were strongly intercorrelated with one another as well as with the non-RRASOR items on Static-99, (2) the PCL-R, MnSOST-R, VRAG, Static-99, and non-RRASOR items on the Static-99 were positively associated with a diagnosis of antisocial personality disorder and negatively associated with a diagnosis of pedophilia, (3) the RRASOR was only modestly positively correlated with the MnSOST-R and the VRAG, and (4) the emergence of two dimensions of underlying risk inherent in the interscale intercorrelation matrix: an Antisocial/Violence component (weighed most heavily on the PCL-R, MnSOST-R, VRAG, non-RRASOR Static-99 items, and diagnosis of antisocial personality disorder) and a

Pedophilic Deviance/Sexual Repetitiveness component (weighed most heavily on the RRASOR and diagnosis of pedophilia). The second study was comprised of 393 adult males released from prison in 1979 in England and Wales. The individual variables used to assess risk were taken from Static-99 and Risk Matrix 2000. The variables were comprised of the following: prior conviction for sexual offenses, any non-contact sexual offense, any male victim of a sex offense, any conviction for a sexual offense against a stranger, burglary involved in index conviction, prior convictions including burglary, prior convictions including nonsexual assault, index convictions including nonsexual assault, age on release between 18-34, and marital status listed as being single (never married). The measure of sexual recidivism was sexual reconviction data that was recorded for 29% of the sample. Variables were added and three dimensions were discovered including Sexual Deviance (any prior sex offense + any male victims + any non-contact offenses), General Criminality (any prior burglary + any prior nonsexual attack; similar to the Antisocial/Violence dimension of study 1), and Detachment (youth + stranger victim + single). The second study replicated the two dimensions developed in the first study and demonstrated that each dimension makes an independent contribution to the prediction of sexual recidivism. The General Criminality/Antisocial-Violence dimensions support the ideas developed by Knight (1999) while the Pedophilic Deviance/Sexual Repetitiveness dimensions support the work developed by Proulx (2000). The third dimension, Detachment, is consistent with work conducted by Smallbone & Dadd (2000). While actuarial instruments measure multiple dimensions, the issue is how the interaction of these dimensions influences risk. The authors suggested that future research examine the development of tools that focused specifically on one dimension or are equipped to address multiple dimensions individually in one instrument as well as address the issue of risk management.

ABEL SCREENING TOOL

ABEL, G.G., LAWRY, S.S., KARLSTROM, E., OSBORN, C.A., & GILLESPIE, C.F. (1994). SCREENING TESTS FOR PEDOPHILIA. *CRIMINAL JUSTICE AND BEHAVIOR, 21*(1), 115-131.

This article compared the different methods used to screen individuals for pedophilia. The authors asserted that by identifying those who are high risk, organizations can be proactive in addressing a potential problem. The article cited case studies in order for the reader to gain an understanding of the nature of pedophilia. Screening methods for pedophilia have existed for years (interviews, questionnaires, home visits, police reports, etc.), and institutions have even implemented various policies aimed at managing child molestation (education/ training, elimination of individual staff-child interactions), yet these methods all have their pros and cons. The article discussed the importance of true positives, true negatives, and false positives in establishing an effective screening device. The Abel Screen displayed high specificity (77%-98%), sensitivity (76%-91%), and efficiency (77.5%-96.9%) when applied in a setting that assumes a 5% prevalence rate of child molestation. The volumetric phallometer (sensitivity 86.7%; specificity 95%; and efficiency 94.6%) and circumferential plethysmograph (sensitivity 47.5%; specificity 100%; efficiency 97.4%) also displayed respectable sensitivity, specificity, and efficiency but are much more intrusive, expensive, and problematic than the Abel Screen. The Abel Screen entails a questionnaire and slides depicting children, adolescents, and adults. The individual then rates these images based upon on how sexually arousing they are. A psycho-physiological hand monitor then records physiological responses. The efficacy of the instrument was established by comparing the responses of a self-selecting sample of "normal" participants to those of pedophiles that had molested pubescent males and prepubescent males/females. The question as to whether an individual can fake pedophilia on the Abel Screen is still being investigated, but preliminary data suggested that there is no difference between those instructed to fake and those who disclose. Through cross-validation it was found that the Abel Screen has a false positive rate of 2%, which may be reduced further through use of other screening techniques. The authors cautioned that while the Abel Screen is able to identify most pedophiles, its sensitivity is below the 90th percentile.

SEX OFFENDER NEED ASSESSMENT RATING

HANSON, R.K. & HARRIS, A.J.R. (2001). A STRUCTURES APPROACH TO EVALUATING CHANGE AMONG SEXUAL OFFENDERS. *SEXUAL ABUSE: A JOURNAL OF RESEARCH AND TREATMENT, 13* (2), 105-122.

This study attempted to extrapolate upon the findings of Hanson & Harris (2000) by creating an instrument to evaluate dynamic risk factors. The Sex Offender Need Assessment Rating (SONAR) consists of items that evaluate intimacy deficits, negative social influences, sexual self- regulation, general self-regulation, and acute risk factors (substance abuse, negative mood, anger, and victim access). The scale was then used to analyze the data present in the files of 208 sex offender recidivists and 201 non-recidivists. The scale showed moderate reliability and was capable of discerning between the two groups. Findings indicated that dynamic risk factors may play an important role in risk assessment, but it is not clear as to the extent of their importance in predicting long-term recidivism.

STATIC-99

HANSON, R.K. & THORNTON, D. (2000). IMPROVING RISK ASSESSMENTS FOR SEX OFFENDERS: A COMPARISON OF THREE ACTUARIAL SCALES. *LAW AND HUMAN BEHAVIOR, 24* (1), 119-136.

This study compared the predictive accuracy of the RRASOR (weighs factors related to sexual deviancy most heavily) and the SACJ-Min (some items deal with sexual deviancy but the focus is upon factors dealing with nonsexual criminal history). A goal of the researchers was to combine the two scales in order to evaluate whether or not predictive accuracy would be greater than either of the original scales. This hybrid scale was dubbed Static-99 because it included only static risk factors. These three instruments were then applied across four data sets that had been used in previous studies. The RRASOR and SACJ-Min were roughly equivalent when it came to predictive accuracy and the combination of the two scales (Static-99) was more accurate than either original scale. Any variations that were encountered were no more than would be expected by chance. Static-99 also showed reasonable accuracy in the prediction of any violent recidivism among sex offenders. While these results have shown promise for Static-99, the authors contend that the inclusion of dynamic risk factors is necessary in order to assess treatment needs and predict when and under what circumstances offenders are at risk.

SJÖESTEDT, G. & LÅNGSTRÖM, N. (2001). ACTUARIAL ASSESSMENT OF SEX OFFENDER RECIDIVISM RISK: A CROSS-VALIDATION OF THE RRASOR AND THE STATIC-99 IN SWEDEN. *LAW AND HUMAN BEHAVIOR, 25* (6), 629-645.

The goal of this study was to cross-validate the RRASOR and Static-99 in a different sociocultual and legal context than the original constructions samples. The sample consisted of all sex offenders released from Swedish prisons from 1993-1997 (1,400 subjects in total, of which 43% were child molesters and 45% rapists). Sexual offenses were operationally defined according to Swedish penal code that accounts for crimes involving physical and noncontact offenses. Researchers acquired files from the national Prison and Probation Administration and then coded the data according to the risk factors of each instrument. The follow-up period lasted for 3.69 years and files were coded for sexual reconviction according to Swedish penal code, any violent reconviction, and violent nonsexual reoffenses. The authors found that both instruments displayed moderate predictive accuracy regarding short-term sexual recidivism. However, Static-99 was found to have greater predictive accuracy when it came to assessing violent recidivism, but not for sexual recidivism. Seven out of the 10 risk factors individually contributed to an increased risk of sexual reoffending. Young age, any male victim, and index nonsexual violence appeared not to be related to sexual recidivism. The authors suggested that their findings illustrated that these two instruments should not be used as stand-alone devices for rule-out decisions due to their low validity. The article included a brief discussion of other actuarial instruments including suggestions on their use. Limitations of this study included a short follow-up period, focus only upon offenders sentenced to prison, and a statistical analysis that increased the risk of Type I errors.

VIOLENCE RISK APPRAISAL GUIDE

RICE, M.E. & HARRIS, G.T. (1997). CROSS-VALIDATION AND EXTENSION OF THE VIOLENCE RISK APPRAISAL GUIDE FOR CHILD MOLESTERS AND RAPISTS. *LAW AND HUMAN BEHAVIOR, 21* (2), 231-241.

This study used the VRAG on a sample of 159 child molesters and rapists who were not involved in the original scale construction sample. The scale was also used to evaluate its performance on a 10-year follow-up using the original construction sample and the new sample. The men were serious offenders with criminal histories, poor childhood adjustment, and inadequate adult social adjustment. One hundred and four had received psychiatric treatment in a maximum security psychiatric facility, but few met diagnostic criteria for mental illness. All study variables were coded from clinical files with the exception of those pertaining to recidivism. Sexual recidivism was operationally defined as the subject being charged with a new sexual offense while violent recidivism was defined as being charged with or returning to prison for a violent offense. Reoffense time was from the subject first being at risk to January 1993 (mean =119.3 months). The results supported use of the VRAG in predicting violence among high risk offenders and it performed well upon cross-validation and follow up when the two samples were combined. The authors posited that from a practical standpoint the focus should be placed upon predictions of future violence, not necessarily a differentiation between sexual and nonsexual violence. The results also yielded evidence supporting an interaction between psychopathy and sexual deviancy resulting in sexual recidivism. Those who offend against women and children are at a higher risk of violent recidivism while child molesters are at a higher risk for sexual recidivism. Limitations of the study include the fact that the two samples were drawn from one Canadian maximum-security psychiatric facility (yet previous studies have illustrated that this population was similar to other prison populations). Future research possibilities focus on the development of a scale similar to the VRAG but pertaining solely to sex offenders.

EVALUATING CLERIC OFFENDERS

CIMBOLIC, P., WISE, R.A., ROSSETTI, S., & SAFER, M. (1999). DEVELOPMENT OF A COMBINED OBJECTIVE EPHEBOPHILE SCALE. *SEXUAL ADDICTION & COMPULSIVITY*, 6 (3), 253-266.

The authors attempted to develop a combined scale (11 items from the MCMI-II and 16 items from the MMPI-2) that would differentiate same-sex ephebophile clerics from priests with nonsexual psychiatric disorders. The sample consisted of 165 adult male Catholic priests in treatment who had participated in two prior studies. The results showed that when used individually both scales are capable of differentiating these groups. However, a combination of the two scales showed greater accuracy and internal consistency on the MCMI-II. Regardless of the accuracy of this combined scale, it was still unable to identify many of the ephebophiles in this sample. The authors urge that a multidimensional approach be utilized when assessing child molesters.

GONSIOREK, J.C. (1999). FORENSIC PSYCHOLOGICAL EVALUATIONS IN CLERGY ABUSE. IN T.G. PLANTE (ED.). *BLESS ME FATHER FOR I HAVE SINNED: PERSPECTIVES ON SEXUAL ABUSE COMMITTED BY ROMAN CATHOLIC PRIESTS.* (PP. 27-57). WESTPORT, CT: PRAEGER PUBLISHERS.

This chapter provided a discussion of two evaluative methods used to assess clergy who abuse children. In discussing the population of professional perpetrators, the author described the priests as fitting into one of the following typologies: naïve, normal and/or mildly neurotic, severely neurotic and/or socially isolated, impulsive character disorders, sociopathic or narcissistic character disorders, psychotics, classic sex offenders (true pedophiles), medically disabled, and masochistic/self defeating. These typologies were created for health professionals and thus may differ when applied to clerics. The first assessment discussed evaluates the potential for rehabilitation. The main purpose of this evaluation was to ascertain the facts of what led to the offending behavior and what can be done to rectify the situation. Different types of evidence may be evaluated in order to formulate a hypothesis. Once the hypothesis as to why the cleric offends is developed, rehabilitation potential and goals are expanded upon. A religious superior then evaluates this outline and the cleric must decide whether or not they are willing to undergo the treatment process. Once treatment is in place, steps must be taken in order to ensure compliance. It is also important that the mental health professionals and religious superiors keep in mind that treatment and punishment are two separate notions. A discussion of professional sexual misconduct recidivism is included and the rate estimate varies. The second type of evaluation discussed deals with damages allotted in civil cases. The assessment for damages is standard in most civil trials. The mental health professional should obtain a complete personal and family history from the victim. Inquiry should be made into the victim's level of functioning as well as utilization of validated psychological tests. A discussion of the standard of care and delayed discovery controversies are also included.

IRONS, R. & LAASER, M. (1994). THE ABDUCTION OF FIDELITY: SEXUAL EXPLOITATION BY CLERGY-EXPERIENCE WITH INPATIENT ASSESSMENT. *SEXUAL ADDICTION & COMPULSIVITY, 1* (2), 119-129.

This article presented the results of the five-day long assessments of 25 male clerics who had been referred for sexual misconduct, primarily with adults. Assessments included administration of the MMPI, MCMI, Thematic Apperception Test, Rorschach, WAIS-R, and sentence completion tasks. Each patient's history was recorded (although the authors believe that much of it was incomplete, especially in regard to childhood abuse or family dysfunction) and clinical diagnoses were based on DSM-III-R criteria. The results of the study were so diverse that a classification system or treatment model could not be created. However, the authors found various commonalities concerning the background of these clerics. They came from rigid backgrounds and lacked insight into their problems and professional boundaries. It was also found that the clerics had no training in the area of transference/countertransference or training concerning sexual abuse. Most of the individuals in the sample met the diagnosis for personality disorders with features of antisocial/psychopathic traits or paranoid, sadistic, or schizoid features. The results illustrated that narcissistic and dependant traits cluster together and were modeled in an exploitive way. The authors suggested the use of multidisciplinary evaluations. If these evaluations are conducted early enough in the process, the prognosis of rehabilitation improves.

MUSSER, P., CIMBOLIC, P., & ROSSETTI, S. (1995). EPHEBOPHILIA AND THE MCMI-II. *SEXUAL ADDICTION & COMPULSIVITY, 2* (3), 214-222.

Researchers used the MCMI-II to determine if it was capable of differentiating same-sex priest ephebophiles (N=101) from priests with psychiatric illnesses of a nonsexual nature (N=99). Through analyses of variance, it was determined that the MCMI-II was not able to differentiate between the groups. Item-level analyses were then conducted in order to determine which items would discriminate the offenders from the non-offenders in the hopes of constructing a priest ephebophile scale. The results suggested that the MCMI-II cannot distinguish between sexually offending clerics and those with mental illnesses. Since the sample consisted of only Catholic priests, the authors suggested that the MCMI-II may be effective when used on a sample of non-priest sex offenders.

WASYLIW, O.E., BENN, A.F., GROSSMAN, L.S., & HAYWOOD, T.W. (1998). DETECTION OF MINIMIZATION OF PSYCHOPATHOLOGY ON THE RORSCHACH IN CLERIC AND NON-CLERIC ALLEGED SEX OFFENDERS. *ASSESSMENT, 5* (4), 389-397.

The goal of this study was to examine the ability of the Rorschach in assessing defensiveness. The hypothesis was based on prior research that illustrated that minimization on the Rorschach would be reflected by higher P, D, A, Lambda, PER, and lower R, Blends, and ZF. The sample consisted of 33 clergymen and 27 non-cleric sex offenders who had been referred for forensic evaluations. Eighty percent of the participants in the sample were facing allegations of child sexual abuse. The clerics were significantly older and more educated than the non-clerics. All participants were administered the MMPI or MMPI-II and the Rorschach. The Rorschach failed to detect minimization or was not sensitive to the same type of response bias as the MMPI validity scales. There was no difference in scores between those who admitted to their crime and those who denied their involvement. Interestingly, the authors reported that two participants exaggerated psychopathology. The authors asserted that minimization and education have been shown to be correlated on certain MMPI validity scales, but this was controlled for in the present study. The authors recommended that other well-established psychometric instruments that are used in the detection of minimization be utilized as opposed to reliance upon Rorschach scores.

MODELS OF TREATMENT FOR OFFENDERS WHO ABUSE CHILDREN

OVERVIEW OF SEX OFFENDER TREATMENT PROGRAMS

ABEL, G.G., OSBORN, C., ANTHONY, D., & GARDOS, P. (1992). CURRENT TREATMENTS OF PARAPHILIACS. ANNUAL REVIEW OF SEX RESEARCH, 225-290.

The authors provided an update of treatment components over the past 10 years (circa 1992). The advances made in behavior therapy include covert sensitization, olfactory aversion, combined covert sensitization and olfactory aversion, imagined desensitization therapy, modified aversive behavioral rehearsal, masturbatory reconditioning, thematic shift, fantasy alternation, directed masturbation, satiation, and electrical aversion. The developments made in pro-social behavior development include social skills training, assertiveness training, and sex education. Advances made in cognitive interventions have consisted of cognitive restructuring and victim awareness. The authors provided a detailed description of the relapse prevention model, in conjunction with an overview concerning the outcome data of cognitive behavioral and relapse prevention treatment programs. A discussion is included concerning the various pharmacological treatment interventions, hormonal agents (CPA and MPA), as well as the legal and ethical issues associated with their use. The authors concluded that treatment with cognitive behavioral and pharmacological intervention is effective and incarceration without treatment appears destined to produce relapse.

BARBAREE, H.E., & MARSHALL, W.L. (1991). TREATMENT OF THE ADULT MALE CHILD MOLESTER. IN C.R. BAGLEY & R.J. THOMLISON (EDS.). CHILD SEXUAL ABUSE: CRITICAL PERSPECTIVES ON PREVENTION, INTERVENTION, AND TREATMENT (PP. 217-256). TORONTO, ONT.: WALL & EMERSON.

This article is a critical review of a wide range of approaches to the treatment of sex offenders. It provided a brief outline on the characteristics of child molesters and discusses the methodological issues associated with evaluating treatment outcome. In addition, it discussed various treatment approaches, including organic treatment, non-behavioral psychotherapy, comprehensive cognitive-behavioral therapy, and the treatment of the sex offender in the context of the mental health and correctional systems. The discussion pointed to the difficulties in conducting treatment outcome research in this area and offers suggestions as to what might be considered the minimum requirements of a treatment outcome study. The authors reported that applying these criteria to the extant reports of treatment for the sex offender leads to the conclusion that the reports to date are not sufficient to evaluate most treatment programs; however, they outlined a number of guidelines for treatment.

BARBAREE, H.E., PEACOCK, E.J., CORTONI, F., MARSHALL, W.L., & SETO, M. (1998). ONTARIO PENITENTIARIES' PROGRAM. IN W.L. MARSHALL (ED.). SOURCEBOOK OF TREATMENT PROGRAMS FOR SEXUAL OFFENDERS (PP. 59-77). NEW YORK: PLENUM PRESS.

The authors described the treatment programs for incarcerated sex offenders sponsored by the Correctional Services of Canada with emphasis on the Warkworth Sexual Behavioral Clinic and the Bath Institution Sex Offenders' Program. The programs utilized a cognitive behavioral approach and group therapy. The Warkworth program was established in 1989 in a medium security federal penitentiary located in Toronto and houses 650 inmates serving sentences of two or more years. Approximately half of these offenders were convicted of a sexual offense or a violent offense in which sexual motivation or behavior was considered to be important. In a follow-up group of 202 offenders, 13 individuals committed a new sexual offense and an additional four individuals committed a new violent offense but not a sexual offense. A total of 36 individuals committed a new offense of any kind. After an average follow-up period of 2.5 years there was a sexual offense recidivism rate of 6.4%. These rates compare favorably with the re-offense rates reported by other larger treatment programs. However, they are too low to conduct discriminate function or logistic regression analysis. The Bath program, which operates within a federal penitentiary, was established in 1991 and is directed by William Marshall. The penitentiary is a "step down" from medium security but offers more constraints than a minimum security facility and houses 300 inmates, 50% of which are sex offenders. The program offers two levels of treatment – offenders who are deemed to be low/low-moderate risk (open groups) and moderate or above (closed groups). Tentative outcome evaluations of the first 107 men treated and released revealed a 2.7% recidivism rate, but so far it has been impossible to estimate the untreated base rate.

BECKETT, R. (1998). COMMUNITY TREATMENT IN THE UNITED KINGDOM. IN W.L. MARSHALL (ED.). *SOURCEBOOK OF TREATMENT PROGRAMS FOR SEXUAL OFFENDERS* (PP. 133-152). NEW YORK: PLENUM PRESS.

Beckett discussed the STEP study (Beckett et al., 1994) that evaluated six representative community-based treatment programs for sex offenders, in conjunction with the Gracewell Clinic, a specialist residential treatment program for child abusers. Beckett examined the impact treatment had on the clients in order to identify which elements of the treatment programs were the most effective and to formulate recommendations on how programs might improve their effectiveness as well as to collect data for a long-term reconviction study. Of the programs selected, two were rolling long-term, open-ended programs and three were short-term, intensive programs offering on average 54 hours of treatment over two weeks. The other was a short-term intensive week program followed by the client seeing his own probation officer and one of the group leaders as a team. In total, 52 child abusers were systematically assessed before and after 54 hours of community-based treatment and these were compared with clients treated by the residential program who had on average received 462 hours of therapy. Cognitive behavioral methods were utilized in all of the programs. Clients were tested pre and post participation in treatment on personality and offense-specific measures. At the end of treatment, 54% of child abusers displayed profiles that fell largely within the non-offending range. The results also illustrated the relationship between treatment change and length of time in therapy. Highly deviant child abusers needed a considerably longer amount of time in treatment before they reached a non-deviant "successfully treated" profile. Overall, 65% of the men who began treatment with a low deviancy profile were successfully treated, compared to only 42% of men who started treatment with a highly deviant profile. Short-term group work successfully treated 65% of offenders entering treatment with low deviancy profiles. With highly deviant men, however, short-term programs were largely unsuccessful. Less than 20% of these offenders had treated profiles by the end of treatment. Long-term therapy, averaging 462 hours of treatment, was more successful than short-term therapy in treating low deviancy men (80% compared with 62%), and considerably more successful in treating highly deviant men (60%). In addition to reducing denial, justifications, and cognitive distortions, long-term treatment was particularly successful in improving the self-esteem, assertiveness, and intimacy skills of these highly deviant child molesters. Currently treatment programs still vary considerably in the number of treatment hours they offer. The amount of time spent in treatment, per offender, can range from 8 to 225 hours per year, with an average of 81 hours. Seventy-percent of the programs offer weekly treatment sessions, with 31% offering intensive treatment on a daily basis. Group work remains the most common form of treatment intervention (97%), though in the majority of programs, co-working, ongoing supervision by individual probation officers, and involvement with mental health professionals are also cited as parallel treatment interventions. With regard to treatment intervention, the most commonly cited goals are increasing victim empathy, controlling sexual arousal, reducing denial, and improving family relationships. Interestingly, less than half of the programs surveyed still cite relapse prevention as an explicit goal.

ECCLES, A., & WALKER, W. (1998). COMMUNITY-BASED TREATMENT WITH SEX OFFENDERS. IN W.L. MARSHALL (ED.). *SOURCEBOOK OF TREATMENT PROGRAMS FOR SEXUAL OFFENDERS.* (PP. 93-103). NEW YORK: PLENUM PRESS.

Eccles & Walker focused on Forensic Behavior Services, which utilizes a cognitive behavioral perspective in conjunction with a relapse prevention approach. The authors stated that in general, there is sufficient evidence to provide optimism that child abusers can receive treatment that lowers their risk to re-offend. With regard to treatment efficacy, the article refers to Marshall & Barbaree (1988), who followed child sexual offenders treated at the Kingston Sexual Behavior Clinic for an average of approximately four years. They found that recidivism rates were markedly lower for treated than for untreated groups. Specifically, the comparisons of recidivism rates for treated versus untreated groups were 18% for molesters of non-familial male children, and 8% versus 22% for incest offenders.

FISHER, D., & BEECH, A.R. (1999). CURRENT PRACTICE IN BRITAIN WITH SEXUAL OFFENDERS. *JOURNAL OF INTERPERSONAL VIOLENCE, 14* (3), 240-256.

Discussed the management and treatment of sex offenders in Britain and provides a brief overview of the first in a series of treatment evaluation studies commissioned by the British government. According to a 1993 survey of the provision of community-based treatment programs for sex offenders, only three of the 63 treatment programs were in existence for more than five years. The increase in treatment programs has been attributed to an increased awareness by the public owing to media attention given to the recidivism of sexual offenders and the realization that these offenders rarely receive any treatment. The authors analyzed sex offender treatment in the community, hospitals, and prisons. An overview of the Sexual Offender Treatment Evaluation Project is also discussed. Cognitive behavioral therapy with reliance on Finkelhor's four preconditions model and the offense cycle was found to be widely used by probation services. Even though the programs were generally successful in covering the specific cognitive areas of therapy, they had little or no behavioral component. Little evidence was found in any of the programs of offenders having been given any formal training in relapse prevention skills. Prior to treatment, the child abusers in the sample were found to be significantly different from the comparison group of non-offenders. Typically, they were emotionally isolated individuals, lacking self-confidence. There were under-assertive, poor at appreciating the perspective of others, and ill-equipped to deal with emotional distress. They characteristically denied or minimized the extent of their sexual offending and problems. A significant portion were found to have little empathy for their victims, strong emotional attachments to children, and a range of distorted attitudes and beliefs in which they portrayed children as able to consent to-and not be harmed by sexual contact with adults. Treatment effectiveness was measured using a battery of psychological tests that measured the areas covered in the treatment program. Individuals were regarded as having shown a treatment effect when their post-treatment test profiles were within a normal range of responding on the measures used. The results revealed that more than half of the total sample showed a treatment effect. All of the programs were found to have a significant effect on offenders' willingness to admit to their offenses and sexual problems. The programs appeared to have significantly reduced the extent to which offenders justified their offending as well as the offenders' distorted thinking about children and sexuality.

GORDON, A., & HOVER, G. (1998). THE TWIN RIVERS SEX OFFENDER TREATMENT PROGRAM. IN W.L. MARSHALL (ED.). *SOURCEBOOK OF TREATMENT PROGRAMS FOR SEXUAL OFFENDERS.* (PP. 3-15). NEW YORK: PLENUM PRESS.

The Twin Rivers Sex Offender Treatment Program was established in 1988 and operates within an 816-bed medium security prison. Of those 816-beds, 200 are dedicated to the sex offender treatment program that consists of a staff of 27 individuals. The therapy utilized by the program consists of cognitive behavioral treatment techniques placed within a relapse prevention framework. Most treatment occurs in both group and individual formats. As of July 1996, 11.4% of the 132 released offenders who completed treatment between 1988 and 1992 had returned to prison for a new sexual offense; of the 235 released offenders who completed treatment between 1993 and 1995, only 4.3% had returned to prison for a new sexual offense.

HORTON, T. (2002). *DUCKING FROM ANGELS - FALLING FROM GRACE: A TREATMENT SUPPLEMENT FOR CLERGY WHO SEXUALLY OFFEND.* BLOOMINGTON, IL: ACME HALO PUBLISHING.

Ducking from Angels is a treatment supplement for sex offender treatment providers to utilize when treating sexually offending clergy of all faiths. It focuses on the authority and trust that was broken by clergy offenders and the unique trauma that the victims of clergy offenders have endured. It is not a treatment program, but as the title implies it is a treatment supplement meant to augment existing sex offender treatment curriculums. The main premise of the supplement is to counteract the cognitive distortions that religious sex offenders hold in order to carry on their misdeeds. It is argued that many of these offenders use Biblical verses as an excuse to commit sexual acts on children. To that end, this guide enables clinicians to use other quotes from the Bible to help encourage change, closure, and empathy in these offenders. In a respectful but powerful way, *Ducking from Angels* becomes a mirror for the offender, encouraging him to honestly look at himself and the damage he has done beyond any potential facades that religious titles or clergy collars can provide.

HUDSON, S.M., WALES, D.S., & WARD, T. (1998). KIA MARAMA: A TREATMENT PROGRAM FOR CHILD MOLESTERS IN NEW ZEALAND. IN W.L. MARSHALL (ED.), *SOURCEBOOK OF TREATMENT PROGRAMS FOR SEXUAL OFFENDERS.* (PP. 17-28). NEW YORK: PLENUM PRESS.

This program in New Zealand was established in 1989 and is housed in a sex offender specific unit with 60 self-contained rooms. The structure of the program is entirely group based and utilizes behavioral treatment within a relapse prevention framework, where individual therapy is kept to a minimum. As of November 1996, 335 men successfully completed the program and have been released. The mean period individuals are considered to be "at risk" is three years and two months (range, 0-5 years 9 months). Twelve of these men have been reconvicted of a sexual crime yielding a reconviction rate of 3.6%.

KEAR-COLWELL, J., & BOER, D.P. (2000). THE TREATMENT OF PEDOPHILES: CLINICAL EXPERIENCE AND THE IMPLICATIONS OF RECENT RESEARCH. *INTERNATIONAL JOURNAL OF OFFENDER THERAPY AND COMPARATIVE CRIMINOLOGY*, 44 (5), 593-605.

The authors contend that the present approaches utilized to treat the pedophile are not as effective as they should be. The recent developments in the application of attachment theory and the treatment of the "difficult client" may lead to improvements in the treatment of such individuals. Attention is drawn to some of the characteristics that pedophiles have in common with personality disordered individuals and with the difficult client. One conclusion is that confrontation during treatment could be counter therapeutic, if not anti-therapeutic, when used in treating the pedophile. It is postulated that other more empathic and supportive approaches are needed, at least at the beginning of the treatment process. The authors discussed the incorporation of the tenets of attachment theory at the initial stages of treatment in order to develop a therapeutic alliance as opposed to a confrontational approach.

LAWS, D.R., MARSHALL, W.L. (2003). A BRIEF HISTORY OF BEHAVIORAL AND COGNITIVE BEHAVIORAL APPROACHES TO SEX OFFENDERS: PART 1. EARLY DEVELOPMENTS. *SEXUAL ABUSE: A JOURNAL OF RESEARCH AND TREATMENT*, 15 (2), 75-92.

This article outlined the development of behavioral and cognitive behavioral treatment of sex offenders from the mid-1800s to 1969. It explored the role of Sigmund Freud and noted that a broad scientific interest in deviant sexual behavior was well established by 1900. John B. Watson and Alfred Kinsey were prominent in the development of behavioral approaches in the early to mid-20th century. A combination of behavioral and cognitive behavioral treatments began to emerge in the late 1960s. Penile Plethysmography (PPG) was developed in 1957, by Kurt Freund, in response to the sexual preference hypothesis. Despite many criticisms of the PPG, it remains a popular assessment tool and continues to be widely used. Earlier non-behavioral treatment approaches were important in establishing that sexual offenders could be engaged in treatment. It is now evident that the sexual preference hypothesis, underpinning behavioral approaches to deviant sexuality, failed to account for the complexity of such behaviors. Gebhard et al. (1965) provided extensive details of the features of sexual offenders, many of which distinguished them from nonsexual offenders and from non-offenders. On these bases, Gebhard et al. were able to classify sexual offenders into subtypes that differed on specific features. This empirically derived classification began a process that recently resulted in the sophisticated systems of Knight and Prentky (1990, 1993). Gebhard et al (1965) were also among the first researchers to demonstrate that some child molesters were violent toward their victims, an observation subsequently confirmed by Marshall and Christie (1981). The earliest behavioral approaches reflected the view that deviant sexual behavior was a distorted manifestation for pedophilia and other paraphilias. Exhibitionists and child molesters were treated with electrical aversion therapy; the modification of sexual fantasies was the target of efforts applied to sadists and voyeurs. However, there was limited evidence on the long-term effects on overt behavior using these techniques.

LAWS, D.R., MARSHALL, W.L. (2003). A BRIEF HISTORY OF BEHAVIORAL AND COGNITIVE BEHAVIORAL APPROACHES TO SEX OFFENDERS: PART 2. THE MODERN ERA. SEXUAL ABUSE: A JOURNAL OF RESEARCH AND TREATMENT, 15 (2), 93-120.

The authors continued their review of the treatment literature by providing an overview of the advances in treatment during the 1970s. The most important developments in the 1970s include: further development of phallometric evaluations in assessment and the associated focus on modifying sexual preferences; introduction of cognitive processes; and the first description of more comprehensive treatment programs. In the early 1970s cognitive psychology began to penetrate the field with particular emphasis upon social skills training, assertiveness, sexual dysfunctions, and gender role behavior. The first conference, at which sexual offender issues were discussed from a behavioral or cognitive behavioral perspective was in 1975 and later became known as the Association for the Treatment of Sexual Abusers (ATSA). The most significant innovation of the 1980s was the adaptation from the addictions field of the relapse prevention model, as well as the formulation of social learning theories of sexual offending. Further, a wide variety of programs described targets such as sexual preferences, sex education, empathy, social skills, self-esteem, substance abuse, anger management, and relapse prevention. The final important development of the

1980s was the beginnings of the work on classificatory (or taxonomic) systems applied to sexual offending. Unlike prior attempts at classification, these models were empirically driven and refined by repeated research. The 1990s were characterized by an explosion of treatment programs and a remarkable increase in the publication of research articles; the emergence of strictly actuarial approaches to risk assessment; the construction of theories describing the cognitions, emotions, and intimacy in sexual offenders; and the introduction of the "self-regulation" model as a revision of the relapse prevention model.

MANN, R.E., & THORNTON, D. (1998). THE EVOLUTION OF A MULTISITE SEXUAL OFFENDER TREATMENT PROGRAM. IN W.L. MARSHALL (ED.). SOURCEBOOK OF TREATMENT PROGRAMS FOR SEXUAL OFFENDERS (PP. 47-57). NEW YORK: PLENUM PRESS.

The authors discussed a national strategy for the treatment of sex offenders in England. Since then, the Sex Offender Treatment Program (SOTP) has been established in 25 correctional facilities. The program utilizes a cognitive behavioral approach and group therapy. No outcome results are present at this time.

MARSHALL, W.L. (1999). CURRENT STATUS OF NORTH AMERICAN ASSESSMENT AND TREATMENT PROGRAMS FOR SEXUAL OFFENDERS. JOURNAL OF INTERPERSONAL VIOLENCE, 14 (3), 221-239.

The author discussed how treatment programs have become more empirically based since the advent of cognitive behavioral therapy in the early 1970s. Marshall described a hypothetical program that includes the assessment of offenders in eight areas – sexual behavior, social functioning, life history, cognitive processes, personality, substance use, physical problems, and relapse-related issues. Further, he went on to describe the structure, process, and content of treatment.

MARSHALL, W.L. (1996). ASSESSMENT, TREATMENT, AND THEORIZING ABOUT SEX OFFENDERS: DEVELOPMENTS DURING THE PAST TWENTY YEARS AND FUTURE DIRECTIONS. CRIMINAL JUSTICE AND BEHAVIOR, 23 (1), 162-199.

This article considered developments during the past 20 years in the assessment and treatment of sex offenders and in theoretical interpretations of their behavior. Marshall reviewed research indicating that in the field of assessments there is a move toward including more cognitive features. One interpretation of the evidence to date suggests that phallometry has been overvalued and that considerable work remains to be done on the psychometric aspects of erectile measurement. Treatment also has moved in a more cognitive direction, but the addition of a relapse prevention approach has been the most significant innovation. Theory development is accelerating, but there needs to be more emphasis on developing and refining our specific constructs rather than elaborating broad explanatory theories.

MATSON, S. (2002). SEX OFFENDER TREATMENT: A CRITICAL MANAGEMENT TOOL. CORRECTIONS TODAY, 64 (6), 114-118.

The author described the uses of cognitive behavioral and psychotropic interventions (SSRIs) to treat sex offenders. Matson concluded that effective treatment interventions incorporate a variety of approaches, including cognitive behavioral techniques, relapse prevention strategies, psychopharmacology, group therapy, and treatment planning that addresses both the risks and needs of individual offenders. He suggested that the most comprehensive approach to managing sex offenders involves strategies that emphasize collaboration and information-sharing while employing individualized supervision plans and the use of sex offender specific treatment.

POLIZZI, D.M., MACKENZIE, D.L., & HICKMAN, L.J. (1999). WHAT WORKS IN ADULT SEX OFFENDER TREATMENT? A REVIEW OF PRISON-AND NON PRISON-BASED TREATMENT PROGRAMS. INTERNATIONAL JOURNAL OF OFFENDER THERAPY AND COMPARATIVE CRIMINOLOGY, 43 (3), 357-374.

An evaluation of 21 sex offender prison and non-prison-based treatment programs was undertaken using the format of the University of Maryland's 1997 report to the U.S. Congress. Eight of the studies were deemed as being too low in scientific merit to include in assessing the effectiveness of the treatment. Of the remaining studies, approximately 50% showed statistically significant findings in favor of sex offender treatment programs. Of six studies that showed a positive treatment effect, four incorporated a cognitive-behavioral approach. Non prison-based sex offender treatment programs were deemed as being effective in curtailing future criminal activity. Prison-based treatment programs displayed promise, but the evidence is not strong enough to support a conclusion that such programs are effective. Few of the studies focused on particular types of sex offenders. Thus, the researchers were unable to formulate any type of conclusion concerning the effectiveness of programs for different sex offender typologies.

SPENCER, A. (1998). PETERHEAD PRISON PROGRAM. IN W.L. MARSHALL (ED.). SOURCEBOOK OF TREATMENT PROGRAMS FOR SEXUAL OFFENDERS (PP. 29-46). NEW YORK: PLENUM PRESS.

The Peterhead Prison Program operates out of a maximum security penitentiary and is owned and operated by basic prison (correctional) staff. Sex offenders comprise at least 85% of the prison population. The program is group based and employs cognitive behavioral techniques. There are no outcome results for this program available at this time.

COGNITIVE BEHAVIORAL TREATMENT AND RELAPSE PREVENTION

AYTES, K.E., OLSEN, S.S., ZAKRAJSEK, T., MURRAY, P., & IRESON, R. (2001). COGNITIVE/ BEHAVIORAL TREATMENT FOR SEXUAL OFFENDERS: AN EXAMINATION OF RECIDIVISM. SEXUAL ABUSE: A JOURNAL OF RESEARCH AND TREATMENT, 13 (4), 223-231.

The authors reviewed a cognitive behavioral treatment program in Jackson County, Oregon, that was established in 1982. Offenders were mandated to participate in this community-based program upon conviction of a felony or misdemeanor sexual offense. These offenders averaged between two and three years of participation. A group of offenders who participated in the Jackson County program between 1985 and 1995 was identified through archival data from the Oregon Department of Corrections. The data revealed success or non success in treatment, as well as any new convictions for sexual or nonsexual offenses. A control group of nonsexual offenders in Jackson County, and a group of sexual offenders in Linn County who were not in a treatment program were also studied. As hypothesized, those Jackson County offenders who successfully completed treatment had lower recidivism rates than those who were unsuccessful in the program. The observed effect of the program was particularly strong for offenders who remained in treatment for one year or more. When review was restricted solely to those participants, the re-offense rate for Jackson County offenders was reduced by over 40% when compared with Linn County offenders. These optimistic findings support the need for comprehensive treatment programs with a cognitive behavioral emphasis.

BEECH, A., & FISHER, D. (2000). MAINTAINING RELAPSE PREVENTION SKILL AND STRATEGIES IN TREATED CHILD ABUSERS. IN D.R. LAWS (ED.). *REMAKING RELAPSE PREVENTION WITH SEX OFFENDERS* (PP. 455-465). CALIFORNIA: SAGE PUBLICATIONS.

This chapter described a relatively quick and easy way of evaluating the extent to which offenders have successfully engaged in the relapse prevention (RP) part of treatment. A newly developed questionnaire was utilized in order to measure change in behavior as a function of treatment. This measurement assesses an offenders' awareness of their own risk situations and use of appropriate coping strategies to deal with such risky situations. An evaluation of a treatment program for imprisoned sex offenders in the United Kingdom found that this instrument was effective in measuring changes in RP skills from the beginning to the end of treatment. More interestingly, when completed again some months after the end of treatment, results from the measure indicated that only men who had also shown significant changes in areas typically targeted in cognitive-behavioral therapy maintained their RP skills. This was not noticeable among men who were no longer in prison and who had gone through a fairly regular treatment regime. Results support the need for both maintenance programs to prevent deterioration in the community and follow-up testing to assess current level of relapse prevention skills.

ECCLES, A., & MARSHALL, W.L. (1999). RELAPSE PREVENTION. IN W.L. MARSHALL (ED.). *THE DEVELOPMENT OF COGNITIVE BEHAVIORAL TREATMENT OF SEX OFFENDERS* (PP. 127-146). ENGLAND: JOHN WILEY & SONS, LTD.

This chapter discussed the development of the relapse prevention model by Marlatt in response to the clinical difficulties associated with the treatment of substance abusers. The authors reviewed and critiqued the Marque-Pithers Model as well as Ward's Model of the offense chain. They noted two potential problems with relapse prevention: (1) clients would be overwhelmed by having to learn the complex language of Relapse Prevention, by having to detail each feature of their offense chain, and by having to provide a lengthy series of plans to prevent a relapse; (2) making treatment (i.e., the aspect of the Relapse model that Pithers, 1990, refers to as the "internal self-management dimension") overly elaborate, and coupling that with extensive post-release supervision, send a message to the client that we believe they can manage their lives on their own. The authors outlined their attempt to apply a modified Relapse Prevention approach (which includes some cognitive approaches) with three main features: (1) the development of the offense chain; (2) the generation of plans to deal with potential future problems; and (3) the delineation of warning signs that serve to indicate to the offender and his supervisor that he is slipping back into problematic behavior. However, the authors noted that even though they have not yet evaluated the Relapse Prevention component, other researchers have and found support for the value of the Relapse component in achieving its goals. Despite this evidence these studies are limited due to methodological problems.

FERNANDEZ, Y.M., & MARSHALL, W.L. (2000). CONTEXTUAL ISSUES IN RELAPSE PREVENTION TREATMENT. IN D.R. LAWS (ED.). *REMAKING RELAPSE PREVENTION WITH SEX OFFENDERS* (PP. 225-235). CALIFORNIA: SAGE PUBLICATIONS.

This chapter suggested that the context within which treatment is provided can have a significant influence on the degree to which the clients change. The article attempted to answer the following questions: Is it best to adopt an individual one-on-one approach or does all or most of treatment occur in groups; Should we employ open or closed-group formats; Or should treatment be seen as a set of psycho-educational components or as a therapeutic process having a guide set of treatment targets? The authors discussed their sex offender program at the Bath Institution, which includes a Relapse model with open group formats. The focus of this program is placed on approach goals rather than avoidance goals.

HANSON, K. (2000). WHAT IS SO SPECIAL ABOUT RELAPSE PREVENTION? IN D.R. LAWS (ED.). *REMAKING RELAPSE PREVENTION WITH SEX OFFENDERS* (PP. 27-38). CALIFORNIA: SAGE PUBLICATIONS.

This chapter discussed the basic principles of Relapse Prevention (RP) and outlined some of the positive and negative aspects of this treatment approach. Hanson promoted the Relapse model as a means of identifying and avoiding high-risk situations and providing a medium through which therapists and offenders can discuss offense behavior. However, he argued that some implications of Relapse Prevention have generated pointless distractions for both therapists and offenders. The chapter also questioned how the more innovative concepts of Relapse Prevention, such as the abstinence violation effect or the lapse/relapse distinction, accurately describe the problem faced by sex offenders. The author offered evidence that sex offenders often lack the motivation that is the prerequisite of Relapse Prevention's interventions and that offenders whose crime patterns do not match the assumption of the model's approach (i.e., negative affect, covert planning, etc.) are unlikely to derive benefit from attempts to force their accounts into a standard Relapse Prevention mold. The model's inability to conceive of untreated, low-risk offenders has diverted attention away from the majority of offenders who naturally desist and has contributed to some sex offenders receiving interventions poorly suited to their needs.

HUDSON, S.M., & WARD, T. (2000). RELAPSE PREVENTION: ASSESSMENT AND TREATMENT IMPLICATIONS. IN D. R. LAWS (EDS). *REMAKING RELAPSE PREVENTION WITH SEX OFFENDERS* (PP. 102-121). CALIFORNIA: SAGE PUBLICATIONS.

The authors discussed the problems of the Relapse Prevention model as it pertains to treatment and maintenance. They presented a brief summary of the model and examine what the assessment and treatment agenda might look like for each of the pathways of offending patterns associated with the major goals (avoidance vs. approach) and predominant strategy (passive vs. active). They make the point that unless we understand the processes involved for an individual offender, how can we credibly identify areas for clinical intervention? The article proposed having assessment and intervention strategies that reflect the heterogeneity present in the offending process. Further, the authors suggested that we need to gain greater clarity concerning the type of offense process exhibited by various offenders (i.e., an adequate taxonomy) in order to differentially evaluate intervention outcomes. The authors asserted that the global strategy of whether treatment works is inadequate because we predict that some types of the offending process are likely to be more difficult to change and maintain.

LAUNAY, G. (2001). RELAPSE PREVENTION WITH SEX OFFENDERS: PRACTICE, THEORY AND RESEARCH. *CRIMINAL BEHAVIOR AND MENTAL HEALTH, 11*, 38-54.

The aim of this article was to evaluate the Relapse Prevention (RP) technique by looking at evidence presented by the Rochester Relapse Prevention program as well as reviewing the theoretical and research basis for the program. Relapse Prevention is used to help offenders understand the interaction of the behavioral, affective and cognitive factors as well as the steps involved that lead to the offending behavior. The program enabled them to generate and practice alternative strategies in order to halt this cycle. The theory on which relapse prevention for sex offenders is based is sound in essence, but the Relapse model suffers from an overlay of cumbersome vocabulary and from the recent addition of some complex constructs that are not clinically useful. Second, there is some reliable research to support the practice of RP even though the crucial findings that would inform its development are still missing. Launay concluded that the original model provides sound principles for therapy to which the modern revisions add little.

LAWS, D.R., HUDSON, S.M., & WARD, T. (2000). THE ORIGINAL MODEL OF RELAPSE PREVENTION WITH SEX OFFENDERS: PROMISES UNFULFILLED. IN D.R. LAWS (ED.). *REMAKING RELAPSE PREVENTION WITH SEX OFFENDERS* (PP. 3-24). CALIFORNIA: SAGE PUBLICATIONS.

This chapter provided an historical background of the Relapse model and critiqued the original model. The authors questioned whether the Relapse model, as was intended, provides us with insight into offending behavior as well as its efficacy in reducing recidivism. They concluded that the issue of scope, or the lack thereof, is a fundamental criticism of the model. Furthermore, it is reported that the model is contradictory with respect to the mechanisms proposed. For example, sometimes phenomena are simply being described while at other times, incompatible mechanisms are proposed in addition to mechanisms that are more complex than required.

LAWS, D.R. (1999). RELAPSE PREVENTION: THE STATE OF THE ART. *JOURNAL OF INTERPERSONAL VIOLENCE*, *14* (3), 285-302.

This article summarized the development of the Relapse Prevention treatment model through the past 20 years. The author described the original model applied to addictive behavior as conceived by Marlatt and his associates. It proved necessary to make alterations to the classical model in order to make it applicable to sexual offenders. The author postulated that the use of the RP model should be confined to disorders of impulse control. Present and future developments in RP include recognition of the concept of harm reduction, use of stepped care, emphasis on motivational interviewing, the revised cognitive-behavior chain, and recognition of cognitive deconstructionism. The greatest weakness of the RP model is that it has escaped empirical evaluation. Future prospects for the model are discussed, and it is recommended that a revised RP be the model for sexual offender treatment for the foreseeable future.

MCGRATH, R.J., HOKE, S.E., & VOJTISEK, J.E. (1998). COGNITIVE-BEHAVIORAL TREATMENT OF SEX OFFENDERS: A TREATMENT COMPARISON AND LONG-TERM FOLLOW-UP STUDY. *CRIMINAL JUSTICE AND BEHAVIOR*, *25* (2), 203-225.

Recidivism rates were examined for 122 sex offenders from a rural Vermont county who were under correctional supervision from 1984 through 1995. Seventy-one non-randomized participants were enrolled in a comprehensive outpatient cognitive-behavioral and relapse-prevention based treatment program, 32 participants received less specialized mental health treatment, and the remaining 19 participants received no treatment. At follow-up, the cognitive-behavioral treatment group demonstrated a statistically significant treatment benefit. This finding is consistent with previous research findings.

MARSHALL, W.L., ANDERSON D., & FERNANDEZ, Y. (1999). *THE DEVELOPMENT OF COGNITIVE BEHAVIORAL TREATMENT OF SEX OFFENDERS* (PP. 9-31). ENGLAND: JOHN WILEY & SONS, LTD.

This chapter provided an historical overview of sex offender treatment up to the development of cognitive behavioral approaches. Cognitive issues were directly brought into mainstream behavior therapy in the mid-1970s. The authors discussed the use of attachment theory and its relevance to sex offender treatment.

PITHERS, W.D. (1990). RELAPSE PREVENTION WITH SEXUAL AGGRESSORS: A METHOD FOR MAINTAINING THERAPEUTIC GAIN AND ENHANCING EXTERNAL SUPERVISION. IN W.L. MARSHALL (ED.). *HANDBOOK OF SEXUAL ASSAULT: ISSUES, THEORIES, AND TREATMENT OF THE OFFENDER* (PP. 343-361). NEW YORK: PLENUM PRESS.

This chapter described the premise behind Relapse Prevention (RP) and treatment procedures. Pithers stressed that since RP is a highly individualized approach to therapy, thorough assessment is necessary in order to determine the issues to focus upon in treatment. The assessment of high-risk situations is outlined and an External Supervisory Dimension of the RP model is discussed. In conclusion, the author reported data from a five-year follow-up study of 167 offenders (20 rapists, 147 pedophiles) who were treated under the RP model. The data revealed a 4% relapse rate. The author claimed that this initial data suggests that relapse prevention represents an effective means of enhancing maintenance of change in sexual aggressors.

PITHERS, W.D., KASHIMA, K.M., CUMMING, G.F., BEAL, L.S., & BUELL, M.M. (1988). RELAPSE PREVENTION OF SEXUAL AGGRESSION. *ANNALS OF THE NEW YORK ACADEMY OF SCIENCES, 528,* 244-260.

The authors reported that an early meta-analysis of relapse data revealed that nearly 66% of all relapses occurred within the first 90 days after the end of treatment. The probability of relapse decreased markedly after that period. However, when it comes to sex offenders, the first nine months after discharge is the time period marked by the highest recidivism rate. The authors attributed the longer period prior to relapse for sex offenders to the more severe violations of social norms inherent in their acts and the greater penalties imposed for their behavior than for the relapse of a substance abuser. The authors outlined a study that they had conducted that analyzed precursors to offenses of 136 pedophiles and 64 rapists. They looked at multiple determinants of sexual aggression in an effort to identify a relapse process occurring over a longer time. They found that 89% of the subjects reported experiencing strong emotional states prior to relapse; 46% of pedophiles more frequently recalled having felt anxious or depressed (38%), generally as a consequence, or cause, of prolonged social disaffiliation. In analyzing precursors, a common sequence of changes that ultimately led to a sexual offense was often found. The first change in the relapse process from the client's typical function was a change in affect. They referred to themselves as "feeling moody," or "brooding." The second alteration involved fantasies of performing the aberrant sexual act. These fantasies were converted into thoughts, often cognitive distortions, in the third step of the relapse process. As fantasies and thoughts continued, the clients engaged in a process of passive planning, cognitively refining the circumstances that would permit commission of a sexual offense. In the final step of the relapse process, the plan was manifested behaviorally. The article went on to outline Relapse Prevention (RP) assessment and treatment procedures. The authors concluded that RP serves as a comprehensive training program designed to help sex offender avoid reoffenses. It is stressed that RP is not an activity that a sex offender completes and the crucial lesson is that maintenance is forever.

PITHERS, W.D., MARQUES, J.K., GIBAT, C.C., & MARLATT, G.A. (1983). RELAPSE PREVENTION WITH SEXUAL AGGRESSIVES: A SELF-CONTROL MODEL OF TREATMENT AND MAINTENANCE CHANGE. IN J.G. GREER (ED.). *THE SEXUAL AGGRESSOR: CURRENT PERSPECTIVES ON TREATMENT* (PP. 214-239). NEW YORK: VAN NOSTRAND REINHOLD.

This chapter described Relapse Prevention (RP) as a systematic assessment and treatment program designed to provide sexually aggressive individuals with cognitive and behavioral skills that will reduce the probability of another offense. The model enhances maintenance of changes that have been induced by other treatments (e.g. presents a description of the sequence of behavioral changes that ultimately culminates in relapse). The authors outlined the basic concepts and terms of relapse prevention and provided a thorough description of the behavioral assessment and treatment components of the relapse prevention treatment model for sexual aggressors.

STONER, S.A., & GEORGE, W.H. (2000). RELAPSE PREVENTION WITH HARM REDUCTION: AREAS OF OVERLAP. IN D.R. LAWS (ED.). *REMAKING RELAPSE PREVENTION WITH SEX OFFENDERS* (PP. 56-75). CALIFORNIA: SAGE PUBLICATIONS.

The authors considered the merits of applying harm reduction to sex offender treatment paradigms. They described harm reduction and reviewed and updated key Relapse Prevention constructs in order to foster better reconciling with harm reduction. The authors also addressed several of the challenges involved with translating harm reduction to sex offender work. The issues of lapse and relapse, the cognitive-behavioral offense chain, and the abstinence violation effect, concepts that are central to RP, are also central to an understanding of how a harm reduction philosophy might be beneficial. In conclusion, the authors were optimistic that harm reduction may be profitably applied to sex offender treatment protocols; however, they acknowledge that this concept is still relatively new and requires further investigation.

WARD, T., & HUDSON, S.M. (2000). A SELF-REGULATION MODEL OF RELAPSE PREVENTION. IN D.R. LAWS (ED.). *REMAKING RELAPSE PREVENTION WITH SEX OFFENDERS* (PP. 79-101). CALIFORNIA: SAGE PUBLICATIONS.

This chapter described a self-regulation model of the relapse process. Initially, the authors gave a brief review of the relevant research and theory on self-regulation in order to provide a conceptual basis for the model. They then presented their model of the relapse process, which contains nine phases and four pathways. Finally, they briefly discussed the research and clinical implications of the model. In conclusion, the authors suggested that the self-regulation model can provide a more comprehensive understanding of the factors associated with relapse and consequently assist clinicians in tailoring treatment to individual offenders. This is in complete contrast to Pither's Relapse model, which provides clinicians with a conceptual map of the factors associated with an offenders' sexually deviant behavior.

WOOD, M.R., GROSSMAN, L.S., & FICHTNER, C.G. (2000). PSYCHOLOGICAL ASSESSMENT, TREATMENT, AND OUTCOME WITH SEX OFFENDERS. *BEHAVIORAL SCIENCES AND THE LAW, 18*, 23-41.

The authors provided an historical review of sex offender treatment as well as programs based on psychodynamic, behavioral, and cognitive-behavioral theories. The authors concluded that cognitive behavioral treatment is effective. More specifically, offenders can use the concepts and procedures generated by cognitive-behavioral models to reduce risk of sexual offending.

HOLISTIC THEARPY

LONGO, R.E. (2002). A HOLISTIC/INTEGRATED APPROACH TO TREATING SEX OFFENDERS. IN B. SCHWARTZ (ED.). *THE SEX OFFENDER: CURRENT TREATMENT MODALITIES AND SYSTEMS ISSUES*, VOL. IV (2). NEW JERSEY: CIVIC RESEARCH INSTITUTE, INC.

Longo addressed "the danger of labeling," and stated that it is important when looking to a holistic model for treatment to be sensitive to the client's culture, race, and spirituality. A holistic approach sees the whole person as made up of many parts: family, friends, community, work, school, intimate relationships, etc. The approach purports that negative labels (i.e., sex offender) do not help people heal, but rather reinforce their staying in the unhealthy state. As out-

lined in "the theory of multiple intelligences," holistic treatment seeks to bring a variety of theories and models into the treatment process in order to enhance a person's potential. The areas this paradigm seeks to address include intrapersonal intelligence, interpersonal intelligence, visual/special intelligence, verbal/linguistic intelligence, logical mathematical intelligence, musical/rhythmic intelligence, and body/kinesthetic intelligence. "Wellness" as a whole and "Transforming Power" are also discussed as well as the therapeutic relationship placed within the holistic model and holistic treatment as a process. In conclusion, the author reported that holistic treatment with sex offenders is quickly growing in acceptance since the field is recognizing shortcomings in the RP model and in using strictly cognitive behavioral techniques.

PHARMACOLOGICAL INTERVENTION

BERLIN, F.S. (1983). SEX OFFENDERS: A BIOMEDICAL PERSPECTIVE AND A STATUS REPORT ON BIOMEDICAL TREATMENT: IN J.G. GREER (ED.). *THE SEXUAL AGGRESSOR: CURRENT PERSPECTIVES ON TREATMENT* (PP. 83-123). NEW YORK: VAN NOSTRAND REINHOLD.

Paraphilias are diagnosable psychiatric conditions manifested by recurrent deviant fantasies, intense erotic cravings, and relatively stereotyped behaviors as a response to those cravings. The behaviors are stereotyped in the sense that exhibitionists expose themselves, whereas pedophiles seek out children and transvestites cross-dress. Paraphilic syndromes are not necessarily mutually exclusive, but like conventional heterosexuality, their course is chronic. They may respond to biological treatments and organic pathologies, but their etiologies are poorly understood. Sexual offenses, as defined legally, may or may not be perpetrated by persons with one of these syndromes. When offending behavior is related to such a syndrome, intramuscularly administered medroxyprogesterone acetate (MPA), orchidectomy to diminish testosterone or cyproterone acetate (CPA) may be helpful. However, antiandrogenic medication can only help if the offender is compliant. Orally administered MPA (at a daily dosage of 150mg) has not been shown to be helpful. It is not known if antiandrogenic medication is useful when offending behavior is unrelated to deviant sexual cravings, as when rape is committed opportunistically or in response to anger and hostility. Stereotactic psychosurgery is still a somewhat controversial procedure that is not yet widely available to be considered a practical treatment option for sexual deviation syndromes at this time. However, behavioral therapy may help some offenders learn how to better resist their urges.

BRADFORD, J.M. (1990). THE ANTIANDROGEN AND HORMONAL TREATMENT OF SEX OFFENDERS. IN W.L. MARSHALL (ED.). *HANDBOOK OF SEXUAL ASSAULT: ISSUES, THEORIES, AND TREATMENT OF THE OFFENDER* (PP. 297-310). NEW YORK: PLENUM PRESS.

This article outlined the use of hormones and other agents in the treatment of sexually deviant behavior. It discussed hormonal controls over sexual behavior, MPA and CPA, and included a review of clinical studies in order to explain both treatment methods. In conclusion, the author provided evidence that the treatment of sex offenders with antiandrogens is clearly successful in reducing recidivism rates. However, he implied that CPA should have limited use in a correctional facility owing to the uncertainty that informed consent may not be gotten freely. There is the danger that CPA is too likely to become part of a subtle coercion process involving the offer of parole contingent on accepting treatment, without a truly independent psychiatric consultation prior to its use. Further, the author indicated that after a treatment period of 6 to 12 months, CPA can be gradually tapered off in a significant number of individuals, without causing relapses, which does not seem to be true for MPA.

GRUBIN, D. (2000). COMPLEMENTING RELAPSE PREVENTION WITH MEDICAL INTERVENTION. IN D.R. LAWS (ED.). *REMAKING RELAPSE PREVENTION WITH SEX OFFENDERS* (PP. 201-212). CALIFORNIA: SAGE PUBLICATIONS.

Grubin discussed the use of medications such as CPA, Depo-Provera and Selective Serotonin Reuptake Inhibitors (SSRI's) in conjunction with cognitive-behavioral treatment. While acknowledging the message that the use of medication sends to the offender (i.e., that his drives are not wholly under his power, and that he has only a limited ability to control his offending behavior), the author supported the notion that medication can assist in identifying thoughts and emotions that can disrupt self-regulation, as well as providing a means to facilitate it.

HUCKER, S.J., & BAIN, J. (1990). ANDROGENIC HORMONES AND SEXUAL ASSAULT. IN W.L. MARSHALL (ED.). *HANDBOOK OF SEXUAL ASSAULT: ISSUES, THEORIES, AND TREATMENT OF THE OFFENDER* (PP. 93-102). NEW YORK: PLENUM PRESS.

The authors reviewed studies that have evaluated interactions among hormones, sex, and aggression. It discussed the basic physiology of sex hormones in the human male, hormones and sex drive, testosterone-level responses to erotic stimulation, treatment of hypogonadal men with testosterone, the behavioral effects of castration, testosterone and aggression in normal males, testosterone and aggression in male offenders, and hormones and sexual aggression. The authors concluded that the studies reviewed in this article are characterized by small groups of subjects and that results are conflicting. Further evidence suggests that there may be an abnormality of androgen metabolism in individuals who display aberrant sexual behavior, though this is not well supported by empirical evidence.

RÖSLER, A., & WITZTUM, E. (2000). PHARMACOTHERAPY OF PARAPHILIAS IN THE NEXT MILLENNIUM. *BEHAVIORAL SCIENCES AND THE LAW, 18,* 43-56.

This article discussed how CPA, MPA, GnRH and psychotropic drugs work to decrease sex offending behavior. It stated that psychotropic drugs are highly controversial because of the erratic results and lack of permanent eradication of paraphilic manifestations. Long-acting gonadotropin-releasing hormone (GnRH) agonist analogues are the most potent antiandrogens that selectively abolish testosterone secretion in a totally reversible fashion. The article indicated that GnRH analogues, together with psychotherapy, are highly effective in controlling selected paraphilias (pedophilia, exhibitionism, and voyeurism), and these are the most promising mode of therapy in the next millennium. Further, the authors reported that there is an urgent need for strong methodological research. These would consist of carefully designed double-blind controlled studies with a large number of subjects in order to validate or not the use of the various pharmacological therapies.

CLERIC SEX OFFENDERS
AND TREATMENT

BRYANT, C. (1999). PSYCHOLOGICAL TREATMENT OF PRIEST SEX OFFENDERS. IN T.G. PLANTE (ED). *BLESS ME FATHER FOR I HAVE SINNED: PERSPECTIVES ON SEXUAL ABUSE COMMITTED BY ROMAN CATHOLIC PRIESTS* (PP. 87-110). WESTPORT, CT: PRAEGER PUBLISHERS.

This chapter provided an overview of theories concerning offending and treatment. The literature is reviewed in order to provide the reader with different possibilities as to why an individual molests a child. A brief discussion of assessment is included and the author made a distinction between assessment and treatment. Several goals of inpatient treatment are outlined. The priest must acknowledge that he has a sexual problem and that something must be done. This first step facilitates the acceptance of responsibility. It is important that the offender understands what initiates his offending and that he has a firm grasp of the tools used to manage his behavior. The offender must also appreciate the inappropriateness of his behavior and recognize the fact that he can be treated, but never cured. A brief overview of cognitive-behavioral treatment and relapse prevention is included.

HAYWOOD, T.W. & GREEN, J. (2000). CLERIC SERIAL OFFENDERS: CLINICAL CHARACTERISTICS AND TREATMENT APPROACHES. IN LOUIS B. SCHLESINGER (ED.). *SERIAL OFFENDERS: CURRENT THOUGHTS, RECENT FINDINGS* (PP. 247-262). BOCA RATON, FL: CRC PRESS.

Haywood and Green provided an overview of the literature pertaining to prevalence, offense/victim characteristics, and evaluation of cleric serial offenders. Depending upon the study, prevalence rates ranged from 2% to 6% (pedophiliac and ephebophiliac clerics), 20% to 40% (sexual misconduct with adults), 8.4% (in a sample of 1322), and 5.8% to 24% (boundary violations with adults) (Sipes, 1990; Loftus & Camargo, 1993; Friel & Friel, 1988; Goetz, 1992; Seat et al., 1993). In examining offense/victim characteristics, the authors concluded that clerics are more likely to engage in sexual misconduct with adults than minors. Of those who offend against children they are more likely to favor adolescent males and they are less likely than non-clerics to be serial offenders or have multiple paraphilias. In examining the literature concerning characteristics of the offender, it is illustrated that in regards to cognitive distortions cleric offenders displayed extreme minimization of personal problems and were less likely to rationalize and justify child molestation. The chapter also provided two case studies, which illustrated offending behavior, evaluation and outcome. In evaluating sex offenders, it is recommended that clinical and actuarial methods be utilized. It is also important to assess sexual preference and the extent of cognitive distortions. The "being a person" (BAP) treatment paradigm is discussed, which includes 100 items that help mold the course of therapy. In discussing relapse prevention the red light/green light metaphor is used to help teach offenders how to manage their behavior.

HUDSON, P.E. (1997). SPIRITUALITY AS A COMPONENT IN A TREATMENT PROGRAM FOR SEXUALLY ADDICTED ROMAN CATHOLIC CLERGY. *COUNSELING & VALUES, 41 (2)*, 174-183.

This article described a European program for clergy sex offenders that is based on spirituality. The article also featured an interview with the head of the treatment program, David Fitzgerald. The program includes only Roman Catholic priests and brothers from Africa and Europe who are typically fixated/regressed pedophiles and ephebophiles. The philosophy of this 12-step program is that addiction results from a spiritual void that is combated through prayer, meditation, and scripture reading. Success is measured through identification of high-risk situations and mastery of the tools presented in the program for managing offending behavior. It is required that the men participate in two years of aftercare. Fitzgerald asserted that those individuals for whom treatment had proved unsuccessful will be reported to civil authorities if there is an indication that the Diocese or community would fail to report that person.

KELLY, A.F. (1998). CLERGY OFFENDERS. IN W.L. MARSHALL ET AL. (EDS.). *SOURCEBOOK OF TREATMENT PROGRAMS FOR SEXUAL OFFENDERS* (PP. 303-318). NEW YORK, NY: PLENUM PRESS.

This chapter provided an overview of the problems associated with managing cleric offenders. The author cited the reforms made by the Chicago Archdiocese in 1992, which instituted a policy of removal for any priests who had been accused of abuse. The Archdiocese also established a review board comprised of lay persons not associated with the Church, as well as psychologists, psychiatrists, and lawyers. This revision is concurrent with the suggestions made by the Canadian bishops Ad Hoc Committee on Child Sexual Abuse in 1992. In 1993, various experts in the field of child sexual abuse met with the National Conference of Catholic Bishops in order to evaluate the problems in the Church. Among the suggestions included improving the care allotted to victims, improving education and the screening of candidates for the seminary, and creating guidelines for relapse prevention and reassignment. The author posited that the abuse is made possible by the cleric's position of power and that the problem extends beyond the individual. Among the problems involved in establishing treatment facilities include the societal stigma associated with clergy offenders. Since child sexual abuse by members of the clergy has become a public issue, some hospitals may not want to institute a program for fear of having to deal with the swarms of media. Thus, this hinders the treatment program, which may be forced to act in secrecy. The surrounding community will also pose a challenge to establishing a program as the offender may resist treatment for fear of being ostracized by fellow priests. In combating these issues, confidentiality must be handled with care. The therapeutic alliance may be hindered when the treatment referral is mandatory and the cleric may feel that there is a political motive behind the referral. These ulterior motives foster a sense of resistance to cooperation and the offender becomes defensive in talking about himself. Cleric offenders differ from the general population in the fact that they have a built in alliance and sense of caring and community as a result of their work. This may assist is creating a helpful, productive relationship. In assessing the clergy, Kelly asserted that the assessment at the very least should consists of a series of clinical interviews, a complete sexual history, personality testing, cognitive and neuropsychological testing, and a physical examination. The treatment center must be viewed a neutral party and may accomplish this by

having a Church representative clearly spell out the allegations in front of the cleric and evaluator. According to Kelly, this creates an air of openness and implies that "yes, we know all of this, and we still care about you and want to help you." During the course of the evaluation, a spiritual assessment should be conducted because clerics often profess that at the time of the offense their prayer life was seriously hindered. The Church is expected to refer all alleged offenders for an evaluation in order to defend against an allegation. Another issue, which must be addressed in evaluations, is the vague criteria for what constitutes an effective cleric. Kelly asserted that psychosis, antisocial characteristic traits and paraphilias are definite rule outs, but the positive behaviors are more vague and possibly immeasurable. There has also been resistance directed towards the use of the penile plethysmograph (PPG) to evaluate sexual deviancy due to its intrusive nature and stimulus material. Thus, this assessment technique is not used often with the clergy. The true prevalence of cleric abuse is unknown but it has been estimated that 2% to 3% may have acted out sexually with a child. There is also the myth that these offenders are true pedophiles who engage in predatory acts, but Kelly contends that this is false. In citing the work of Father Canice Connors, former director of St. Luke's Institute, 44 priests were diagnosed as pedophiles, 185 were ephebophiles, 142 were compulsives, and 165 were diagnosed with unintegrated sexuality. The treatment center must also be prepared to respond to the needs of the parish. This can be achieved through organizing educational programs and providing counseling to those members of the laity who are likely to feel hurt and betrayed. In communicating with the Church regarding the progress of the cleric, it is recommended that the clerics review every written communication and sign it before it is shared. While the treatment center should not be biased in any manner, being biased in favor of the cleric can enable treatment progress since they usually display a trust of self and others. Characteristics of clergy offenders are discussed and the subjugation of self makes treatment very difficult in the beginning. They have limited awareness of their emotional life, poor use of leisure time, poor physical health, and underdeveloped relations and may also profess that their role is to be concerned with the well being of others and not themselves. This idea must be challenged in treatment and it must be explained that if they can not help themselves then they will be ineffective in helping others. Intimacy must be addressed during treatment in order to develop a sense of interpersonal security. Intimacy building also allows the treatment provider to teach the cleric healthy strategies to deal with emotions. Shame and guilt must also be addressed during the treatment progress since shame reinforces denial, which is an unfavorable evaluation of the self. Shame may also serve to annihilate the self for those clerics who have not developed a sense of self, which is separate from their vocation. Clerics are placed upon a moral pedestal by the parish and a lapse in moral behavior is devastating because of these high standards. Guilt may be used in a healthy manner since it is an unfavorable view of behavior, not the self, and may be used to prevent future behavior whereas shame may perpetuate it. The presence of grandiosity in the cleric results in a minimization of abuse and blame being directed towards the victim. This is evident in those clerics who have an insecure sense of self and display a need to rely on the parishioners who idolize him. This idolatry and lack of intimacy play a role in facilitating boundary violations. Once the initial denial stage has been combated, clerics are likely to regret their actions and vow never to do it again. Due to their intelligence and alienation from emotions, these vows are hollow because while they may have made up their minds, they have not yet found a way to control their emotions. Empathy deficits may be present in those clerics who have lost touch with the needs of others and only seek to fulfill their selfish wishes and issues with authority may be played out in the boundary violation. Treatment aftercare is discussed and it is emphasized that psychotherapy should be continued for a minimum of 6 months to a year. A support team should also be established with at least one member of the Church hierarchy on the committee. This team would enable the cleric to communicate his feelings with someone whom he knows will be there to care for him whenever he needs it. The cleric should also be required to attend a 12-Step meeting and discuss it with his therapist in order to ensure that the program is meeting his needs. The issue of reassignment and the legal implications associated with child abuse are briefly discussed.

LOFTUS, J.A. & CAMARGO, R.J. (1993). TREATING THE CLERGY. ANNALS OF SEX RESEARCH, 6, 287-303.

This article described a study conducted over a two-year period at the Southdown Treatment Center for cleric offenders. WAIS and MMPI scores from the past 25 years were compared for the sample that was comprised of clerics described as age inappropriate offenders, homosexual, heterosexual, and bisexual. These scores were then compared to those of a control group comprised of clerics in order to establish a baseline. The authors found evidence that 2.7% of the clerics in the age inappropriate group had contact with children under age of 13. The following characteristics emerged in analyzing the data concerning the age inappropriate group: most were priests from Dioceses, they were between the ages of 49 and 60 when they were first refereed for treatment, they ministered in parishes and educational settings, there was no criminal or psychiatric history for the individual clerics or their families, and they had no history of substance abuse. The offense data illustrated that the abuse occurred frequently (four or more times) and the ages of the victims varied. The MMPI data suggested that the personality profile for the clerics was comprised of shy, passive, and lonely characteristics. In evaluating their treatment, the authors urged that clerics should be treated no differently from other sex offenders. They have had some evidence that nonverbal psychotherapies have been helpful because the patients show signs of being alienated from their body before entering treatment. Recidivism is discussed with caution because out of the 111 men in the sample, the treatment providers know the status of only 40 individuals. Based upon these figures, there appeared to be a recidivism rate of 10%.

MANUEL, G. (1999). BEGINNING AN INTERVENTION IN CLERGY SEXUAL ABUSE. IN T.G. PLANTE (ED). BLESS ME FATHER FOR I HAVE SINNED: PERSPECTIVES ON SEXUAL ABUSE COMMITTED BY ROMAN CATHOLIC PRIESTS (PP. 22-26). WESTPORT, CT: PRAEGER PUBLISHERS.

This chapter is based upon the author's own experience as a clinician and provided a brief overview of the various considerations that must be taken into account when staging an intervention. The mental health professional must be aware of the mandatory reporting laws for child sexual abuse as well as the sexual misconduct policies and procedures the institution. It is important that the mental health professional alert Church authorities that they must pay serious attention to their reactions and they must be made aware of the issue of denial. Withdrawing from the intervention is appropriate if the religious superior will not allow for a fair intervention. The issues of shame and guilt must be addressed in order to make religious superiors aware of the need for neutrality. The mental health professional is also responsible for educating the religious superiors as to how they should address the victim and the perpetrator in a manner that is clear and effective.

VALCOUR, F. (1990). THE TREATMENT OF CHILD SEXUAL ABUSERS IN THE CHURCH. IN S.J. ROSSETTI (ED.). *SLAYER OF THE SOUL: CHILD SEXUAL ABUSE AND THE CATHOLIC CHURCH* (PP. 45-66). MYSTIC, CT: TWENTY-THIRD PUBLICATIONS.

Valcour described different forms of treatment and risk factors associated with sexual offending. The author asserts that while sexual deviancy is not curable, it can be treated and cites the success of the Saint Luke Institute (of the 55 child molesting priests none are known to have relapsed). Certain risk factors such as chromosomal abnormalities are unalterable and the evaluator must pay attention to the perpetrators own childhood trauma because the offending may be a form of acting out. These traumas also stunt the psychological development of these individuals. Valcour asserts that in conjunction with the previously mentioned risk factors, early experiences, hormonal problems, neuropsychological deficits, denial, and countertransference also play a role in the offending behavior and treatment survival. The problems involved in psychotherapeutic interventions include idealization, authority conflict, control issues, self-loathing, and a need for forgiveness. While these are fairly common, the individual may be hindered by other problems such as paraphilias, eating disorders, and depression. An alternative form of treatment involves the hormone Depo-Provera, which stifles sexual arousal but has numerous side effects. Valcour contends that before reassignment can be considered for the priests, a formal appraisal of the individual's risk of reoffending must be obtained from the treatment center. It is considered encouraging if the priest has

displayed insight into his disorder and is committed to preventing the recurrence of the behavior. Insight into one's own risk factors, a willingness to disclose problems, and participation in an aftercare program are also encouraging. In order for aftercare to be successful the diocese needs to create and enforce certain guidelines that spell out the conditions for reassignment.

WARBERG, B.W., ABEL, G.G., & OSBORN, C. (1996). COGNITIVE-BEHAVIORAL TREATMENT FOR PROFESSIONAL SEXUAL MISCONDUCT AMONG THE CLERGY. *PASTORAL PSYCHOLOGY, 45 (1)*, 49-63.

This article explained cognitive-behavioral therapy with clerics through discussion of case studies. The authors asserted that clergy offenders describe their misconduct as being sudden, impulsive, and unplanned. Through various methods, therapists are able to teach clerics that the behavior is anything but impulsive and can be interrupted early in the process. The authors also discussed the role of cognitive distortions and their impact on treatment outcome. Professional sexual misconduct treatment failures are more prone to have sustained rationalizations and justifications. Victim empathy in clerics is examined and certain factors prevent the minister from understanding the harm he has inflicted. Failure to appreciate the power differentiation between minister and parishioner, naivety about sexual issues/minimal training in transference/countertransference, and desensitization of the intimacy of the minister/laity relationship all combine to affect victim empathy. The presence of paraphilias must also be evaluated when assessing treatment needs. The authors asserted that 20% of professional sexual misconduct cases were found to have a history of prior paraphilias. It is stressed that interpersonal and emotional factors (anxiety, stress, depression, deficits in social/assertive skills, alcohol/drug abuse, personality disorders/intrapsychic conflicts) play a role in the development of professional sexual misconduct. In order to ensure the safety of the minister and congregation, those who have engaged in sexual misconduct must be thoroughly evaluated and placed under constant surveillance by staff. These individuals must be trained in recognizing the ministers offending behavior. The congregation can also serve as a source for evaluating the minister's behavior through the administration of a "bill of rights", which outlines appropriate minister/Church member behavior. When the sexual misconduct is rampant, steps must be taken in order to manage the clerics. Prohibitions may be implemented that prevent the minister from working with parishioners. In order to protect the congregation, the authors recommend that close monitoring be implemented. Thus far, group therapy sessions that include various professional who have been involved in sexual misconduct have shown promise.

ASSESSMENT OF SEX OFFENDER TREATMENT

GENERAL RECIDIVISM RATES

HANSON, R.K., SCOTT, H., & STEFFY, R.A. (1995). A COMPARISON OF CHILD MOLESTERS AND NONSEXUAL CRIMINALS: RISK PREDICTORS AND LONG-TERM RECIDIVISM. *JOURNAL OF RESEARCH IN CRIME AND DELINQUENCY, 32 (3), 325-337.*

This study compared the recidivism rates of a sample comprised of 191 child molesters and 137 nonsexual offenders over a 15 to 30-year period. During this time period, 83.2% of the nonsexual criminals recidivated while only 61.8% of the child molesters reoffended. In analyzing the characteristics of the offending behavior, the authors reported that when the child molesters reoffended the crime was of a sexual nature whereas the nonsexual criminals were responsible for the majority of nonsexual violent crimes.

PRENTKY, R.A., LEE, A.F.S., KNIGHT, R.A., & CERCE, D. (1997). RECIDIVISM RATES AMONG CHILD MOLESTERS AND RAPISTS: A METHODOLOGICAL ANALYSIS. *LAW AND HUMAN BEHAVIOR, 31 (6), 635-659.*

The authors attempted to evaluate the inconsistencies involved in recidivism research through the examination of various methodological applications. A data set of 251 sex offenders (136 rapists and 115 child molesters), which spanned a time period of 25 years, was analyzed in an attempt to understand differences in recidivism rates. The authors postulated that these changes in recidivism rates resulted from differences in the operationalization of recidivism, criminal offenses, and follow-up period. In analyzing this data, the researchers found that figures were underestimated when the definition of recidivism was based on conviction or imprisonment. It was also concluded that sexual offenders are at risk of reoffending for a long period of time.

RICE, M.E., QUINSEY, V.L., HARRIS, G.T. (1991). SEXUAL RECIDIVISM AMONG CHILD MOLESTERS RELEASED FROM A MAXIMUM-SECURITY PSYCHIATRIC INSTITUTION. *JOURNAL OF CONSULTING AND CLINICAL PSYCHOLOGY, 59 (3), 381-386.*

Recidivism rates for 136 extrafamilial child molesters were evaluated during a follow up period of 6.3 years. Of the 136 participants 31% were convicted of a new sexual offense, 43% committed a violent or sexual offense, and 58% were arrested or returned to the penitentiary. In analyzing these recidivism rates, the researchers looked at the following variables: sexual assessment measures, treatment variables, and outcome variables. Of these variables, marital status, previous time spent in a penitentiary, previous property convictions, previous sexual convictions, diagnosis of a personality disorder, and sexual age preference as indicated by phallometric responses were found to be the strongest predictor variables of sexual recidivism. Fifty percent of the child molesters in the sample had participated in behavioral therapy. However, therapy did not affect recidivism with this sample.

OVERVIEW OF TREATMENT OUTCOMES

ABRACEN, J., & LOOMAN, J. (2001). ISSUES IN THE TREATMENT OF SEXUAL OFFENDERS: RECENT DEVELOPMENTS AND DIRECTIONS FOR FUTURE RESEARCH. *AGGRESSION AND VIOLENT BEHAVIOR, 1, 1-19.*

This article discussed what constitutes effective treatment through evaluation of the Regional Treatment Centre Sex Offender Treatment Program (RTCSOP) and the California Department of Mental Health's Sex Offender Treatment and Evaluation Project (SOTEP). In addition, it included a discussion about in-treatment changes on dynamic variables that entails looking at the treatment of minimization and denial, as well as reviewing individual versus group treatment. The article also presented data from several studies that frequently discussed the association of alcohol and sexual offending. In summary, the authors concluded that cognitive-behavioral treatment geared to the principles of risk/need/responsivity can be effective at reducing recidivism in sex offenders.

BECKER, J.R. (1994). OFFENDERS: CHARACTERISTICS AND TREATMENT. *THE FUTURE OF CHILDREN: SEXUAL ABUSE OF CHILDREN, 4* (2), 176-197.

This article reviewed what is known about offenders and treatment. First, the role of paraphilias in child molestation is discussed. Second, the article looked at what is known about offenders, including data on juvenile offenders and incest offenders. Third, the article discussed recidivism and the difficulty of determining recidivism rates, with a summary of what is known about recidivism of untreated offenders. Fourth, the article looked at treatment, including mechanisms for getting offenders into treatment, goals and types of treatment, the efficacy of treatment, and the need for post-incarceration monitoring and long term treatment. Low recidivism rates have been reported with cognitive-behavioral treatment.

BURDON, W.M., & GALLAGHER, C.A. (2002). COERCION AND SEX OFFENDERS: CONTROLLING SEX-OFFENDING BEHAVIOR THROUGH INCAPACITATION AND TREATMENT. *CRIMINAL JUSTICE AND BEHAVIOR, 29* (1), 87-109.

This article examined the dual roles that coercion has played in treating sex offenders and controlling their behavior. In addition, the article suggested a theoretical explanation for the apparent effectiveness of cognitive-behavioral approaches to treating sex offenders. The authors suggested that coercion has served two primary and important roles: incapacitation and ensuring entry into and retention in treatment. However, the authors reported that as efforts to assess the overall effectiveness of sex offender treatment continue, self-determination theory and organism integration theory offer some possible insight into the apparent effectiveness of cognitive-behavioral therapy and suggest a number of alternative dependent measures that can be used to assess overall effectiveness of sex offender treatment. Although the current reliance on dependent measures such as recidivism and refunding may speak to the overall effectiveness of treatment, it does not reveal much about the treatment process itself. According to the authors, this knowledge is essential in terms of ongoing efforts to further improve treatment effectiveness.

CRAIG, L.A., BROWNE, K.D., & STRINGER, I. (2003). TREATMENT AND SEXUAL OFFENSE RECIDIVISM. *TRAUMA, VIOLENCE, & ABUSE, 4* (1), 70-89.

This article points out that cognitive-behavioral treatment has emerged as the principal type of sex offender treatment targeting deviant arousal, increasing appropriate sexual desires, modifying distorted thinking, and improving interpersonal coping skills. The authors indicated that since 1995, 19 treatment studies have been published, and a third demonstrated positive treatment effects and used sound methodological principals to establish the most effective way of reducing sexual reoffending. This article reviewed such studies and concluded that meta-analytical studies of treatment efficacy provide conflicting viewpoints. Furby et al. (1989) and Quinsey et al. (1993) previously found no convincing evidence that treatment reduces recidivism, whereas W. L. Marshall and Barbaree (1988) and W. L. Marshall, Eccles, et al. (1991) demonstrated positive treatment results in reducing sexual offense recidivism. Further, the meta-analysis by Hall (1995) reported a small but robust treatment effect. The authors contend that although sex offender treatment programs appear to reduce sex offense recidivism, what is not clear is whether this is specific to particular types of sex offenders (adult or adolescent offenders, exhibitionists, child molesters, adult rapists, personality disordered), which may in turn be limited to specific modalities of treatment (cognitive-behavioral, MST, chemical castration, and behavioral therapy). Further, the authors suggested that treatment efficacy may be better served by exploring which dynamic factors affect recidivism in order to facilitate the forensic practitioner when assessing if the offender is released back into the community. Research on those dynamic factors associated with the environment, opportunity to offend, and changes in criminogenic factors, once integrated into treatment programs, would contribute to reducing the recidivism rates. One reason some studies fail to find significant treatment results is that the base rates for sexual reoffending are relatively small. By virtue of the sample, programs that target lower risk offenders are likely to have difficulty in demonstrating treatment effects in already low rates of recidivism.

THE EFFECTIVENESS OF TREATMENT OF SEXUAL
OFFENDERS: REPORT OF THE ASSOCIATION FOR THE
TREATMENT OF SEXUAL ABUSERS, COLLABORATIVE
DATA RESEARCH COMMITTEE, NOVEMBER 3, 2000.

This report outlined the treatment effectiveness for
reducing sexual offense recidivism and general
recidivism through evaluation of studies used in the
meta-analysis. The studies evaluated were predomin-
inantly cognitive behavioral. Found that reductions
in both sexual recidivism (17% to 10%) and general recidivism (51% to 32%) are possible when
current treatment programs are evaluated with
credible designs.

HALL, G.C.N. (1995). SEXUAL OFFENDER RECIDIVISM
REVISITED: A META-ANALYSIS OF RECENT TREATMENT
STUDIES. JOURNAL OF CONSULTING AND CLINICAL
PSYCHOLOGY, 63 (5), 802-809.

Hall performed a meta-analysis on 12 studies of
treatment with sexual offenders (N=1,313). A
small, but robust, overall effect size was found for
treatment versus non-treatment. Cognitive-behavioral treatment and hormonal treatment reduced
recidivism by approximately 30% (from 27% to
19%). He also found that studies with longer follow-up periods that included outpatients in their
samples had larger effects as did those with higher
base-rates. Cognitive-behavioral treatment was
found to be superior to behavioral treatment and as
effective as hormonal treatment.

HANSON, K., & BUSSIÈRE, M.T. (1998). PREDICTING
RELAPSE: A META-ANALYSIS OF SEXUAL OFFENDER
RECIDIVISM STUDIES. JOURNAL OF CONSULTING AND
CLINICAL PSYCHOLOGY, 66 (2), 348-362.

Even though this article primarily reviewed recidivism studies, it does discuss treatment effectiveness
with regard to recidivism. Evidence from 61 follow-
up studies was examined to identify the factors
most strongly related to recidivism among sexual
offenders. With regard to treatment, examination
of these studies found that offenders who failed to
complete treatment were at increased risk for both
sexual and general recidivism. The article stated
that reduced risk could be due to treatment effectiveness; alternatively, high-risk offenders may be
those most likely to quit, or be terminated, from

treatment. The current review suggested that treatment programs can contribute to community safety
through their ability to monitor risk. Further, there is
reliable evidence that those offenders who attend and
cooperate with treatment programs are less likely to
re-offend than those who rejected intervention.

HANSON, K.R., GORDON, A., HARRIS, A.J.R.,
MARQUES, J.K., MURPHY, W., QUINSEY, V.L., &
SETO, M.C. (2002). FIRST REPORT OF THE COLLABO-
RATIVE OUTCOME DATA PROJECT ON THE EFFECTIVE-
NESS OF PSYCHOLOGICAL TREATMENT FOR SEX OFFEND-
ERS. SEXUAL ABUSE: A JOURNAL OF RESEARCH AND
TREATMENT, 14 (2), 169-194.

This meta-analytic review examined the effectiveness of treatment by summarizing data from 43
studies (combined n = 9,454). Most of the studies in
the review were produced after 1995 and 23% were
only available after 1999. Forms of treatment oper-
ating prior to 1980 appeared to have little effect.
When averaged across all studies, the sexual offense
recidivism rate was lower for the treatment groups.
Current treatments were associated with reductions
in sexual recidivism and general recidivism. The
recidivism rates for treated sex offenders were
lower than the recidivism rates of untreated sex
offenders. Studies comparing treatment completers
to dropouts consistently found higher recidivism
rates for the dropouts, regardless of the type of
treatment provided.

HANSON, R.K., STEFFY, R.A., & GAUTHIER, R.
(1993). LONG-TERM RECIDIVISM OF CHILD MOLES-
TERS. JOURNAL OF CONSULTING AND CLINICAL
PSYCHOLOGY, 61 (4).

This study examined the long-term recidivism rates
of male child molesters who were released from a
maximum-security Ontario provincial prison
between 1958 and 1974. The treatment group in
this study included child molesters who were
treated between 1965 and 1973. The treatment
program aimed to increase the social competence of
the offenders through individual and group counseling and by creating a therapeutic milieu that
encouraged the men to recognize and correct social
and sexual adjustment problems. The offenders also
received aversive conditioning training to decrease
their sexual interest in children. Because the

program was designed in the 1960s, it was not informed by the subsequent developments in the field, such as relapse prevention and various cognitive-behavioral techniques. Results of this study found that the child molesters who were enrolled in the treatment program showed clinically significant improvements on almost all of the mental health and personality measures used in this study. Forty-two percent of the sample engaged in another sexual of serious offense and ten percent of the participants were reconvicted. The factors found to have an affect on recidivism include previous sexual offenses, never having been married, and victim preference. Incest offenders were the least likely to recidivate whereas those who selected only male victims were at the greatest risk of recidivism. However, the lack of equivalent measures on a control group limited the extent to which these changes could be attributed to the treatment program itself. The authors concluded that sexual offense recidivism is most likely to be prevented when interventions attempt to address the life-long potential for re-offense and do not expect child molesters to be permanently "cured" following a single set of treatment sessions.

LOOMAN, J., ABRACEN, J., & NICHOLAICHUK, T.P. (2000). RECIDIVISM AMONG TREATED SEXUAL OFFENDERS AND MATCHED CONTROLS: DATA FROM THE REGIONAL TREATMENT CENTRE. JOURNAL OF INTERPERSONAL VIOLENCE, 15 (3), 279-290.

Follow-up data are reported on 89 sexual offenders at the Regional Treatment Centre in Ontario and 89 untreated sex offenders matched for pretreatment risk. The average time at risk was 9.9 years. It was found that the treated group had a sexual recidivism rate of 23.6%, whereas the untreated group had a sexual recidivism rate of 51.7%. The treated participants were less likely to be convicted for either sexual or nonsexual offenses, and those who were reconvicted spent significantly less time incarcerated than the untreated participants at the time of follow-up. These data suggested not only that treatment resulted in fewer incarcerations but also that when the treated participants were convicted, they tended to receive shorter sentences than the untreated group. The authors suggested that if shorter sentences reflect less severe offenses, then treatment had an impact not only on the number of offenses but also on the

severity of these offenses. The data concerning the actual number of offenses indicated that treatment was effective in reducing the number of new offenses when offenders do recidivate.

MALETZKY, B.M. (2002). A 25-YEAR FOLLOW-UP OF COGNITIVE-BEHAVIORAL THERAPY WITH 7,275 SEXUAL OFFENDERS. BEHAVIOR MODIFICATION, 26 (2), 123-148.

Outcome data is presented, grouped into five year cohorts, for 7,275 sexual offenders entering a cognitive-behavioral treatment program. The assessment variables included treatment completion, self-admission of covert and/or overt deviant behaviors, the presence of deviant sexual arousal, or being recharged for any sexual crime (regardless of plea or conviction). It proved possible to follow 62% for the cohort at five years after initiating treatment, but follow-up completion rates decreased with time. Outcomes were significantly different based on offender subtype, with child molesters and exhibitionists achieving better overall success than pedophiles or rapists. Prematurely terminating treatment was a strong indicator of committing a new sexual offense. Of interest was the general improvement of success rates over each successive five year period of many types of offenders. Unfortunately, failure rates remained comparatively high for rapists (20%) and homosexual pedophiles (16%), regardless of when they were treated over the 25-year period.

MARQUES, J.K., NELSON, C., ALARCON, J.M., & DAY, D.M. (2000). PREVENTION RELAPSE IN SEX OFFENDERS: WHAT WE LEARNED FROM SOTEP'S EXPERIMENTAL TREATMENT PROGRAM. IN D.R. LAWS (ED.). REMAKING RELAPSE PREVENTION WITH SEX OFFENDERS (PP. 321-340). CALIFORNIA: SAGE PUBLICATIONS.

The authors provided an overview of the Sex Offender Treatment and Evaluation Project (SOTEP), which is housed at Atascadero State Hospital in California. The SOTEP is a longitudinal research program (1985-1995) that was designed to evaluate the effectiveness of an innovative relapse prevention program for sex offenders who are under civil commitment as sexually violent predators. The project is now in the follow-up phase, in which recidivism data are being collected on both treated and untreated study participants. The article described some of the lessons learned from SOTEP, particularly those that highlighted the strengths and weaknesses of the Relapse Prevention model as was applied in the treatment program. It is acknowledged that some of the information is based on preliminary analyses of the recidivism data, as well as informal and qualitative data sources. In addition, the authors indicated some specific ways that the model could be improved and describe their newest application of the RP model.

MARQUES, J.K. (1999). HOW TO ANSWER THE QUESTION "DOES SEX OFFENDER TREATMENT WORK?" JOURNAL OF INTERPERSONAL VIOLENCE, 14 (4), 437-451.

The author focused on the Sex Offender Treatment and Evaluation Project (SOTEP), which is a longitudinal research program that the author and her colleagues have been conducting in California for the past ten years. The overall design of the study is discussed as well as some of the problems that the researchers encountered when conducting treatment outcome studies. In conclusion, a summary of the preliminary findings is given which suggest that treating the more serious offender is worthwhile and that their relapse prevention program seems to be teaching some skills that can be important to high-risk offenders.

MARSHALL, W.L. (1993). THE TREATMENT OF SEX OFFENDERS: WHAT DOES THE OUTCOME DATA TELL US? A REPLY TO QUINSEY, HARRIS, RICE AND LALUMIERE. JOURNAL OF INTERPERSONAL VIOLENCE, 8 (4), 524-530.

Marshall agreed with Quinsey et al. (1993) that the application of rigorous methodological standards needs to be applied to a well developed field of sex offender treatment outcome studies; however, this field is still in its early stages. On the other hand, Marshall disagreed with these authors' conclusion regarding controlled, random-design study, and meta-analytic approaches to evaluation because there is little data on which to base our inferences about effectiveness.

MARSHALL, W.L., & ANDERSON, D. (2000). DO RELAPSE PREVENTION COMPONENTS ENHANCE TREATMENT EFFECTIVENESS? IN D.R. LAWS (ED.). REMAKING RELAPSE PREVENTION WITH SEX OFFENDERS (PP. 39-55). CALIFORNIA: SAGE PUBLICATIONS.

This article attempted to evaluate the effectiveness of the Relapse Prevention (RP) model by discussing achievement of within-treatment goals, issues in evaluating treatment (i.e., indices of reoffending and duration of follow-up), features to be evaluated (i.e., the components of RP and the effects of adding RP components to standard cognitive-behavioral treatment), and looking at programs without RP. The authors concluded that this review offered strong support for the idea that sexual offenders can be effectively treated. Cognitive-behavioral programs utilizing an internal self-management RP component that is not too elaborate appear to be the most successful.

MARSHALL, W.L., ANDERSON, D., & FERNANDEZ, Y. (1999). THE DEVELOPMENT OF COGNITIVE BEHAVIORAL TREATMENT OF SEX OFFENDERS (PP. 146-163). ENGLAND: JOHN WILEY & SONS, LTD.

The authors discussed ways to evaluate treatment programs. They concluded that treatment with sex offenders can be effective and that the balance of the evidence weighs in favor of a positive treatment outcome. Cost-benefit analyses are discussed but they exclude the cost of therapy for the victims. Cohen and Miller (1998) derived data relevant to this issue from various American organizations. Based on means for 1991, the total cost of treatment for victims of recent child sexual abuse exceeded $600 million. For victims of historical childhood sexual abuse, the total was over $4 billion whereas for adult victims of attempted or completed rape, the cost of their treatment exceeded $800 million. The value of treatment with sex offenders far exceeds the obvious benefits of reduced recidivism. From these types of analyses, it appears that out of every 100 sex offenders treated, we only have to prevent 3 or 4 who would otherwise have offended from reoffending in order to cover the costs of treatment.

Marshall, W.L., & Barbaree, H.E. (1990). Outcome of comprehensive cognitive-behavioral treatment programs. In W.L. Marshall (Ed.). *Handbook of sexual assault: Issues, theories, and treatment of the offender* (pp. 363-385). New York: Plenum Press.

This article outlined the nature of comprehensive cognitive-behavioral treatment programs for the treatment of sex offenders. It discussed the content of these programs and outlined the major treatment targets that included (1) sexual behaviors and interests, (2) a broad range of social difficulties, and (3) cognitive distortions about the offensive behavior. Further, the article discussed how cognitive-behavioral treatment programs are evaluated and included a revision of both institutional and outpatient programs. The article concluded that cognitive-behavioral programs for the treatment of sex offenders offer encouragement for the continued application and development of such programs. However, according to the article, there are some inconsistencies in observed outcome across studies. For instance, some programs are very effective in treating exhibitionists, while others are not. Similarly, some programs seemed to be relatively more effective with men who molest boys than with men who molest girls, while the reverse seems to be true for other offenders. The authors surmised that the future of cognitive-behavioral approaches to the treatment of sex offenders appears to be positive, although there is much work still to be done.

Marshall, W.L., & Eccles, A. (1991). Issues in clinical practice with sex offenders. *Journal of Interpersonal Violence, 6* (1), 68-93.

This article addressed issues that the authors believed to be the most relevant to clinical work with sex offenders, including: Assessment (Diagnosis & Evaluation) and Treatment (Antiandrogens, Non-behavioral Psychotherapy, & Cognitive-Behavioral Therapy). The authors concluded that assessments are essential because they allow us to define the individual's problem, determine his risk for reoffending, specify his treatment needs, and evaluate the effectiveness of treatment. The authors asserted that the treatment of sex offenders is effective. Overall, cognitive-behavioral

programs seem to offer the best hope, with antiandrogens having a valuable adjunctive role for some individuals.

Marshall, W.L., Jones, R., Ward, T., Johnston, P., & Barbaree, H. (1991). Treatment outcome with sex offenders. *Clinical Psychology Review, 11* (4), 465-485.

The article discusses the methodological stances that guide the review of the effectiveness of sex offender treatment in the literature. In determining the value of treating sex offenders, the authors followed in the tradition of reporting failure rates that are typically derived from official records, re-arrest or reconviction, and that report the percentage of men who re-offend (recidivism rates). They stated that the most common criticism of treatment studies is the failure to provide a controlled comparison with untreated offenders. When reviewing outcome studies, the authors considered: physical treatments (psychosurgery, castration), pharmacological interventions (MPA and CPA), non-behavioral approaches (programs considered were offered within prisons, or at least with maximum security settings), cognitive behavioral programs, institutional based programs, and outpatient programs. The article concluded that the most effective treatment approaches are a combination of pharmacological and psychological treatment and cognitive behavioral treatment.

Marshall, W.L., & Pithers, W.D. (1994). A reconsideration of treatment outcome with sex offenders. *Criminal Justice and Behavior, 21* (4), 10-27.

This article presented an optimistic view of the literature, asserting that recent, relatively well-controlled evaluations have shown that treatment can be effective. To be maximally effective, according to this appraisal of the literature, treatment must be comprehensive, cognitive-behaviorally based, and include a relapse prevention component. According to the article, earlier outcome research that produced either treatment failure, or at best equivocal results, did not meet these criteria. The article reviewed two sets of publications – Furby, Weinrott, & Blackshaw, 1989, and reports by the

Penetanguishene Group – concerning therapeutic efficacy with sex offenders that in both cases present "gloomy" conclusions. The authors outlined the limitations of the studies considered by both sets of publications. With regard to Furby et al, they discussed such issues as including outdated programs in their review, potential biases against treatment effects, and duplication of data. With regard to the reports by the Penetanguishene Group, the authors discussed methodological problems such as the limited scope of the Pentanguishene treatment program, the problem of matching treated with untreated subjects, and the fact that subjects were not randomly assigned. The article also discussed more recent evaluations of treatment efficacy and concluded that even though these studies converge on the conclusion that sex offenders who have engaged in specialized treatment re-offend at lower rates than offenders who have not participated in treatment, the authors noted that many of the evaluations do not include comparison with an untreated group. However, they referred to a study conducted by Marques et al. (1993), which was able to compare three groups of sex offenders. Their research design matched volunteers who were randomly allocated to treatment or no treatment, and non-volunteers who were matched with the volunteers.

McGrath, R.J., Cumming, G., Livingston, J.A., & Hoke, S.E. (2003). Outcome of a treatment program for adult sex offenders: From prison to community. Journal of Interpersonal Violence, 18 (1), 3-17.

The study, which is a retrospective study wherein random assignment was not possible, was an evaluation of a component of the Vermont Treatment Program for Sexual Aggressors (VTPSA). It is a prison-based treatment program for adult male sex offenders that include a community aftercare component. The study extended a preliminary evaluation of the program presented by increasing the sample size and lengthening the follow-up period. The purpose of this study was to identify the characteristics of men who completed treatment and compare them with those who refused or dropped out of treatment and then to compare the re-offense rates among these three groups. Treatment was cognitive-behavioral and relapse-prevention in nature. The results of this study had several implications

for how to manage sex offenders. The data from this study highlighted the importance of considering sex offender treatment completion as a factor in making release decisions. In this study, the reduction in the sexual recidivism rate among participants who completed treatment was statistically as well as clinically significant. Treatment completers were almost six times less likely to be charged for committing a new sexual offense than were participants who refused, dropped out, or were terminated from treatment. The authors acknowledged that these results were consistent with other recent outcome results, however, they caution, that despite the fact that treatment completion was strongly associated with reductions in sexual recidivism, inferences about the meaning of this association are confounded by some methodological difficulties. The difficulties included the degree to which treatment groups were equivalent and the trouble involved in sorting out the relative effects of the three interventions (prison treatment, community treatment, and community supervision).

Nicholaichuk, T., Gordon, A., Gu, D., & Wong, S. (2002). Outcome of an institutional sexual offender treatment program: A comparison between treated and matched untreated offenders. Sexual Abuse: A Journal of Research and Treatment, 12 (2), 139-153.

Data from a sex offender treatment program operated by the Correctional Service of Canada at the Regional Psychiatric Center in Saskatoon supported the conclusion that cognitive behavioral treatment with high risk/need offenders can reduce sexual offense recidivism. The study compared 296 treated and 283 untreated offenders followed for a mean of six years after their release. An untreated comparison subject was located for each treated offender on three dimensions (1) age at index offense, (2) date of index offense, (3) prior criminal history. Convictions for new sexual offenses among treated offenders were 14.5% versus 33.2% for untreated offenders. During the follow-up period, 48% of treated offenders remained out of prison compared to 28.3% of untreated offenders. Time series comparisons of treated and comparison samples also showed that treated men reoffended at significantly lower rates after ten years. This article stressed that a necessary step in evaluating treatment outcomes is to ensure that proper comparison samples are identified rather than relying upon samples of convenience.

NICHOLAICHUK, T., & YATES, P. (2002). TREATMENT EFFICACY: OUTCOMES OF THE CLEARWATER SEX OFFENDER PROGRAM. IN B. SCHWARTZ (ED.). *THE SEX OFFENDER: CURRENT TREATMENT MODALITIES AND SYSTEMS ISSUES* (CH. 3). NEW JERSEY: CIVIC RESEARCH INSTITUTE, INC.

This chapter discussed the controversy over the effectiveness of cognitive-behavioral intervention with sexual offenders and provided both qualitative and quantitative reviews of sex offender treatment efficacy with particular attention devoted to the methodological limitations of treatment effectiveness research. Further, the authors described the "Clearwater Study," which supports the findings of prior research that postulated that cognitive-behavioral treatment, when applied to appropriate subjects, can reduce the occurrence of post treatment sexual offending. This article highlighted the importance of addressing responsivity in treatment. Specifically, findings indicated that risk for post-treatment recidivism is differentially associated with age, sexual offense history, type of offender, deviant sexual arousal, psychopathy, and severity of pre-treatment offense history.

QUINSEY, V.L., HARRIS, G.T., RICE, M.E., & LALUMIERE, M.L. (1993). ASSESSING TREATMENT EFFICACY IN OUTCOME STUDIES OF SEX OFFENDERS. *JOURNAL OF INTERPERSONAL VIOLENCE, 8* (4), 512-523.

The authors provided a critique of a study by Marshall et al. They argued that the treatment literature does not support the conclusions of Marshall et al., and that the approach taken in Marshall et al.'s review is unable to provide scientifically satisfactory answers to questions concerning treatment efficacy. The article discussed the methodological issues of the Marshall et al.'s review and enumerated the principle threats to the validity of the conclusions. The authors endorsed Marshall et al.'s view with regard to cost-benefit analyses; however, the authors recognized that it is completely dependent on whether the recidivism associated with treatment is statistically significant. The authors concluded that outcome research with sex offenders has so seriously failed to demonstrate effectiveness that a controlled, random-design study is demanded and that meta-analysis is the best evaluative approach.

QUINSEY, V.L., KHANNA, A., & MALCOLM, P.B. (1998). A RETROSPECTIVE EVALUATION OF THE REGIONAL TREATMENT CENTRE SEX OFFENDER TREATMENT PROGRAM. *JOURNAL OF INTERPERSONAL VIOLENCE, 13* (5), 621-644.

The purpose of this study was to examine the relationship of psychological assessment data, provision of treatment, and progress in treatment to subsequent recidivism among inmates treated in the Regional Treatment Centre (RTC) Sex Offender Treatment Program between the years 1976 and 1989. The program employed behavioral and cognitive-behavioral approaches to treatment while utilizing both individual and group therapy in three to four month cycles. The follow-up period ended in 1992 and a total of 483 inmates were followed. Of these men, 213 received sex offender treatment, 183 were assessed for the program but were judged as not requiring it, 52 refused to be assessed, 27 were assessed but judged to be unsuitable, and nine were considered to require treatment but did not receive it for various reasons, such as being released before they could enter the program. Outcome data were gathered from the Royal Canadian Mounted Police computerized arrest and convictions records. Sexual and violent offenses were defined as mutually exclusive. Of 483 inmates who were referred to the sex offender treatment program and followed for an average of 44 months of opportunity to re-offend, 38% were arrested for new violent or sexual offenses. The treated offenders were the most frequently rearrested for sex offenses. Inmates judged unsuitable for treatment were rearrested less frequently, particularly for sex offenses. Inmates judged to not require treatment and those who refused treatment also had fewer re-arrests for sex offenses than did treated participants, although they had more re-arrests for violent offenses. After statistically controlling for the static variables that predicted reoffending, the treatment program was associated with a higher rate of sexual re-arrests but had no effect on the composite variable, which was violent or sexual re-arrests. Among treated offenders, clinical assessment of treatment gains was not significantly associated with recidivism. Overall the results of this study mirrored the state of the literature on sex offenders. According to the authors, we are much better at measuring risk than we are at modifying it, although substantial changes can be made in proximal measures of treatment change. The study found that the best prerelease predictors were static historical variables.

SWAFFER, T., HOLLIN, C., BEECH, A., BECKETT, R., & FISHER, D. (2000). AN EXPLORATION OF CHILD SEXUAL ABUSERS' SEXUAL FANTASIES BEFORE AND AFTER TREATMENT. *SEXUAL ABUSE: A JOURNAL OF RESEARCH AND TREATMENT, 12*, 1.

This study looked at the content, type, and frequency of deviant fantasies, both pre- and post psychotherapy, of 30 males with an average age of 43 years and seven months. Subjects were selected at random from a larger group who participated in the Sex Offender Treatment Evaluation Program (SOTEP). Sixty percent of the subjects had been convicted of an extra familial act of abuse. Sixty percent of the victims were female, and 83.3% were 12 years old or younger when the abuse first began. The men had been convicted of a range of sexual offenses, including indecent assault (57%), incest (10%), and anal intercourse (7%). The study used both qualitative and quantitative methodologies and described the frequency, content of, and triggers for child sexual abusers' deviant fantasies as reported both pre- and post therapy. Of the eight questions asked on a semi-structured interview, a significant difference in the offenders' responses were found on three of the items. A significant difference was found on pairing sexual fantasies with masturbation directly after offending, fantasy triggers associated with the offender, and age of child in sexual fantasies. A significant difference was not found in time spent fantasizing about children before the offense, fantasy triggers associated with children, developmental factors associated with sexual fantasies, and gender of child in sexual fantasies. The authors outlined the limitations of this study, which included the issue that it was conducted on a small number of participants who were being treated in the community, excluded a measure of social desirability, and excluded questions about other types of sexual fantasies. The article does not, however, specify what treatment approach was used with the participants.

WEISS, P. (1999). ASSESSMENT AND TREATMENT OF SEX OFFENDERS IN THE CZECH REPUBLIC AND IN EASTERN EUROPE. *JOURNAL OF INTERPERSONAL VIOLENCE, 14* (4), 411-421.

The author described the experiences with the comprehensive therapeutic program for sexual offenders in the Czech Republic. Since 1976, specialized departments for the treatment of sex offenders were established in psychiatric hospitals. The treatment is imposed by the court as per the recommendations of forensic experts. As a rule, inpatient therapy is followed by treatment in outpatient "sexological" departments. The therapeutic goals are as follows: adjustment of behavior, acquisition of information, overcoming defensive mechanisms and creating insight, strengthening of conscious control, changes in attitudes and values, sexual adaptation, and social reintegration. These goals are achieved by means of a set of diagnostic, psychotherapeutic, pharmocotherapeutic, and social measures including penile plethysmography, individual and group psychotherapy (in their psychodynamic and cognitive-behavioral forms), antiandrogen suppression, and social interventions. After 20 years (1976-1996), the author claimed that the recidivism rate of 953 treated offenders is 17.1%. He reported that this rate compares very favorably with the observed relapses of those offenders who did not receive comprehensive treatment (approximately 80% during one- year after release). The author acknowledged that the low recidivism rate might not be entirely the effect of the therapy per se and postulated that it may also be attributed to the lengthy period of outpatient aftercare and the close supervision by social workers given to the offenders after discharge from the program. According to the author, of all the ex-communist countries, only the Czech Republic has developed a special model of sex offender treatment.

CLERIC OFFENDERS AND TREATMENT OUTCOMES

Fones, C.S.L., Levine, S.B., Althof, S.E., & Risen, C.B. (1999). The sexual struggles of 23 clergymen: A follow-up study. *Journal of Sex & Marital Therapy*, 25, 183-195.

Researchers followed 19 clergymen (17 Roman Catholic priests) for a period of one to six years after their evaluation in the Program for Professionals sex offender treatment program. It was found that 39% of the sample had offended against adolescents. Of that percentage, 52% characterized their sexual behavior as being of a deliberate nature. Through clinical interviewing and administration of the MCMI-III and PPG/Abel Assessment it was found that the majority of subjects returned to previous or higher levels of vocational functioning and felt that the treatment had been beneficial. It was found that the clerics in this sample struggled with loneliness, masturbatory conflicts, and displayed a desire to have others perceive them beyond their vocational roles. Those priests identified as homosexual engaged in the following sexual behavior that was initially labeled as compulsive: frequent, occasional, or self thwarted procurement of anonymous sex, attempts to begin a relationship with a rejecting individual, entitled, defiant, rebellious sexual relationships with a gay man, and use of pornography. Upon follow-up it was found that these behaviors thought to have been compulsive had subsided and none of the clerics had relapsed.

INSTITUTIONAL RESPONSES TO SEXUAL ABUSE BY CLERICS

OVERVIEW

BURKETT, E. & BRUNIE, F. (1993). *A GOSPEL OF SHAME: CHILDREN, SEXUAL ABUSE, AND THE CATHOLIC CHURCH*. NEW YORK, NY: PENGUIN BOOKS.

This book provided an overview of the various cases of child sexual abuse surrounding the Catholic Church. The authors contend that one of the reasons why the Church is an appealing target is due to the fact that the Bishops are able to handle these cases in secrecy. While abuse undoubtedly occurs in other religious organizations and professions, none of them have the ability and power to bury these issues in the way the Catholic Church has. The structure of the Church and the notion of celibacy are discussed in relation to creating a pro-offending environment. The authors contend that the Bishops failed to realize their oversight in the management of sex offenders because they did not know the true scope of the problem. The effects of the sexual abuse scandal are discussed in relation to the parish and the Church's financial holdings.

ROSSETTI, S.J. (1996). *A TRAGIC GRACE: THE CATHOLIC CHURCH AND CHILD SEXUAL ABUSE*. COLLEGEVILLE, MN: THE LITURGICAL PRESS.

This book provided an overview of the problem of child sexual abuse in the Catholic Church. Chapter 1 provided an overview of the problem thus far and the responses of the Church hierarchy. Chapter 2 presented original research conducted by the author concerning the feelings of the Church and laity concerning the current crisis. Survey research was conducted on 1,013 lay persons and illustrated a general sense of dissatisfaction displayed by those who had experienced a crisis in their parish. The majority of the respondents reported anger concerning the crisis and expected better behavior from their priests. However, those who had experienced abuse within their parish were less likely to expect priests to be better than anyone else and less likely to look to the clergy for moral leadership. They were also less likely to trust the priesthood and the incident of cleric abuse negatively impacted vocational desires associated with the Church. The actions of a single priest appeared to have a negative effect on people's satisfaction with the clergy. The survey was also sent to 314 priests who felt positive about their vocation and about the Catholic Church. However, the majority of ministers reported feeling that they were not kept informed by the Church and that the hierarchy did not want to deal with sexual abuse in an open manner. Rossetti concluded that exposure to the abuse heightens dissatisfaction, confidence in leadership declines, few trust priests with their children after having their own priest accused, endorsements of celibacy decrease, and satisfaction with the Church decreases. Chapter 3 built upon these findings in explaining the parish as a victim of sexual abuse. Rossetti asserted that parishioners require knowledge about the sexual abuse and that interventions should be set in place in order to heal the parish. Chapter 4 presented red flags for identifying sexual abuse. The author emphasized the need to evaluate an individual's psychosexual history as well as the importance of training and educating the clergy. Six factors are also identified as red flags for abusers and include confusion about sexual orientation, childish interests and behavior, lack of peer relations, extremes in developmental sexual experiences, personal history of childhood sexual abuse and/or deviant sexual experience, and an excessively passive, dependant, and conforming personality. Chapter 5 addressed the impact of the crisis on the offenders. The author contends that cleric suicides are increasing and that society ostracizes the sex offender through interventions such as Megan's Law. There is also mismanagement of cleric offenders, but Rossetti contends that perpetrators can be successfully treated. Recidivism is briefly discussed as well as the role of chemical castration in treatment. Saint Luke Institute has shown success in utilizing Depo-Provera to treat cleric offenders and claims a relapse rate of only two priests during the ten years it has been in operation. In surveying the attitudes of the laity, the majority of individuals are unwilling to allow a cleric offender into their parish. However, if the priest had undergone treatment and is under supervision then the laity was willing to accept him. The author argued that the following factors must be evaluated when examining the extent of the situation: clinical diagnosis and abuse history, quality of treatment and response to treatment, aftercare program, availability of supervision and ministry not involving minors, a considered waiting period, and various other pastoral considerations. In discussing suicide amongst priests, Rossetti asserted that the most difficult time is right after the perpetrator has been confronted because they become overwhelmed. It is at this point that they must be supported and interventions must be provided. While the majority of priests do not commit suicide when confronted with allegations of abuse, this may be due in part to their faith. The last two chapters of the book included a discussion of suggested reforms in addressing the issue of cleric abuse.

SIPE, A.R. (1999). THE PROBLEM OF PREVENTION IN CLERGY SEXUAL ABUSE. IN T.G. PLANTE (ED). *BLESS ME FATHER FOR I HAVE SINNED: PERSPECTIVES ON SEXUAL ABUSE COMMITTED BY ROMAN CATHOLIC PRIESTS* (PP. 111-134). WESTPORT, CT: PRAEGER PUBLISHERS.

Sipe posits four problems that hinder the development of a program of prevention of sexual abuse in the Church. The first problem was the lack of screening methods to eliminate sex offenders from entering the clergy. The problem with this is that while some individuals may have a history of offending prior to joining the seminary, many begin acting out once they have entered the institution. While screening tests have improved, they continue to fail in certain areas. The second problem was the widespread denial of the abuse by Church officials. This results in rationalization, avoidance, and the shifting of blame. Third, certain elements of Church doctrine facilitated the creation of a pro-offending environment. Finally, the clergy was lacking in professional ethical standards regarding sexuality.

AVENUES OF LEGAL REDRESS FOR VICTIMS

SMITH, L.M. (1994). LIFTING THE VEIL OF SECRECY: MANDATORY CHILD ABUSE REPORTING STATUTES MAY ENCOURAGE THE CATHOLIC CHURCH TO REPORT PRIESTS WHO MOLEST CHILDREN. *LAW & PSYCHOLOGY REVIEW 18*, 409-421.

This article argued that state laws which mandate the reporting of child abuse should be used as a tool in clergy sexual abuse cases in order to stop Church officials from denying the incidents. The first part of the article discusses the hierarchy of the Church. The issue of celibacy as a cause of sexual abuse is discussed in conjunction with the theory that those entering the seminary are already underdeveloped. Smith then discussed in the second part of the article the Child Abuse Prevention and Treatment Act, which requires that all states "establish provisions for the reporting of known and suspected instances of child abuse and neglect." However, some states do not have universal reporting requirements and only those designated professionals (i.e. doctors, teachers, and psychologists) have a duty to report. If implemented, there would be no conflict with the First Amendment because as set forth in *Forest Hills Early Learning Ctr. V. Lukhard*, "the reporting requirements do not burden the Church's free exercise of religion, are justified by a compelling state interest, and are the least restrictive means available for protecting this interest." Reporting would be required once there is "reasonable cause to believe" (*State v. Hurd*). In regards to the Church, a reasonable belief that the child had been molested may be sufficient grounds to report the incident. Under the Child Abuse Prevention and Treatment Act, the reporters of the abuse are allowed immunity whereas failure to alert the authorities may result in criminal procedures. While one may potentially sue the Catholic Church concerning their failure to report the abuse, the doctrine of charitable immunity forbids lawsuits against charities (this also includes Churches).

STEINHAUSER, K. (1993). LEGAL ISSUES IN SEXUAL ABUSE AND DOMESTIC VIOLENCE. *PASTORAL PSYCHOLOGY, 41 (5)*, 321-336.

Steinhauser answered various frequently asked questions concerning the reporting of sexual abuse and domestic violence. It informed the clergy of the responsibility to report, myths concerning domestic violence/sexual abuse, and the consequences of failure to report these issues. The author recommended that if there is a child in the parish who is suspected of being a victim of abuse, the parishioner should try to develop a rapport with the child and assess the situation before reporting it. The article also contains a discussion concerning the affect of sexual abuse on the victim as well as the process involved in removing the child from the home. It is stressed that as long as one makes a report in good faith the person will be protected from civil litigation.

YOUNG, J.L. & GRIFFITH, E.E.H. (1999). DEVELOPMENTS IN CLERGY MALPRACTICE: THE CASE OF SANDERS V. CASA VIEW BAPTIST CHURCH. *JOURNAL OF THE AMERICAN ACADEMY OF PSYCHIATRY & THE LAW, 27 (1)*, 143-147.

This article was a review of a legal case that extrapolated upon the authors' 1995 research concerning clergy malpractice in civil suits. While the 1995 article outlined the various reasons why the courts have been unwilling to institute a complaint on the basis of clergy malpractice, the authors argued that the current trend appears to be to award on the basis of a breach of fiduciary duty. However, courts have been willing to evaluate the secular nature of a situation and award on the basis of professional malpractice, as was the finding in the present case. Even though it is stated that the relationship between cleric and parishioner is not a fiduciary one, much is involved in proving that it is. The authors contend that in order to establish the presence of a fiduciary relationship it has to be illustrated that the individual is acting in a manner that would allow them to gain influence over the person and gain their trust.

YOUNG, J.L. & GRIFFITH, E.E.H. (1998). RECONSIDERATION OF SEXUAL MISCONDUCT BY CLERGY COUNSELORS: THE CASE OF F.G. V. MACDONELL. *JOURNAL OF THE AMERICAN ACADEMY OF PSYCHIATRY & THE LAW, 26 (2)*, 289-293.

The authors discussed the complaint of fiduciary duty in the present case. Based upon the 1995 research conducted by the authors, it was concluded that while there is no complaint of clergy malpractice for fear of implicating the First Amendment, the complaint of breach of fiduciary duty may prove successful in prosecuting the clergy. In the present case, the New Jersey Supreme Court also viewed the breach of fiduciary duty was a more appropriate complaint than clergy malpractice.

YOUNG, J.L. & GRIFFITH, E.E.H. (1995). REGULATING PASTORAL COUNSELING PRACTICE: THE PROBLEM OF SEXUAL MISCONDUCT. *BULLETIN OF THE AMERICAN ACADEMY OF PSYCHIATRY AND LAW, 23 (3)*, 421-432.

This article reviewed various cases and examined the justifications given by the courts in not expanding malpractice theory towards clergy counselors who sexually abuse their clients. Though they are governed by various professional organizations (i.e. the American Association of Pastoral Counselors, the Christian Association for Psychological Studies), some clergy counselors practice outside of these organizations. The allegation of clergy malpractice is problematic in legal proceedings due to the lack of precedents in this area. The courts also argue that a clergy malpractice tort would in fact be redundant since sexual misconduct with a patient already violates the law. Courts have also cited a conflict with the First Amendment and the mishandling of transference as reasons why clergy malpractice should not be pursued. Many of these cases also claimed intentional infliction of emotional distress, which is problematic to establish and prove intent. Fraud is sometimes claimed against sexually abusive clergy but the courts are reluctant to shy away from the traditional definition of this tort, which involves commercial transactions. Vicarious liability is another frequent claim made against the Church, but it was often rejected by lower courts because no complaint was left after granting a motion for summary judgment in favor of the individual judgment. The authors suggested specific legal means of prosecuting sexually abusive clergy counselors that do not implicate the First Amendment.

HISTORICAL CHURCH RESPONSES

BLANCHARD, G.T. (1991). SEXUALLY ABUSIVE CLERGYMEN: A CONCEPTUAL FRAMEWORK FOR INTERVENTION AND RECOVERY. *PASTORAL PSYCHOLOGY, 39 (4)*, 237-245.

This article sought to place the issue of clergy sexual misconduct in a framework, which equated the exploitation to that of father/daughter incest. Blanchard has isolated several variables, which are similar to both situations and include the issues of power, trust, authority, intellectual and educational differences, idealization, and vulnerability. The article provided a brief discussion about how social attitudes influence the treatment of the cleric and provides an outline for an intervention strategy.

DOYLE, T.P. (2003). ROMAN CATHOLIC CLERICALISM, RELIGIOUS DURESS, AND CLERGY SEXUAL ABUSE. *PASTORAL PSYCHOLOGY, 51 (3)*, 189-231.

This article presented a review of the historical precedents to the problem of sexual abuse of children by clergy as well as the impact of clericalism on the psychological and emotional development of the victims. A review of the cases pertaining to sexual abuse in the clergy illustrated the following common themes: the victims were from families who are involved in the Church, the abuse was chronic, the victim's claims were dismissed by family and friends, when the Church was alerted they attempted to silence the victim to avoid scandal, many victims did not disclose the abuse until they were adults, and many victims experienced significant trauma and abuse after the incident occurred. In combating these claims, the Church has minimized the extent of the abuse by first denying its existence. When that failed, it was claimed that the problem was not rampant. During this crisis, Doyle discussed the various claims that the Church made in order to deal with the problem of sexual abuse. First, they claimed to not have understood the nature of child sexual abuse until recently when it was no longer regarded as a moral lapse made right through penance. A second assertion made in civil cases was that the civil law doctrine of "respondent superior" does not apply because the Church has no financial responsibility to the victims or control over the priest's actions when he is not performing his official duties. This came into conflict with Church Canon, which took steps to ensure the moral and spiritual protection of the congregation in situations that include the solicitation for sexual favors by priests hearing confession and sexual the abuse of minors (*Code of Canon Law,* 1917, 1983). Doyle examined Church doctrine dating back to the middle ages in which the issue of sexual misconduct was first brought to light. In his citation of *Body of Canon Law,* the author points out that in the section concerning penance (*De Poenitentia*), Gratian asserts that clerics who engage in sexual abuse should be subjected to the same punishment as lay people and should be excommunicated from the Church. Pope Pius V issued *Horrendum,* which stated that priests who abuse are deprived of all offices, benefits, and privileges. These clerics would also be degraded, and turned over to a Church tribunal for further punishment. Doyle then examined the state of the Church post-*Vatican II* in which membership in the priesthood and seminaries dwindled. The unpublished work by Baars & Terruwe (1971) revealed that 20-25% of the priests had serious psychiatric difficulties while 60-70% suffered from emotional immaturity. They concluded that some of the priests experienced psychological disturbances that developed in childhood while others developed difficulties while in the seminary. The authors recommended a screening process for candidates entering the seminary. These results are consistent with the findings of Kennedy (1972), which concluded that 6% of priests were psychologically and emotionally developed, 29% were still developing, 57% were underdeveloped, and 8% were maldeveloped. Those who were underdeveloped were more comfortable with teenagers, had few friends their own age, and used intellectualization as a coping device. Despite these studies, sexual abuse and dysfunction were still viewed as a sin having resulted from social disorganization and moral decay. Doyle contends that the official Church has refused to acknowledge the structure of the Catholic Church as a cause of sexual abuse. Doyle cited speeches from the pope at various gatherings (an address to the Irish Bishops 1999, World Youth Day, 1993) that fail to acknowledge the responsibility of the Church. As a result, a decree from the Congregation for the Doctrine of the Faith outlined a new and secret process for investigating clergy abuse. Mention of the issue was made in the pope's Holy Thursday letter to priests and attributes the abuse to sinfulness and evil while making little mention of the victims. Until 1984 and the much publicized case of Fr. Gilbert Gauthe in Louisiana, claims of sexual abuse were handled by the Bishop in private. In 1984 victim's claims were seen as being genuine yet the same secretive practices were implemented. Doyle also discussed the different meanings of Church and how it shaped the response towards victims of sexual abuse. By shifting focus and painting the Church as the victim, it served to minimize and abuse the victim further. A discussion of clericalism is included in order to help the reader understand its impact on the victim. Clericalism was rampant pre-*Vatican II* as members of the clergy derived their identity and power from their association with the Church, resulting in a power differentiation with the laity. Doyle asserted that clericalism is directly related to the victim's decision to remain silent about the abuse as well as the Church's response to the abuse (denial, scapegoating, etc.). Along with clericalism, religious duress (which causes people to react to abuse in bizarre ways) and the trauma bond (the victim's attitude towards the abuser) also influenced the victim's response to cleric sexual abuse. The victim is susceptible to clergy abuse because along with having authority by way of being older, he is a familiar authority figure. This authoritarianism is increased by his pastoral role. Part of the seduction process involves a secret and special relationship that traps the victim. The trauma bond is subsequently sanctioned/approved by the Church. The author discussed the *Myth of Complicity*, which is where the victim is somehow led to believe that the abuse is normal behavior and not a violation. This exploitive bond is strengthened by the repetition of abuse, victim's belief in their uniqueness, and fear. The fact that the abuser is a trusted person as well as the extreme reaction of the community also affects the trauma bond. The civil courts have begun to recognize the effect of these factors on victims' responses as apparent in *Parke v. Kownacki*, which recognized the Church's attempt to deny abuse.

FERDER, F. & HEAGLE, J. (1995). CLERGY PEDOPHILES AND MINISTRY: ANOTHER PERSPECTIVE. AMERICA, 173 (14), 6-11.

This article is a response to Rossetti's "Mark of Cain: Reintegrating pedophiles" article. The authors asserted their concern over the use of terminology and clinical data cited by Rossetti. The failure to distinguish the types of child molesters and the neglectful attention paid to the published data raises concerns. One particular criticism concerns the recidivism data for Saint Luke Institute, in which Rossetti neglected to acknowledge that child molesters lie, minimize, and distort the truth. The authors also raised the question of the lack of credible data concerning the characteristics of clergy offenders. The authors concluded that it is too early in the stages of research and treatment to assert that any of these findings are conclusive.

GOETZ, D. (1992). IS THE PASTOR'S FAMILY SAFE AT HOME? LEADERSHIP, 13, 38-44.

This author surveyed 374 pastors concerning their marriage and family life. Nineteen percent of those surveyed admitted to having extramarital affairs and 15% admitted that they had sought counseling for this reason. Another factor affecting the pastor's ability to cope with these feelings of sexual temptation is their sense of isolation. Fifty-five percent of the pastors said they had no close friends or family members with which they could discuss their problems. This is coupled with the pressure of having to give the appearance of being a perfect family, which 94% of pastor's reported as being problematic.

HUGHES, A.A. (1996). SEXUAL ABUSE: HELPING THE CHURCH RECOGNIZE AND RESPOND TO VICTIMS. PASTORAL PSYCHOLOGY, 45 (2), 119-127.

This article argued that the Church does not know how to reach out to victims of sexual abuse within the parish. The author stated that, "Problems these victims have are sometimes masked by smiles and extra involvement, deceiving other Church members and leaders into thinking they are bold and committed Christians." If the Church hired counselors trained in treating victims of sexual abuse, then they can begin to reach out to the victims and offer them proper help. Educating members of the Church concerning the signs of sexual abuse may make it less challenging to help these victims. The author also called for pastors to receive training in counseling skills so that they can better comfort their parishioners. The Church community is also called upon to be supportive and patient with the victim.

ISLEY, P.J. (1997). CHILD SEXUAL ABUSE AND THE CATHOLIC CHURCH: AN HISTORICAL AND CONTEMPORARY REVIEW. PASTORAL PSYCHOLOGY, 45 (4), 277-299.

This article reviewed the literature pertaining to clergy offenders and the history of molestation in the Catholic Church through examination of various Church documents. Isley asserted that the problem of sexual abuse in the Church has been present for years and that contrary to the claims of the Church, it is not a recent phenomenon. The historical examination began in the tenth and eleventh centuries in which Church doctrine focused upon "clerical sexual immorality", which included bestiality, homosexuality, incest, and sodomy. In the Middle Ages the practice of child oblation was instituted by the Benedictine Order where parents would send their male children to the monastery until they were 15 years old. While Church treatise still condemned sexual misconduct, the victim and the abusive monk were both subjected to penance. This was publicly condemned in the eleventh century document *Book of Gomorrah* written by Fr. Peter Damian who spoke out against "sexual immorality of the clergy and the laxness of superiors who refused to take a strong hand against it." Isley noted that there have been common themes surfacing in criminal and civil litigation that involve the Church. It has often come to light that the priest's history of offending had been known by the Church and that the complaints of victims were ignored. The Church has claimed that in light of these accusations they have been unfairly portrayed in the media and that they were lacking in knowledge concerning sex offender recidivism. Isley pointed out that a claim of ignorance concerning sex offender risk factors and recidivism rates is unwarranted because the field was ripe with literature concerning these issues at the height of the abuse scandal. As of 1990, two thousand cases were pending in the state courts, but the judicial system has been reluctant to prosecute such cases and they are often dismissed on procedural grounds. Despite public outcry, some Church officials such as Philip Jenkins claimed that the situation has been blown out of proportion and that the Church is in fact the victim of various interests groups with private agendas. Isley also points out that none of the treatment centers for cleric offenders

(Institute of Living in Hartford, CT; Saint Luke Institute in Suitland, MD; Servants of the Paraclete in Albuquerque, NM) have ever conducted qualitative or quantitative research on their offenders despite the Church's claims of success. The studies that are available suffer from methodological problems and must be interpreted with caution. Those who treat cleric offenders also assert that because they offend against teenage boys this puts them at a lower risk of recidivism. This statement was in complete contrast to the present scientific findings in the field of sex offender recidivism. What makes the issue of recidivism even more problematic is that many offenses may go underreported due to the priest's position in the community.

ISLEY, P.J. & ISLEY, P. (1990). THE SEXUAL ABUSE OF MALE CHILDREN BY CHURCH PERSONNEL: INTERVENTION AND PREVENTION. PASTORAL PSYCHOLOGY, 39 (2), 85-99.

This article provided a review of the literature pertaining to sexual abuse of children by the clergy. The literature in the field circa 1991 is outlined in order for the reader to get an idea of what constitutes child sexual abuse, the male victim, the offender, and the scandal in the Church. The authors contend that it is probable that the structure of the Church facilitated offending behavior. This is apparent in the fact that offenders are often protected, have the ability to shun responsibility for their actions, and have free access to children. A brief discussion is included concerning the minimal literature devoted to interventions with male victims. The authors urged that the intervention be handled in an authoritative manner and be turned over to the legal system, not the institution. The legal system will provide more helpful solutions to the problem than the institution in question, which is often concerned with the preservation of its reputation.

McCALL, D. (2002). SEX AND THE CLERGY. SEXUAL ADDICTION & COMPULSIVITY, 9, 89-95.

This article reviewed the literature pertaining to sexual behavior within the clergy. McCall posits that the purpose of the literature review is not to provide the reader with the history of sexuality in the Church, but to acknowledge that it does occur.

While sexual behavior can be no less addictive/compulsive than it is in other professions, it has far reaching ramifications. The author argued that there are not only ramifications between the victim and abuser, but that the family, congregation, and institution are also affected. The article provided a brief overview of a variety of issues including prevalence of sexual abuse (ranging from an unknown figure to Sipe's estimation of 6% of priest), the problem of sexual misconduct in other religious and professional systems, and victims (including a discussion of subpopulations).

PLACA, A.J. (1990). LEGAL ASPECTS OF THE SEXUAL ABUSE OF CHILDREN. IN S.J. ROSSETTI (ED.). *SLAYER OF THE SOUL: CHILD SEXUAL ABUSE AND THE CATHOLIC CHURCH* (PP. 149-173). MYSTIC, CT: TWENTY-THIRD PUBLICATIONS.

This chapter provided a brief overview of the legislation concerning child sexual abuse and included a discussion concerning the investigative, criminal, and civil processes as well as reporting laws. Pastoral responses should be carried out in a compassionate and helpful manner. Even if a child makes an allegation that is false, the child still needs some kind of help. The Church's investigative process should not be as confrontational as the legal process because parishioners are members of the religious family and should be treated as such. When allegations are made, Placa suggested that they be handled in a manner in which clear concern for the victim and future victims is expressed in a compassionate and realistic manner. It is also urged that the priests express concern for the interests of the Church and the accused person, who should receive any clinical or legal help necessary. In discussing whether or not an individual should be reintegrated into the ministry, it is suggested that they participate in treatment and that reintegration be considered only after a thorough evaluation. Conditions for reintegration would involve that the perpetrator have no unsupervised contact with children for a specified period of time, participate in a twelve-step self help group, and that they be appointed a mentor who will supervise his behavior.

RIGALI, N.J. (1994). CHURCH RESPONSES TO PEDOPHILIA. *THEOLOGICAL STUDIES, 55 (1)*, 124-140.

This article reviewed the response of the Catholic Church to sexual abuse by the clergy in Canada and the United States. It outlined the main points of the Canadian bishops 1992 report *From Pain to Hope*, which called for more openness and truth when investigating allegations of child sexual abuse. The committee noted that by isolating priests and placing them above other members of society, the Church was creating an environment where relationships were stunted and susceptible to sexual abuse. The committee recommended that Bishops establish delegates and committees to handle the allegations of sexual abuse made by parishioners. The Canadian committee also called for more relationship/human sexuality education in the seminary as well as establishing a hot line for troubled youth. In contrast, the response of the Catholic Church in the US was first addressed in the USCCB Statement in 1988, which was far less open or committed as the Canadian report. This same document was issued a year later after further allegations of child sexual abuse were reported with an addendum that stated that the problem was being examined in all seriousness. It was not until 1991 that the Church made a public statement through Archbishop Pilarczyk, which acknowledged that the Church recognized child molestation as a disease and not a moral failing. This approach drew fire from critics who saw the Church response as an attempt to medicalize the problem. In 1990, the US Diocesan policies called for the establishment of delegates to handle and evaluate accusations of sexual abuse as well as a new screening system for candidates entering the seminary. In 1993 a committee was established to review the issue of sexual abuse in the clergy and Canice Connors called for the establishment of a national minimal standard for the seminary candidates as well as the public disclosure of the assessment and treatment of clergy offenders. The Think Tank Report called for a more open, non-secular approach to addressing the issue of abuse (i.e. settling civil suits in public, meetings on abuse be held in public, review board comprised of local lay people, and the establishment of research centers).

ROSSETTI, S.J. (2002). THE CATHOLIC CHURCH AND CHILD SEXUAL ABUSE. *AMERICA, 186 (13)*, 8-16.

This article addressed some common misconceptions concerning clergy sexual abuse. The myth that all child molesters are incurable pedophiles who engage in chronic abuse is discussed. Rossetti claims that there is some truth to this myth, however not all abusers are pedophiles and relapse has been reported at 2.9%. The second myth that priests abuse children because they are celibate is dismissed. Rossetti acknowledged that some dysfunctional individuals may join the clergy in order to manage their behavior through celibacy, but he cautioned against generalizing this theory. He also warned that we do not yet know whether or not priests or more likely to be child abusers than other individuals. The third myth that the priesthood attracts homosexuals and that this is the reason why it has so many child abusers was dismissed on the grounds that there is no common link between homosexuality and true pedophilia. He proposed that the Church attracts stunted/regressed homosexuals and that this is a possible reason why there may be abuse. The fifth myth is that the Bishops are covering up these cases. Rossetti asserts that the Bishops are not reporting child sexual abuse because the law requires that suspected incidents be reported only if the victim who comes forward is a minor. The final myth addressed was that the safest step to take in managing child sexual abuse is to defrock the priest, which the Church has failed to do. Rossetti agreed with the steps the Church has taken in treating priests and raised the issue that by defrocking priests, they do not receive treatment and are free to continue offending. In conclusion, the author asserted that the Church has failed to appear "humble and chaste" and until it does, the media will continue to vilify the Church. He recommended that the Bishops handle these cases in a public manner and revamp their teachings concerning human sexuality.

ROSSETTI, S.J. (1995). THE MARK OF CAIN: REINTEGRATING PEDOPHILES. *AMERICA, 173(6)*, 9-18.

This article addressed the reinstitution of child sexual abusers to the clergy by drawing parallels between the Biblical story of Cain and sex offender legislation in the US. The call to ostracize these priests has led to the creation of "cleric warehouses" that provide long term care for these individuals. Rossetti asserts that, "our myths about child molesters come more from the projection of what lies within our own inner psyches than from the truth about who these men are." Relapse statistics for the St. Luke Institute are cited; the author asserts that of the 300 priests they have treated only two have relapsed. Among the characteristics that predict poor treatment outcome include violent behavior, low IQ, lack of insight, choice of young victims, organic brain deficits, and severe character disorder. Rossetti argued that the priests who do offend against minors do not display these characteristics and are in fact likely to commit fewer acts against fewer victims. Despite these issues, Roman Catholics still feel that these individuals should not be allowed back into the priesthood. In a survey conducted by Rossetti, 42% agreed that they should not be allowed to return to the ministry while 27% disagreed and 31% were unsure. However, 51% agreed with allowing former child abusers back into the ministry if they had received treatment while 22% disagreed and 27% felt unsure. In deciding whether or not a priest should be returned to the ministry it is stressed that evaluation of clinical diagnosis, abuse history, the quality of treatment and responsiveness to treatment must first take place. An individual's after-care program, the availability of supervision, placement in a ministry not involving minors, other pastoral considerations, and a waiting period must also be considered.

STANTON, C. (1990). OFFICIALLY RESPONDING TO AN ACCUSATION OF SEXUAL ABUSE: REFLECTIONS OF A DIOCESAN COMMUNICATIONS DIRECTOR. IN S.J. ROSSETTI (ED.). *SLAYER OF THE SOUL: CHILD SEXUAL ABUSE AND THE CATHOLIC CHURCH* (PP. 143-148). MYSTIC, CT: TWENTY-THIRD PUBLICATIONS.

The author provided the reader with a five-point response plan for officially responding to allegations of abuse within the Church. The first step was to establish a media crisis team comprised of the bishop, chancellor, vicar general, communications director, lawyer, and diocesan officials. This will ensure that there will always be somebody present to address the media's questions. The second step was to provide an immediate and personal response in order to fulfill legal and pastoral responsibilities.

Third, remove the accused in order to protect future victims. Fourth, the media crisis team must meet in order to designate a spokesperson and draft a concise public statement. The final step was to ensure that the truth is told as opposed to doing more harm by keeping the facts secret.

TESTIMONY OF VICTIMS

BLAND, M.J. (2002). THE PSYCHOLOGICAL AND SPIRITUAL EFFECTS OF CHILD SEXUAL ABUSE WHEN THE PERPETRATOR IS A CATHOLIC PRIEST. *DISSERTATION ABSTRACTS INTERNATIONAL, 63 (4-A)*, 1253.

Participants were divided into three groups: Abused by priest (N = 48), no abuse (N = 76), and childhood sexual abuse history (N = 20). Each subject completed a background data questionnaire, religiosity index, spiritual injury scale, and trauma symptoms checklist. The abused by priest group scored higher than the group who experienced no abuse on guilt, dissociation, sexual abuse trauma index, and the trauma symptoms checklist. There were no difference between the two concerning Church attendance, but those abused by priests were more likely to no longer identify themselves as Roman Catholic. When compared to both groups those abused by priests had higher symptoms of grief, anger, a sense of meaninglessness, feelings that God treated them unfairly, dissociation, depression, sexual problems, sleep disturbances, higher scores on the sexual abuse trauma index, and higher scores on the trauma symptom checklist. Cardock, C. & Gardner, J.R. (1990). Psychological intervention for parishes following accusations of child sexual abuse. In S.J. Rossetti (Ed.). *Slayer of the soul: Child sexual abuse and the Catholic Church* (pp. 123-142). Mystic, CT: Twenty-Third Publications.

The authors of this chapter described the impact child sexual abuse has on the religious community. "Target populations," which are comprised of the victim, victim's family, perpetrator, other children and their families, and the parish itself are affected by the abuse either directly or indirectly as rumors and media attention swell. The parish's resources must be utilized in order to address the specific needs of each group who may be experiencing anger, confusion, and disillusionment. The emotional reaction of adults varied as certain basic assumptions about the Church and clergy are shattered by the revelation of abuse. These emotions may also spark a religious crisis where the parishioner experiences a sense of betrayal and loss of trust in Church and God. These emotions and thoughts are compounded by problems presented by the legal system, which may make the victim feel uncomfortable and re-victimized. The psychological reaction of child victims varies as the offender has created a unique relationship with the child. Psychological reactions may include denial, anxiety, anger, guilt, concerns about sexuality, and confusion. The authors presented three general principles for Church intervention that include the suggestion that the Church reach out as opposed to retreat from the parish community, that forums be established in which parishioners can express themselves and gain information, and that the Church uses its network with other professions to gain the support as needed. In assisting adults, it is important that the helpers validate the reactions the individual is feeling as well as provides information and education about the situation. Some individuals may want to pray about the situation and making the effort to return to a sense of normalcy as quickly as possible is also therapeutic. In helping children, helpers and the family are urged to create a safe and stable environment. It is also recommended that the parents first raise the issue of abuse with the child as opposed to a stranger. In doing this, it is important that the parents speak honestly and not avoid the topic.

DE FUENTES, N. (1999). HEAR OUR CRIES: VICTIM-SURVIVORS OF CLERGY SEXUAL MISCONDUCT. IN T.G. PLANTE (ED.). *BLESS ME FATHER FOR I HAVE SINNED: PERSPECTIVES ON SEXUAL ABUSE COMMITTED BY ROMAN CATHOLIC PRIESTS* (PP. 135-167). WESTPORT, CT: PRAEGER PUBLISHERS.

The purpose of this chapter was to provide Church officials with an overview of the issues concerning victims of clergy sexual misconduct. Discussions concerning the various definitions of misconduct, prevalence, and dynamics are included. Risk factors that may play a role in rendering an individual susceptible to clergy sexual abuse include age, gender, history of abuse, access/availability, substance abuse, over idealization of the cleric/Church, clinical and character disorders, ethnic, racial, and cultural influences, illness and physical disability, and lack of training concerning the dynamics of clergy sexual misconduct. The author urged that each Church have a multi-disciplinary Sexual Abuse Advisory Board, which will respond to allegations and provide victim support.

FATER, K. & MULLANEY, J. (2000). THE LIVED EXPERIENCES OF ADULT MALE SURVIVORS WHO ALLEGE CHILDHOOD SEXUAL ABUSE BY CLERGY. *ISSUES IN MENTAL HEALTH NURSING, 21,* 281-295.

This article reported the results of a phenomenological study of seven adult male survivors of childhood sexual abuse by clergy. Data was gathered through semi-structured interviews that revealed that the survivors experienced a bifurcated rage (self directed and outwardly directed) and spiritual distress. This rage was found to be present in every aspect of their lives. Participants were solicited through survivor programs and ranged in age from 28-48. One Catholic priest abused four of the participants, another Catholic priest abused two other participants, and an Episcopalian priest abused one. Some of the participants removed themselves from the Church as a result of the rage they felt while others continued their involvement.

HOPKINS, N.M. (1991). CONGREGATIONAL INTERVENTION WHEN THE PASTOR HAS COMMITTED SEXUAL MISCONDUCT. *PASTORAL PSYCHOLOGY, 39 (4),* 247-255.

This article discussed the impact of sexual misconduct on the parish and the need for intervention. The author posits that since the congregation reacts with feelings of denial and anger, Church officials may avoid providing assistance. The cleric's behavior impacts not only the individuals directly involved, but the entire congregation. The author discussed the psychoanalytical concepts of projection and transference as causes, which facilitate denial. The pastor is looked upon as the embodiment of spirituality and when they lapse in their behavior it shatters the congregation's image. Anger is discussed in terms of displacement, repression, and exploding. The author recommended that the leaders of the intervention pay attention to the

following points: that the intervention be comprised of two individuals, small group work should be utilized, denial must be handled with sensitivity, feelings of anger should be validated, dependency of the congregation will have to be addressed as well as the issues of transference, projection, and the embodiment of the divine. The intervention will also have to focus on teachings about sexuality and victimization.

LUEPKER, E.T. (1999). EFFECTS OF PRACTITIONERS' SEXUAL MISCONDUCT: A FOLLOW-UP STUDY. *JOURNAL OF THE AMERICAN ACADEMY OF PSYCHIATRY & THE LAW, 27 (1),* 51-63.

The author surveyed 107 women who had been victims of clergy or professional sexual misconduct in order to assess their situations before and after the misconduct. Through the Impact of Event Scale and Vinson's Scale, symptoms of posttraumatic stress were measured. Post-misconduct status was characterized by an increase in post traumatic stress disorder, major depressive disorders, suicidality, use of prescription drugs, concern over substance abuse, disrupted relationships, and disruptions in work or earning potential. Eighteen percent of the women had been re-victimized by a different professional. They also reported that they contacted an average of 2.36 professionals before finding one, which provided adequate assistance. Once engaged in therapy at least 100 hours were devoted to the therapeutic alliance. The author contends that the victims were more satisfied with the steps taken by a professional review boards than the Church. In conclusion, these victims required intense therapy but are at risk of enduring re-victimization and must be handled with care.

MCLAUGHLIN, B.R. (1994). DEVASTATED SPIRITUALITY: THE IMPACT OF CLERGY SEXUAL ABUSE ON THE SURVIVOR'S RELATIONSHIP WITH GOD AND THE CHURCH. *SEXUAL ADDICTION & COMPULSIVITY, 1 (2),* 145- 158.

This study examined the impact of sexual abuse on the victims' Church attendance, participation, and relationship with God. An original 15-item scale was constructed in order to gauge spirituality. Forty-three usable surveys were analyzed from a sample comprised of 35 Catholics (26 of which were survivors and nine were co-victims) and eight Protestants. Results illustrated that spiritual development and sense of spiritual self at the time of the victimization determined their method of coping with the trauma. It was found that those abused by the clergy distanced themselves from the Church in order to avoid being victimized again. While it was clearly proven that clergy sexual abuse affected Church attendance and participation, the results are not as clear pertaining to its effect on the victim's relationship with God.

MYER HOPKINS, N. (1999). THE USE AND LIMITATIONS OF VARIOUS MODELS FOR UNDERSTANDING CLERGY SEXUAL MISCONDUCT: THE IMPACT ON THE CONGREGATION. *JOURNAL OF SEX EDUCATION AND THERAPY, 24 (4),* 268-276.

The uses and limitations of the systems model, psychoanalytic model, and the conflict resolution/mediation model in responding to clergy sexual abuse are discussed. The systems model assumes that everything is connected and that an intervention can impact the entire institution. Some strategies that characterized this model included exploring a congregation's history, working intensively with clergy who are asked to carry the burden for the congregation, carefully challenging the tendency for the congregation to keep secrets, and looking for larger ways to open up a system. This model was limited by the assumption that one individual can effect another and create a cycle of mutually reinforcing behaviors. One strength of this system model is that it draws attention to the fact that the system is comprised of individuals who do not share the same level of power. In combating this problem it is recommended that educational sources be utilized as well as small discussion groups where parishioners can discuss topics such as gender, sexual harassment, and race. The psychoanalytic model explains misconduct as resulting from transference and projection. This model is characterized by strategies in which education is provided about psychoanalytical concepts in order for individuals to understand these unconscious processes. These strategies also seek to provide minimal information pertaining to the diagnosis of the individual in question in order to maintain confidentiality. The limitation of this model is that it places the focus upon the individual and not the system. In order to assist people in recognizing the complexities of the situation, the author recommended that you encourage people to see things "in shades of gray," ask them to talk about their experiences in the ministry, and encourage them to embrace ambiguity. The conflict resolution/mediation model is utilized when a conflict arises between those loyal to the accused cleric and those who sympathize with the victim. The author contends that mediation should not even be attempted until a full investigation of all of the facts has taken place. Some of the strategies utilized in this model include group discussion and work, which is aimed at the entire community. It is also important to manage those who may become abusive towards others in the community, provide guidelines for people engaging in conflict resolution, suggest the involvement of a third party to help mediate the situation, and assist the congregation in examining their vision statements. The limitation of this model is that it is only useful once all of the pain associated with the situation is addressed. The author recommends that individuals not rely solely upon one of these systems and that an integration of all three may prove beneficial. The issues of damaged spirituality and ethical/moral considerations are also included in the conclusion of this article.

NASON-CLARK, N. (1998). THE IMPACT OF ABUSES OF CLERGY TRUST ON FEMALE CONGREGANTS' FAITH AND PRACTICE. IN A. SHUPE (ED.). *WOLVES WITHIN THE FOLD: RELIGIOUS LEADERSHIP AND ABUSES OF POWER* (PP.85-100). NEW BRUNSWICK, NJ: RUTGERS UNIVERSITY PRESS.

This chapter attempted to answer why the sexual abuse scandal in Newfoundland sparked such public outrage. In past work, Nason-Clark has posited that the following factors have played a role: (1) greater public knowledge of the prevalence and consequences of child sexual assault; (2) the women's movement; (3) the changing relationship between Church and state; (4) the geographical, economic, and political realities of Newfoundland; (5) the media; and (6) the judicial systems responses to child sexual abuse. The author interviewed twenty-four Roman Catholic women to assess their reaction to the scandal. Every woman in the sample could remember where they were when they first heard about the story and all reacted initially with disbelief. Nineteen of the 24 women reported anger as one of the emotions they felt after the scandal. The anger was targeted at the offending priests, bishop, other Catholic priests, Church hierarchy, and some were angry with the Catholics who lived in the parish where the priests were charged. They also experienced a sense of betrayal and guilt that caused them to alter their relationship with the Church. Four years after the initial interview, the author conducted a follow-up study and found some women had made their way back to the Church while others had decided to stay away. They claim that the Church in Newfoundland had not recovered from the scandal and that they will never regard priests in the same manner again.

PULLEN, E. (1998). AN ADVOCACY GROUP FOR VICTIMS OF CLERICAL SEXUAL ABUSE. IN A. SHUPE (ED.). *WOLVES WITHIN THE FOLD: RELIGIOUS LEADERSHIP AND ABUSES OF POWER* (PP. 67-84). NEW BRUNSWICK, NJ: RUTGERS UNIVERSITY PRESS.

This chapter presented a case study concerning the Saint Anthony's Seminary Support Group. The study is meant to illustrate how communities respond to disclosures of sexual abuse. According to Pullen, these support groups discussed the "spiritual abuse" they have experienced as a result of clergy misconduct. This feeling of betrayal is increased as a result of the steps the institution takes in order to cover up the abuse, minimizes the impact of the abuse on the community, isolated the victim, and controlled the facts of the scandal. St. Anthony's Seminary saw allegations of abuse in 1989 directed towards Fr. Philip Mark Wolfe. Not long after the allegations, a group began to meet to discuss the situation. This meeting resulted in various letters, which urged the institution to be open and honest in the resolution of this problem. After further allegations were made, the support group was formed in 1993. This victims' support group is a network, which keeps members abreast of the status of the survivors. Once it is apparent that the survivors are experiencing problems, the group bands together to provide assistance. The group sees itself as helping the community heal from the sexual abuse and assists in educating the community about child sexual abuse. A great deal of time is spent evaluating the efforts the Franciscans have made in addressing the abuse at St. Anthony's.

ROSSETTI, S.J. (1997). THE EFFECTS OF PRIEST-PERPETRATION OF CHILD SEXUAL ABUSE ON THE TRUST OF CATHOLICS IN PRIESTHOOD, CHURCH, AND GOD. *JOURNAL OF PSYCHOLOGY AND CHRISTIANITY, 16 (3)*, 197-209.

The author surveyed 1,775 Catholics in North America concerning their feelings for the clergy, Church, and God. The sample was divided into three groups: those who had no awareness of charges of sexual abuse within their parish (N = 501), those who were aware that a priest in their diocese had been accused (N = 1,097), and those whose own parish priest had been charged (N = 177). The results illustrated that while trust declined in the priesthood and Church across the three groups, trust in God remained consistent. The study also illustrated that parishioners are more likely to distrust the Church's handling of sexual misconduct and less likely to accept Church doctrine on sexuality and morals. North American Catholics viewed new priests in the parish with suspicion, were less willing to allow offending clerics back into the parish, and were less likely to believe that the modern Church is better than the Church in the past. Rossetti discussed the need to expand the concept of victim to include the parishioners and Church. The need to extend counseling to these individuals is stressed in order to combat the damage done by offending clerics.

ROSSETTI, S.J. (1995). THE IMPACT OF CHILD SEXUAL ABUSE ON ATTITUDES TOWARD GOD AND THE CATHOLIC CHURCH. *CHILD ABUSE & NEGLECT, 19 (12)*, 1469-1481.

This study examined the effects of childhood sexual abuse on attitudes towards the Catholic Church, clergy, and God. The sample of adult Catholics was divided into three groups: no childhood sexual abuse (N = 1,376), sexually abused but not by a priest (N = 307), and those who had been sexually abused by a priest (N = 40). Those who had been sexually victimized by a priest displayed less trust in the Catholic Church, clergy, and their relationship with God than those who were not abused. While the data was inconclusive for the group that had been sexually abused but not by a priest, there is some evidence that the abuse had a negative effect on their trust in the Church, clergy, and God. The findings also illustrated that female victims of sexual abuse displayed a decline in trust in God, but the male victims did not. The author's hypothesis that those victims who had been in therapy would express less trust in the Church, clergy, and God when compared with those who had not been in therapy was supported by these findings. Author cited the low response rate (25%) and reliance upon a Catholic sample was limitations.